The Christian Tradition

The Christian Tradition
A History of the Development of Doctrine

Jaroslav Pelikan

2 The Spirit
of Eastern
Christendom
(600–1700)

The University of Chicago Press

Chicago and London

THE UNIVERSITY OF CHICAGO PRESS, CHICAGO 60637
THE UNIVERSITY OF CHICAGO PRESS, LTD., LONDON

© 1974 by The University of Chicago
Published 1974. Phoenix Edition 1977

Printed in the United States of America

90 89 88 87 86 85 84   98765
International Standard Book Number: 0–226–65373–0
Library of Congress Catalog Card Number: 79–142042

Contents

Preface

The Spirit of Eastern Christendom is the second volume
of my five-volume history of Christian doctrine. It is intended to continue the narrative begun with the first
volume and to bring the account through its Byzantine,
Syriac, and early Russian developments to the end of the
seventeenth century. The continuity of this history with
that set forth in *The Emergence of the Catholic Tradition*
is in many ways the most obvious feature of this recital:
the greatest insult one could pay to any theologian interpreted here—be he Chalcedonian, Monophysite, Nestorian, iconoclast, or whatever—would be to call him a
"creative mind." As I have noted repeatedly in this volume, quotations could often be transposed across two or
three or even five centuries without doing violence to the
texts. Yet there is more change and development (what
we usually mean by "history") here than the participants
recognized. I have tried to do justice to the continuity and
to the change, as well as to the subtle relations between
continuity and change.

One editorial problem raised by this circumstance is the
relation between the second volume and the first. By my
own definition, set forth in the preface to the first volume,
I intend each volume to stand on its own feet; this second
volume is no exception. Yet the very traditionalism of the
theologians with whom I have been dealing makes cross-
references to the first five centuries of the church unavoidable. I have sought to obviate the necessity of retelling
the entire story of volume 1 by recapitulating that story
as it was understood by the seventh century and by those
that followed it, without at this time entering directly on

the question of how accurately they may have interpreted their tradition. For this volume it is more important to know what Maximus Confessor or Photius thought about the Council of Nicea than to know how the creed of Nicea itself evolved. This is how I have attempted to preserve the autonomy of each volume and yet to maintain the unity of the work as a whole.

In keeping with this working principle, I have here treated the first five or six centuries of the history of Christian doctrine as a given, even though I am quite aware of their heterogeneity. In the bibliography to this volume, I have likewise concentrated my attention on those works that carry the story into the centuries being covered here. If I were writing the history of Christian doctrine backwards, beginning with the nineteenth and twentieth centuries and working my way to the beginnings—an intriguing idea intellectually, and an impossible one methodologically—I would, I am sure, look at the seventh century in quite another way and would also produce another kind of bibliography. But I have included in the bibliography those works that are the most instructive about the career of Eastern Christian thought. These I have selected on the basis of a combination of two criteria: those that have taught me the most, and those that will carry my readers to the next stage of the scholarly discussion. As is obvious from the list of works cited, these two criteria are frequently discordant; for I have been the beneficiary chiefly of Eastern scholarship, especially Russian (to some of which I have paid my tribute), while my bibliography has works in Western languages that are less influential in determining my own interpretations but are more available. An additional factor determining the bibliography is the sheer problem of quantity. Without counting items in anyone's list, I am sure that there are more first-rate monographs on the theology of Augustine than on the entire theological history of Byzantium. This has compelled me to include works whose counterparts in the scholarly literature about the early centuries I did not cite in volume 1. Conversely, I have not repeated works cited there unless they were essential to my account of these centuries. One place, however, where I did not make such compromises is in the citation of primary sources; these I have continued to quote, as I did in vol-

ume 1, in the best available edition of the original text,
regardless of its provenance.

The title of this volume does perhaps deserve comment.
In the précis and prospectus of the entire work, which I
first formulated in 1950, this section bore the title "The
Mind of Eastern Orthodox Christendom." Of the two
major revisions in that title, the elimination of the term
"Orthodox" is justified by my deepening awareness that
the non-Chalcedonian churches, to whom the term "Orthodox" is usually not applied by anyone except themselves, do have a legitimate place in this history. The
substitution of "spirit" for "mind" is a more subtle question. It was motivated in part by my expectation, shared
with all serious students of this period, of the publication
of *The Mind of Byzantium* by Milton V. Anastos, which
thus preempted the term "mind"; I wish I could have had
the benefit of its appearance while I was undertaking this
project. Another source of the word "spirit" is, I suppose,
the literature of German *Geistesgeschichte,* to which I
owe a considerable debt. In the present case, however, that
debt is largely an indirect one, having been acquired
through my borrowings from the work of scholars of
Slavic origin, above all, from that of T. G. Masaryk, whose
Rusko a Evropa was my earliest textbook for the study of
"the spirit of Eastern Christendom"; interestingly, the
English translation of Masaryk's book is entitled *The
Spirit of Russia.* I am not unaware of the problematic
nature of *Geistesgeschichte,* but for my purposes this lia-
bility seems to turn out to be an asset.

The linguistic problem, as represented especially by the
transliteration of names and the translation of technical
terms, has probably caused me more hours of trouble than
the methodological one. Transliteration is especially awk-
ward where the same name has been used in more than
one alphabet. I have tried to steer a middle course between
literalistic pedantry and thoughtless uniformity. The
translation of technical theological words is, obviously,
much more delicate. Perhaps the best illustration of the
problem occurs in chapter 2, where ἐνέργεια could easily
have been rendered as "energy" (except that this is not
what the word "energy" means to us) or as "operation" to
conform with the Latin (except that this is even more
opaque); after trying different sets of terms, I finally

settled on "act," "action," and "activity," partly because these terms enabled me to make some of the distinctions made by the Greek. For similar reasons, I have used "image," "idol," and "icon" in chapter 3, even though these English words often render the same Greek term.

Finally, I want to acknowledge my gratitude to those who have contributed to this book. In addition to those whose names I have cited in the preface to volume 1 as my benefactors for the entire work, I should single out several Byzantinists, who have graciously welcomed an amateur to their charmed circle and have given him the benefit of their counsel: George V. Florovsky, my beloved mentor, who has shaped my basic perspective on Eastern Christianity; Francis Dvornik, whose Czech works were my introduction to Byzantine history; Deno Geanakoplos, my colleague and friend, whose contribution to these pages extends far beyond my explicit references to his published works; and John Meyendorff, whose history of Byzantine theology appeared too late for me to use it, but whose historical erudition and theological learning have informed much of my own account. With thanks to these scholars and to the others whose advice has helped me over many difficulties, I must nevertheless follow the conventions of historical authorship and admit that all the mistakes that remain in this book are my own.

Primary Sources

Authors and Texts

Abd.*Margar.*	Abdiša of Nisibis. *The Book of the Pearl {Liber Margaritae}*
Act.&script.*Wirt.*	*Acta & scripta theologorum Wirtembergensium et Patriarchae Constantinopolitani D. Hieremiae.* Wittenberg, 1584
Ado.*Chron.*	Ado of Vienne. *Chronicle*
Aen.Par.*Graec.*	Aeneas of Paris. *Book against the Greeks*
Agap.*Cap.*	Agapetus, deacon of Constantinople. *Chapters of Admonition {Capita admonitoria}*
Agath.*Ep.*	Pope Agatho I. *Epistles*
Alc.*Trin.*	Alcuin. *The Faith of the Holy and Undivided Trinity*
Ps.Alc.*Proc.*	Pseudo-Alcuin. *Book on the Procession of the Holy Spirit, Addressed to Charlemagne*
An.Comn.*Alex.*	Anna Comnena. *Alexiad*
Anaph.*Jac.*	*Anaphora of the Holy Mar Jacob {i.e., James} Brother of Our Lord and Bishop of Jerusalem*
Anast.Bibl.CCP(869)pr.	Anastasius Bibliothecarius. Preface to *Acts* of the Fourth Council of Constantinople (869)
Anast.S. *Hex.*	Anastasius of Sinai. *Anagogical Contemplations on the Hexaemeron*
Ps.Anast.S.	Pseudo-Anastasius of Sinai
Jud.*al.*	*Second Dialogue against the Jews {Adversus Judaeos dialogus alius}*
Jud.*dial.*	*Dialogue against the Jews*
Jud.*parv.*	*Short Dialogue against the Jews {Adversus Judaeos dialogus parvus}*
Anath.*Sar.*	*Anathema against the Saracens*
Andr.Cr.*Imag.*	Andrew of Crete. *On the Veneration of the Holy Images*
Ps.Andron.Comn.*Jud.*	Pseudo-Andronicus I Comnenus, Emperor. *Dialogue of a Christian and a Jew against the Jews*
Ans.*Proc.*	Anselm of Canterbury. *On the Procession of the Holy Spirit*
Ans.Hav.*Dial.*	Anselm of Havelberg. *Dialogues in Constantinople with Nicetas of Nicomedia*
Arist.*An.*	Aristotle. *On the Soul {De anima}*

xi

Arnob.*Nat.*   Arnobius of Sicca. *Against the Nations*
Ath.   Athanasius of Alexandria
  Ar.   *Orations against the Arians*
  Exp.Ps.   *Exposition of the Psalms*
  Tom.   *Tome to the Antiochenes*
Ps-Ath.   Pseudo-Athanasius
  Az.   *Treatise on the Azymes*
  Chr.un.   *That Christ Is One {Quod unus sit Christus}*
  Exp.fid.   *Exposition of the Faith {Expositio fidei}*
Aug.   Augustine of Hippo
  Ev.Joh.   *Exposition of the Gospel of John*
  Grat.   *On Grace {De gratia}*
  Quaest.Ex.   *Questions on Exodus*
  Serm.Dom.   *Our Lord's Sermon on the Mount {De sermone Domini
                        in monte}*
  Trin.   *On the Trinity*
Avell.   Avellan Collection
Bab.   Babai of Kaškar
  Evagr.   *Exposition of the Book of Centuries by Evagrius Ponticus*
  Tract.   *Tractate against Those Who Say: "As the Soul and the
                        Body Are One Hypostasis, so God the Logos and the
                        Man Are One Hypostasis"*
  Un.   *On the Union*
Barl.   Barlaam of Calabria
  Ep.   *Epistles*
  Lat.   *Against the Latins*
  Or.Un.   *Oration for the Union*
Barth.Ed.   Bartholomew of Edessa
  Agar.   *Refutation of the Hagarene*
  Moh.   *Against Mohammed*
Bas.   Basil of Caesarea
  Ep.   *Epistles*
  Hom.   *Homilies*
  Spir.   *On the Holy Spirit*
Bas.I.Mac.ap.CCP(869) Basil I the Macedonian, emperor, at the Fourth Council of
                        Constantinople (869)
Bas.Ochr.*Ep.*   Basil of Ochrida (Bulgaria). *Epistles*
Bess.   John Bessarion
  Consec.   *On the Words of Consecration*
  Plat.   *Against the Calumniator of Plato*
  Proc.   *On the Procession of the Holy Spirit*
C.A.   *Augsburg Confession*
Calv.*Inst.*(1559)   John Calvin. *Institutes of the Christian Religion* (edition of
                        1559)
CChalc.   Council of Chalcedon
  Act.   *Acts*
  Can.   *Canons*
CCP(681)   Third Council of Constantinople
  Act.   *Acts*
  Or.imp.   *Oration to the Emperor*
CCP(754)*Decr.*   (Iconoclast) Synod of 754 in Hiereia and Constantinople.
                        Decrees
CCP(869)*Act.*   Fourth Council of Constantinople. *Acts*

Cerul.	Patriarch Michael Cerularius
Ep.Petr.Ant.	*Epistles to Peter of Antioch*
Panop.	*Panoply*
Sem.	Edict *{Σημείωμα}* on the Projected Excommunication of *Patriarch Michael*
CFlor.(1439)	Council of Florence
Decr.Arm.	*Decree on the Armenians*
Def.	*Definition*
CFor.(796)	Council of Fréjus-Toulon [Concilium Forojuliense]
Chrys.	John Chrysostom
Prod.Jud.	*On the Betrayal of Judas {De proditione Judae}*
Sac.	*On the Priesthood {De sacerdotio}*
Chyt.*Or.*	David Chytraeus. *Oratio de statu ecclesiarum hoc tempore in Graecia, Asia, Africa, Ungaria, Boëmia, etc. {Oration on the Present State of the Churches in Greece, Asia, Africa, Hungary, Bohemia, etc.}.* Wittenberg, 1580
CLater.(649)	First Lateran Council
Act.	*Acts*
Can.	*Canons*
Clem.	Clement of Alexandria
Paed.	*Tutor {Paedagogus}*
Pasch.fr.	*On the Passover. Fragments*
Prot.	*Exhortation to the Greeks {Protrepticus}*
CLug.(1274) *Const.*	Second Council of Lyons. *Constitution*
CNic.(787)	Second Council of Nicea
Act.	*Acts*
Can.	*Canons*
Col.Afr.*Ep.Thdr.*	Columbus of Africa et al. *Epistle to Pope Theodore*
Conf.Dosith.	*Confession of Dositheus*
q.	*Questions*
Conf.Petr.Mog.	Peter Mogila. *Orthodox Confession of the Faith of the Catholic and Apostolic Eastern Church.*
Conf.Sar.	*Confession of the Christian Faith against the Saracens*
Const.Pogon.	Emperor Constantine IV Pogonatus
Edict.	*Edict*
Sacr.	*Sacred Epistles*
Const.V.	Emperor Constantine V
Corp.iur.civ.Nov.	*Code of Justinian {Corpus iuris civilis}. Novellae*
Cosm.*Sl.*	Cosmas the Presbyter. *Message {Slovo}*
Cydon.*Moh.*	Demetrius Cydonius. Translation of Richardus. *Against the Followers of Mohammed*
Cypr.*Unit.eccl.*	Cyprian of Carthage. *On the Unity of the Church {De unitate ecclesiae}*
Cyr.	Cyril of Alexandria
Chr.un.	*That Christ Is One {Quod unus sit Christus}*
Ep.	*Epistles*
Cyr.H.*Catech.*	Cyril of Jerusalem. *Catechetical Lectures*
Cyr.Luc.	Patriarch Cyril Lucaris
Conf.	*Eastern Confession of the Christian Faith*
Ep.	*Epistles*
Cyrus.Al.	Cyrus of Alexandria
Cap.	*Chapters {Capitula}*
Ep.	*Epistles*

fr.	*Fragments*
Dial.Papisc.	*Dialogue of the Jews Papiscus and Philo with a Certain Monk*
Didym.*Spir.*	Didymus of Alexandria. *On the Holy Spirit*
Dion.Ar.	Pseudo-Dionysius the Areopagite
C.h.	*Celestial Hierarchy*
D.n.	*On the Divine Names*
Ep.	*Epistles*
E.h.	*Ecclesiastical Hierarchy*
Dion.BarSal.*Exp.lit.*	Dionysius Bar Salibi. *Exposition of the Liturgy*
Dion.CP.*Tom.syn.*	Dionysius of Constantinople. *Synodical Tome*
Doct.Ad.	*The Doctrine of Addai*
Doct.Jac.	*The Doctrine of Jacob, Recently Baptized*
Doct.patr.	*The Doctrine of the Fathers on the Incarnation of the Logos {Doctrina patrum de incarnatione Verbi}*
Dom.Ven.*Ep.Petr.Ant.*	Dominicus of Venice. *Epistle to Peter of Antioch*
Ein.*Ann.*	Einhard. *Annals*
Ep.Oliv.	*Epistle of Pilgrim Monks on the Mount of Olives to Pope Leo III*
Epiph.	Epiphanius of Salamis
fr.	*Fragments*
Haer.	*Against Eighty Heresies*
Epiph.M.*V.Serg.*	Epiphanius the Monk [Epifanij Mnich]. *Life of Sergius of Radonež*
Episc.CP.*Ep.*	Bishops of Constantinople. *Epistle*
Episc.Ger.*Graec.*	Bishops of Germany. *Response at Worms on the Faith of the Holy Trinity, against the Heresy of the Greeks*
Episc.Or.*Ep.*	Bishops of the Orient. *Epistle*
Eug.IV.*Ep.*	Pope Eugenius IV. *Epistles*
Eus.	Eusebius of Caesarea
Ep.Const.Aug.	*Epistle to the Empress Constantia*
H.e.	*Ecclesiastical History*
Eus.Bass.*Ep.Thds.Al.*	Eusebius of Mar Bassi et al. *Epistle to Theodosius of Alexandria*
Euth.Zig.	Euthymius Zigabenus
Anath.	*Fourteen Anathemas against the Bogomils*
Bog.	*Narrative of the Heresy of the Bogomils*
Panop.	*Panoply*
Ps.	*Commentary on the Psalter*
Sar.	*Disputation on the Faith with a Saracen Philosopher*
Evagr.*H.e.*	Evagrius Scholasticus. *Ecclesiastical History*
Gel.I.*Ep.*	Pope Gelasius I. *Epistles*
Ps.Geo.Arb.*Exp.*	Pseudo-George of Arbela. *Exposition of the Offices of the Church*
Geo.Kiev.*Lat.*	George of Kiev. *Against the Latins*
Geo.Schol.*Sal.*	George Scholarius. *Concerning the Only Way for the Salvation of Men*
Germ.I.*Dorm.*	Patriarch Germanus I of Constantinople. *On the Dormition of the Theotokos*
Germ.II.*Bog.*	Patriarch Germanus II of Constantinople. *Homily against the Bogomils*
Goth.*Deit.*	Gottschalk of Orbais. *That it is Permissible to Speak of the Deity as Trine*

Gr.M.	Gregory the Great
Ep.	*Epistles*
Ev.	*Homilies on the Gospels*
Gr.Naz.	Gregory of Nazianzus
Carm.	*Poems {Carmina}*
Ep.	*Epistles*
Hom.	*Homilies*
Or.	*Orations*
Gr.Nyss.	Gregory of Nyssa
Deit.	*On the Deity of the Son and of the Holy Spirit*
Hom.opific.	*On the Creation of Man {De hominis opificio}*
Thdr.	*On Theodore the Martyr*
Gr.Pal.	Gregory Palamas
Ak.	*Against Akindynus*
Cap.	*150 Physical, Theological, Moral, and Practical Chapters {Capitula}*
Conf.	*Confession of the Orthodox Faith*
Dec.	*Exposition of the Decalogue*
Hom.	*Homilies*
Theoph.	*Theophanes*
Tr.	*Triads*
Gregent.*Herb.*	Gregentius of Taphar. *Disputation with the Jew Herbanus*
Hadr.*Ep.*	Pope Hadrian I. *Epistles*
Hag.*Tom.*	*Hagioretic Tome {ἀγιορειτικὸς τόμος}*
Heracl.*Ecth.*	Emperor Heraclius. *Ecthesis*
Herodot.*Hist.*	Herodotus. *History*
Hil.*Trin.*	Hilary of Poitiers. *On the Trinity*
Hil.Kiev.*Sl.*	Hilarion of Kiev. *Message {Slovo}*
Hinc.R.	Hincmar of Reims
Deit.	*On the Deity as One and Not Three*
Opusc.Hinc.L.	*Opusculum against Hincmar of Laon*
Hom.*Il.*	Homer. *Iliad*
Hon.I.*Ep.*	Pope Honorius I. *Epistles*
Hor.*A.p.*	Horace. *Art of Poetry*
Horm.*Ep.*	Pope Hormisdas. *Epistles*
Humb.	Humbert of Silva Candida
Dial.	*Dialogue*
Proc.	*On the Procession of the Holy Spirit from the Father and the Son*
Resp.Nicet.	*Response to the Book of Nicetas Stethatos*
Isid.Sev.*Eccl.off.*	Isidore of Seville. *Ecclesiastical Offices*
Išo'yahb.*Ep.*	Išo'yahb III. *Epistles*
Jac.Bar.*Ep.Thds.*	Jacob Baradaeus. *Epistle to Theodosius of Alexandria*
Jac.Ed.	Jacob of Edessa
Can.	*Canons*
Conf.	*Confession*
Ep.*Thos.*	*Epistle to Thomas the Presbyter*
Hex.	*Exposition of the Hexaemeron*
Jer.CP.*Ep.Tüb.*	Patriarch Jeremiah of Constantinople. *Epistle to the Lutheran Theologians at Tübingen*
Joh.Ant.*Az.*	John of Antioch. *Treatise on the Azymes*
Joh.Argyr.*Proc.*	John Argyropoulos. *On the Procession of the Holy Spirit*
Joh.Bek.	John Bekkos

Apol.	*Apology for the Union of 1274*
Ep.Joh.XXI.	*Epistle to Pope John XXI*
Un.	*On the Union of the Churches of Old and New Rome*
Joh.Cant.	Emperor John VI Cantacuzenus
Apol.	*Apologies for the Christian Religion against the Mohammedan Sect*
Or.	*Orations against Mohammed*
Joh.D.	John of Damascus
1 Cor.	*Exposition of 1 Corinthians from John Chrysostom*
Dialect.	*Dialectic*
Dialex.	*Dispute {Διαλέξις} with a Manichean*
Disp.Sar.	*Dispute of a Saracen and a Christian*
F.o.	*The Orthodox Faith*
Haer.	*On Heresies*
Imag.	*Orations on the Images*
Jacob.	*Against the Jacobites*
Man.	*Dialogue against the Manicheans*
Parall.	*Sacred Parallels*
Rect.sent.	*On the Correct Thought {De recta sententia}*
Volunt.	*On Two Wills in Christ {De duabus in Christo voluntatibus}*
Ps.Joh.D.*Trin.*	Pseudo-John of Damascus. *On the Trinity*
Joh.Diac.	John the Deacon
Joh.H.	John V of Jerusalem
Const.	*Against Constantinus Cabalinus on the Images*
Icon.	*Against the Iconoclasts*
Joh.Maur.*Carm.*	John Mauropus. *Poems {Carmina}*
Just.*Dial.*	Justin Martyr. *Dialogue with Trypho*
LeoM.*Tom.*	Pope Leo I (the Great). *Tome*
Leo II.*Ep.*	Pope Leo II. *Epistles*
Leo III.*Ep.*	Emperor Leo III. *Epistle to 'Umar {Omar}, Chief of the Saracens*
Leo IX.*Ep.Petr.Ant.*	Pope Leo IX. *Epistle to Peter of Antioch*
Leo Ochr.*Enc.*	Leo of Ochrida (Bulgaria). *Encyclical*
Leo Per.*Lat.*	Leo of Perejaslav. *Against the Latins*
Leont.B.*Nest.etEut.*	Leontius of Byzantium. *Against the Nestorians and Eutychians*
Leont.N.	Leontius of Neapolis (Cyprus)
fr.	*Fragments*
Serm.	*Sermons*
Lib.Car.	*Caroline Books {Libri Carolini}*
Lib.diurn.	*Daybook of the Roman Pontiffs {Liber diurnus Romanorum pontificum}*
Lit.Bas.	*Liturgy of Basil*
Lit.Chrys.	*Liturgy of Saint John Chrysostom*
Lit.Clem.	*Clementine Liturgy*
Lit.Praesanct.	*Liturgy of the Presanctified*
Liut.*Leg.*	Liutprand of Cremona. *Narrative of the Legation to Constantinople*
Luth.	Martin Luther
Ep.	*Epistles*
Rom.Leip.	*Against the Famous Romanist in Leipzig*
Mac.Ant.*Symb.*	Macarius of Antioch. *Symbol*

Man.II.Pal.*Dial.*	Emperor Manuel II Palaeologus. *Dialogues with a Persian*
Marc.Eph.	Mark of Ephesus
Conf.	*Confession of Faith at Florence*
Consec.	*On the Consecration of the Eucharist*
Dial.	*Dialogue on the Addition to the Symbol by the Latins*
Or.Purg.	*Orations on Purgatory*
Mart.I.*Ep.*	Pope Martin I. *Epistles*
Maur.Rav.*Ep.*	Maurus of Ravenna. *Epistle*
Max.	Maximus Confessor
Ambig.	*Book of Ambiguities*
Ascet.	*Ascetic Book*
Carit.	*400 Chapters on Charity*
Disp.Byz.	*Disputation Held in Byzantium*
Ep.	*Epistles*
Myst.	*Mystagogy*
Opusc.	*Theological and Polemical Opuscula*
Or.dom.	*Brief Exposition of the Lord's Prayer {Orationis dominicae brevis expositio}*
Pyrr.	*Disputation with Pyrrhus*
Qu.dub.	*Questions and Doubts*
Qu.Thal.	*Questions to Thalassius on the Scripture*
Rel.mot.	*Relation about the Motion*
Schol.C.h.	*Scholia on the "Celestial Hierarchy" of Dionysius the Areopagite*
Schol.D.n.	*Scholia on the "On the Divine Names" of Dionysius the Areopagite*
Schol.E.h.	*Scholia on the "Ecclesiastical Hierarchy" of Dionysius the Areopagite*
Schol.Ep.Dion.Ar.	*Scholia on the "Epistles" of Dionysius the Areopagite*
Schol.Myst.	*Scholia on the "Mystical Theology" of Dionysius the Areopagite*
Max.Aquil.	Maximus of Aquileia
Max.Plan.*Aug.*	Maximus Planudes. Greek translation of Augustine. *On the Trinity*
Mel.*Ep.*	Philip Melanchthon. *Epistles*
Meth.CP.*Syn.*	Patriarch Methodius II of Constantinople. *Synodicon*
Metr.Crit.*Conf.*	Metrophanes Critopoulos. *Confession*
Metrop.	*The Prerogatives of Metropolitans*
Mich.Anch.	Michael III Anchialu, patriarch of Constantinople
Arm.	*Epistle on the Armenians*
Dial.	*Dialogue with Emperor Manuel Comnenus*
Min.Fel.*Oct.*	Minucius Felix. *Octavianus*
Nars.*Hom.*	Narsai. *Liturgical Homilies*
Niceph.	Patriarch Nicephorus of Constantinople
Antirr.	*Refutation {Antirrheticus}*
Apol.	*Shorter Apology for the Holy Images*
Ep.Leo III	*Epistle to Pope Leo III*
Epiph.	*Against Epiphanius*
Imag.	*Greater Apology for the Holy Images*
Niceph.Kiev.	Nicephorus of Kiev
Posl.	*Message {Poslanie}*
Nicet.Amas.*Patr.*	Nicetas of Amasia. *On the Patriarchs*
Nicet.Byz.	Nicetas of Byzantium

Arab.	*Refutation of the Falsely Written Book of the Arab Mohammed*
Arm.	*Refutation of the Epistle Sent by the Prince of the Armenians*
Lat.	*Against the Latins*
Ref.Ep.	*Refutation of the Epistles of the Hagarenes*
Nicet.Chon.*Thes.*	Nicetas Choniata. *Thesaurus of the Orthodox Faith*
Nicet.Nicom.	Nicetas of Nicomedia
Nicet.Steth.	Nicetas Stethatos
Antidial.	*Antidialogue*
Arm.etLat.	*Against the Armenians and the Latins*
Nicol.I.*Ep.*	Pope Nicholas I. *Epistles*
Nil.Cab.	Nilus Cabasilas of Thessalonica
Caus.Diss.	*On the Causes of Dissensions in the Church*
Prim.	*On the Primacy of the Pope*
Nil.Dox.*Not.*	Nilus Doxopatres. *The Order of the Patriarchal Sees {Notitia thronorum patriarchalium}*
Nil.Sor.	Nilus Sorskij
Pred.	*Legacy to His Disciples {Predanie učenikom}*
Ustav	*Monastic Rule {Monastyrskij ustav}*
Or.	Origen of Alexandria
Cels.	*Against Celsus*
Jos.	*Homilies on Joshua*
Luc.	*Homilies on the Gospel of Luke*
Patr.Job.	*Excerpt from the Record of the Installation of Patriarch Job {Otvyrok iz zapiski o postavlenij patriarcha Iova}*
Patr.Mosc.	*Establishment of the Patriarchate of Moscow*
Paul.I.*Ep.*	Pope Paul I. *Epistles*
Paul.Ant.*Ep.Thds.Al.*	Paul of Antioch. *Epistle to Theodosius of Alexandria*
Paul.II.CP.*Ep.Thdr.*	Paul II of Constantinople. *Epistle to Pope Theodore*
Paulin.Aquil.	Paulinus of Aquileia
Carm.	*Poems {Carmina}*
CFor.(796)	Council of Fréjus-Toulon [Concilium Forojuliense]
Fel.	*Against Felix of Urgel*
Paulin.N.*Ep.*	Paulinus of Nola. *Epistles*
Petr.Ant.	Peter of Antioch
Ep.Al.	*Epistle to the Patriarch of Alexandria*
Ep.Cerul.	*Epistle to Michael Cerularius*
Ep.Dom.	*Epistle to Dominicus of Venice*
Ep.H.	*Epistle to the Patriarch of Jerusalem*
Ep.Leo IX.	*Epistles to Pope Leo IX*
Petr.Chrys.*Serm.*	Peter Chrysologus. *Sermons*
Petr.Dam.*Proc.*	Peter Damian. *Against the Error of the Greeks on the Procession of the Holy Spirit*
Petr.Lomb.*Sent.*	Peter Lombard. *Sentences*
Petr.Sic.	Peter of Sicily
Hist.	*History of the Heresy of the Manicheans, Who Are Also Called Paulicians*
Serm.	*Sermons against the Manicheans, Who Are Also Called Paulicians*
Philoth.*Posl.*	Philotheus of Pskov. *Message {Poslanie}*
Philox.*Diss.*	Philoxenus of Mabbug. *Dissertations*
Phot.	Patriarch Photius of Constantinople

Amph.	*Amphilochia*
Enc.	*Encyclical*
Ep.	*Epistles*
Hom.	*Homilies*
Man.	*Against the Manicheans*
Myst.	*Mystagogy Concerning the Doctrine of the Holy Spirit*
Syn.	*Collections and Demonstrations {Συναγωγαὶ καὶ ἀποδείξεις}*
Ps.Phot.	Pseudo-Photius
Franc.	*Against the Franks*
Rom.	*Against Those Who Say that Rome Is the First See*
Pos.*V.Aug.*	Possidius. *Life of Augustine*
Psell.	Michael Psellus
Acc.Cerul.	*Accusation against Michael Cerularius*
Cant.	*Commentary on the Book of Canticles*
Char.Gr.Theol.	*Character of Gregory the Theologian*
Char.Joh.Chrys.	*Character of John Chrysostom*
Chron.	*Chronography*
Com.Sim.Met.	*Commemoration of Simeon Metaphrastes*
Daem.	*On the Activity of Demons*
Enc.Sim.Met.	*Encomium of Simeon Metaphrastes*
Ep.	*Epistles*
Exeg.Phdr.	*Exegesis of the "Phaedrus"*
Id.	*On Plato's Doctrine of Ideas*
Om.doct.	*Omnifarious Doctrine*
Pr.Phil.Sol.	*Preface to Philip the Solitary*
Salut.	*Oration on the Salutation {to Mary}*
Pyrr.	Pyrrhus of Constantinople
Radb.*Cog.*	Paschasius Radbertus. *You Compel Me {Cogitis me}*
Ratr.*Graec.*	Ratramnus. *Against the Greeks*
Reg.*Chron.*	Regino of Prüm. *Chronicle*
Rom.Mel.	Romanus the Melodist
Akath.	*Akathistos*
Kont.	*Kontakion*
Oik.	*Oikioi*
Hymn.	*Hymns*
Se'ert.*Chron.*	*Chronicle of Se'ert* (Kurdistan)
Serg.*Ep.*	Sergius of Constantinople. *Epistles*
Serg.Cyp.*Ep.Thdr.*	Sergius of Cyprus. *Epistle to Pope Theodore*
Sev.Ant.	Severus of Antioch
Ep.Thds.	*Epistle to Theodosius*
Gram.	*Against the Godless Grammarian*
Hom.cathed.	*Cathedral Homilies*
Neph.	*To Nephalius*
Sim.N.Th.	Simeon (Symeon) the New Theologian
Catech.	*Catechetical Sermons*
Eth.	*Ethical Orations*
Hymn.	*Hymns*
Myst.	*Mystical Prayer*
Or.	*Orations*
Theol.	*Theological Orations*
Sim.Thess.*Haer.*	Simeon of Thessalonica. *Against All Heresies*
Smarag.	Smaragdus
Acta	*Acts of the Conference in Rome {810}*

Spir.	*On the Holy Spirit*
Soph.	Sophronius of Jerusalem
Ep.syn.	*Synodical Epistle*
Or.	*Orations*
Steph.Bostr.*fr.*	Stephen of Bostra. *Fragments*
Steph.Dor.*Ep.*	Stephen of Dora (Palestine). *Epistle*
Symb.Ath.	*Athanasian Creed {Symbolum Athanasianum}*
Symb.CP(681)	*Symbol of the Third Council of Constantinople*
Symb.Leo III.	*Symbol of Pope Leo III*
Syn.CP.(1638)	Synod of Constantinople (1638)
Syn.CP.(1672)	Synod of Constantinople (1672)
Syn.H.(1672)	Synod of Jerusalem (1672)
Syn.Jass.(1643)	Synod of Jassy, Moldavia (1643)
Syn.Jes.(585)	Synod of Jesuyahb I (585)
Syn.Kos.(612)	Synod of King Kosran (612)
Syn.Pal.(1341)	Palamite Synod (1341)
Syn.Pal.(1351)	Palamite Synod (1351)
Syn.Pal.(1368)	Palamite Synod (1368)
Syn.Sel.(486)*Can.*	Synod of Seleucia (486). *Canons*
Syndoct.post.	*Later Agreement {Syndocticon posterius}*
Tert.	Tertullian of Carthage
Praescrip.	*Prescription of Heretics*
Prax.	*Against Praxeas*
Thdr.AbuQ.	Theodore Abû Qurra
Conc.	*Conflicts with the Saracens, from the Mouth of John of Damascus {Concertationes cum Saracenis}*
Imag.	*On the Cult of Images*
Mim.	*Address {Mîmar}*
Opusc.	*Opuscula*
Thdr.Agall.*Argyr.*	Theodore Agallianus. *Refutation of John Argyropoulos*
Thdr.CP.*Qu.Max.*	Theodore, deacon of Constantinople. *Questions to Maximus*
Thdr.H.	Theodore of Jerusalem
Thdr.Phar.*fr.*	Theodore of Pharan. *Fragments*
Thdr.Stud.	Theodore of Studios
Antirr.	*Refutations {Antirrhetica} of the Iconoclasts*
Can.imag.	*Canon for the Establishment of the Holy Images*
Ep.	*Epistles*
Ep.imag.	*Epistle to Plato on the Cult of the Holy Images*
Icon.	*Chapters against the Iconoclasts*
Or.	*Orations*
Praesanct.	*Exposition of the Liturgy of the Presanctified*
Prob.	*Problems for the Iconoclasts*
Ref.	*Refutation of the Poems of the Iconoclasts*
Thds.Al.	Theodosius of Alexandria
Ep.	*Epistle*
Ep.Paul.Ant.	*Epistle to Paul of Antioch*
Or.	*Oration*
Thds.Peč.*Lat.*	Theodosius of Pečerskaja Lavra. *Against the Latins {Slovo}*
Thdt.*H.r.*	Theodoret of Cyrrhus. *History of Religion*
Them.*fr.*	Themistius of Alexandria. *Fragments*
Theod.Aur.*Spir.*	Theodulph of Orléans [Aurelianensis]. *On the Holy Spirit*
Theoph.*Chron.*	Theophanes the Confessor. *Chronography*
Theoph.Nic.*Theot.*	Theophanes of Nicea. *Sermon on the Theotokos*

Theor.*Disp.*	Theorianus. *Disputations with Narsai IV*
Theot.	*Demonstration That Mary Is Theotokos*
Thos.Aq.*Graec.*	Thomas Aquinas. *Against the Errors of the Greeks*
Thos.Ed.*Nat.*	Thomas of Edessa. *Treatise on the Nativity of Our Lord Jesus Christ*
Thphyl.CP.*Ep.Petr.Bulg.*	Patriarch Theophylact of Constantinople. *Epistle to Czar Peter of Bulgaria*
Thphyl.Ochr.*Lat.*	Theophylact of Ochrida (Bulgaria). *On the Things of Which the Latins Are Accused*
Tim.I.*Ep.*	Timothy I, Nestorian patriarch. *Epistles*
Tim.Ael.*Chalc.*	Timothy Aelurus, Monophysite patriarch of Alexandria. *Critique and Refutation of the Definition at Chalcedon*
Troph.Dam.	*Trophies of the Divine and Unconquerable Church of God and of the Truth against the Jews in Damascus*
Verg.*Aen.*	Vergil. *Aeneid*
V.Moh.	*Life of Mohammed*
Vosk.Chron.	*Chronicle of Voskrosensk {Voskrosenskaja lĕtopis'}*

Editions and Collections

ACO	*Acta conciliorum oecumenicorum.* Strasbourg, 1914–.
Allacci	Allacci, Leone [Leo Allatius]. *De ecclesiae occidentalis atque orientalis perpetua consensione.* Cologne, 1648.
Arendzen	Arendzen, Johann, ed. *Theodori Abu Kurra De cultu imaginum libellus.* Bonn, 1897.
Badger	Badger, George Percy. *The Nestorians and Their Rituals.* Vol. 2. London, 1852.
Barth-Niesel	Barth, Peter, and Niesel, Wilhelm, eds. *Joannis Calvini Opera Selecta.* 5 vols. Munich, 1926–36.
Bek.	*Die Bekenntnisschriften der evangelisch-lutherischen Kirche.* 2d ed. Göttingen, 1952.
Bidez-Parmentier	Bidez, Joseph, and Parmentier, Léon, eds. *The Ecclesiastical History of Evagrius with the Scholia* London, 1898.
Bonwetsch	Bonwetsch, G. Nathanael, ed. *Doctrina Jacobi nuper baptizati.* Berlin, 1910.
Boor	Boor, Carl Gotthard de, ed. *Theophanis Chronographia.* 2 vols. Leipzig, 1883–85.
Borovkova-Majkova	Borovkova-Majkova, M. S., ed. *Nila Sorskago Predanie i Ustav so vstupitel'noju stat'ej.* St. Petersburg, 1912.
Brightman	Brightman, Frank Edward, ed. *Liturgies Eastern and Western.* Vol. 1: *Eastern Liturgies* (no more published). Oxford, 1896.
Carr	Carr, Simon Joseph, ed. Thomas of Edessa. *Treatise on the Nativity of Our Lord Christ.* Rome, 1898.
CCSL	*Corpus christianorum. Series latina.* Turnhout, Belgium, 1953–.
Chabot	Chabot, Jean Baptiste, ed. *Synodicon Orientale ou recueil de synodes nestoriens.* Paris, 1902.
Connolly	Connolly, Richard Hugh, ed. Narsai. *Liturgical Homilies.* Cambridge, 1909.

Connolly-Codrington   Connolly, Richard Hugh, and Codrington, Humphrey William, eds. *Two Commentaries on the Jacobite Liturgy.* London, 1913.

Contos   Contos, Leonidas. *The Concept of Theosis in Saint Gregory Palamas. With Critical Text of the "Contra Akindynum."* Vol. 2: Text. Los Angeles, 1963.

CR   *Corpus Reformatorum.* Berlin and Leipzig, 1834–.

CSCO   *Corpus scriptorum christianorum orientalium.* Paris, 1903–.

CSEL   *Corpus scriptorum ecclesiasticorum latinorum.* Vienna, 1866–.

DAI   *Dopolnenija k Aktam istoričeskim.* St. Petersburg, 1846–72.

Darrouzès   Darrouzès, Jean, ed. *Documents inédits d'ecclésiologie byzantine.* Paris, 1966.

Diekamp   Diekamp, Franz, ed. *Doctrina patrum de incarnatione Verbi.* Münster, 1907.

Ed.Leon.   *S. Thomae Aquinatis opera omnia, iussu Leonis XIII edita.* Rome, 1882–.

Eustratiades   Eustratiades, Sophronius, ed. Ῥωμανὸς ὁ Μελῳδὸς καὶ ἡ Ἀκάθιστος. Thessalonica, 1917.

Ficker   Ficker, Gerhard, ed. *Die Phundagiagiten: Ein Beitrag zur Ketzergeschichte des byzantinischen Mittelalters.* Leipzig, 1908.

Foerster   Foerster, Hans, ed. *Liber diurnus Romanorum pontificum.* Bern, 1958.

Frankenberg   Frankenberg, Wilhelm, ed. *Euagrius Ponticus* (with Babai's exposition). Berlin, 1912.

GCS   *Die griechischen christlichen Schriftsteller der ersten drei Jahrhunderte.* Berlin, 1897–.

Goodspeed   Goodspeed, Edgar Johnson, ed. *Die ältesten Apologeten.* Göttingen, 1915.

Gordillo   Gordillo, Maurice. "Photius et primatus Romanus." *Orientalia Christiana Periodica* 6(1940):1–39.

Gouillard   Gouillard, Jean, ed. *Le Synodicon de l'Orthodoxie: édition et commentaire.* Centre de recherche d'histoire et civilisation byzantines: *Travaux et Mémoires.* Vol. 2:1–316. Paris, 1967.

Graf   Graf, Georg, ed. *Die arabischen Schriften des Theodor Abû Qurra.* Paderborn, 1910.

Hergenröther   Hergenröther, Joseph Adam Gustav, ed. *Monumenta Graeca ad Photium pertinentia.* Regensburg, 1869.

Hofmann   Hofmann, Georg, ed. *Concilium Florentinum.* 3 vols. Rome, 1929–31.

Holl   Holl, Karl. "Die Schriften des Epiphanius gegen die Bilderverehrung." *Gesammelte Aufsätze zur Kirchengeschichte.* Vol. 2: *Der Osten,* pp. 351–87. Tübingen, 1928.

Jeffery   Jeffery, Arthur. "Ghevond's Text of the Correspondence between 'Umar II and Leo III." *Harvard Theological Review* 37 (1944):269–332.

Jugie   Jugie, Martin, ed. Theophanes Nicaenus. *Sermo in Sanctissimam Deiparam.* Rome, 1935.

Karmirēs   Karmirēs, Iōannēs N., ed. Τὰ δογματικὰ καὶ συμβολικὰ μνημεία τῆς ὀρθοδόξου καθολικῆς ἐκκλησίας. 2 vols. 2d ed. Athens and Graz, 1960–68.

Kayser	Kayser, C. *Die Canones Jacob's von Edessa übersetzt und erläutert, zum Theil auch zuerst im Grundtext veröffentlicht.* Leipzig, 1886.
Kmosko	Kmosko, M., ed. *Demonstratio inedita probans Mariam Dei genitricem esse.* In "Analecta Syriaca e codicibus Musei Britannici excerpta." *Oriens Christianus* 2 (1902): 39–57.
Kotter	Kotter, Bonifatius, ed. *Die Schriften des Johannes von Damaskus.* Berlin, 1969–.
Kurtz-Drexl	Kurtz, Eduard, and Drexl, Franz, eds. *Michaelis Pselli Scripta minora.* 2 vols. Milan, 1936–41.
Lagarde	Lagarde, Paul de, ed. *Iohannis Euchaitorum metropolitae quae in codice vaticano Graeco 676 supersunt.* Göttingen, 1882.
Lambot	Lambot, Cyrille, ed. *Oeuvres théologiques et grammaticales de Godescalc d'Orbais.* Louvain, 1945.
Laourdas	Laourdas, Basil S., ed. Φωτίου ὁμιλίαι. Thessalonica, 1959.
Legrand	Legrand, Emile Louis Jean, ed. *Bibliographie hellénique ou Description raisonée des ouvrages publiés par des Grecs au dix-septième siècle.* 5 vols. Paris, 1894–1903.
Leib	Leib, Bernard, ed. *Deux inédits byzantins sur les azymes au début du XIIe siècle.* Rome, 1924.
Leonid	Leonid, Metropolitan, ed. *Žitie prepodobnago . . . Sergija čudotvorca i Pochval'noe emu slovo.* St. Petersburg, 1885.
Levy	Levy, Paul, ed. Michael Psellus. *De Gregorii theologi charactere iudicium, accedit eiusdem de Ioannis Chrysostomi charactere iudicium ineditum.* Leipzig, 1912.
Lietzmann	Lietzmann, Hans, ed. *Das Leben des heiligen Symeon Stylites.* Leipzig, 1908.
Loparev	Loparev, Chr. "Ob Uniatstvě Imperatora Manuila Komnina." *Vizantijskij Vremennik* 14 (1907):344–57.
McGiffert	McGiffert, Arthur Cushman, ed. *Dialogue between a Christian and a Jew Entitled* Ἀντιβολὴ Παπίσκου καὶ Φίλωνος Ἰουδαίου πρὸς μοναχόν τινα. New York, 1889.
Mai	Mai, Angelo, ed. *Scriptorum veterum nova collectio e vaticanis codicibus.* 10 vols. Rome, 1825–38.
Makarij	Makarij, Metropolitan. *Istorija russkoj cerkvi.* 3d ed. 12 vols. in 8. St. Petersburg, 1877–91.
Malinin	Malinin, V. N. *Starec Eleazarova monastyrja Filofej i ego poslanija.* Kiev, 1901.
Mansi	Mansi, J. D., ed. *Sacrorum conciliorum nova et amplissima collectio.* Florence, 1759–98.
Meyendorff	Meyendorff, Jean, ed. Grégoire Palamas. *Défense des saints hésychastes.* 2 vols. Louvain, 1959.
MGH	*Monumenta Germaniae Historica.* Berlin, 1826–.
Conc.	*Concilia.*
Conc.Sup.	*Conciliorum Supplementa.*
Ep.	*Epistolae.*
Poet.	*Poetae.*
Scrip.	*Scriptores.*
Michalcescu	Michǎlcescu, Jon, ed. Θησαυρὸς τῆς ὀρθοδοξίας: *Die Bekenntnisse und die wichtigsten Glaubenszeugnisse der griechisch-orientalischen Kirche im Originaltext, nebst einleitenden Bemerkungen.* Leipzig, 1904.

Michel — Michel, Anton. *Humbert und Kerularios: Quellen und Studien zum Schisma des XI. Jahrhunderts.* 2 vols. Paderborn, 1924–30.

Mohler — Mohler, Ludwig, ed. *Bessarionis in calumniatorem Platonis libri IV.* Paderborn, 1927.

Montet — Montet, Édouard Louis. "Un rituel d'abjuration des musulmans dans l'église grecque." *Revue de l'histoire des religions* 53 (1906): 145–63.

Müller — Müller, Ludolf, ed. *Des Metropoliten Ilarion Lobrede auf Vladimir den Heiligen und Glaubensbekenntnis nach der Erstausgabe von 1844 neu herausgegeben, eingeleitet und erläutert.* Wiesbaden, 1962.

Nairn — Nairn, J. A., ed. *"De Sacerdotio" of St. John Chrysostom.* Cambridge, 1906.

Pavlov — Pavlov, Alexsandr S. *Kritičeskje opyty po istorii drevnejšej greko-russkoj polemiki protiv Latinjan.* St. Petersburg, 1878.

Petit — Petit, Louis, et al. *Oeuvres complètes de Georges (Gennade) Scholarios.* 8 vols. Paris, 1928–36.

Petrovskij — Petrovskij, N., ed. "Pis'mo patriarcha Konstantinopol'skago Feofilakta Carju Bolgarii Petru." *Izvěstija otdělenija russkago jazika i slovesnosti imperatorskoj Akademii Nauk 1913 g.,* pp. 356–72. St. Petersburg, 1913.

PG — *Patrologia graeca.* Paris, 1857–66.

Phillips — Phillips, George, ed. *The Doctrine of Addai.* London, 1876.

Pitra — Pitra, Jean Baptiste, ed. *Spicilegium Solesmense.* 4 vols. Paris, 1852–58.

PL — *Patrologia latina.* Paris, 1878–90.

PO — *Patrologia orientalis.* Paris, 1903–.

Popov — Popov, Andrej N. *Istoriko-literaturnyj obzor drevnerusskich polemičeskich sočinenij protiv Latinjan.* Moscow, 1875.

Popruženko — Popruženko, Michail Georgevič, ed. *Kozma presbiter. Bolgarskij pisatel' X. věka.* Sofia, 1936.

PSRL — *Polnoe sobranie russkich lětopisej.* St. Petersburg, 1841–1968.

Reifferscheid — Reifferscheid, August, ed. *Annae Comnenae Porphyrogenitae Alexias.* 2 vols. Leipzig, 1884.

Reischl-Rupp — Reischl, W. K., and Rupp, J., eds. Cyril of Jerusalem. *Opera.* 2 vols. Munich, 1848–60.

Renauld — Renauld, Émile, ed. Michael Psellus. *Chronographia.* 2 vols. Paris, 1926–28.

RIB — *Russkaja istoričeskaja biblioteka.* St. Petersburg, 1872–1927.

Rücker — Rücker, Adolf, ed. *Die syrische Jakobosanaphora nach der Rezension des Ja'qôb(h) von Edessa.* Münster, 1923.

Sathas — Sathas, Kōnstantinos N., ed. Μεσαιωνική βιβλιοθήκη ἢ Συλλογὴ ἀνεκδότων μνημείων τῆς ἑλληνικῆς ἱστορίας. 7 vols. Venice, 1872–94.

SC — *Sources chrétiennes.* Paris, 1940–.

Schaff — Schaff, Philip, ed. *Creeds of Christendom.* 3 vols. 6th ed. New York, 1919.

Schirò — Schirò, Giuseppe, ed. Barlaam Calabro. *Epistole greche i primordi episodici e dottrinari delle lotte esicaste: Studio introduttivo e testi.* Palermo, 1954.

Schmitt   Schmitt, F. S., ed. *Sancti Anselmi opera omnia.* Seckau, Rome, Edinburgh, 1938–61.

Schoell-Kroll   Schoell, Rudolf, and Kroll, Wilhelm, eds. *Corpus iuris civilis.* vol. 3: *Novellae.* Berlin, 1912.

ST   *Studi e testi.* Rome, 1900–.

Trapp   Trapp, Erich, ed. Manuel II. Palaiologos. *Dialoge mit einem "Perser."* Vienna, 1966.

WA   D. *Martin Luthers Werke.* Weimar, 1883 ff.

Br.   *Briefe*

Weiskotten   Weiskotten, Herbert T., ed. *Sancti Augustini vita scripta a Possidio episcopo.* Princeton, 1919.

Westerink   Westerink, Leendert Gerrīt, ed. Michael Psellus. *De omnifaria doctrina.* Nijmegen, 1948.

Will   Will, Cornelius, ed. *Acta et scripta quae de controversiis ecclesiae graecae et latinae saeculo undecimo composita extant.* Leipzig, 1861.

Ex Oriente Lux

Harnack (1931) 2:511

The seventh century is known as the time when "the history of dogma in the Greek church came to an end, [so that] any revival of that history is difficult to imagine." *The Spirit of Eastern Christendom* begins its account with the seventh century. From then on, we are told elsewhere, Eastern Christians "held in their lifeless hands the riches of their fathers, without inheriting the spirit which had created and improved that sacred patrimony. . . . In the revolution of ten centuries, not a single discovery was made to exalt the dignity or promote the

Gibbon (1896) 6:107

happiness of mankind." *The Spirit of Eastern Christendom* is a history of those ten centuries.

These quotations from two of the most eminent historians of modern times illustrate an attitude toward the history of Eastern Christianity and of its doctrine that has been all but canonical in Western historiography. Multivolume histories of the church—even one that was published within the past decade—have been able simply to ignore most of the development of non-Western Christendom except for those episodes, such as the schism or the Crusades, that involved the history of the West as well. Greek Orthodox Christianity is widely thought to have been characterized by "degradation of will, and slavery of the whole episcopate to the whims of the emperors. . . , that narrow pietism, that formalism and ritualism in devotion, consisting altogether in the ex-

Vailhé (1913) 763,761

ternals of religion." Linguistic barriers, political divisions, and liturgical differences helped to isolate the two cultures from one another and thus to perpetuate a schism of mind and spirit even among those (for example, the two

1

historians quoted earlier) for whom the ecclesiastical
and confessional schism was not theologically normative.

Alongside this isolation—partly reacting against it and
partly stemming from it—was an ecumenical and sometimes romantic yearning for Eastern Christianity. Martin
Luther appealed to the example of the East as proof that
one could be catholic and orthodox without being papal.
Military conflict between Anglicans and Russian Orthodox during the Crimean War made it necessary to
consider the problems, if not of intercommunion, then
at least of interburial. The monumental *Patrologia
Graeca,* published between 1857 and 1866; the scientific
work of the Pontifical Oriental Institute and, before its
establishment, of individual Roman Catholic scholars
such as Cardinals Mai and Pitra; the editions and monographs of Western Byzantinists—all these contributed to
a better understanding of the East by the West and, for
that matter, to a better understanding of the East by the
East itself, for, even in the distinguished publications of
the Greek and Russian historians listed in our bibliography, the East could not match the West in either quality
or quantity of scholarship. In the aftermath of the Russian Revolution, theologians and other intellectuals came
to the centers of Western thought and life, bringing with
them the treasures of the Eastern tradition, as the "Greek
scholars in Venice" had on the eve of the Renaissance.
Western historians of art have been intrigued by icons
and mosaics, while men of thought and letters have discovered the philosophical and theological power of
Dostoevski and Tolstoi. And William Butler Yeats
described how he had

... sailed the seas and come
To the holy city of Byzantium.

Yeats's attitude, not surprisingly, comes close to the
estimate of Eastern Christianity on the part of its own
adherents. The orthodox churches of the East were joined
by the separated, "non-Chalcedonian" churches (to whose
christological doctrines we shall turn in chapter 2) in
an affirmation of the special destiny of the East. The
East represented the rising sun and its illumination, the
West symbolized "the godless souls in the deep hell of
ignorance." Prelates of the Latin church, in the land of
the sunset, could be dismissed as "the bishops of darkness." It was also from the East that Christ had come.

See p. 281 below

Geanakoplos (1962)

Bab.*Evagr.*3.60 (Frankenberg
231[230])

Phot.*Enc.*24 (*PG* 102:732)
Tim.I.*Ep.*26 (*CSCO*
75:100–101[74:148–49])

Gregent.*Herb*.2 (*PG* 86:669);
Tim.I.*Ep*.2.3 (*CSCO* 75:31
[74:50])

Orthodox and Nestorians were agreed that "we have been taught to pray toward the East, because we find that God created man there," in the Garden of Eden. In fact, the East had been the source of life and light from the beginning. "Ex Oriente lux! The Christian church on earth began in the East. In the East lay Paradise, the location of the 'primitive church'; out of the East came the ancestor of Israel, Abraham, led by the great promise of God; Jesus was born in the East; out of the East came the Magi to the manger of Christ as emissaries of the

Heiler (1937) 125

entire Gentile world." Much of Christian liturgy and most of Christian dogma had arisen in the East, as Greek theologians frequently reminded their Western opponents. The principal symbol of the superiority of Eastern over Western theology was the preeminence of Greek as the language for expressing Christian doctrine with due precision. Various doctrinal controversies showed that "there are not even any Latin terms to correspond to the

Elert (1957) 186

more subtle conceptual distinctions" of Greek theology.

One feature of Greek theology has special pertinence, and creates special complications, for the historical study of the development of doctrine. According to its leading proponents, orthodox doctrine did not really have a history, but had been changeless from the beginning. Their Nestorian and Jacobite adversaries were no less insistent upon the immutability of Christian truth. In some ways, indeed, the documentary evidence would seem to bear out this assumption. In theology, as in rhetoric, there was "a great consensus binding together authors who are widely separated in time, so that one cannot in a precise sense

Böhlig (1956) 248

speak of a 'development,' but only of a tradition." In some cases (for example, in the glosses on Dionysius the Areopagite ascribed to Maximus Confessor) literary analysis shows that authentic paragraphs have probably been conflated with later ones, but even this analysis seems sufficiently tenuous to warrant our citing the glosses under the name of Maximus. If the assumption of changeless truth were carried to its ultimate conclusion, this would, of course, preclude the writing of a history of doctrine in our sense of the word "history," which is based on the assumption that the study of a development in chronological sequence helps to make the past intelligible. In this volume as in its predecessor, our own procedure has been basically chronological, with each doctrine in-

See vol. 1:279–92

troduced at the point when it became historically decisive. But as the earlier development of the Christian doctrine of man was described in connection with Augustine, so here we have violated chronology by usually including the preceding and the subsequent history of a doctrine in the chapter dealing with its principal historical manifestation. The major exceptions to this basically chronological structure are the chapters dealing with non-Chalcedonian christology and with the relations between orthodox Christianity and other religions. Both seem to lend themselves better to synthetic than to sequential treatment. It must, moreover, be emphasized again that the

See vol. 1:85

discussion of non-Christian religions has dealt only with their significance for Christianity as this significance was seen by Christians: Christian distortions of Jewish or Muslim doctrine were what made Christian doctrinal history, and we have taken them largely as they stand.

The relation of Christianity to these non-Christian religions, especially to Islam, belongs to political and to military history at least as much as to the history of doctrine. Similarly, the relation of orthodox to heretical Christianity, in the debates over the two natures in Christ or over the icons, was in large measure a political as well as a doctrinal matter. While the controversy over one will or two wills in Christ was raging during the seventh century, Sophronius, patriarch of Jerusalem, took Stephen, bishop of Dora, to Calvary and spoke of the need for

Steph.Dor.*Ep.* (Mansi 10:896)

christological orthodoxy amid the terrors of the Muslims. In a Christmas sermon in 638, Sophronius lamented his inability this year to maintain his usual custom of following the path of the shepherds to Bethlehem, for one must now fear not the flaming sword before Paradise,

Soph.*Or.*1 (*PG* 87:3206)

but the sword of the Saracen conquerors. Jerusalem came into Muslim hands in 638, Antioch in the same year, and Alexandria in 642–43: of the five patriarchates in which, by Eastern theory, lay the ultimate earthly authority over the church, three were conquered in the

See pp. 164–66 below

space of half a decade. Hence it is understandable that a christological confession would contain the plea to be delivered from "the domination of tyrants and the imposture of the Persians . . . and the willfulness of the

Cyrus.Al.*Ep.*1 (Mansi 10:1005)

Saracens"; or that in the middle of a conventional Eastern restatement of the Nicene Creed against the Latins, an eleventh-century patriarch of Antioch should suddenly

Petr.Ant.*Ep.H*.5.3 (Michel 2:442)

break into an anathema upon "the Arabian wolves, who have ravaged every one of the churches."

It is not, therefore, an effort to deny the importance of these portentous historical events when we turn our attention to the doctrinal developments and theological issues of the seventh and subsequent centuries. As the Roman persecution of Christians or Constantine's suspension of that persecution belonged to our account only insofar as the former determined the doctrinal answer See vol. 1:37–38 of the church to classicism and the latter determined the See vol. 1:200–210 form of the dogma of the Trinity, so here we shall treat even such awesome political and military cataclysms as the fall of Constantinople in 1204 and again in 1453 only in connection with the conflict between Eastern and Western Christianity, or between Christianity and Islam, over Christian doctrine, which we have defined as "what the church of Jesus Christ believes, teaches, and conSee vol. 1:1fesses on the basis of the word of God." It is worth noting that the conflict with Islam was responsible for an emphasis upon the relation between believing, teaching, and confessing. Against the Arabs Nicetas of Byzantium Nicet.Byz.*Arab*.1.10 (*PG* 105:681) asserted "what is confessed and believed among us Christians"; and John VI Cantacuzenus, emperor and theologian, at the opening of his *Apologies* against Islam, declared: "That God is the Maker of all things, visible Joh.Cant.*Apol*.1.1 (*PG* 154:381) and invisible—this we have been taught and have come to know and believe and confess." Even the Byzantine theory that the emperor occupied a special place in the church belongs to our account only as a chapter in ecSee pp. 144–45, 168 belowclesiology (which it certainly was), not as a concept in Byzantine statesmanship or jurisprudence (which it also was).

The same principle of definition and of exclusion applies to the institutional history of the Eastern churches. Eastern monasticism gave the impetus to the religious life in the West through the *Life of Antony,* written by Athanasius and translated into Latin very early. In the social and political history of Byzantium the monks were a powerful force, and such establishments as Studios under Theodore or the various communities of Athos, "the holy mountain," played an influential role in many aspects of Byzantine life. One such aspect was Christian doctrine, and therefore the monks will appear repeatedly in our narrative and will sometimes even

See pp. 254–70 below

See pp. 133–45 below

Lemerle (1971) 203
Phot.*Ep*.2.48 (*PG* 102:865)

Phot.*Ep*.2.39 (*PG* 102:853–57)

See vol. 1:339–49

dominate it. Yet the distinctive features of ascetic practice will be strictly ancillary to our main business, despite their importance and interest. A similar function will be assigned to the history of the liturgy. It will occupy an even more prominent place in this second volume than it did in the first. Not only the iconoclastic controversy, but many other doctrinal discussions make sense only in a liturgical context. But we must leave to other works the account of how Greek and Syriac worship has evolved or of how the Old Church Slavic liturgies arose, and concentrate on liturgy as "the melody of theology." Finally, Byzantine theology included a force virtually unknown in the West until the Renaissance or even later: the theological speculations of an educated laity. Before he became patriarch in 858, Photius had been "not a professor, not the occupant of a chair," but a lay intellectual. He could address a poet as "the Homerizer" or could discourse about the Greek theater, including the comedies of Aristophanes, and then turn to polemics against the Western doctrine of Filioque. The Christian Hellenism of Michael Psellus two centuries later is probably an even better illustration. For our purposes, this Christian Hellenism represents chiefly the intellectual substratum of the doctrinal developments and, as such, can never be ignored, even though it is not the object of our research for its own sake.

By the seventh century, what we have called "catholic orthodoxy in the East" bore its own doctrinal identity and had begun to move in its own theological direction. Some of the questions that had been agitating it since the fourth and fifth centuries continued to be central to the doctrinal life of the church. It was above all the christological question—or cluster of questions—that refused to remain settled in the East, as one council after another, one theologian after another, one emperor after another, came up with supposedly definitive solutions that failed. And even when it had finally been settled, it not only left in its wake a series of lasting schisms; it also reappeared as the form for the solution of the controversy over icons. No comparable christological development was taking place in the West, which dealt instead with the problems of nature and grace or with the meaning of the sacraments—both christological questions by Eastern definition (or perhaps by any definition), but not questions for explicit controversy among Greek Christians. The theological debate between East and West became an epitome of the situation that had produced it: the two parties would not have been able to understand each other even if the Westerners had been able to read Greek or the Easterners had been able to read Latin.

It is fallacious and presumptuous to suppose, as many Western historians have, that the only worthwhile chapters in the doctrinal history of the East are those that deal with the West. On the contrary, even the student of Western history may benefit from a better acquaintance with specifically Eastern developments. Although the reader will undoubtedly discern the profound affinities of the author, in piety and in theology, with "the spirit of Eastern Christendom," this is nevertheless a history for Western readers and in a Western context. It was, after all, a Westerner, whether a pagan or a Christian, who coined the Latin proverb "Ex Oriente lux."

1　The Authority of the Fathers

The dominant figure in the development of Christian doctrine in the East during the seventh century was Maximus Confessor, whom modern historians have acclaimed as "the most universal spirit of the seventh century and perhaps the last independent thinker among the theologians of the Byzantine church," as "probably the only productive thinker of the entire century," and as "the real father of Byzantine theology." He was acknowledged as a saint very early, perhaps even during his own lifetime, and a century or so later was hailed as "a saintly veteran of many contests." Yet the same theologians who used such epithets in praise of Maximus Confessor also made clear that the very title of confessor implied anything but being independent, original, or productive; "that which is confessed among us" was intended "for the support of the dogma of theology." As a confessor and theologian, Maximus was obligated to preserve, protect, and defend the doctrine that had been handed down by the fathers; for to "confess with soul and mouth" meant to affirm "what the fathers have taught us." In any theological argument, therefore, it was necessary to produce "the voices of the fathers as evidence for the faith of the church." For that was what "theology" was, the study of the relation between Father, Son, and Holy Spirit in the Trinity, while "economy" referred to the incarnation of the Logos. A cognate distinction was that between "commandments" and "dogmas": through the former God set apart those who obeyed them, but through the latter he bestowed on them "the illumination of knowledge," for doctrines dealt either with God or with things visible

H.G.Beck (1959) 436
Elert (1957) 259
Meyendorff (1969) 99
Doct.patr.21.9 (Diekamp 137)

Thdr. Stud. Antirr.2.40 (PG 99:381)

Thdr.Stud.Antirr.2.26 (PG 99:369)

Max.Ep.12 (PG 91:465)

Max.Ep.13 (PG 91:532)

Max.Or.dom. (PG 90:876)
Max.Ep.13 (PG 91:524)
Max.Carit.2.24 (PG 90:992)

Max.*Carit*.1.77–78 (*PG* 90:977)

Max.*Ep*.2 (*PG* 91:494)

Hussey (1937) 29

Const.V.ap.Niceph.*Antirr*.1.11 (*PG* 100:220)

Joh.H.*Icon*.2 (*PG* 96:1349)

Thdr.Stud.*Antirr*.2.18 (*PG* 99:364)

Gal.1:8

Joh.D.*Imag*.2.6 (*PG* 94:1288)

Theor.*Disp*.2 (*PG* 133:289)

Sim.Thess.*Haer*. (*PG* 155:33)

and invisible or with the providence and judgment of God. For the same reason, "doctrine" and "love" had to be distinguished.

This understanding of the authority of the fathers was not peculiar either to Maximus or to his party; "the Byzantines never forgot their inheritance." All parties of Christians in all the controversies to be described here had in common a wish to conform themselves to that authority. For example, the iconoclasts had to claim in support of their position that they were "confessing what the holy catholic church had handed down," while their opponents likewise appealed to the church fathers, "whose sayings and whose virtues stand as a support and a pillar of the catholic and apostolic church." The same was true of the various sides in the conflict over the person of Christ, of the Eastern and Western positions on the Filioque, and of all the other theologies that arose. Almost any of the opponents in almost any of the disputes could have said with Theodore of Studios: "For the substantiation of what has been said it would be necessary to have the statement confirmed by patristic testimony." This testimony could not be contradicted by any other authority; for "if anyone announces to you another gospel than that which the catholic church has received from the holy apostles, fathers, and councils, and has guarded until now, do not listen to him. . . . If an angel or an emperor announces to you a gospel other than the one you have received, close your ears." Unquestioning loyalty to the fathers was a continuing characteristic of Eastern thought. A twelfth-century theologian observed that "the Romans [that is, the Byzantines] are exceedingly manly in other respects; but when it comes to transgressing the boundaries of the holy fathers, they are extremely cowardly." In the fifteenth century, the very title of the *Against Heresies* of Simeon of Thessalonica included the statement: "He has inserted nothing of his own, but has collected everything from the Holy Scriptures and from the fathers." Therefore it is important to pay attention not only to what the theologians of these centuries said themselves, but to which patristic authorities they cited and how. The selection and the arrangement of patristic testimonies in their theological treatises may be a more reliable index to their thought than are their own ex professo statements. For when a theologian undertook

Max.*Or.dom.* (*PG* 90:873)

to explain any issue or to expound any text, he had to acknowledge that he was setting forth not his own ideas, but what God had willed.

The Changeless Truth of Salvation

Epifanovič (1915) 125

See vol. 1:155; 233–34

Max.*Or.dom.* (*PG* 90:905)

Max.*Ascet*.2 (*PG* 90:913)

John 2:10

Max.*Qu.Thal*.40 (*PG* 90:396)
Max.*Qu.Thal*.9 (*PG* 90: 288)
1 John 3:2

Max.*Qu.Thal*.9 (*PG* 90:285)
Eph.1:18
Max.*Qu.Thal*.22 (*PG* 90:317)

Ps.82:6; John 10:34

2 Peter 1:4
Max.*Schol.D.n*.8.3 (*PG*
4:360); Max.*Schol.C.h*.12.3
(*PG* 4:96)
Max.*Schol.E.h*.3.13 (*PG*
4:152)
Max.*Schol.C.h*.7.2 (*PG* 4:69)

Max.*Ambig*.20 (*PG* 91:1241)
See vol. 1:348

Max.*Schol.Ep.Dion.Ar*.2 (*PG*
4:529)

Max.*Ascet*.1 (*PG* 90:912)

"The chief idea of St. Maximus, as of all of Eastern theology, [was] the idea of deification." Like all of his theological ideas, it had come to him from Christian antiquity and had been formulated by the Greek fathers. Salvation defined as deification was the theme of Christian faith and of the biblical message. The purpose of the Lord's Prayer was to point to the mystery of deification. Baptism was "in the name of the life-giving and deifying Trinity." When the guests at the wedding in Cana of Galilee, as described in the Gospel of John, said that their host had "kept the good wine until now," they were referring to the word of God, saved for the last, by which men were made divine. When, in the epistles of the same apostle John, "the Theologian," it was said that "it does not yet appear what we shall be," this was a reference to "the future deification of those who have now been made children of God." When the apostle Paul spoke of "the riches" of the saints, this, too, meant deification. But there were two principal passages of the Bible in which the definition of salvation as deification was set forth: the declaration of the psalm, "I say, 'You are gods,'" which was quoted in the New Testament; and the promise of the New Testament that believers would "become partakers of the divine nature." The first of these meant that righteous men and angels would become divine, the second that "being united with Christ" was the means of deification. For similarity to Christ was a deifying force, making men divine. Greek paganism had already known that one should rise from the active life to the contemplative, but Greek Christianity discovered that there was a third step beyond both of these, when one was taken up and was made divine. From the writings of Dionysius the Areopagite the devotees of contemplation had learned that God was not only beyond all existing realities, but beyond essence itself; and thus they had come to the true meaning of deification.

The presupposition of salvation as deification was the incarnation of the Logos of God, for "the purpose of the Lord's becoming man was our salvation." In fact, "the-

Max.*Schol.D.n.*2.9 (*PG* 4:225)

Max.*Ambig.*42 (*PG* 91:1348–49)

Max.*Ambig.*64 (*PG* 91:1389)

Max.*Qu.Thal.*61 (*PG* 90:637)
Max.*Ambig.*50 (*PG* 91:1368)

Thunberg (1965) 457–58

Max.*Ambig.*20 (*PG* 91:1237)

Max.*Qu.Thal.*22 (*PG* 90:321)

Max.*Opusc.*1 (*PG* 91:33)

ology" was sometimes used by such writers as Dionysius to refer to the mystery of the incarnation and related issues. Originally man had been created for "a mode of propagation that was deifying, divine, and nonmaterial," but his fall into sin meant that this divine plan was replaced and that man would be trapped in a material mode of propagation, one dominated by sexual passion. For this reason the Logos of God became man, to set man free from this passion and to restore him to the condition for which he had been created. And so God became human in order that man might become divine. Easter Sunday, "the first Sunday," could be seen either as "a symbol of the future physical resurrection and incorruptibility" or as "an image of the future deification by grace." Ultimately, of course, these were identical for the believer. The very definition of the gospel was tied to this definition of salvation; it was "an embassy from God and a summons to man through the incarnate Son and the reconciliation [He wrought] with the Father, granting a reward as a gift to those who have believed Him, namely, eternal deification." And even though deification was not explicitly mentioned in every definition of the gospel, it was present implicitly as the content of the salvation proclaimed by the gospel.

The phrase, "granting a reward as a gift," suggests an ambiguity in the idea of deification; for it is "possible for Maximus to say, on the one hand, that there is no power inherent in human nature which is able to deify man, and yet, on the other, that God becomes man *insofar* as man has deified himself." The biblical declaration, "You are gods," was not to be understood to mean that man had the capacity by nature or by his present condition to achieve deification; he could achieve it and receive this sublime name only by the adoption and the grace of God. Otherwise deification would not be the gift of God, but a work of human nature itself. "No creature is capable of deification by its own nature, since it is not capable of grasping God. This can happen only by the grace of God." Deification was not a matter of human power, but of divine power alone. Yet this repeated and unequivocal insistence upon grace as essential to deification was not intended to exclude the free will of man from participation in the process. For "the Spirit does not generate a will that is not willing, but he transforms into deification a will

Max.*Qu.Thal*.6 (*PG* 90:280)

See pp. 234–35 below

Max.*Opusc*.7 (*PG* 91:76)

Max.*Schol.D.n*.1.3 (*PG* 4:197)

Max.*Schol.E.h*.5.3 (*PG* 4:161)

Max.*Ambig*.60 (*PG* 91:1385)

Max.*Ambig*.47 (*PG* 91:1360)

that has the desire." Thus the antithesis between divine grace and human freedom, which dogged Western theology for many centuries, did not present a problem in that form for Eastern Christian thought. It is perhaps significant that some of the most extensive discussions of the question came in the controversies with Islam.

The gift of deification achieved by the incarnation of the Logos was not, however, intended to be kept hidden. It was a matter of divine revelation, made known to men through sacred teaching. Therefore, "perfect salvation" had as its counterpart "perfect confession," and heretics opposed them both. Because divinely revealed doctrine contained the truth of salvation, it was appropriate to call "the doctrines of the saints deifying lights," for they illumined believers with the light of reliable knowledge and made them divine. It was, then, characteristic of the means of grace and revelation that they communicated a knowledge of divine truth, even as they transformed mortal men by deification. On the one hand, Scripture did not only present the history of revelation and salvation, for "through the divine Scriptures we are purified and illumined for the sacred birth from God." On the other hand, the sacraments did not only convey grace, for "through the communion and through the rite of anointing we are made perfect in our knowledge." The truth of salvation conferred more than knowledge, but not less. One could rise from a knowledge of the saving history of the incarnation, death, and resurrection of Christ to a contemplation of glory, and ultimately to mystical union with God; but it was with such knowledge that one nevertheless had to begin. Through "practical philosophy" or the active life of the Christian some believers rose from the flesh of Christ to his soul; through contemplation others were enabled to go on from the soul of Christ to the "mind" of Christ; and through mystical union some few were able to move further still, from the mind of Christ to his very Godhead. But the true knowledge of God in Christ was indispensable to all of them.

Union with God and its preliminary, purification, were, therefore, closely tied to knowledge. Commenting on a passage in Gregory of Nazianzus, Maximus asserted that a "mystagogy through knowledge" was fundamental to the purification of the mind through the Holy Spirit, even though this gift was granted only to those who

Max.*Ambig*.19 (*PG* 91:1233)

already had the gift of holiness. Faith was to be defined as "the foundation underlying the deeds of piety, that which gives assurance that God is and that things divine are

Max.*Ep*.2 (*PG* 91:393, 396)

real." As such, it was the basis both of hope and of love, neither of which could be firm without it. The kingdom of God, which effected union with God, was "faith in

Max.*Qu.Thal*.33 (*PG* 90:373)

action." Such faith was quite specific in its content and object. It was "the faith of the church . . . through which

Max.*Qu.Thal*.48 (*PG* 90:440)

we are led into the inheritance of the good." The faith was attached to the orthodox dogmas of the church, which made both hope and love possible. Without faith it was impossible to attain to salvation. Believers had been taught that the necessary discipline for the attainment of

Max.*Ep*.12 (*PG* 91:504)

life eternal was nothing less than this faith; orthodox belief was necessary for salvation. And so the warning of the apostle Paul against "those who create dissensions and difficulties, in opposition to the doctrine which you

Rom.16:17

have been taught" was taken as an attack on "those who

Max.*Ep*.12 (*PG* 91:497)

do not accept the devout and saving dogmas of the church."

These devout and saving dogmas of the church were divinely revealed truth, and as such were changeless. When a theologian came, for example, to define "the supreme state of prayer," the definition was introduced

Max.*Carit*.2.61 (*PG* 90:1004)

with the formula, "they say," because manuals of prayer and ascetic practice, like other compendia of church doctrine, did not claim to be original at all. The richest legacy that anyone could bequeath to posterity, according to Theodore of Studios, was the orthodox faith of the

Thdr.Stud.*Or*.11.7.43 (*PG* 99:845)

church, together with the monastic rule. Quoting Maximus, this same theologian identified as "the dogma of truth" that which had been spoken in Christian antiquity by the fathers; his opponents agreed with him on the formal principle, disagreeing only on the material content

Thdr.Stud.*Antirr*.2.39-40 (*PG* 99:380-81)

of that tradition. Everyone on both sides of each of the controversies with which we shall be dealing accepted the principle of a changeless truth. Monotheletes and Dyotheletes, iconoclasts and iconodules, Greeks and Latins—all laid claim to this principle and insisted that they held to this changeless truth. "The word of truth is such," any of them might have said, "that it is uniform and unshakable by its very nature, and it cannot be subjected to differences of viewpoint or to temporal changes. It is always the same, teaching and advocating the same thing, because it transcends all addition or subtraction." It was characteristic of falsehood, by contrast, that it was "splintered into many parts and many theories, changing suddenly from one thing to another. At one moment it maintains this, at the next it teaches the very opposite; and it never remains fixed in the same place, for it is subject to changes and to the exigencies of mutation." And therefore when an ecumenical council promulgated a doctrine, under the leading of the Holy Spirit, this was acknowledged as the "ancient and originally authoritative tradition in the church . . . and in no sense an innovation."

Underlying this definition of divine truth as changeless was a definition of the divine itself as changeless and absolute. Because God transcended change, the truth about him also had to do so. It was characteristic of the nature of God to be impassible and indestructible. God was "both ancient and new," as Hebrews 13:8 also made clear. It was impossible to predicate any change of God or to attribute to him any movement of mind or will. When the biblical accounts, especially those of the Old Testament, ascribed "repentance" to God, this was not to be understood in a literal sense as some sort of anthropopathism, but, in keeping with the character of biblical language, as an accommodation to human ways of speaking. Scripture spoke in a way that was not literally accurate, in order to enable its readers to grasp what transcended literal accuracy. Thus only God was changeless by his very nature; yet others could receive the gift of being "immovable" as a kind of habitude. God was "by nature good and impassible," and he loved all his creatures alike; therefore a man who "by good will is good and impassible loves all men alike." Part of the process of salvation as deification was the gradual assimilation of the mind of man to the mind of God. Through the grace of prayer it was joined to God and it learned to associate only with God, becoming ever more godlike and withdrawing itself more and more from the dominance of this mortal life. The judgment of God did not proceed "according to time and the body," and so the soul, which transcended time and body, was assimilated to this divine quality. The use of the same vocabulary, and especially of the key term "changeless," both for the nature of God and for the distinctive character of truth about God, seems to imply a connection between the two.

Thdr.Stud.*Antirr*.2.pr. (*PG* 99:352)

Niceph.*Apol*.5 (*PG* 100:839)

Max.*Schol.Ep.Dion.Ar*.9.1 (*PG* 4:560)
Max.*Schol.D.n*.10.2 (*PG* 4:385)

Max.*Qu.Thal*.60 (*PG* 90:621)

Max.*Qu.dub*.32 (*PG* 90:812–13)

Max.*Schol.C.h*.2.2 (*PG* 4:37)

Max.*Schol.C.h*.7.2 (*PG* 4:68)

Max.*Carit*.1.25 (*PG* 90:965)

Max.*Ascet*.24 (*PG* 90:929)

Max.*Qu.dub*.60 (*PG* 90:832)

The contrast between the orthodox truth about God and its heretical distortions was to be found specifically in this distinctive character. For it was a mark of the heretics that they set forth "the innovation of those who are making the gospel worthless." A heretic was one who could be labeled as "the discoverer of these novel dogmas." The Montanist movement of the second and third centuries, with its claim to new prophecy, was rejected as a product not of the Holy Spirit of God but of the evil and demonic spirit. Origen's theory of the preexistence of the soul, as well as theories of the preexistence of the body, negated the "royal way" of the ancient patristic tradition, which taught that soul and body came into existence simultaneously. In contrast to this tradition, which was modest in its claims of knowledge about God, heretics such as Eunomius had presumed "to know God as well as he knows himself," which was madness and blasphemy. "Innovation" and "blasphemy" were almost synonymous, for both were opposed to divine truth, as the Arian heresy showed. This hostility to theological innovation appeared with at least equal vigor in the advocates of positions that eventually came to be acknowledged as heretical. Thus a christological position against which Maximus wrote was based on the presupposition that "every formula and term that is not found in the fathers is shown to be obviously an innovation," and that those who taught as Maximus did were inventing their own doctrine in opposition to the formula of the fathers. Another of his opponents insisted that it should be enough to stick to the language of the earlier councils and not to say more than they had said, even though new questions had arisen. Everyone agreed that heresy was simply "a new faith," one that taught "an alien god"; therefore it was to be rejected. It contradicted not only the ancient and traditional truth, but its own statements as well.

The changeless truth of salvation was therefore not subject to negotiation. When someone asked for forgiveness on the basis of his ignorance of the orthodox doctrine, it was essential to distinguish between a forgiveness extended to a person for his failings (which was required by the gospel) and a forgiveness extended to false dogmas (which was prohibited by the very same gospel). Doctrinal controversy was a difference not over vocabulary but over the very substance of Christian faith; this could

Max.*Ep*.13 (*PG* 91:517)

Niceph.*Antirr*.1.23 (*PG* 100:257)

See vol. 1:97–108

Max.*Ambig*.68 (*PG* 91:1405)

See vol. 1:337–38

Max.*Ambig*.42 (*PG* 91:1325)

Max.*Ambig*.18 (*PG* 91:1232)

Max.*Ambig*.24 (*PG* 91:1261)

Thdr.CP.*Qu.Max*.2 ap.Max. *Opusc*.19 (*PG* 91:216–17)

Pyrr.ap.Max.*Pyrr*. (*PG* 91:300)
Niceph.*Antirr*.1.20 (*PG* 100:244)

Niceph.*Antirr*.1.43 (*PG* 100:309)

Max.*Pyrr*. (*PG* 91:352)

Max.*Opusc*.16 (*PG* 91:189)

Pyrr.ap.Max.*Pyrr.* (*PG* 91:296)

Niceph.*Antirr*.3.34 (*PG* 100:428)

Max.*Ep*.12 (*PG* 91:500)

Max.*Qu.Thal*.63 (*PG* 90:665)

Max.*Pyrr.* (*PG* 91:328)

Max.*Qu.Thal*.40 (*PG* 90:400)
Max.*Schol.Myst*.1.3 (*PG* 4:420)

Max.*Ascet*.18 (*PG* 90:925)

Max.*Qu.Thal*.50 (*PG* 90:465)

Niceph.*Imag*.3 (*PG* 100:537)
Max.*Qu.Thal*.28 (*PG* 90:365);
Max.*Schol.D.n*.2.11 (*PG* 4:232); Max.*Schol.C.h*.6.2 (*PG* 4:64)

Max.*Ep*.7 (*PG* 91:433)

not be dismissed as logomachy. Sometimes it was suggested that the two sides in the controversy over the wills of Christ differed "not at all except in mere formulas," but this suggestion was repudiated as a betrayal of the true faith. To those who were faithful, there could be no distinction within the tradition between those things that were primary and those that were secondary, between what was to be respected more and what less; for the doctrine had come from the fathers and was to be revered. This was the ancient and changeless faith of the church. Those who accepted it were "those who graze on the divine and pure pasture of the doctrine of the church." The church was "pure and undefiled, immaculate and unadulterated," and in its message there was nothing alien or confused. The truth of the gospel was present in the church as it had been in the beginning, was now, and ever would be, world without end.

The Norms of Traditional Doctrine

The source of this changeless truth was to be found in "the dogmas of the evangelists and apostles and prophets." The saving knowledge of this truth, the source of life, had been drawn through a succession of witnesses in the Old and in the New Testament, beginning with the patriarchs, the lawgivers, and the leaders, continuing with the judges and the kings, and coming all the way to the prophets and to the evangelists and apostles. Their words, contained in the inspired Scriptures, were not of earth but of heaven. The lifelong study and "continuous meditation on the divine Scriptures" was the path to spiritual health. It was, therefore, not permissible for anyone to refuse to believe what Scripture said. Rather, one was to heed its word; for if it was God who had spoken and if he was uncircumscribed in his essence, then it was obvious that the word which had been spoken by him was uncircumscribed also. The foundation of faith was the authority of the apostles, the architects and heralds of the truth. Thus the apostle Paul was a servant of superhuman mysteries, the universal leader and guide, a veritable high priest. Not only the inspiration, but also the clarity of Scripture certified it as the supreme authority of Christian doctrine.

Yet the controversies of the centuries over the meaning of Christian doctrine made it obvious that, inspired and

Max.*Schol.D.n.*8.10 (*PG* 4:368)

Max.*Qu.Thal.*43 (*PG* 90:413)

Max.*Schol.D.n.*2.2 (*PG* 4:213)

Max.*Qu.Thal.*28 (*PG* 90:361)
Max.*Schol.C.h.*2.2 (*PG* 4:37)

Max.*Qu.Thal.*64 (*PG* 90:693)

Max.*Qu.Thal.*17 (*PG* 90:305)
Max.*Schol.Ep.Dion.Ar.*9.2 (*PG* 4:568)

Max.*Ambig.*46 (*PG* 91:1356)

Max.*Schol.Ep.Dion.Ar.*9.1 (*PG* 4:561)
Max.*Qu.Thal.*28 (*PG* 90:365)

Neh.7:66–70 (LXX)
Max.*Qu.Thal.*55 (*PG* 90:544–45)

Max.*Schol.E.h.*5.2 (*PG* 4:161)

clear though Scripture was, theologians could read and understand it in different, indeed contradictory, ways. It was essential not to go "outside the intent of Scripture." For "those who do not read the words of the Spirit wisely and carefully" could fall "into many kinds of error" and had done so. It was not enough to know the Scriptures thoroughly and to have been trained in them; the heretics, despite these advantages, still managed to deceive themselves. They distorted the Scriptures to suit their own minds, which were hostile to God. Such false interpretation happened when the reader, through ignorance and especially through deliberate distortion, failed to observe the distinctiveness of the biblical way of speaking. It was "the custom of Scripture to explain the ineffable and hidden counsels of God in a bodily manner, so that we might be able to know divine matters on the basis of words and sounds that are cognate; for otherwise the mind of God remains unknown, his word unspoken, his life incomprehensible." This meant that these things were not in fact as Scripture described them, but Scripture was true even when it was not literally accurate. Anyone who sought to grasp the meaning of the Scriptures had to pay very careful attention to their way of speaking. He had also to observe that a word or a proper name used in them was multiple in meaning. Scripture consistently placed its real and spiritual meaning "before what it tells in historical accounts," but this was evident only to those who looked at it with sound vision and healthy eyes. The historical accounts in the Bible were never merely historical.

Above all, this characteristic of Scripture was important for a proper understanding of what it had to say about Christ and about salvation. "Our Savior has many names," and there were many methods of contemplating him through the types and symbols of the natural world as these were employed in the Scriptures. The proper interpretation of Scripture was a symbolic and sacramental interpretation because of the nature of the ineffable truth communicated by it. For while it was true that "the prophetic charisma is far inferior to the apostolic," the writings of the prophets, if properly understood, were replete with testimony to Christ. The three thousand who came out of Babylon were a witness to the Trinity. The hierarchy of the church was a fulfillment of the Old Testament priesthood. The Old Testament was a shadow

Max.*Schol.E.h*.3.2;3.5 (*PG*
4:137; 141)

Thdr.AbuQ.*Mim*.1.18 (Graf
104)

Max.*Qu.Thal*.62 (*PG* 90:648)

Max.*Qu.Thal*.32 (*PG* 90:372)

Max.*Qu.Thal*.63 (*PG* 90:669)

Troph.Dam.2.4.1 (*PO* 15:223)

Max.*Qu.Thal*.54 (*PG* 90:521)
Max.*Qu.dub*.8 (*PG* 90:792)

Max.*Qu.Thal*.52 (*PG* 90:492)

Max.*Qu.Thal*.38 (*PG* 90:389)

Max.*Qu.Thal*.65 (*PG* 90:745)

Max.*Ambig*.42 (*PG* 91:1345)

Max.*Qu.Thal*.65 (*PG* 90:737)

Max.*Schol.C.h*.1.2 (*PG* 4:32)

Max.*Qu.Thal*.63 (*PG*
90:676–77)

1 Cor.12:28

Max.*Rel.mot*.9 (*PG* 90:124)

Max.*Opusc*.15 (*PG* 91:160)

Max.*Pyrr.* (*PG* 91:320)

of the New, in which the promise of deification had now
come true. All Christians were agreed in their acceptance
of the Old Testament together with the New, even though
they differed in its interpretation. God had, by all sorts
of symbols, prefigured the incarnation of his Son in the
person of Jesus Christ. It was the task of the faithful
exegete to find these symbols and to apply them to the
incarnation. He had to understand Scripture according
to the spirit as well as the letter; without the spirit, the
full meaning could not be found. Anyone who paid attention only to the letter would understand only the natural,
not the supernatural, meaning. This was the reason for the
failure of Jewish exegesis to understand the Old Testament properly. When it was obvious that a text could not
be taken as it stood, a deeper, spiritual sense had to be
sought. This spiritual sense could be called either allegor-
ical or tropological. There were some exegetes who "in-
dustriously stick only to the letter of Scripture," but those
who loved God had to concentrate on the spiritual meaning, because the word of truth meant more to them than
the mere letter of what had been written. For example,
this was the proper way to deal with those things in
Scripture which had been spoken by evil men. Because the
purpose of Scripture was not only to provide natural
information, but to confer the gift of deification, the
spiritual sense was fundamental. The true authorities for
the understanding of this spiritual sense were those who
dealt with the words of God "mystically"; this understanding was given only to those who were "worthy" of
the Holy Spirit.

But those who were truly "worthy" were the fathers
of the church and their spiritual descendants in the orthodox tradition, those who had given it its dogma. The
lamp of Scripture could be seen only when it stood on
the lampstand of the church. The statement of the apostle
Paul, that Christ had instituted not only apostles and
prophets but also teachers in the church, meant that "we
are taught by all of the Holy Scripture, by the Old and
the New Testament, and by the holy teachers and councils." The apostles had instructed their successors, and
these instructed their successors in turn, "the divinely
guided fathers of the catholic church." To be sure, what
the fathers taught had not come from their own resources
but was drawn from the Scriptures. But anyone who

took it upon himself to expound "the complete doctrine" of Scripture could not do so without the guidance of those who had developed the exact understanding of the mysteries of Scripture. Such guidance in the understanding of the sublime teaching of Scripture came from "the mystae and mystagogues" who had exercised themselves in it. Heresies, whether of former times or of the present, could be denounced as lacking the authority either of the Bible or of the fathers, while the orthodox doctrine was one that was "in accordance with the tradition both of the Sacred Oracles and of the patristic teachings." The authority of Scripture, then, was the authority of a Scripture properly interpreted, that is, interpreted according to the spiritual sense and in harmony with patristic exegesis. The fathers were "coryphaei" of the church; and even though one could and did diverge from their exegesis in some detail or other, this did not change one's dependence on them "more than on our very breath."

So intimate was the connection between the Scripture and the fathers that in one sentence "the holy apostle Paul and . . . Gregory [of Nazianzus], the great and wondrous teacher," could be invoked together. The difference between the apostle and the church father seems to have been one more of degree than of kind. The fathers and theologians of the church could have spoken on many questions that they did not discuss, for there was a grace in them that would have authorized them to do so, but they preferred to keep silence. The sayings of the church fathers did not belong to them, but came from the grace of Christ granted to them. The authority of "our holy fathers and teachers" was in fact not theirs, "but rather that of the truth that speaks and has spoken through them." And so the attribute "inspired by God [$\theta\epsilon\acuteo\pi\nu\epsilon\upsilon\sigma\tau\sigma$]," which the New Testament used only once and applied to the Old Testament, could be applied also to the church fathers. The attributes and epithets that came to be attached to the names of individual church fathers are a significant index of their special grace and inspiration. Athanasius was "this God-bearing teacher" and "the inerrant winner of contests"; Basil was "the great eye of the church," meaning perhaps "the leading light"; Clement of Alexandria was "the philosopher of philosophers," whose adaptations of Platonic theories had special force in the church; Dionysius the Areopagite, whose authen-

Max.*Ambig*.37 (*PG* 91:1293)

Max.*Ambig*.67 (*PG* 91:1400)

Max.*Schol.E.h*.6.6 (*PG* 4:172); Max.*Opusc*.9 (*PG* 91:117)

Max.*Opusc*.20 (*PG* 91:245); Max.*Schol.D.n*.1.3 (*PG* 4:197)

Thdr.Stud.*Antirr*.2.37 (*PG* 99:376)

Thdr.Stud.*Or*.7.7 (*PG* 99:753) Thdr.AbuQ.*Mim*.10.16 (Graf 252)

Max.*Ambig*.71 (*PG* 91:1409)

Max.*Qu.Thal*.43 (*PG* 90:412)

Max.*Ambig*.pr. (*PG* 91:1033)

Max.*Ambig*.42 (*PG* 91:1341)

2 Tim.3:16

Max.*Or.dom*. (*PG* 90:881); Thdr.Stud.*Ep*.1.19 (*PG* 99:968); Phot.*Myst*.79 (*PG* 102:361)

Max.*Ambig*.10 (*PG* 91:1105) Const.Pogon.*Edict*. (Mansi 11:704); Phot.*Ep*.1.16 (*PG* 102:768)

Max.*Pyrr*. (*PG* 91:309); Lampe (1961) 988; Bab.*Evagr*. 1.35 (Frankenberg 81[80])

Max.*Pyrr*. (*PG* 91:317); Max.*Schol.D.n*.5.8 (*PG* 4:332)

Max.*Schol.D.n.*4.12; 8.6; 11.1
(*PG* 4:264; 360; 393)
Max.*Ambig.*41 (*PG* 91:1312–13)
Max.*Schol.D.n.*12.4 (*PG* 4:405)
Max.*Schol.D.n.*6.2 (*PG* 4:337)
Max.*Ambig.*7; 23 (*PG* 91:1080; 1260)
Max.*Ambig.*7 (*PG* 91:1077)
Max.*Ambig.*conc. (*PG* 91:1417)

Max.*Opusc.*15 (*PG* 91:165–68)

Max.*Pyrr.* (*PG* 91:296–97)

Max.*Opusc.*9 (*PG* 91:128)

Max.*Opusc.*16 (*PG* 91:209);
Max.*Schol.E.h.*1.3 (*PG* 4:117)

Max.*Qu.Thal.*63 (*PG* 90:673);
Niceph.*Antirr.*3.41 (*PG* 100:460)
Max.*Opusc.*7 (*PG* 91:72)

Max.*Carit.*pr. (*PG* 90:960)

Max.*Ep.*12 (*PG* 91:465)

Max.*Opusc.*19 (*PG* 91:224–25)

ticity and antiquity had to be defended against critics, was "the one who truly spoke of God, the great and holy Dionysius," "this blessed one who was made worthy of divine inspiration," one who had in a marvelous way taught all the dogmas of the faith correctly, and even "the revealer of God [ϑεοφάντωρ]"; Gregory of Nazianzus was not only a "God-bearing teacher," as was Athanasius, but his sayings were "most divine." Even some of the Latin fathers came in for recognition, especially Ambrose and, above all, Pope Leo I.

Taken together, these inspired and holy fathers of the church catholic, Eastern and Western, were the norm of traditional doctrine and the standard of Christian orthodoxy. When Maximus's opponent Pyrrhus asserted that the sayings of the fathers were "the law and canon of the church," Maximus could only agree, declaring that "in this, as in everything, we follow the holy fathers." To other opponents he proclaimed: "First let them prove this on the basis of the determinations of the fathers! . . . If this is impossible, then let them leave these opinions behind and join us in conforming to what has been reverently determined by the divinely inspired fathers of the catholic church and the five ecumenical councils." To identify the orthodox doctrine of the catholic church meant to hold to that which the fathers had handed down by tradition. A wise and orthodox teacher of church dogma was like a lantern, safely illuminating the obscure mysteries that were invisible to the many; this light was "the knowledge and power of the patristic sayings and dogmas." For his ascetic instruction, Maximus relied not on his own thought but on the writings of the fathers, which he compiled for the edification of his brethren. When ascetics forsook "the way of the holy fathers," they became deficient in every spiritual work. "Let us," said Maximus, "guard the great and first remedy of our salvation (I am referring to the beautiful heritage of the faith). Let our soul and our mouth confess it with assurance, as the fathers have taught us." Or, as he summarized his position elsewhere, "We do not invent new formulas as our opponents charge, but we confess the statements of the fathers. Nor do we make up terms according to our own ideas, for this is a presumptuous thing to do, the work and invention of a heretical and deranged mind. But what has been understood and stated by the saints, that we reverently adduce as our authority."

Yet as it was not enough to cite the authority of Scripture when both sides in every controversy were claiming that authority, so it did not suffice simply to declare that one stood with the orthodox tradition of the fathers in their interpretation of the faith on the basis of Scripture when both the orthodox and the heretic were claiming this authority as well. Such an exhortation as "Let us reverently hold fast to the confession of the fathers" seemed to assume, by its use of "confession" in the singular and of "fathers" in the plural, that there was readily available a patristic consensus on the doctrines with which the fathers had dealt in previous controversy and on the doctrines over which debate had not yet arisen—but was, in some cases, about to arise. When it did arise, the existence of such a patristic consensus became problematical. In principle everyone agreed that "with a loud voice the holy fathers . . . , all of them everywhere, confess and steadfastly believe in an orthodox manner" about the dogmas of the Trinity and the person of the God-man. But when one or another of them was found to speak in a manner that came to be identified as doctrinally suspect only after his death, this was to be understood "in a nontechnical and inexact sense [καταχρηστικῶς]." It was harsh, indeed it was unthinkable, to suggest that Athanasius and Gregory of Nazianzus could be in disagreement. The same formula, "God forbid!" was also invoked in response to the rhetorical question: "Can it be that St. Dionysius is contradicting himself?" When an orthodox church father such as Gregory of Nyssa appeared to be in agreement with a heretic such as Origen on the eventual salvation of all men, it was necessary to explain away this agreement. When it appeared that there was a contradiction between two passages in Gregory of Nazianzus, closer study would show "their true harmony."

Therefore when two statements of the fathers seemed to mean different things, they were not to be interpreted as though they were contradictory. The same word could be used with various meanings, and it was necessary to distinguish among these. In this way it could be shown that the fathers did not "disagree with one another or with the truth," but were in agreement with "the catholic and apostolic church of God" and with the "correct faith." Those who sought contradictions or errors in the fathers were "like thieves." "It was precisely the *consensus patrum* which was authoritative and binding, and not their pri-

Max.*Opusc*.7 (*PG* 91:81)

Max.*Ambig*.5 (*PG* 91:1056–60)

Max.*Opusc*.7 (*PG* 91:73)

Max.*Pyrr*. (*PG* 91:292)

Max.*Ambig*.13 (*PG* 91:1208)

Max.*Schol.D.n*.5.8 (*PG* 4:328)

See vol. 1:151–52

Max.*Qu.dub*.13 (*PG* 90:796)

Max.*Ambig*.1 (*PG* 91:1036)

Max.*Opusc*.7(*PG* 91:88)

vate opinions or views, although even they should not be hastily dismissed. Again, this *consensus* was much more than just an empirical agreement of individuals. The true and authentic *consensus* was that which reflected the mind of the Catholic and Universal Church—τὸ ἐκκλησιαστικὸν

Florovsky (1972) 1:103

φρόνημα." Patriarch Sophronius of Jerusalem, a contemporary of Maximus, summarized this idea of patristic consensus in a similar way: "An apostolic and ancient tradition has prevailed in the holy churches throughout the world, so that those who are inducted into the hierarchy sincerely refer everything they think and believe to those who have held the hierarchy before them. For . . . all their running would be in vain if an injustice were to be done

Soph.*Ep.syn.* (*PG* 87:3149–52)

to the faith in any respect." Sophronius's formula, "an apostolic and ancient tradition," did not mean that everything "ancient" was therefore automatically "apostolic."

Max.*Schol.D.n.*6.2 (*PG* 4:337)
See vol. 1:124
Max.*Schol.E.h.*7.1 (*PG* 4:176)

All the orthodox theologians knew that in some instances "antiquity means foolishness." Even Irenaeus had erred in teaching the idea of the millennium. But while all that was ancient was not apostolic or orthodox, all that was orthodox had to have been apostolic and was therefore ancient. True doctrine, as Theodore of Studios was to assert, was "the excellence of the apostles, the foundation of the fathers, the keys of the dogmas, the standard of orthodoxy," and anyone who contradicted it, even if he

Gal.1:8

were an angel, was to be excommunicated and anathe-

Thdr.Stud.*Ref.*28 (*PG* 99:469)

matized. On the other hand, one whom Theodore of Studios regarded as a herald of Antichrist, Emperor

Thdr.Stud.*Ep.*2.15 (*PG* 99:1161)

Constantine V, was to say, in formal agreement with Theodore, that he held to "the apostolic and patristic doctrines" and that he followed "the holy councils that had

ap.Thdr.Stud.*Ref.*18 (*PG* 99:465)

taken place before him." And another opponent of iconoclasm asserted: "I could also tell you of other things, which Christ did not say. But what is the point of that? As we have received from the holy fathers, so we believe, be-

Joh.H.*Const.*5 (*PG* 95:320)

cause they were taught these things from God." This was the changeless truth taught in Scripture, confessed by the fathers, and formulated in the orthodox creeds, "the apostolic and patristic doctrine . . . the ordinance of the church, the six holy and ecumenical councils . . . and the

Thdr.Stud.*Ref.*17; 35 (*PG* 99:465; 473–76)

orthodox dogmas laid down by these."

The Councils and Their Achievements

"Who has illumined you with the faith of the holy, consubstantial, and worshipful Trinity? Or who has made

Max.*Carit*.4.77 (*PG* 90:1068)

Max.*Opusc*.15(*PG* 91:180)

Max.*Opusc*.9 (*PG* 91:128)

Acts 15:6–29

Thdr.AbuQ.*Mim*.1.22 (Graf 111)

Joh.H.*Icon*.11 (*PG* 96:1357)

Max.*Schol.C.h*.1.2 (*PG* 4:32)

Max.*Rel.mot*.9 (*PG* 90:124)

Max.*Pyrr*. (*PG* 91:352)

Florovsky (1972) 1:96

known to you the incarnate economy of one of the Holy Trinity?" Although Maximus's immediate answer to these questions was that this illumination and knowledge had come from "the grace of Christ dwelling in you, the pledge of the Holy Spirit," he knew, and elsewhere argued with force, that the historical medium through which doctrinal illumination had been transmitted was the ecumenical council. In opposition to heretics he asserted the authority "of a council or of a father or of Scripture." For as the authority of Scripture was concretely worked out in the consensus of the fathers about the teaching of Scripture, so this consensus in turn was expressed in the creeds and doctrinal decrees of the councils; those who disagreed should "follow those things which have been reverently decreed by the holy fathers of the catholic church and by the five holy and ecumenical councils." The account of the apostolic assembly in the Book of Acts showed that when there was a conflict of opinion among the apostles, the various sides did not appeal to Paul or even to James, but to a council. Nor was this practice confined to the apostolic era. For "the catholic church cannot be only apostolic," but had to be gathered into a "thousand-tongued assemblage" in the one true faith; one of the places where this happened was an ecumenical council. The fathers of the church were, by definition, "those who have handed down the dogma to us by tradition," but the councils were a primary channel for that tradition. In any complete enumeration of the means of instruction in Christian doctrine, the Scriptures of the Old and New Testament, the doctors of the church, and the councils all had to be cited.

Yet the authority of the councils, as indeed that of the doctors and even of the Scriptures, was the authority of the one changeless truth. When it was necessary, one could list reasons for declaring a particular council null and void, because it had not been "convened in accordance with the laws and canons of councils and with the rules of the church." These included the requirement that an encyclical letter from the patriarchs announce the council, as well as the time and place for it to convene, and that the delegates have proper credentials from their superiors. But in fact "no Council was accepted as valid in advance." The early councils of the church were convoked on the authority of the emperor, not on that of the bishops. The right of the bishops, specifically of the bishop of Rome, to convoke or to validate an ecumenical council was a matter

See pp. 166–68 below

of controversy between East and West. Even in the East there were some who objected to the imperial authority in the councils, and this was to become a crucial issue in

See pp. 108, 143–44 below

the eighth century. Some gatherings properly summoned by the Byzantine emperor were eventually branded as illegitimate, notably the council held at Ephesus in 449 at the summons of Emperor Theodosius II, which came

See vol. 1:262–63

to be called "the robber synod." It was rejected because its doctrine was rejected. Fundamentally, then, a doctrine did not become orthodox because a council said it was, but a council was orthodox—and therefore binding— because the doctrine it confessed was orthodox. The canon law of the church accepted those councils which were

Max.*Disp.Byz.*12 (*PG* 90:148)

known for their right doctrine.

In a particular case, therefore, one could appeal to the conciliar principle, insisting that "the law of the church ever since the beginning" had specified that controversies were to be "resolved by ecumenical councils," but this always included the proviso that it be done with the "consensus and determination of the bishops who adorn

Niceph. *Imag.*25 (*PG* 100:597)

the apostolic sees," who were, in turn, determined by the consensus of the fathers. Because "the Holy Spirit does not contradict himself," it followed that authentic councils

Thdr.AbuQ.*Mim.*1.33 (Graf 122)

had to be in agreement with one another. The truth was not only changeless, it was uniform. Now it was obvious that the texts of the doctrinal decrees of the various councils contained many variations and additions. Yet when one had enumerated these various decrees and quoted the various texts, one had to affirm that they were various witnesses to one and the same faith. "Following these five holy and blessed councils, I acknowledge one single standard of faith, one teaching, and one creed," as this had been defined by the 318 fathers of the Council of

Soph.*Ep.syn.* (*PG* 87:3188)

Nicea in 325. Although the councils, whether ecumenical or regional, were many in number, they were—if they were truly orthodox—one in their acceptance of divine

Thdr.Stud.*Ref.*30 (*PG* 99:472); CCP (754) *Decr.*ap. CNic. (787) (Mansi 13:217)

authority and in their confession of the truth of the mind of God. Yet this one changeless doctrine had in fact been confessed amid the vicissitudes of various controversies, whose recital became a favorite method of affirming one's orthodoxy.

Thus the council held at Constantinople in 680–81 led up to its redefinition of the doctrine of the person

CCP (681) *Act*.18 (Mansi 11:632–33)

CCP (754) ap.CNic. (787) (Mansi 13:232–37)

Niceph.*Ep.Leo III* (PG 100:192–93)

Thdr.Stud.*Ref*.30 (PG 99:472–73)

Phot.*Ep*.1.8.6–18 (PG 102:632–52)

Soph.*Ep.syn*. (PG 87:3184–87)

Soph.*Ep.syn*. (PG 87:3184)

of Christ with a résumé of the dogmas promulgated by its predecessors, and the iconoclastic synod of 754 prefaced its christological denunciation of images by recounting the christological decrees of the six ecumenical councils. The patriarch Nicephorus, leader of the opposition to this synod, declared: "I honor the seven holy and ecumenical councils," together with the "divine, transcendent, and saving dogmas" proclaimed by them; and he followed this declaration with a rehearsal of the seven councils, one by one, enumerating the dogmas they had formulated and the heretics they had condemned. His contemporary, Theodore of Studios, asserted that if one accepted the doctrine of the first ecumenical council as binding, one was thereby committed to all of them; and he proceeded to quote the christological portion of the Nicene Creed and to apply it to the decisions of each of the successive councils. Photius, as a successor of Nicephorus, employed the same technique, listing the achievements of the seven councils one by one. But this custom had been in practice earlier, and already here in the seventh century it provided Sophronius with a way of describing the achievements of the ecumenical councils (which at this time numbered only five). So pervasive was this method and so thorough its documentation that if the creeds and doctrinal decrees of the first five councils had been lost, it would be possible to recover their substance from the writings of Sophronius or of Maximus or of their successors. It would be impossible, however, to reconstruct their exact texts, because theologians had the habit of pleonastically recasting the creed to suit the controversy of the moment, and because the history of the several councils and of their creedal formulations (for example, of the creed supposedly adopted at Constantinople in 381) had become confused very early.

The first of the ecumenical councils—first in time, but also first in eminence and in significance for all that followed—was the Council of Nicea in 325. "Of these [councils]," said Sophronius, "we say that the first is the assembly of the 318 divinely inspired fathers in Nicea"; and as its achievement he cited its having, "by divine summons, cleansed away the stains of the madness of Arius." In opposition to the teachings of Arius, Nicea had defined the dogma of the Trinity, which had thereby become the norm of orthodoxy for all of Christendom

Max.*Schol.D.n*.7.1 (*PG*
4:344); Max.*Or.dom.* (*PG*
90:876)

Dion.Ar.*D.n*.2.1 (*PG* 3:636)

Max.*Schol.D.n*.2.1
(*PG* 4:209–12)

Max.*Schol.D.n*.2.6 (*PG*
4:224)

See vol. 1:200–210

Max.*Schol.Myst*.3 (*PG* 4:424)

Ps.36:9
Max.*Schol.Ep.Dion.Ar*.9.1
(*PG* 4:557)

in all the centuries to follow. Therefore "the proclamation
of the Trinity as alone deserving of worship, in three
undivided and unseparated hypostases" was the very
content of theology for someone like Maximus. The use
of the phrase "the entire substance" in Pseudo-Dionysius
provided Maximus with the occasion for a summary of the
Nicene faith. The phrase referred to "the deity of the
holy and only worshipful Trinity, which is made known
in three hypostases." Hence it did not mean a solitary
divine essence, for it was customary to use "entire divine
substance" for the Trinity, revealed in the plurality of
persons as "Father and Son and Holy Spirit; for these three
are the one entire and single Deity." He likewise took the
opportunity of this summary, as well as other opportu-
nities when they arose, to condemn Arians, Eunomians,
and other heretics anathematized at Nicea, either by name
or in substance, even though in some cases (for example,
the Nestorians) these were parties whose formal loyalty
to Nicea was as uncompromising as his own.

As a confession of the one unalterable faith of Christendom, the creed of Nicea had nevertheless permitted
itself some neologisms, notably the title "homoousios."
For various reasons, including its heretical provenance,
the term seemed to stand as a refutation of the claim that
orthodoxy was ever and always the same. To this Maximus
replied by acknowledging that it had been "some recent
fathers" who had adopted the term, together with the
term "of three hypostases." But these terms were ways of
affirming "the universal divine and enlightened knowledge and orthodoxy" of one divine nature that was nevertheless trine, with each of the Three possessing certain
unique properties, such as fatherhood, sonship, and the
sanctifying power of the Holy Spirit. The term "homoousios" was no more than a way of stating what was
implied in such metaphors as the designation of the
Father as "fountain of life," which proved that the divine
monad proceeded as Trinity. The content of "homoousios"
had been believed and taught all along, but it had now
come to be confessed. As Nicea was seen to be only the
explicit elaboration in confession of the unchanging faith
and doctrine of the orthodox church, so the councils that
followed Nicea also stood in continuity with Nicea and
with orthodoxy. "All the fathers chosen by God after the
Council of Nicea, and every council of orthodox and

holy men, did not . . . introduce another definition of faith by adding their own words . . . but solemnly confirmed the one identical definition as the first and only one legislated by the 318 fathers." What they had done was to "give it an exegesis and work out its implications on account of those who were giving a false exegesis and a distorted explanation to its dogmas." When the debates over two wills in Christ threatened the unity of orthodox believers, this one Nicene faith, by means of such exegesis and discovery of implications, could be applied to the new issues that had arisen. "Let us guard the great and first remedy of our salvation," Maximus exhorted, "the beautiful heritage of the faith, confessing with soul and mouth in confidence what the fathers have taught us." There followed an extended paraphrase of the Nicene Creed, slanted toward the christological controversies of the hour. And when the issue had shifted from the wills of Christ to the images of Christ, it was once more by means of such a paraphrase that Nicephorus could simultaneously reaffirm his allegiance to the changeless faith of the 318 fathers of the Council of Nicea and define the orthodox position against the iconoclasts.

"Coming after this [the Council of Nicea], not in glory or in grace but only in time," Sophronius continued, was "the second council, assembled in the imperial city" of Constantinople in 381. It had been provoked by various heresies, including those of Macedonius and of Apollinaris: the first of these was a denial of the full deity of the Holy Spirit, a question that "had not yet been raised" at Nicea and therefore required further clarification; the second was a theory of the hypostatic union in Christ that interpreted the formula "Logos plus flesh" for the incarnation in such a way as to seem to deny the presence of a human soul in Christ. Against these teachings the council reaffirmed the Nicene doctrine of the Trinity, articulating more fully the place of the Holy Spirit as well as the relation between the One and the Three, and condemning "those who are hostile to the Spirit" together with "the Apollinarists." While this settled the doctrine of the Holy Spirit and of the Trinity, it did not dispose of the christological questions raised by Apollinarism. These came up again at what Sophronius called "the third council—third only in time—which was the first to hold its sessions in Ephesus by the will of God," in

Max.*Opusc*.22 (PG 91:260)

Max.*Ep*.12 (PG 91:465)

Niceph.*Imag*.18 (PG 100:580–81)

Soph.*Ep.syn*. (PG 87:3184–85)

Max.*Opusc*.22 (PG 91:260)

See vol. 1:248

Soph. *Ep.syn.* (PG 87:3185)

Max.*Schol.D.n.2.3* (PG 4:216)

431. If Constantinople condemned "those who are hostile to the Spirit," Ephesus anathematized "the man-worshiper Nestorius and his entire impiety, which is hostile to Christ." Now it became customary to cite Nestorianism and Apollinarism as two extremes, both rejected by orthodoxy. Sophronius made it a point to distinguish the Council of Ephesus in 431 from the so-called "robber synod" of Ephesus of 449, which had not been convened "by the will of God" and which had formulated the doctrine of the person of Christ in a way that did not conform to the truth of the changeless orthodox faith.

Soph.*Ep.syn.*(PG 87:3185)

The definitive formulation of that doctrine was the achievement of "the assembly, filled with the wisdom of God, of the 630 celebrated fathers and torchbearers of the faith, the assembly of divine origin that carried out its divine convention in Chalcedon" in 451. Here it had been determined that the person of Jesus Christ, the God-man, was a person "in two natures" without separation or confusion. This terminology had not been used in the Nicene definition. Was it therefore an innovation? By no means, for the controversy had not yet arisen at Nicea, and therefore the greater precision of such terminology had not been necessary; yet the faith of Nicea was the faith of Chalcedon. Because of the controversies that

Max.*Opusc.22* (PG 91:257)

swirled over the christological issue in the seventh century and because of the use of christology as the principle for the resolution of the iconoclastic issues in the eighth and ninth centuries, Chalcedon came to occupy a place right alongside Nicea as the second major watershed for the development of doctrine. "Leo, the exarch of the great Roman church, the all-powerful and all-holy," had been

Max.*Opusc.15* (PG 91:168)

the one to carry the day at Chalcedon, providing the formulas on the basis of which, with significant additions from other sources, the council was able to agree. When Eutyches and Dioscurus had set forth their christological teachings, "the church did not accept either these two or those who were fighting against them, but, as was its cus-

Thdr.AbuQ.*Mim.*1.27 (Graf 115)

tom, referred them both to the holy council" of Chalcedon. Here "the true dogma of the confession of Christ" had been adopted as "the definition of the divine council of

Thdr.AbuQ.*Opusc.4* (PG 97:1508)

holy fathers in Chalcedon." And when the defense of the use of icons in the church came to base its case on christological arguments, it could accuse its opponents of trying to abolish the dogmatic decisions of Chalcedon,

Niceph.*Antirr*.1.40 (*PG* 100:300)

which had articulated the mystery of the divine dispensation in Christ with such clarity and precision. As the leaders of Eastern Christianity during the seventh century, especially Maximus Confessor himself, were to learn to their chagrin, professions of loyalty to Chalcedon were not enough to ward off severe conflict over the person of Christ; but the issues of the conflict and the terms of the solution were all cast in the framework that came from the fourth of the ecumenical councils.

Soph.*Ep.syn.* (*PG* 87:3184)
See vol. 1:335

These four councils occupied a special place in the structure of dogmatic authority, corresponding to that of the four Gospels—a parallel that was also employed by Pope Gregory I. Even after there had been additional councils that were acknowledged by both East and West as ecumenical and authoritative, Nicea, Constantinople, Ephesus, and Chalcedon continued to have a special aura. Hence Sophronius, writing in about 633, still put the first four councils into a class apart, but he continued: "Over and above these four great and ecumenical, all-sacred and all-holy assemblies of holy and blessed fathers, which are worthy of equal honor, I also receive another holy and ecumenical council in addition to these, a fifth one, held in the imperial city while Justinian was wielding the scepter of the Roman Empire" in 553. Its achievement was "the reconfirmation of the celebrated Council of Chalcedon," together with condemnation of "that madman Origen" and of "the three chapters" to which Nestorians appealed. Either because it was so recent or because his own position on some questions bore affinities to those condemned there, this council and its controversies figured prominently in the writings of Maximus. It was obvious that he could condemn the theories of Theodore of Mopsuestia about the proper interpretation of such a book as the Song of Solomon. But he likewise had to condemn Origenism. Therefore he rejected the notion of the preexistence of rational beings. With it he repudiated the idea of a prehistorical fall, which was supported by neither the Scriptures nor the fathers. It was the way of the fathers, in opposition to Origen's theory of the preexistence of the soul and in opposition to theories of the preexistence of the body, to follow the royal road, the via media, and to teach that soul and body come into existence simultaneously. He spoke of what "Origenists teach and believe," using the present tense. A

Soph.*Ep.syn.* (*PG* 87:3185);
Cerul.*Ep.Petr.Ant*.1.9 (Will 178–79)

Max.*Schol.Ep.Dion.Ar*.9.1 (*PG* 4:561)

Max.*Qu.Thal*.60 (*PG* 90:625)

Max.*Schol.E.h*.6.6 (*PG* 4:172)

See vol. 1:350

Max.*Ambig*.42 (*PG* 91:1325)
Max.*Schol.Ep.Dion.Ar*.8.1 (*PG* 4:545)

century later, Theodore Abû Qurra felt able to say: "As
for the fifth council, there is no one who defends the
heresies condemned by it," presumably including overt
Origenism.

Thdr.AbuQ.*Mim*.1.28 (Graf
117)

Sophronius's catalog of the councils stopped at five,
which is the number included in the first volume of this
work; but as the sixth and the seventh councils, which
are to be discussed in the present volume, became part of
the body of orthodox dogma, they were added to the
catalogs of his successors. Thus, for example, the patriarch
Nicephorus, in the catalog already cited, went on from
these five to the sixth and seventh; and he defended
the seventh, in which he himself had participated, as
"notable" and "ecumenical." Yet this proliferation of
councils, while it could not be taken to mean that any new
doctrines had been formulated, did raise a question about
the relation between council and doctrine. It had to be
admitted that not all the doctrine of the church was expressed in the dogmatic decrees of the councils. Specifically, Maximus raised, but left to "wise men" to answer,
the question why "if this dogma [of salvation as deifica-
tion] belongs to the mystery of the faith of the church,
it was not included with the other [dogmas] in the
symbol expounding the utterly pure faith of Christians,
composed by our holy and blessed fathers," presumably
the 318 fathers of the Council of Nicea. Dogma was
indeed the changeless truth of salvation, but it was not
exhausted by the councils and their achievements. There
was more to the knowledge of God than could be known
even from these.

Niceph.*Ep.Leo III* (PG
100:192)

Niceph.*Imag*.25 (PG
100:597)

Max.*Opusc*.28 (PG 91:300)

Max.*Ambig*.42 (PG 91:1336)

Knowing the Unknowable

Authority in Christian doctrine was, then, the authority
"of a council or of a father or of Scripture." Yet each of
these norms pointed beyond itself to something that
seriously qualified it. Councils were authoritative; but
there were central dogmas, such as salvation through
deification, that were not contained in their decrees, and
true "theological mystagogy" transcended the dogmas
formulated by councils. The church fathers had prescribed
the content of orthodoxy; but the true fathers were those
who, like Dionysius the Areopagite, had taught that "negative statements about divine matters are the true ones" and
who therefore imposed limits on their thought and lan-

Max.*Opusc*.15 (PG 91:180)

Max.*Qu.dub*.73 (PG 90:845)

Max.*Ambig.*20 (*PG* 91:1241)

guage. Scripture had the first and the last word in determining doctrine; but even in accepting the words of Scripture one had to keep in mind that "every word of God written for men according to the present age is a forerunner of the more perfect word to be revealed by him

Max.*Ambig.*21 (*PG* 91:1252)

in an unwritten way in the Spirit." All three components of the system of orthodox authority were thus transcended by their own content, and the knowledge they conveyed was a unique species of knowledge, one that affirmed the unknowability of what it knew. It was important for theology to know the relation between "the things that are spoken and the things that are ineffable, the things that are known and the things that are unknow-

Joh.D.*F.o.*2 (Kotter 2:8–10)

able."

Alongside the objectivity of the knowledge available through councils, fathers, and Scripture, there arose a theology of subjective knowledge and of religious experience, which came to occupy a large place in Byzantine dogmatics. "Whence does it come that the church fathers regard it as necessary to deal with these questions in dogmatics? There is no other answer than this, that monasticism had drawn attention to the significance of psycho-

Holl (1928) 2:278

logical problems." The truth was changeless and static, but the experience of it was dynamic and variable. There had long been a distinction between "theology" and "economy," between the study of the Trinity in itself and the study of the incarnation and salvation achieved through the history of Jesus Christ; that distinction was

Max.*Ambig.*56 (*PG* 91:1380)

maintained. Also important was the distinction between a theology that dealt with the symbols of revelation and

Max.*Schol.Ep.Dion.Ar.*9.1 (*PG* 4:564)

a theology that proceeded demonstratively. But this implied that theology was obliged to recognize at one and the same time its validity and its limitations, shunning speculation as well as doctrinal indifference, and concentrating on the task of communication: "neither to concern ourselves with those things that are above us, nor

Max.*Schol.D.n.*3.1 (*PG* 4:237)

to neglect the knowledge of God, but to give to others of the things that have been granted to us." As a warrant for this procedure one cited Scripture, which urged: "Seek not what is too difficult for you, nor investigate what is beyond your power. Reflect upon what has been

Ecclus.3:21–22

assigned to you, for you do not need what is hidden."

The two exhortations of this passage—to avoid what is beyond us and to reflect on what has been vouchsafed

Max.*Ambig*.7 (*PG* 91:1081)

John 1:18
Max.*Schol.D.n*.1.2 (*PG* 4:192)

Max.*Schol.D.n*.13.1; 5.7 (*PG* 4:405; 324)

Ex.3:14
See vol. 1:54
Max.*Schol.D.n*.5.5 (*PG* 4:317)

Max.*Schol.D.n*.5.4 (*PG* 4:313)
Max.*Schol.Ep.Dion.Ar*.1 (*PG* 4:529); Max.*Schol.D.n*.5.8 (*PG* 4:328)

Max.*Schol.D.n*.1.5 (*PG* 4:201)

Max.*Schol.D.n*.1.5 (*PG* 4:204)
Dion.Ar.*C.h*.2.3 (*PG* 3:140–41)

Max.*Schol.C.h*.2.3 (*PG* 4:40–41)
Max.*Schol.D.n*.7.2 (*PG* 4:349)
Max.*Schol.E.h*.7.11 (*PG* 4:184)
Max.*Schol.C.h*.13.4 (*PG* 4:100)

Max.*Schol.D.n*.1.1 (*PG* 4:188)

Max.*Schol.D.n*.7.3 (*PG* 4:352)

Max.*Schol.D.n*.2.6 (*PG* 4:221)

to us by revelation—constituted the program of theology. Theology was, at one and the same time, sublime and "apophatic," that is, based on negation. As the evangelist John had said, "no one has ever seen God," which meant that one could see the glory of God, but not God himself. For God was his own place and his own boundary, and stability as well as movement was defined by him. From very early times the word from the burning bush, "I am who I am," had been taken to mean that God was "he who is" in a special sense. Maximus not only took this word as a "title" for God, but insisted that when God was called "that which is," this referred to "the whole of being collectively." But strictly speaking, God transcended being, for he was the Creator of all. The treatise of Pseudo-Dionysius *On the Divine Names* provided the basis for this clarification of the symbolic terms, including even the term "being," with which men could entitle the unnameable God. It was no less accurate to identify God as "nothing," for one did not use the verb "to be" univocally in speaking of the Creator and of creatures. Therefore God was unknown, according to Dionysius—not in the sense that the name "God" had no meaning, but in the sense that it transcended all meaning and all understanding. Although angels had an elevated form of knowledge, not acquired through sense experience, even they could not understand many things about the divine mystery, but, as in Isaiah 6:2, had to veil their faces. The knowledge of God was revealed to each creature in accordance with its capacity; therefore it was measured knowledge, but the true knowledge of God in himself would have to be as unmeasured as God. If God, who was literally "immense [ἀμέτρητος]" (that is, not large but beyond measure), were to reveal himself in his true being, the trauma to the human mind would be the same as that inflicted by the unveiled sun on the naked eye.

The most accurate way to speak of the knowledge of God, therefore, was to describe it as a "knowing ignorance," and the most accurate way to speak of God himself was to speak in negatives. God was known through contraries, since he transcended both affirmation and negation. He participated in the reality of his creatures —but "in a nonparticipatory way," retaining his absoluteness even in his sovereignty as Creator. In fact, "negative statements about divine matters are the only true

Max.*Ambig*.20 (*PG* 91:1241)

Max.*Schol.C.h*.2.3 (*PG* 4:41)

Max.*Ambig*.5 (*PG* 91:1057)

Max.*Schol.D.n*.2.3 (*PG* 4:217)

Max.*Carit*.1.100 (*PG* 90:984)

Max.*Schol.D.n*.2.4 (*PG* 4:216–17)

Max.*Ambig*.18 (*PG* 91:1233)

Max.*Carit*.3.99 (*PG* 90:1048)

Max.*Schol.D.n*.7.3 (*PG* 4:352–53)

Max.*Carit*.1.96(*PG* 90:981)

Max.*Schol.D.n*.1.5 (*PG* 4:205)

Max.*Schol.D.n*.2.7 (*PG* 4:224)

ones." This applied not only to the language about God, but to the language about everything divine, so that even terms such as "life" and "light" did not mean the same in this context. The answer to the question, "Who knows how God is made flesh and yet remains God?" could not be supplied by positive formulations or by speculations about the divine nature. "This only faith can grasp, as in silence it adores the Logos." Silence thus became a means of communication and of understanding, through which faith learned. Hence "the very fact of knowing nothing is knowledge surpassing the mind," as had been said by Gregory of Nazianzus and Dionysius. God was unknown and yet known, for "God becomes knowable by means of ignorance." In the same way he was nowhere (in the sense that his being was not confined to space) and yet everywhere (in the sense that he filled all things); in relation to time as well as in relation to space, he both contained and transcended the ages and tenses by which men measured temporal sequence. In short, "a perfect mind is one which, by true faith, in supreme ignorance knows the supremely unknowable one."

But, as Maximus continued in this same passage, a perfect mind was one "which, in gazing upon the universe of his handiwork, has received from God comprehensive knowledge of his providence and judgment." For it was on the basis of his creatures that men perceived *that* God is, but they were not able to understand *what* God is. Not from his ousia, but from the magnificence of his handiwork and from his providence for his creation was God to be known. It was the consensus of the theologians that God was not to be worshiped on the basis of his essence, which was supremely unknowable, but on the basis of his procession "outward," that is, his providence and foreknowledge as a cause of his creation. This was the content of true theological knowledge. One could go as far as to say that the very name "God" did not refer to the essence of God in himself, but to his loving-kindness toward mankind. This meant that "we construct the nomenclature of God on the basis of the forms of participation which he has conferred on us." Theology was not a science of divine ontology but of divine revelation. If "knowledge" were to mean only the former, then theological knowledge was not knowledge; but if it could mean a knowledge about the authentic word and the

Max.*Schol.D.n*.2.2 (*PG* 4:213)

Max.*Schol.D.n*.1.3 (*PG* 4:193)

Thdr.AbuQ.*Mim*.4.6 (Graf 164–65)

Max.*Schol.D.n*.7.1 (*PG* 4:341)

true praise of God, then theological knowledge did have a right to be called knowledge. It was impossible to know God as he was in himself, for he was the cause of all things and "the very simplicity of all simple things, the life of living things, in essence transcending all essences." To gain this species of theological knowledge, it was necessary, after having used various created realities as analogies for God, "to take away from him completely each of the things with which we have compared God." The task of the true knowledge of God was to cleanse itself of these images and thus in its ignorance to know God. "For the ignorance about God on the part of those who are wise in divine things is not a lack of learning, but a knowledge that knows by silence that God is unknown."

In this way the warning of Ecclesiasticus 3:21–22 was obeyed: "Seek not what is too difficult for you, nor investigate what is beyond your power." But the warning had as its counterpart the command: "Reflect upon what has been assigned to you." Not in spite of, but because of, the apophatic character of reliable knowledge about God, it was the duty of the mind that had accepted the doctrine of the fathers to move toward understanding. "Faith in search of understanding" is a formula identified with a Latin theologian, Anselm of Canterbury, in the second half of the eleventh century; but it applies no less to the enterprise carried on by Greek theologians, including Maximus, John of Damascus, and others. "The life of the mind is the illumination of knowledge, and this springs from love for God." Such love for God was, however, based on true faith, and had to be distinguished from doctrine, without which it could not exist. On the other hand, this doctrine, changeless and final though it was, demanded rational reflection. For "the grace of God does not effect wisdom in the saints without the mind that grasps it; nor knowledge without the power of the reason that is capable of it; nor faith apart from the fullness of the mind and reason concerning the things that are to come. . . . On the other hand, none of the things listed does a man acquire by his natural powers, apart from the divine power that bestows them." The context for such a faith in search of understanding was the church's worship. Deification had not been adequately defined in the creeds and dogmas of the church, because "this release from all evils and shortcut to salvation, the true love of

Joh.Cant.*Apol*.1.19 (*PG* 154:436)

Max.*Carit*.1.9 (*PG* 90:964)

Max.*Ep*.2 (*PG* 91:393, 396, 404)

Max.*Qu.Thal*.59 (*PG* 90:605)

God with understanding . . . [is] a worship that is true
and genuinely acceptable to God." Such worship was a
"cosmic liturgy," in which the believing mind found an
expression that was appropriate to the nature of revelation.
The rituals and sacraments performed by men on earth
were an imitation of the heavenly hierarchy. And therefore "imitating the angels in heaven, we are found to be
worshiping God through all things." The theological implications of this liturgical life were to be of concern
to Eastern thought in the next century.

Worship was, however, more than the performance of
the divine liturgy, for faith in search of understanding
was also engaged in worship, the worship of God by
the mind. The mind worshiped God in spirit and in truth
when it concentrated on those things which God had
revealed in such a form that they could be apprehended
by it. It was true, to be sure, that the written word of
Scripture was only a "forerunner," as John the Baptist
had been, preparing the way for the more perfect word
to follow. Moreover, even the terms and names that were
used about God in Scripture, although true, had to be
regarded as inappropriate and in this sense "unworthy"
of him. But the recognition of this unworthiness was
itself derived from the revelation of God in Scripture,
so that true fidelity to Scripture did not consist in claiming that its language was a disclosure of the inner being
of God but in recognizing that it spoke about the saving
will of God toward the world. For that very reason, the
mind had the obligation to pay careful attention to the
revelation of his saving will. This meant that in speaking
about God one should be careful to stick to those things
that had been disclosed in Scripture. The use of the same
word in different senses by Scripture and the fathers was
the source of much confusion, but it had to be remembered
that what mattered to the fathers was not terminology but
content.

Faith in search of understanding, therefore, had the
duty of clarifying these various senses in which words
were used. "To say something without first distinguishing
the meanings of what is said is nothing less than to confuse everything" and to obscure instead of clarifying.
Specifically, the appearance of the same terms in pagan
philosophers and in Christian theologians could lead to
such confusion unless it were recognized that what had

Max.*Qu.Thal*.pr. (*PG* 90:260)
Balthasar (1947)

Max.*Schol.C.h*.1.3 (*PG* 4:33)

Max.*Or.dom.* (*PG* 90:896)

See pp. 133–45 below

Matt.22:37

Max.*Schol.D.n*.1.2 (*PG* 4:192)

Max.*Ambig*.21 (*PG* 91:1252)

Max.*Schol.D.n*.9.1 (*PG* 4:369)

Max.*Schol.D.n*.1.1 (*PG* 4:188)

Max.*Opusc*.25 (*PG* 91:273)

Max.*Pyrr.* (*PG* 91:289)

Max.*Schol.Ep.Dion.Ar*.8.6
(*PG* 4:556)

Max.*Schol.D.n*.10.3 (*PG* 4:388)

Max.*Pyrr*. (*PG* 91:296)

Max.*Schol.D.n*.7.1 (*PG* 4:340)

been said among the Greeks in an irreligious sense had been taken over by such Christian thinkers as Dionysius for the articulation of the mystery of truth. By a proper use of words, Dionysius had adapted these Greek terms to theological purposes. But one had to be careful to note the distinctive meaning acquired by such philosophical terms when they were employed for Christian doctrine. Nevertheless, the meaning of the term "composite," for example, when applied to the relation of the divine and the human nature of Christ, could be established by consulting "both the philosophers outside [the church] and the divinely wise mystagogues of the church." Yet when the exponent of Christian doctrines used the writings of the philosophers this way, he had to remember that the God to whom these doctrines referred transcended such philosophical categories as wisdom or hypostasis or ousia. The knowledge of God was a knowledge of the unknown and the unknowable, in continuity with the witness of Scripture and the teachings of the fathers.

2   Union and Division in Christ

Abd.*Margar.* (Mai 10–II:353 [Badger 399])

The doctrine of the person of Christ formulated at the ecumenical councils achieved and expressed the unity of orthodox catholic Christendom. It also produced the most prolonged schisms in the history of Christendom. Ironically, it was the orthodox doctrine of union and division in the person of Christ that was responsible for these divisions in the body of Christ—an irony not lost on the participants in the divisions. The time when the unity of the person of Christ was affirmed was the time "from which the church began to be divided," claimed the Nestorians, referring to the Council of Ephesus in 431. Twenty years later, in 451, the Council of Chalcedon brought about a schism with the "Monophysites." The ecclesiastical and political division took place through those fifth-century councils, but the "intellectual and cultural division was consummated a hundred years or so after the political." Doctrinally, the period from the seventh until the ninth century was even more decisive; for it was during this period that each of the three major Eastern parties—the Nestorian, the Monophysite, and the Chalcedonian—articulated its distinctive christological position in a way that perpetuated division and precluded retreat (or advance) toward a formula of union. After the definition of Nicea there had also been a time of troubles and of redefinition, but this had lasted about half a century. The time of troubles after Ephesus and Chalcedon has lasted for fifteen centuries.

Abramowski (1940) 78

Although the reasons for this continuing schism over the dogma of the person of Christ lie in large measure outside the history of doctrine, it would be sheer reduc-

37

tionism to suppose, as many modern interpreters have, that there were no genuine doctrinal issues at stake. The effort to encompass in a set of dogmatic formulas the union and the division of the divine and the human in Christ was inadequate at best—and it was not always at its best. "Of all the divine mysteries," said Maximus, "the mystery that has to do with Christ stands out as the most mysterious." It was well and good for orthodox theologians to state that "we proclaim . . . the duality of the essences that come together in him, as well as of their properties . . . , but we likewise declare the combination of these ontologically into a unity of person by means of the hypostatic union"; but this did not necessarily yield a doctrinal position that could meet the criterion of consistency. As the prophecy of Simeon about the infant Jesus had stated, the doctrine of the person of Christ had been "set for the fall and rising of many, or for the rising of many and for their fall." The subsequent history of this doctrine, also in its orthodox form, suggests that the definitions of Ephesus and Chalcedon still left much to be desired. Even if there had not been a continuing need for the defense and clarification of these definitions against the critics, on what were conventionally supposed to be the two extremes, the Nestorian and the Monophysite, the "middle way" within Chalcedonian orthodoxy itself would have demanded further refinement of the union of divine and human in Christ and of the distinction between them.

Although our primary concentration here is on the development of orthodoxy as the church's doctrine about Christ, the complex interrelations between the three parties require us to pay at least some attention to each, following "the historical order: first Nestorian theology, then Monophysite, then Greek." We have discussed them earlier as part of the outcome of fifth-century disputes; now their continuing history must claim our attention in its own right. Only on this basis can we interpret the theory of Christ as universal man that came out of the conflicts within and between the parties. Because it was this version of orthodox teaching that was to prove useful in coming to the rescue of orthodoxy when the opponents of the use of images in the church had invoked christological arguments for their position, it acquired a significance that went even beyond the interpretation of the

Max.*Ambig.*42 (*PG* 91:1332)

Niceph.*Imag.*21 (*PG* 100:588)

Luke 2:34

Tim.I.*Ep.*14 (*CSCO* 75:77 [74:117])

Joh.D.*Imag.*3.2 (*PG* 94: 1285); Thdr. AbuQ.*Mim.* 8.3–4 (Graf 200–201)

Jugie (1926) 1:13
See vol. 1:266–77

person and work of Christ. Moreover, our summary of what was eventually identified as orthodox doctrine must also include the responses of Chalcedonian theology to Nestorian and to Monophysite teaching. It was declared by all three parties that the unity of mankind, lost through sin, had now been restored in Christ. Yet they themselves could not achieve unity in their doctrine of who or what Christ was.

Duality of Hypostases

As part of its affirmation of the authority of the councils, orthodoxy identified itself with the anathema pronounced at Ephesus in 431 upon "the man-worshiper Nestorius" and his theology of the incarnation as the indwelling of the Logos. Yet the adherents of that theology continued to resist the anathema and to declare that their view of the relation between the divine and the human in Christ was the only correct one and that "we, the church of Christ our Lord, hold the truth of the gospel," while all the others had fallen away from it. Much more, even, than in Byzantine orthodoxy, truth here was changeless, so that it is possible to quote writers separated by many centuries, between Babai the Great early in the seventh and Abdiša late in the thirteenth, almost without attention to their place in time. The persistent and fundamental question that Nestorian christology went on putting to its opponents was: "What, then, is to be done with the duality [of] divinity and humanity" in Christ?

Denied though it had been in 431, this duality was, in Nestorian eyes, reaffirmed by the orthodox twenty years later at Chalcedon, even though this council also repeated the condemnation of Nestorius and declared its approval of Cyril of Alexandria. When these latter actions of Chalcedon were at issue, Nestorians attacked it as "the origin of the abyss" separating them from other Christians and as the place where the digging of the abyss had begun. The teaching of the Council of Chalcedon that there was "one hypostasis" in Christ was denounced as "an insane error" and "a corruption of our faith." Still the very terminology of Chalcedon could be used by Nestorians to define their own teaching of duality: "The natures are preserved . . . without confusion, without mixture, without separation." The true doctrine was neither that of Ephesus nor that of Chalcedon, but that of "my fathers,

Išo'yahb.*Ep.*3.22 (*CSCO* 12:208[11:288])

See pp. 13–16 above

Tim.I.*Ep.*34 (*CSCO* 75:117 [74:172])

ap.*Se'ert.Chron.*94 (*PO* 13:562–63)

Išo'yahb.*Ep.*2.9 (*CSCO* 12:106[11:142])

Bab.*Un.*3.9 (*CSCO* 80:82 [79:88])

ap.Se'ert.Chron.94 (PO
13:568)

Tim.I.Ep.9 (CSCO
75:59[74:92])

Syn.Jes.(585) 1 (Chabot 394)

Thdr.AbuQ.Mim.1.26 (Graf
114–15)
Bab.Un.6.20 (CSCO 80:162
[79:200])

Bab.Un.3.9 (CSCO 80:67
[79:83])

ap.Thdr.AbuQ.Opusc.
29 (PG 97:1576)

See vol. 1:251–56

Bab.Un.6.21; 1.5; 2.8 (CSCO
80:194–95 [79:239–40]; 80:24
[79:29]; 80:49 [79:60])

Bab.Evagr.5.48 (Frankenberg
339[338])

Matt.2:11
Thos.Ed.Nat.3 (Carr 18[13]);
Bab.Un.4.12 (CSCO 80:
108[79:135])
Luke 2:52

See vol. 1:251

Bab.Un.3.9 (CSCO 80:81
[79:87])

my teachers, my predecessors, and my guides, the 318"
fathers of the Council of Nicea. This was "the celebrated
synod of the 318 fathers" to which Nestorian theologians
declared their loyalty. In 585 a Nestorian synod affirmed
the doctrine "which the 318 holy fathers assembled at
Nicea and the 150 fathers assembled at Byzantium declare,
teach, write, and affirm for the churches of all countries."
The first two councils were, then, normative for Nestorian
teaching, but those that had followed were not—a view
that the defenders of Ephesus and Chalcedon found to be
inconsistent. What "we have learned from the true tradition of all the sons of the catholic and apostolic church"
was the confession of these two councils. Sharing this
confession with all orthodox Christians, one could confi-
dently declare that this was "the mind of the Holy Scriptures and the tradition of the entire catholic and apostolic
church." In their disputes with the adherents of Ephesus
and Chalcedon, the Nestorians could identify as their
common starting point "the dogmas that are in accordance with the faith," namely, those of Nicea and Constantinople. What was at issue in the disputes was the
continuity between the first two councils and those that
followed.

In their denial of that continuity, the Nestorians of
later centuries repeated and preserved most of the emphases characteristic of the theology of the indwelling
Logos in the fourth and fifth centuries. Many of the
favorite biblical texts were the same. Especially prominent
was the use of John 2:19: "Destroy this temple, and in
three days I will raise it up," which was in many ways the
key passage in the Nestorian definition of the nature of
the union between divine and human in Christ. In words
that were taken almost verbatim from Nestorius himself,
the leading Nestorian theologian of the seventh century
declared: "Thus we adore God in the temple of his humanity, because he dwells in it as in a temple, united
with it eternally." The frankincense presented to the
Christ child by the Magi had as its purpose "to show that
he who was born is the temple of God." The words of the
Gospel that "Jesus increased," so difficult for the theology
of hypostatic union to handle, were a way for the Nestorians to interpret the events of the Gospel story, such
as the hunger, the sleeping, and the suffering of Christ.

The two Syriac versions of Hebrews 2:9, over which an earlier generation had disputed, were still at issue, with the Nestorians preferring the reading: "Apart from God he tasted death." John 1:14, the proof text for hypostatic union, was taken to mean that "he assumed flesh and made his dwelling in it, that is, in one of the hypostases of our humanity," and it was pointed out that the text did not say "he became man," but "he became flesh." The distinction between "the form of God" and "the form of a servant" was taken to be the equivalent of the Nestorian distinction between "one of the hypostases of the Trinity" and "one of the hypostases" of humanity.

From these passages the Nestorians proved the theology of the indwelling Logos. Colossians 2:9 was paraphrased to mean: "In him God the Logos dwells perfectly." The man whom the Logos had assumed as his temple and dwelling was the Second Adam, made sinless by the grace of God. It was this assumed man, and not the indwelling Logos, who had been crucified. For "if, as the heretics say, God had been crucified or had died, this would not have been of any use to us, but he would have redeemed only his fellow Gods." To the question, "Did he suffer in both, in his divinity and in his flesh, or only in his flesh?" the answer could only be that he had suffered only in the flesh. One point of controversy that continued to be of interest to both sides was the propriety of calling the Virgin Mary Theotokos, God-bearer. An anonymous Syriac treatise, perhaps from the ninth century, argued, in opposition to the Nestorian christology, that the message of the angel to the shepherds at the birth of Christ "demonstrated that he who was born of Mary is God and therefore Mary is the Theotokos." The Nestorians found it obvious that "either the Virgin is a goddess by nature and an infinite spirit . . . or she is a woman . . . and gave birth to a human being in the nature of his humanity"; since the latter was the case, she could not be called Theotokos. This was not intended to demean her position. Deriving the name Mary from "Mar," the Syriac word for "Lord," the Nestorian patriarch Timothy I went so far as to say that Christ was worthy of being called "Lord" partly because his mother had already had this dignity before him. But even that dignity did not qualify her to be called "Mother of God." All these issues in the Nes-

See vol. 1:246

Tim.I.*Ep*.1 (*CSCO* 75:12; 20[74:21; 33]); Bab.*Un*.2.8 (*CSCO* 80:50[79:62])

See vol. 1:247

Bab.*Un*.3.11 (*CSCO* 80:101 [79:126])
Tim.I.*Ep*.34 (*CSCO* 75:108 [74:158–59])

Phil 2:6–7

Bab.*Un*.3.11 (*CSCO* 80:102 [79:127])

Bab.*Evagr*.3.2 (Frankenberg 189[188])

Thos.Ed.*Nat*.7 (Carr 35[47])
Bab.*Evagr*.6.40 (Frankenberg 387[386])

Thos.Ed.*Nat*.7 (Carr 35[47])

Bab.*Un*.7 (*CSCO* 80:209 [79:258])

Thdr.AbuQ.*Opusc*.14 (*PG* 97:1537–40)

Luke 2:11

Theot.3 (Kmosko 55[54])

Bab.*Un*.7 (*CSCO* 80:214; 219–20[79:264; 271–72])

Tim.I.*Ep*.36 (*CSCO* 75:170 [74:246])

torian theology of the seventh and eighth centuries were echoes of the controversies preceding and surrounding the councils of the fifth century.

The polemics, too, were a continuation of old battles: the charges and countercharges of heresy were largely the same, but some new names had been added to the roster of heretics. Cyril of Alexandria was still a major object of attack for his view of the hypostatic union, but a new villain after the Second Council of Constantinople was "this tyrannical emperor, Justinian." It was especially Justinian's condemnation of the "three chapters," and above all his condemnation of Theodore of Mopsuestia, that earned him this reproach. The expansion of the Trisagion to read, "Holy is God, holy and powerful, holy and immortal, who was crucified for us," was still denounced as "blasphemy." The standard word for the adherents of this formula was "Theopaschites," that is, those who said that God had suffered. In the polemical interchange it was still necessary for the Nestorian position to ward off the guilt by association that sought to identify it with earlier (and heretical) views of the humanity of Christ. There were some who, upon hearing the Nestorian doctrine of the humanity of Christ as an "assumed man," would ask: "Was he, then, a mere man, according to your teaching, and could he have redeemed us by himself?" The answer was that the doctrine of the "assumed man" did not make Christ a "mere man." Nor did it mean that he was a man who had been "adopted" to become the Son of God, for this would imply that there were two Sons of God, the man adopted and the second hypostasis of the Trinity. Besides, the notion of adoption had been condemned by the church as Arian, at the council of the 318 fathers of Nicea. Because of the continuous effort to identify this theology with such heresies, its defenders were careful to specify differences between the humanity of Christ and that of all other men, differences such as the virgin birth, incorruptibility, the possession of "all authority in heaven and on earth," and the like. Since this authority was said to have been "given" to him, the passage had to apply to the "assumed man," for the Son of God had had the authority all along.

Although it is "well-nigh impossible to distinguish between [Nestorian] texts that come from vastly different periods," in the period that we are considering here some-

Išo'yahb.*Ep*.2.28 (*CSCO* 12:149[11:205])

See vol. 1:275–77
Bab.*Un*.3.9 (*CSCO* 80:79 [79:98])

Bab.*Evagr*.6.79 (Frankenberg 413[412])

Bab.*Un*.7 (*CSCO* 80:226 [79:279–80])

Bab.*Un*.2.8; 4.15 (*CSCO* 80:51; 123[79:64; 152])

Thos.Ed.*Nat*.8 (Carr 40[55])

Bab.*Un*.3.9; 4.16 (*CSCO* 80:74; 123–24[79:105; 153])

Bab.*Evagr*.4.9 (Frankenberg 265[264])

Tim.I.*Ep*.39 (*CSCO* 75:189–90[74:272–73])

Matt.28:20
Tim.I.*Ep*.34 (*CSCO* 75:120 [74:176–77])

ap.Thdr.AbuQ.*Opusc*.11 (*PG* 97:1536)

Vacant (1903) 11–1:290

thing did change in Nestorian theology, and decisively. The accomplishment of the change was to a considerable

Rücker (1936) 39

degree the work of "the creator of Nestorian dogmatics," Babai the Great. Combining as he did the traditional, the ascetic, and the speculative elements of Nestorian theology and spirituality, Babai gave to the Persian church a position on the doctrine of the person of Christ that was considerably less ambiguous than earlier Nestorian teaching had been. The official acceptance of Nestorianism by the Persian church had taken place already in 486, when a synod at Seleucia, "the Synod of Mar Acacius," had declared its faith "as pertains to the incarnation of Christ, in the confession of the two natures of divinity and humanity." These two natures existed without "mixture or confusion," for each retained the properties peculiar to it. They were united in majesty and in the worship addressed to "the unity of the person [Syriac parsōpā] of our Lord," in whom there were present "a perfect God" and "a perfect human being" in an indissoluble union but with an

Syn.Sel.(486) *Can.*1 (Chabot 302[55])

unimpaired integrity of natures. This committed the church to some version of the theology of the indwelling Logos. What Babai brought to this theology in the first part of the seventh century, and bequeathed to later centuries, was a systematization of these emphases into an integrated and self-consistent outlook. "It was Babai who introduced the formula 'two natures, two hypostases, one

de Vries (1951) 614

person of the sonship.'"

Fundamental to Babai's reconstruction of the doctrine of the person of Christ was the dogma of the Trinity, and

Bab.*Evagr.*5.62; 6.10 (Frankenberg 347[346]; 369[368])

in some ways Nestorian dogmatics may be read as the effort to place christology into the context of orthodox trinitarianism. Formally, there was no conflict on the dogma of the Trinity: "The dispute between us and them is not over baptism, nor over the Godhead in the Trinity, nor over the Trinity in the Godhead, nor over the deity and the humanity of Christ the Lord, but over the

Tim.I.*Ep.*1 (*CSCO* 75:6[74:12–13])

union between the deity and the humanity." It was possible to find the pearl of trinitarian doctrine even among Chalcedonians and among Monophysites, but the pearl

Tim.I.*Ep.*26 (*CSCO* 75:97 [74:144])

had been stained by their christology. In fact, however, the concepts and even the vocabulary of Nicene trinitarianism were assigned a controlling position in Nestorian christology that they did not possess among those for whom the doctrine of God had been defined at Nicea

Bab.*Un*.7 (*CSCO* 80:206
[79:254–55])

Bab.*Tract*. (*CSCO*
80:237[79:294])

Bab.*Un*.4.17 (*CSCO* 80:
129–30[79:159–61])

See vol. 1:264
Psell.*Om.doct*.2 (Westerink
17)

See vol. 1:219

Nars.*Hom*.17 (Connolly 5)

Syn.Kos.(612) (Chabot 592
[575])

Bab.*Tract*. (*CSCO* 80:246
[79:305])

Išo'Yahb.*Ep*.2.7 (*CSCO*
12:97[11:129])
Tim.I.*Ep*.18 (*CSCO*
75:84–85[74:127])
Abd.*Margar*.2.4 (Mai 10–II:
353[Badger 399])

but the doctrine of Christ at Ephesus and Chalcedon. Although John 1:14 said that the Logos had become flesh, the becoming could not be interpreted literally; for if it were, that would impair the doctrine of the Trinity. The Nicene doctrine that the divine in Christ was one hypostasis of the Trinity, not the entire Trinity, necessarily implied that there be one divine hypostasis and one human hypostasis in the person of Christ. The terms "hypostasis," "nature," and "person" had to be used the same way in the doctrine of Christ as they were used in the doctrine of the Trinity.

Part of the difficulty was that in the decree of Chalcedon it had been said that the two natures of Christ had combined "in one person and hypostasis [εἰς ἓν πρόσωπον καὶ μίαν ὑπόστασιν]," so that hypostasis and person were practically synonymous in orthodox usage. At Nicea hypostasis and ousia appeared to be used interchangeably, but subsequent debate and development had made it necessary to distinguish between them. Nestorian theology was based on a similar necessity to distinguish between hypostasis (Syriac qěnomâ) and person (Syriac parṣōpā). It is not clear just how early it began to make this distinction. A homily attributed to Narsai, whose life spanned the entire fifth century, declared: "We believe in one Lord Jesus Christ the Son of God—one person, double in natures and their hypostases," but for that very reason the attribution is suspect. It is clear that at a conference of Nestorian and Monophysite bishops in 612, the former insisted that "Christ is 'one,' not indeed according to the unity of nature or of hypostasis, but rather according to the singleness of his person as Son." They had to acknowledge that church fathers whose orthodoxy they affirmed had spoken of "one hypostasis made up of two natures," but they maintained that even this did not imply an identification of hypostasis and person. Syriac was a richer and more complex language than either Greek or Arabic, and it allowed for more precise distinction.

What exactly was the distinction between hypostasis and person? One had to begin, not with the doctrine of the person of Christ, but with the doctrine of the Trinity. "There are three adorable hypostases in the eternal Trinity." The way to distinguish among the three hypostases was by their respective "persons." For a hypostasis was to be defined as "a singular substance, which subsists in its own unique being and is one in number. . . . It is distinguished from other fellow hypostases through the special property that it possesses in its person." The person of each hypostasis, then, was "that which keeps it from being another [and which] determines what sort of hypostasis it is." Person was a quality of hypostasis. In the Trinity, it was the person of the hypostasis called Father to be unbegotten, and the person of the hypostasis called Son to be begotten. The doctrine of the Trinity meant that no hypostasis could forsake its nature and become homoousios with another. "Because the hypostasis exists in its being, it cannot be assumed or added to by another hypostasis and become one hypostasis with it. . . . But a person can be assumed and yet remain in its own hypostasis." One hypostasis with two natures, therefore, was unthinkable. For the same reason the one person of Jesus Christ could have two hypostases, but it was absurd to say that he was one hypostasis with either two persons or two natures. To the question, "Why is the person granted and assumed, while the hypostasis is neither granted nor assumed?" the answer was that "the hypostasis is fixed . . . and possesses all the properties of its nature," while the "person, though fixed, can be assumed." Whatever affected a hypostasis had to affect its nature—the nature it shared with all other hypostases of its kind. And so Christ must have two hypostases, as he must have two natures in his one person; for if he had only one hypostasis, everything that happened to his hypostasis—such as being born and dying—must happen to his divine nature, and thus to the entire Godhead. Such a Christ would share neither the nature of the Godhead nor the nature of mankind.

It would be a misreading of this terminological difference to conclude from it that what separated Nestorian christology from the doctrines of Ephesus and Chalcedon was no more than a dispute over words or even over abstract philosophical concepts such as nature, hypostasis, and person. The terminology and the abstractions were a way of identifying a distinctive interpretation of the central affirmations of the gospel. There was much in Nestorian thought and language about salvation that did not sound significantly different from what their opponents were saying. They could speak of Christ as "the sacrifice for every man," and affirm that "it was impossible to receive these blessings [of salvation] or to possess them

Bab.*Un*.4.17 (*CSCO* 80: 129–30[79:159–61])

Bab.*Un*.7 (*CSCO* 80:218 [79:270])

Bab.*Tract*.(*CSCO* 80:243[79:301])
Bab.*Un*.3.9 (*CSCO* 80:78[79:97])

Bab.*Un*.4.17 (*CSCO* 80:138[79:171])

Bab.*Tract*. (*CSCO* 80:241–42[79:299])

Tim.I.*Ep*.34 (*CSCO* 75:124[74:182])

Tim.I.*Ep*.35 (*CSCO* 75:158[74:230])

Tim.I.*Ep*.2.6 (*CSCO* 75:35 [74:56])

Thos.Ed.*Nat*.6 (Carr 32[41])

Bab.*Evagr*.2.73 (Frankenberg 179[178])

Thos.Ed.*Nat*.5 (Carr 27[30])

Tim.I.*Ep*.14 (*CSCO* 75:77[74:116])

Išo'yahb.*Ep*.3.22 (*CSCO* 12:207[11:286])

Thos.Ed.*Nat*.7 (Carr 36[48])

Tim.I.*Ep*.14 (*CSCO* 75:74 [74:112])

Ath.*Ar*.1.43 (*PG* 26:100–101)

Tim.I.*Ep*.35 (*CSCO* 75:155[74:226])

Bab.*Un*.4.12 (*CSCO* 80:109 [79:136])

Rücker (1936) 54

without the mediation of someone." Yet there seems to have been a perceptible difference of emphasis in the understanding of mediation. Perhaps more than in Chalcedonian orthodoxy, Christ was thought of here as teacher and example. The Logos had clothed himself in flesh "in order by his word to instruct us about the matters of the age to come." He was born "to teach the perfection of knowledge and to grant the hope and expectation of future blessings." Believers were to follow the example of the fathers, but above all to imitate the pattern that the man assumed by the Logos had set. Moreover, a false understanding of the relation between the divine and the human in Christ deprived human nature of the hope of salvation, for salvation could have come only through a distinct human hypostasis. It would have been easy for God to grant the life eternal by his own fiat, but this would have made him seem an accessory to human sin, "because while we were still in our sins he would have redeemed us, without the mediation of a man from our midst who was righteous."

The coming of that man in the flesh could be called "the incarnation of the Logos and the deification of humanity." The definition of the salvation of man as his deification was a standard element of Eastern theology, and even Nestorian theologians had to have recourse to it. But in doing so they were quick to qualify the term in such a way as to protect duality also here. Athanasius had taught that "because of our relationship to his body we have become the temple of God," thus sounding a theme familiar to Nestorian thought. But he went on in the next sentence to say that "thus even in us the Lord is now worshiped." Patriarch Timothy, by contrast, after asserting that the Holy Spirit transformed believers "into the likeness of the flesh of our Lord," immediately went on to warn that this did not mean that "we become sons of God by nature or that we are worshiped by all men as [our Lord] is." Babai likewise rejected as "wickedness and blasphemy" any suggestion that "we are sons of God as he is and are to be worshiped through our union with God the Logos. God forbid!" The idea of deification had been heightened in Eastern mysticism. In Nestorian mystical thought, however, "the suffering and death of the Redeemer are introduced, but more in the sense of the mystic's dying spiritually with Christ." Even in mystical treatises, therefore, the emphasis on "the union of the infinite with the finite, of the perfect with the imperfect" in Christ, as well as in the believer, stressed their duality. A possible source of this difference between Nestorian mystical theology and that of Chalcedonian orthodoxy is the dependence of the latter on Dionysius the Areopagite and of the former on Evagrius Ponticus. Dionysius had been translated into Syriac, and the Nestorians were aware of the differences between various translations. But except for occasional references to this "disciple of Paul" and to his theory of hierarchies, he was not prominent in Nestorian mystical literature. Evagrius provided a way of understanding the union between God and the mystic that did not impair the absoluteness and impassibility of God.

The differences in the doctrine of redemption can also be seen in the doctrine of the Eucharist. The relation between christological and eucharistic doctrine was made explicit when, for example, it was maintained that "the body of the Lord which is in heaven" and "the body that is broken daily over the altar" were "one person" and yet that the eucharistic body was not identical with "his natural body, which is in heaven." At the consecrating word of the priest the bread became "the body of the Son of God," and yet they remained different by nature; so it was also in Christ. Summarizing the parallel, an expositor of the Nestorian liturgy criticized certain men who "have said that these mysteries are in the precise sense the body and blood of Christ, not the mystery of his body and blood." Both the Eucharist and the person of Christ were a union of two different natures, which remained distinct also after the union. There had to be a duality between the natural, heavenly body and his eucharistic body, for otherwise "what is the purpose of his coming from heaven?" To those who taught otherwise it was necessary to declare that "at the altar each day we do not break and slay that body of the Lord which is in heaven. This was broken once and for all on the cross and has entered into its glory. . . . What we eat is not his body by nature, but is the commemoration of his suffering." The result of eating "this bread which is called the body of Christ" was that the communicant was lifted up to "that body which is in heaven." In short, "as Christ, through the union with the eternal Logos, as interpreted by the Nestorians, is called,

Bab.*Evagr*.4.3 (Frankenberg 261[260])

Bab.*Evagr*.1.58 (Frankenberg 101[100])

Tim.I.*Ep*.33 (*CSCO* 75: 106[74:156])

Bab.*Evagr*.2.17; 78 (Frankenberg 143; 183[142; 182])

Bab.*Evagr*.1.58 (Frankenberg 101[100])

Bab.*Un*.4.16 (*CSCO* 80:124–26[79:154–55])

Tim.I.*Ep*.34 (*CSCO* 75: 119–20[74:175–76])

Ps.Geo.Arb.*Exp*.24 (*CSCO* 76:61–62[72:66–67])

Bab.*Un*.7 (*CSCO* 80:233 [79:288])

Bab.*Un*.7 (*CSCO* 80: 229–30[79:284])

Thos.Ed.*Nat*.7 (Carr 38[51])

and in some way actually is, the Son of God without God's having actually become man, so also the eucharistic bread is in a true sense the body of Christ through its union with the real body of Christ in heaven."

The definition of the union was based on these assumptions. Although the name "Christ" might pertain specifically to the human hypostasis because it was this that was anointed, it more usually referred to the person of the union between divine and human. Such titles as "Logos" and "Son of God" belonged to theology, but "Christ" belonged to the economy of the incarnation. From passages like Psalm 82:6, "I have said, 'You are gods,'" it was clear that "Son of God" was not an inappropriate title even for the man assumed by the Logos. Yet this did not mean, as its opponents charged, that the Nestorian position required the acceptance of a double sonship, one divine and the other human. On the contrary, there was "one lordship and one sonship in the two hypostases, which exists in the hypostasis of the Logos by nature and in the hypostasis of the humanity by the union." Despite such assurances, it was not clear whether the union was chiefly a union of the function carried out by the divine-human person in a duality of hypostases and of the worship addressed to him, or whether it was more than this. The "more" would lie in the traditional idea of the communication of properties, by which the properties characteristic either of the human nature (such as the ability to die) or of the divine nature (such as the ability to perform miracles) were in fact communicated to Jesus Christ in his concrete and single selfhood (or hypostasis). By this idea, Christ the Son of God in his single hypostasis was born (hence his mother could be called "Theotokos") and died, but not the divine nature of the Logos. When Babai came to speak of such communication, it was almost always on the basis of "appellation" or of how "the Scriptures speak" or of biblical attribution of the deeds of one nature to the other. This raises the question whether, in such a definition of the union, the communication of properties was in any sense real or whether it was only verbal, as Babai charged that the flesh and humanity of Christ was in the theory of his opponents. The union was, quite clearly, "an indissoluble one, in the womb of the Virgin, on the cross, in the death and burial." Babai was, moreover, committed to the view

de Vries (1947) 214

Bab.*Evagr*.4.21 (Frankenberg 275[274])
Bab.*Un*.4.12 (*CSCO* 80: 111[79:138])

Bab.*Un*.6.20 (*CSCO* 80:161–84[79:199–227])

See vol. 1:164, 178

Thos.Ed.*Nat*.7 (Carr 38[51])

Philox.*Diss*.2.23 (*PO* 15:507)

Bab.*Un*.4.16 (*CSCO* 80: 123–28[79:152–59])

Tim.I.*Ep*.34 (*CSCO* 75:130 [74:190])

See vol. 1:249–51, 270–74

Bab.*Un*.4.17; 5.18; 2.8 (*CSCO* 80:132; 141; 56–57[79:163; 174; 70])

Bab.*Un*.7 (*CSCO* 80: 206[79:254])

Tim.I.*Ep*.34 (*CSCO* 75:108[74:159])

Bab.*Evagr*.3.1 (Frankenberg 189[188])

Heb.1:2

Tim.I.*Ep*.36 (*CSCO* 75:172–73[74:250])

that the fact of the union was incontestable, but the "how" was unknown. But even such biblical language as "in these last days [God] has spoken to us by a Son" referred "specifically to the union," but "generally to the duality of ousias and of hypostases." This suggests again that they accepted the duality of hypostases because they wanted to, but the unity of person because they had to.

Many centuries after most of the materials we have been citing were written, the metropolitan of Nisibis, Abdišа (Ebedjesus), who died in 1318, composed *The Book of the Pearl,* which "is his most valuable treatise on Nestorian theology and constitutes the official view of the sect." Here most of these themes were systematically formulated. Chalcedon was interpreted as having "confirmed the confession of the two natures and the distinction between the properties of both natures," even though the poverty of Greek and its inability to distinguish between hypostasis and person led the council to assert one hypostasis in Christ. The Trinity consisted of "hypostases rather than accidental powers," because within the hypostases there could not be any change or union. The statement of the Gospel that "the Logos became flesh" was to be understood, therefore, in the sense that the flesh "became" what it had not been before, while the Logos "dwelt in" the flesh. Conflict over this issue, symbolized by the question of the Theotokos, divided Eastern Christendom into three groups: the Monophysites, who taught one hypostasis and one nature; the Melchites (Chalcedonians), who taught one hypostasis and two natures; and the "so-called Nestorians," who taught a duality of hypostases and of natures in the one person of Christ. Much of the book was an expression of the common ground shared by all Christians, especially in the East, but in its doctrine of the person of Christ the division both of the hypostases of Christ and of the church was officially set down.

Atiya (1968) 302

Abd.*Margar*.3.4 (Mai 10–II: 353[Badger 399])

Abd.*Margar*.1.5 (Mai 10–II: 346–47[Badger 386])

John 1:14

Abd.*Margar*.3.1 (Mai 10–II: 350[Badger 394])

Abd.*Margar*.3.4 (Mai 10–II:353–54 [Badger 399–400])

One Incarnate Nature of God the Logos

During the centuries that followed the decision of the Council of Chalcedon, it was not only the "Nestorian" doctrine of the person of Christ, but especially the "Monophysite" doctrine, that continued to oppose the Chalcedonian definition of christological orthodoxy. Most of the adjustments in the orthodox interpretation of that definition, moreover, were slanted in the direction of the doctrine of "one incarnate nature of God the Logos." From the time of Chalcedon and even earlier, the history of this doctrine must be viewed as a distinct branch of the christological development. One of its founding fathers, Severus of Antioch, citing the authority of one of his theological forefathers, Cyril of Alexandria, stated the issue in his rhetorical question: "Why, then, are we being forced to say 'two [natures],' when the doctor [of the church, viz., Cyril] cried out that they are no longer two?"

Although Severus was a founding father, it remained for the period we are considering in this chapter, the end of the seventh and the beginning of the eighth century, to consolidate the tradition that had been transmitted, as a synod of eastern "Monophysite" bishops put it, "from Peter, the chief of the divine band of apostles, all the way to Severus." The vehicle of this consolidation was the West Syrian church, usually called "Jacobite." It received this designation because of its eponymous founder, Jacob Baradaeus, whose action in filling vacancies in the West Syrian hierarchy "was the establishment of a new church." The followers of Jacob Baradaeus thought it fitting that he should have this name because he was "in everything an imitator of the battles of the great Saint Jacob [James], the archbishop and martyr and brother of our Lord Jesus Christ." Their principal liturgy was called *The Anaphora of the Holy Mar Jacob Brother of Our Lord and Bishop of Jerusalem.* In at least some versions of it there was the prayer that God would remember the bishops of the church, "who from Jacob, the chief of bishops, the apostle and martyr, until this very day, have proclaimed the word of the orthodox faith in thy holy church." And it was commonly believed among the Jacobites that "this liturgy of Mar Jacob is more ancient than all the other liturgies, and therefore the others are arranged on the basis of it."

It was, however, a third Jacob, Jacob of Edessa, who gave the Jacobite communion the stamp of his piety and erudition. During the seventh and eighth centuries "there is scarcely anyone in East or West who is his peer in comprehensive learning, literary activity, and unremitting industry." He "founded the grammar of the Syriac language" and was in fact "the first founder of Semitic grammar" altogether. He was "profoundly versed in all the science of this epoch—in physics, in geography, in

Sev.Ant.*Gram*.2.12 (*CSCO* 112:91[111:117])

Episc.Or.*Ep.* (*CSCO* 103: 134[17:192])

Phot.*Enc*.2 (*PG* 102:721)

Joh.D.*Haer*.6 (*PG* 94:744)

Kleyn (1882) 62

Eus.Bass.*Ep.Thds.Al.* (*CSCO* 103:88[17:126]

Anaph.Jac.(Connolly-Codrington 91; Brightman 31)

Anaph.Jac. (*CSCO* 14:25)

Dion.BarSal.*Exp.lit*.8 (*CSCO* 14:61[13:42])

Kayser (1886) 1:49

Merx (1966) 48

Hjelt (1892) 3

Baumstark (1922) 248

Merx (1966) 34

See vol. 1:21

Sev.Ant.*Hom.cathedr.* (*PO* 4:5–94; 8:211–394; 12:5–164; 16:765–862; 20:277–432; 22: 207–312; 23:5–176; 25:5–174; 26:263–450)

Rücker (1923) xxii

Hage (1966) 51

ap.Dion.BarSal.*Exp.lit.*6 (*CSCO* 14:53[13:30])

Jac.Ed.*Conf.* (Kayser 1:62–64 [2:30–31])

Jac.Ed.*Conf.* (Kayser 1:62[2:30])

Jac.Ed.*Conf.* (Kayser 1:63[2:30])

Jac.Ed.*Ep.Thos.*ap.Dion. BarSal.*Exp.lit.*3 (*CSCO* 14:39[13:9])

Jac.Ed.*Hex.*7 (*CSCO* 97:293 [92:344])

Episc.Or.*Ep.* (*CSCO* 103: 133[17:189–90])

astronomy, and in natural history." Therefore he deserves to be called "the outstanding representative [of] Christian Hellenism" in the Semitic Christian tradition. But it is a mistake of some historians to stress this side of Jacob's thought and writing at the expense of his primary vocation as a churchman and theologian. He acquired the title "the interpreter of books" because he knew not only Syriac but also Greek and even Hebrew and therefore, unlike most Christian theologians of his time, was able to read and interpret both the Old Testament and the New Testament in the original. In addition to his output of biblical commentaries, he translated into Syriac the *Cathedral Homilies* of Severus from the original Greek, which has since been lost. He also expounded the *Anaphora of Jacob,* and his exposition has been called "by far the most valuable . . . on account of his comprehensive knowledge and his critical capacities, unusual for that time." Since it is beyond question that "the heart of the Syrian Jacobite Church beat in its liturgy, as did that of other Eastern churches," Jacob's interpretation of the liturgy, which dealt theologically not only with the great themes of the Mass but even with such questions as the role of incense, is a valuable source for the history of Monophysite doctrine. Alongside these sources must, finally, be put a confession that Jacob composed. It summarizes, perhaps more succinctly than any other document of the time, the distinctive christological emphases of the Jacobites. It may also serve, therefore, as an organizing basis for our exposition of their christology.

In the opening sentence of his confession Jacob characterized himself as one "who walks in the footsteps of our devout and holy fathers [and] teaches as they did." Later he spoke of "the sound faith and orthodox confession of the prophets, apostles, and holy fathers." His liturgical exposition, too, was "the tradition [which] I have received from the fathers, which I also transmit." No less bound by the tradition was his biblical exegesis, all of which he claimed to have derived from this source. Among the fathers there were, of course, some who were especially favored by the Monophysites, including "the directors and divine doctors of the holy church of God, Athanasius, Basil, the Gregories [of Nazianzus and of Nyssa], Cyril, and others like them, all the way to the blessed Severus." Severus himself compiled a florilegium

Sev.Ant.*Neph*.2 (*CSCO*
120:36[119:49])

Jac.Ed.*Hex*.7 (*CSCO* 97:
273[92:320])

Sev.Ant.*Ep.Thds*.(*CSCO*
103:18[17:28])
Sev.Ant.*Gram*.2.10 (*CSCO*
112:80[111:102])

Sev.Ant.*Gram*.3.39 (*CSCO*
102:188[101:256])

Max.*Ep*.12 (*PG* 91:472)
Sev.Ant.*Gram*.3.35 (*CSCO*
102:149[101:204–205])

Jac.Ed.*Hex*.7 (*CSCO* 97:270
[92:316–17])

See p. 20 above
Sev.Ant.*Gram*.3.9 (*CSCO* 94:
126[93:180])
Sev.Ant.*Gram*.3.17 (*CSCO*
94:196–99[93:279–83])
Tim.I.*Ep*.19 (*CSCO* 75:86
[74:129])

Jac.Ed.*Ep.Thds*.ap.Dion.
BarSal.*Exp.lit*.3 (*CSCO*
14:37[13:7])

Sev.Ant.*Gram*.2.5 (*CSCO*
112:65[111:82–83])

Philox.*Diss*.1.70 (*PO* 15:
489–90)
Sev.Ant.*Ep.Thds*. (*CSCO*
103:19[17:29–30]); Tim.
Ael.*Chalc*.5 (*PO* 13:223–24)

Philox.*Diss*.1.54 (*PO* 15:480)

Thds.Al.*Ep*. (*CSCO* 103:
2[17:7])

Thdr.AbuQ.*Mim*.1.27
(Graf 116); Phot.*Ep*.1.9.18
(*PG* 102:711)

Paul.Ant.*Ep.Thds.Al*. (*CSCO*
103:75[17:107–8])

Sev.Ant.*Gram*.3.3 (*CSCO*
94:22[93:31])

of quotations from these and other fathers to prove that his position was traditional and hence orthodox. Gregory of Nazianzus, surnamed "the Theologian," had spoken by the inspiration of the Holy Spirit. But it was chiefly the fathers and bishops associated with the see of Alexandria who had been the bearers of genuine orthodoxy. Athanasius was the peer of the twelve apostles; and Severus declared himself willing to accept the Chalcedonian formula if it could be found in Athanasius— which was, of course, unthinkable. The successor of Athanasius in the see of Alexandria, Cyril, was no less eminent. The Chalcedonian opponents of the Jacobite christology quoted Cyril against it, and its defenders had to explain away some of Cyril's language. But Cyril's authority was beyond such reproach; he was "the great master and the treasury of the words of the Spirit." Just as the Chalcedonian theologians had some favorites even among the Western fathers, so, too, Severus, rejecting Leo's christology as a denial of the hypostatic union, found the doctrines of Ambrose much more congenial—even though Nestorians also consulted Ambrose.

The consensus of the fathers to which this appeal was made had been expressed in the orthodox councils. Jacob of Edessa proceeded in his liturgical discussion from "the symbol of the 318 fathers" of the Council of Nicea. The use of the term "homoousios" for Jesus Christ in that symbol was proof that the one incarnate Logos was the proper subject for all christological predications. The 318 fathers at Nicea were followed by the 150 council fathers at Constantinople, who set forth the same faith that had been confessed earlier. The third ecumenical council, held at Ephesus in 431, likewise was approved. The condemnation of Nestorius at Ephesus was defended because it was directed not at his life but at his doctrine. Thus the Jacobites accepted the authority of the same councils regarded by the orthodox as the first three ecumenical councils. Their opponents found this terminus ad quem for the truly ecumenical councils quite arbitrary. The reason for it was, of course, Chalcedon, "which, taking advantage of the pretext of the madness of Eutyches, brought into the churches the Nestorian worship of a man." Both the Chalcedonian formula and the *Tome* of Leo on which it was based were thoroughly Nestorian in their doctrine. Even though his own language about Christ contained

Sev.Ant.*Ep.Thds.* (CSCO 103: 13[17:22])

such echoes of Chalcedon as "without confusion" and "distinctive," Severus refused to accept the claim that "Saint Cyril said that there was absolutely no difference between saying that one nature of God the Logos was incarnate and confessing that Emmanuel is indivisibly united in two natures."

Sev.Ant.*Gram.*3.9 (CSCO 94: 115–34[93:165–92])

On the basis of this understanding of the authority of the councils, the Jacobites charged Chalcedon and its adherents with having broken the continuity of the one true and orthodox faith and with having introduced doctrinal innovations. Jacob of Edessa affirmed in his confession that "we do not alter or disturb these eternal propositions which our fathers have set down." Orthodoxy consisted in adherence to "apostolic and patristic doctrines, which are divine and irreproachable." On the basis of the warning "Remove not the ancient landmark which your fathers have set," it was urged that the boundaries of orthodoxy had been permanently fixed by tradition. When charged with novelty because he had written a new statement of faith, Philoxenus of Mabbug replied that he had in fact merely rehearsed the one faith confessed by many doctors of the church and by the first two councils. It was the Chalcedonians who were guilty of doctrinal innovation when they invented such neologisms as the term "homohypostatos" (of the same hypostasis), corresponding to "homoousios" (of the same ousia). They cited the authority of the fathers, but they either corrupted their meaning or explained it to suit their own purposes; this was tantamount to doctrinal innovation. The "mysteries of the fathers" were such that "neither addition nor subtraction" was permitted.

Jac.Ed.*Conf.* (Kayser 1:64[2:31])

Thds.Al.*Ep.* (CSCO 103: 5[17:11])

Prov.22:28
Episc.CP.*Ep.* (CSCO 103: 104[17:150])

Philox.*Diss.*1.69 (PO 15:489)
Sev.Ant.*Gram.*2.23 (CSCO 112:197[111:252]); Tim.
Ael.*Chalc.*4 (PO 13:222)

Max.*Opusc.*14 (PG 91:152);
Joh.D.*Dialect.*48 (Kotter 1:114)

Sev.Ant.*Neph.*2 (CSCO 120:35[119:47])

Thds.Al.*Or.* (CSCO 103: 28[17:42])

Concretely, however, this declaration of loyalty to the tradition of the fathers could not be taken to mean that one should—or even could—repeat their formulas as they stood. For example, orthodox fathers had been able to speak of the humanity of Christ as an "assumed man" because the Nestorian version of this term had not yet achieved currency and the term could be understood in an orthodox way. Similarly, Athanasius could call the humanity of Christ "the Lordly man," a term that eventually became suspect. The appearance of such terms did not implicate these fathers in the heresies later associated with the terms, but it did not imply either that such terms were acceptable now. There had likewise been

Ps.Ath.*Exp.fid.*1 (PG 25:201)

Sev.Ant.*Neph.*1 (CSCO 120: 2–3[119:3])
Ath.*Exp.Ps.*41.5 (PG 27: 197); Ps.Ath.*Exp.fid.*1 (PG 25:201–4)
Sev.Ant.*Gram.*3.23 (CSCO 102:10[101:15])

Thds.Al.*Or.* (*CSCO* 103:
35[17:53]); Sev.Ant.*Gram.*
2.28 (*CSCO* 112:170–71
[111:218])

Philox.*Diss.*2.26 (*PO* 15:510)

See vol. 1:211

Sev.Ant.*Gram.*3.28 (*CSCO*
102:61[101:85]); Sev.Ant.
*Neph.*1 (*CSCO* 120:3[119:4])

Jac.Ed.*Hex.*5 (*CSCO*
97:159[92:187])

Jac.Ed.*Hex.*1 (*CSCO* 97:
35[92:44])

Sev.Ant.*Gram.*2.17 (*CSCO*
112:125[111:160])

Philox.*Diss.*1.33 (*PO* 15:461)

Sev.Ant.*Gram.*2.1 (*CSCO*
112:51[111:65])

Philox.*Diss.*1.32 (*PO* 15:
460–61)

terminological confusion about "hypostasis." Therefore a willingness "to accept all the words spoken to us by the fathers" carried with it the obligation to "consider their own time, when these things were said, on account of what and on account of whom, what reason impelled them to write this way, and what was the purpose of their statement." For instance, as Gregory of Nazianzus had acknowledged, the Council of Nicea had not considered the doctrine of the Holy Spirit at any length because it was not yet an issue; in the same way the relation between the divine and the human in Christ had not been an issue at that council and therefore had not been adjudicated with precise terminology. This was not in any way a concession that the later development of such terminology was a departure from the faith of Nicea; quite the contrary.

It was essential in the repetition of orthodox formulas to remember that they spoke about mysteries that were beyond formulation. According to Jacob of Edessa, human reason, which doubted divine revelation and went on to investigate what it could not understand, was responsible for a preoccupation with the literal, material sense of Scripture. For example, the creation of the angels was not explicitly described in Scripture; such matters were "hidden and unknown" and were "God's business alone," not to be pried into by man. Even the terms used by the fathers and the councils, such as ousia, hypostasis, and the like, were inadequate; yet they were also unavoidable, since there was no other way to express divine truth. The doctrine of the incarnation had to be recounted in paradoxes; for "such doctrines of Christian faith are mysteries, and whoever knows them knows that they cannot be grasped, and whoever grasps them knows that they cannot be explained." Faith meant a prohibition of curious investigation into the eternal generation of the Son or the eternal procession of the Holy Spirit. Such questions as, "How does the hypostasis of the Son descend from heaven?" or "How did the immortal one die?" were out of order and "not proper for believers, nor does anyone who has felt the mystery of Christian faith inquire about such matters." In this emphasis on knowing the unknowable the Jacobites were stating the common faith which they shared with other Christians, but it took on a special coloring in their system because of the implication that

Jac.Ed.ap.Dion.BarSal.*Exp. lit*.15 (*CSCO* 14:85–86 [13:74–75])

Jac.Ed.*Ep.Thos*.ap.Dion. BarSal.*Exp.lit*.3 (*CSCO* 14:38[13:8])

Sev.Ant.*Ep.Thds*. (*CSCO* 103:11[17:19])

Sev.Ant.*Gram*.3.7 (*CSCO* 94: 73[93:105])

See vol. 1:256–57

Sev.Ant.*Gram*.3.31 (*CSCO* 102:86[101:119])

Sev.Ant.*Gram*.2.5 (*CSCO* 112:65[111:82–83])

Sev.Ant.*Gram*.3.11 (*CSCO* 94: 151[93:216])

Jac.Ed.*Conf*. (Kayser 1:63 [2:30])

Jac.Ed.ap.Dion.BarSal.*Exp. lit*.8 (*CSCO* 14:61[13:41])

Gen.1:3
Jac.Ed.*Hex*.2 (*CSCO* 97: 57[92:71–72])
Jac.Ed.*Hex*.3; 4; 5 (*CSCO* 97:98; 120; 163[92:95–96; 143–44; 191])
Gen.1:26
Jac.Ed.*Hex*.7 (*CSCO* 97: 239–40[92:281–82])

"economy" rather than "theology" was the proper topic of doctrinal affirmations.

The distinction between economy and theology was basic to the Jacobite position. Jacob of Edessa took the words of the Gloria Patri, "As it was in the beginning, is now, and ever shall be," to mean that one was to distinguish between Christ "before he became incarnate" and Christ "in his body." It was the purpose of the entire liturgy to recount "what Christ has accomplished for us" in the "economy which Christ carried out when he suffered for us in the flesh." Severus had recourse to the distinction as a way of explaining how the incarnate Logos, who was one with the Holy Spirit in the Trinity, could nevertheless receive the Holy Spirit at his baptism. Another way of stating the distinction was to speak of the "times" of Christ, namely, "before the incarnation" and "after the incarnation," which corresponded to theology and economy. This distinction of times, which had been articulated by such theologians as Hilary of Poitiers, must not be taken to mean, however, that "they divide the incarnate Logos into two natures." Likewise, the Nicene Creed, in attaching "homoousios" (a term that pertained to theology) to "Jesus Christ" (a title that pertained to economy) was not confusing theology and economy, but confessing the unity of the incarnate Logos. It was clear that the issue between the Monophysite tradition and the others, all of which accepted the Council of Nicea, lay "not in theology but in economy."

Nevertheless, the implications of theology for economy, specifically of trinitarian doctrine and terminology for christological doctrine and terminology, were at issue. The confession of Jacob of Edessa opened its christological affirmations with the declaration that the "Logos, the Creator, [is] homoousios in every way with the Father, who begat him." In his commentary on the liturgy he urged the unity of the Godhead as well as the Trinity, "distinguished without being divided and united without being confused." The words of the Genesis story, "Let there be light," were spoken by the Father to "the creating Logos, his Wisdom." This was true also of other sayings in the creation account. It was true above all of the words, "Let us make man in our image, after our likeness," where the plural pronouns clearly referred to the Trinity. All of this was standard orthodox teaching, since "the term

Philox.*Diss*.2.17 (*PO* 15: 495–96)

Philox.*Diss*.2.21 (*PO* 15:505–506)

Max.*Carit*.2.29 (*PG* 90:993)

See vol. 1:176–80

Syndoct.post.(569) (*CSCO* 103:117[17:167])

Philox.*Diss*.2.9 (*PO* 15: 496–97)

Sev.Ant.*Gram*.2.2 (*CSCO* 112:55[111:70])

Sev.Ant.*Gram*.2.4 (*CSCO* 112: 58–66[111:74–76])
Thds.Al.*Or*.pr. (*CSCO* 103: 25[17:38])

Sev.Ant.*Gram*.2.33 (*CSCO* 112:201–2[111:258])

Sev.Ant.*Gram*.2.17 (*CSCO* 112:122–23[111:157])

'Trinity' ... represents the confession of the entire church," not merely that of the Jacobites. Where the divergence lay was in the definition of this "distinguishing without dividing" and "uniting without confusing," as it applied not to the Godhead as such but to the person of Jesus Christ. For the hypostatic union as taught by the Jacobites represented "a truer union of hypostasis than that which pertains to the Father and the Son." This latter was "not a union of hypostases, but only of nature," while the union in Christ was "a division neither of hypostases nor of natures separated from hypostases." Statements like this, which could be interpreted by an unfriendly critic to mean that the oneness of God was less truly one than the oneness of divine and human in Christ, sounded "tritheistic" not only to unbelievers outside the church but also to other Christians. Clearly there was a danger, which some Jacobites themselves recognized, that in the name of avoiding modalistic monarchianism, their theologians might lapse into "a plurality of gods and a plurality of ousias."

Apparently the unity of the hypostasis of Jesus Christ had to be preserved at almost any cost—even perhaps at the cost of jeopardizing the unity of the hypostases in the Trinity. To the Nestorians, for whom trinitarian doctrine controlled christological doctrine, one said that "on account of the term 'homoousios' you do violence to the economy which was carried out to save our life. For you always make it a practice to err as follows: 'If Father, Son, and Spirit are one nature, how can one of the hypostases operate singly, without the others?' " Part of the confusion seems to have lain in the term "nature," which in patristic usage "sometimes signifies the ousia and sometimes the hypostasis," that is, sometimes what the Three had in common and sometimes what was distinctive of each. Not only had the fathers sometimes used "nature" equivocally; they had also treated "hypostasis" and "person" as synonyms, and had sometimes equated both of these with "ousia" and "nature." Now that the controversy had made precise definitions and careful distinctions necessary, however, "hypostasis" should be taken to mean "neither commonality nor relationship, but what is distinctive of each person or thing." "Ousia," on the other hand, referred to "that which is common" to Father, Son, and Spirit; and "nature" was best used to refer to the ousia, so that Philoxenus preferred to say that the divine nature of the Logos had remained in heaven, but that the divine hypostasis of the Logos had descended from heaven.

It was this divine hypostasis that, in the words of the confession of Jacob of Edessa, "came down from heaven and became flesh from the Holy Spirit and from Mary the Theotokos, flesh with soul and reason." The appropriate term for the incarnation, therefore, was that it was "from two natures" that became a composite hypostasis, rather than "in two natures" that continued to be distinct from each other. Chalcedon had deliberately rejected "from" and had said "in"; at some early date, however, one recension of the Chalcedonian creed had in fact substituted "from two natures," and, at least in the transmitted texts, the repetition of the symbol of Chalcedon at the Lateran Council of 649 used "from two natures" in Greek and "in two natures" in Latin, while the canons of the Council in both languages combined the two formulas and said "from two natures and in two natures." The difference, according to Severus, was that the preposition "in" meant "a duality, representing separation," while "from" indicated "composition and a union without confusion." This difference, moreover, was not merely one of terminology but one of doctrine, and even saying "united in two natures" did not make "in two natures" acceptable. Drawing upon the authority of Cyril of Alexandria, Severus called the formula "from two natures" the anchor of true christological doctrine. The composite of two natures was "neither split nor divided nor separated nor subject to enumeration"; on the other hand, the union had taken place "without any change or mixture or confusion." It also appears that, at least for Severus, the phrase "means more than an affirmation that at the time of the union there was a concurrence of Godhead and manhood. It means also that at every moment in the life of our Lord there was this concurrence."

The formula meant, above all, that the humanity—or, as the advocates of this position still preferred to call it, the flesh—of Christ had never had an existence of its own, but had come into existence with the union. Since there had never been a previous hypostasis of his humanity, only his deity was a hypostasis, the hypostasis of the Logos, and therefore the person of Jesus Christ was "one person and one incarnate nature of God the Logos."

Philox.*Diss*.2.13 (*PO* 15:499)

Jac.Ed.*Conf*. (Kayser 1:63 [2:30])

ap.Max.*Ep*.12 (*PG* 91:493)

Sev.Ant.*Gram*.3.3 (*CSCO* 94:20[93:28])

Urbina (1951) 390–91

CLater.(649)*Act*.5 (Mansi 10:1149–50)

CLater.(649)*Can*.6 (Mansi 10:1153–54)

Sev.Ant.*Gram*.2.29 (*CSCO* 112:177[111:226–27])

Sev.Ant.*Neph*.2 (*CSCO* 120:9[119:11])

Sev.Ant.*Gram*.3.9 (*CSCO* 94:122 [93:174])

Paul.Ant.*Ep.Thds.Al*. (*CSCO* 103:74[17:106–7])

Samuel (1957) 371–72

See vol. 1:247–48

Sev.Ant.*Neph*.2 (*CSCO* 120:30[119:40])

Sev.Ant.*Gram*.2.22 (*CSCO* 112:146[111:187])

Thds.Al.Or.6 (CSCO 103: 50–51[17:73])

This was properly called a "union" by the fathers because it was a composite "from one nature or hypostasis of God the Logos and his own flesh, which was truly animated with a rational and intellectual soul." The anathema against "in two natures" was not directed against those who separated the two natures in their abstract thought or theological speculation, but against those who said that there were still in concrete fact two natures after the union. The union did not require one to overlook the

Sev.Ant.Gram.2.14 (CSCO 112:99[111:128])

differences and distinctive properties of the two natures

Sev.Ant.Gram.3.30 (CSCO 120:75[101:104])

from which Christ had been formed. Behind this was the insistence that the humanity which the Logos had taken up into his one nature "did not omit any of the things of which a human being consists, but [was] . . . of the

Thds.Al.Ep. (CSCO 103: 3[17:8])

same nature as we." That insistence had been put to the test when some maintained that the physical body of Christ had been free of corruption from the moment of

See vol. 1:272
Paul.Ant.Ep.Thds.Al. (CSCO 103:76[17:109–10])

his conception rather than from the resurrection, a view condemned by the main body of "Monophysite" teaching. Also excluded, at another extreme, was any notion that the union was not merely a union of two natures but of two ousias, divine and human; for if "ousia" were taken in its usual and proper significance as referring to that which was common to all the members of a class, a union of ousias would mean that "the Holy Trinity has become incarnate in all of humanity and has become composite

Sev.Ant.Gram.2.26 (CSCO 112:164[111:209])

with our entire race," which would be blasphemous.

"One incarnate nature of God the Logos" was, therefore, the orthodox doctrine of the hypostatic union. Jacob of Edessa found it prefigured already in the creation of

Jac.Ed.Hex.7 (CSCO 97: 272–73[92:318–19])

man as a composite of body and soul. The opponents of the Jacobites, while having to acknowledge that this analogy between the relation of soul and body in man and the relation of divine and human in Christ had been

Thdr.AbuQ.Mim.10.16 (Graf 252); Nicet.Byz.Arm.15 (PG 105:632–36)

used by the fathers, argued that it did not imply the doctrine of one incarnate nature. They likewise claimed that this doctrine taught a mixture and a confusion of deity and humanity in the person of Emmanuel (a favorite title for the incarnate Logos), but the defenders of the

See vol. 1:240
Sev.Ant.Gram.3.14 (CSCO 94:172–73[93:246])

Is.63:7–14(LXX)

See vol. 1:377
Sev.Ant.Gram.3.6 (CSCO 94:63[93:90])

doctrine rejected this as calumny. What it did teach was, in the words of a proof text often employed by earlier theologians, that "neither an emissary nor an angel, but the Lord himself has saved us." Within the composite hypostasis of Christ, according to these words, the sub-

Sev.Ant.*Gram*.3.6 (*CSCO* 94: 59–60[93:85]); Philox.*Diss*. 2.32 (*PO* 15:514)

Sev.Ant.*Gram*.2.37 (*CSCO* 112:224–25[111:288])

Sev.Ant.*Gram*.2.14 (*CSCO* 112:96; 99[111:123; 127])

Sev.Ant.*Neph*.2 (*CSCO* 120:21[119:28])

See vol. 1:249–51

Jac.Ed.*Hex*.7 (*CSCO* 97: 289[92:339–40])

Ps.8:5; Heb.2:7

Jac.Ed.*Hex*.1 (*CSCO* 97: 18[92:24])

Luke 2:52; Mark 13:32

Sev.Ant.*Gram*.3.7 (*CSCO* 94:84[93:121])

Sev.Ant.*Neph*.2 (*CSCO* 120:28[119:38])

Ps.22:1; Matt.27:46

Sev.Ant.*Gram*.3.6 (*CSCO* 94:52[93:74])

Sev.Ant.*Neph*.2 (*CSCO* 120:61[119:83])

Sev.Ant.*Gram*.3.41 (*CSCO* 102:206–49[101:280–338])

Jac.Ed.*Conf*. (Kayser 1:63[2:30–31])
Jac.Ed.*Hex*.5 (*CSCO* 97: 192[92:225])

Jac.Ed.*Hex*.1 (*CSCO* 97: 23–24[92:30–31])
Is.6:3

ject of all the words and actions in the economy was God the Logos, now incarnate: "the divine things because he is God, the human because he has become man." The sharing of the action in this hypostatic union was a special kind of sharing, for in it there was only one center of action, the Logos. To those who taught otherwise it was necessary to say: "Do not use the word 'two' after the union! . . . But if you want to confess two natures after the union, go find yourself some other union!" For when one said "union," one was obliged to confess "one incarnate nature of God the Logos."

To this one subject, the one incarnate nature of God the Logos, all predicates were to be attached by the communication of properties. As body and soul in man functioned together and each performed what properly belonged to the other, so it was in Christ. The predicate in the psalm, "made a little lower than the angels," had to be applied to "Christ, the Logos of God, because he has truly become man on our behalf." The ignorance and growth in knowledge attributed to Christ in the Gospels, which would have been inappropriate before the incarnation, became appropriate through the incarnation and now pertained to the person of the Logos made man. The meanest and most humiliating words of the Gospels about Christ belonged "not to one of his forms or natures (for this would introduce a division) but to the Logos incarnate on our behalf." Even the cry of dereliction on the cross, "My God, my God, why hast thou forsaken me?" had been "spoken, without any division [of natures], by the incarnate Logos of God himself." The same was true of the most exalted statements and actions in the Gospels, such as walking on the water and raising the dead. Humiliating deeds and exalted deeds—"God the Logos incarnate did them both." A lengthy compendium of patristic quotations was assembled to prove that "Emmanuel is one and the same in his miracles and in his sufferings."

This had to mean, as the confession of Jacob of Edessa made clear, that there was no stopping short of saying that "the holy, almighty, immortal God was crucified for us and died. . . . Nor do we maintain, as do the Nestorians, those man-worshipers, that a mortal man died for us." Elsewhere, he defended the liturgical addition to the Trisagion. And since, by the common consent of all theological parties, the seraphic hymn in Isaiah referred to the Trinity, it must have been one of the Trinity who was crucified. If this confession brought on the mocking title of "Theopaschite," one could take comfort in the words of the apostle that "they crucified the Lord of glory." Against the formula of the Chalcedonians, according to which the incarnate Logos "died not in his divine nature, but only in his human nature," the Jacobite version of the doctrine of the hypostatic union insisted that speaking of two natures after the union was a capitulation to Nestorian thought. For "when things are distinct from each other and each of them is considered on its own and looked at individually, then such a 'distinction' is in fact a separation." The doctrine of hypostatic union and the idea of two natures after that union were mutually contradictory.

The slogan for the hypostatic union was the identification of the Virgin Mary as Theotokos. Jacob of Edessa confessed: "Also after he has become man, we hallow and glorify him, together with the Father and the Holy Spirit. Likewise we know and declare that the holy Virgin is Theotokos, and we do not call her Christotokos or Anthropotokos" (an attack on Nestorius's way of speaking about her). Although they regarded Chalcedonian language about Mary as hypocritical, Monophysites joined with Chalcedonians in calling her Theotokos, as when Theodosius of Alexandria asserted that the Logos became incarnate "from the Holy Spirit and from her who is, in the precise and true sense, Theotokos, the ever-Virgin Mary." As the God-bearer, she had not given birth only to the man who had been assumed by the Logos or in whom the Logos dwelt. The Nestorian exegesis of John 2:19 made "Jesus the temple that is dissolved, which the God who was in him raised up." Such a theory was not incarnation, but only inhabitation, as "Athanasius" had pointed out. Consistently thought through, it was saying that "Christ will be found to be not God incarnate but a God-bearing man." The theology of the indwelling Logos, which rejected the idea of Theotokos and affirmed the metaphor of Jesus as temple, was equivalent to the assertion that "it was not the Lord himself who became man, but he who visited was the Lord, while he who was visited was a man and not the Lord."

At stake here was nothing less than the salvation of man. In explaining the liturgy, Jacob of Edessa took the response, "We lift them [our hearts] up to the Lord [or:

See vol. 1:270–71
1 Cor.2:8
Sev.Ant.*Ep.Thds.* (*CSCO* 103:17[17:27])

Thdr.AbuQ.*Mim.*8.18 (Graf 210)

Sev.Ant.*Gram.*2.14 (*CSCO* 112:97[111:124–25])

Philox.*Diss.*2.22 (*PO*.15:506)
Sev.Ant.*Neph.*2 (*CSCO* 120: 13[119:16])

Jac.Ed.*Conf.* (Kayser 1:63[2:31])

See vol. 1:242
Tim.Ael.*Chalc.*6 (*PO* 13: 224–25)

Thds.Al.*Ep.Paul.Ant.* (*CSCO* 103:84[17:121])

Philox.*Diss.*1.35 (*PO* 15:463)

Ps.Ath.*Chr.un.*2 (*PG* 28: 123); Thds.Al.*Or.* (*CSCO* 103:51[17:73])

Sev.Ant.*Neph.*2 (*CSCO* 120:16[119:21])

See pp. 40–41 above

Sev.Ant.*Gram.*3.5 (*CSCO* 94:47[93:67–68])

Jac.Ed.ap.Dion.BarSal. *Exp. lit.*10 (*CSCO* 14:67[13:50])

It is for us with the Lord]" as a reference to "the incarnation of the Son, through which he has redeemed us," to "the mercy of the Father upon us," and to "the enrollment of the Holy Spirit, by which, in baptism, he has enrolled us in the adoption of sons." All of this was lost if the incarnation did not mean one incarnate nature of God the Logos; "for if by division we say that it pertains to the human nature to say such things, then the terms 'economy' and 'humiliation' and 'condescension' amount to absolutely nothing." The patristic theme of Christ as the

Sev.Ant.*Gram*.3.6 (*CSCO* 94:72[93:103])

See vol. 1:149–51

divine conqueror over death and Satan was prominent in Monophysite teaching, for it harmonized well with the idea that the person of the incarnate Logos was a com-

Thds.Al.*Ep.* (*CSCO* 103:3[17:8])

posite, brought about when the one nature of God the Logos became incarnate. The formula of Leo, that "one

Sev.Ant.*Gram*.3.7 (*CSCO* 94:94–95[93:136])

[nature] shines in the miracles, but the other succumbs to

LeoM.*Tom*.4 (*ACO* 2–II–1:28)

the injuries," jeopardized the economy of the incarnation and removed the humanity of Christ (and hence all other humanity) "from victory over sufferings and from their

Sev.Ant.*Gram*.2.37 (*CSCO* 112:226–27[111:291])

complete destruction." The idea of the indwelling Logos removed the qualitative distinction between the incarnation of Emmanuel and that bond with God by which, according to the New Testament, "all of us human beings

2 Pet.1:4
Sev.Ant.*Gram*.2.26 (*CSCO* 112:166[111:212])

have become participants in the divine nature." The Eucharist, whose importance had been fundamental to

See vol. 1:236–38

the development of the theology of the hypostatic union, conveyed this salvation because it was truly the body and blood of Christ, as Jacob of Edessa seems to have taken

Jac.Ed.*Ep.Thos.*ap.Dion. BarSal.*Exp.lit*.3 (*CSCO* 14:38[13:9])

for granted; and it was recognized that there was a connection between Nestorian christology and a view of the Eucharist that stressed its memorial aspect rather than

Philox.*Diss*.1.35 (*PO* 15:465)

the real presence.

Summarizing the controversy between his party and the other two, Severus declared: "The term 'union' is affirmed both by our opponents and by us. It is also acknowledged that a conjunction of two natures has taken place. But that which was accomplished by the union . . . is the basis of the opposition between the doc-

Sev.Ant.*Gram*.2.13 (*CSCO* 112:93[111:119–20])

trines." This was a fair statement of the issues between Nestorian, Jacobite, and Chalcedonian christologies. What it overlooked was the process, beginning already in Severus's time and continuing especially in the period we are discussing in this chapter, by which all three doctrines were achieving definitive formulation.

Actions and Wills in Unison

While the defenders of Chalcedonian orthodoxy were active in combating those who seemed to make too little of the union between the divine and human as well as those who seemed to make too much of it, they were themselves engaged in a conflict over the meaning of christological orthodoxy, which, by the end of the seventh century, produced a further development and reformulation of dogma. "The war over two natures is not yet over," lamented Pope Honorius, "and already we are starting more trouble for ourselves." The relation of the new conflicts to both groups of non-Chalcedonians was itself an issue in the debates, as was the interpretation of the preceding development. Unlike the "Nestorian" and "Monophysite" teachings, the new ideas and formulas that provoked controversy were propagated chiefly within the ranks of the orthodox and within the boundaries of the empire. They could, and did, claim to be carrying out the implications of the reinterpretation of Chalcedon that had been going on ever since the fifth century. The overwhelming tendency of this reinterpretation had been in the direction of finding ways to stress the unity rather than the duality of Christ, yet always, as Chalcedon had insisted, with "the difference of the natures being by no means taken away because of the union, but rather the distinctive character of each nature being preserved."

This stress on the unity of Christ was an expression of the universal Christian consensus that salvation was achieved through the union of divine and human, first through their union in Jesus Christ and then through their union in believers. Nestorians spoke of "the union of the infinite with the finite, of the perfect with the imperfect" and urged that the name "Christ" be applied to the person of the union; Jacobites acknowledged that "the term 'union' is affirmed both by our opponents and by us," and that all Christians were agreed on the doctrine that "a conjunction of two natures has taken place"; the neo-Chalcedonianism of the sixth century asserted "one Christ synthesized from both natures . . . one Lord in each nature." Neither the duality of hypostases in Nestorian doctrine nor the duality of natures in Chalcedonian doctrine could be carried to the point of negating the union; in fact, the very point of the duality was to safeguard the

Hon.I.*Ep*.5 (*PL* 80:476)

Mich.Anch.*Arm.* (*PG* 133:229)

See vol. 1:264

See vol. 1:276

reality of the union by preserving the integrity of its constituent elements. The Chalcedonians maintained that their teaching affirmed a genuine hypostatic union even though it spoke of "two natures after the union." They probed the various meanings of the word "union" in order to clarify the doctrine of union in Christ. And in response to the question, "In which hypostasis do you worship the Son of God?" they would answer: "We worship the one person."

Union between the divine and the human was also the leitmotiv of the doctrine of salvation. Thus Maximus, while still oblivious of the controversy over the divine and the human will in Christ, was able to say: "As we all have one nature, so we are able to have with God and with one another but one mind and one will, being in no way at odds either with God or with one another." It has been observed that this passage, which showed "how apt for confusion such terminology was," also bespoke "a spirituality which places the summit of holiness in the unity of wills [and which] . . . was in large measure common property not only among the Byzantines but also among the Monophysites." The very notion of salvation as deification was the foundation of this spirituality. For the sake of precision, it was necessary to reject the idea that there was "one will shared in every respect . . . by God and those who are saved," especially if this idea was taken to be somehow paradigmatic for the notion of one will shared in every respect by the Logos and the humanity of Christ. Yet the impulse toward union between divine and human, whether in the believer or in Christ, was overwhelming. If the confession adopted at Chalcedon precluded speaking of the result of that union as "one nature," some other formula had to be found to express the union and, amid the political crises of the first half of the seventh century, to conciliate the proponents of "one nature."

Such a formula was found in the concept of "one action" and subsequently in the concept of "one will." The two concepts came in that order chronologically, although discussions of the two sometimes reversed the order, perhaps because "action" seemed to be logically derivative from "will." "Action [ἐνέργεια]" was a technical term used by Aristotle to refer to "operation" (as it was translated into Latin), as well as to actuality as distinguished

Max.*Ep*.12 (*PG* 91:484)

Max.*Opusc*.18 (*PG* 91:213–16)

Ps.Joh.D.*Trin*.5 (*PG* 95:17)

Max.*Ep*.2 (*PG* 91:396)

Sherwood (1952) 3

Max.*Opusc*.1 (*PG* 91:25)

Max.*Opusc*.1 (*PG* 91:29–32)

Max.*Pyrr*. (*PG* 91:333); CLater(649) *Can*.10–11 (Mansi 10:1153–56); Mart.I. *Ep*.1 (*PL* 87:125)

Pyrr.ap.Max.*Pyrr.* (*PG* 91:341)

Max.*Ep.*19 (*PG* 91:596)

Joh.D.*F.o.*59 (Kotter 2:144)

Const.Pogon.*Edict.* (Mansi 11:705)

Sev.Ant.*Gram.*2.37 (*CSCO* 112:224–25[111:288]); Sev. Ant.*Neph.*2 (*CSCO* 120:61 [119:83])

Steph.Dor.*Ep.* (Mansi 10:893)

Tim.I.*Ep.*36 (*CSCO* 75:177[74:256])

Hon.I.*Ep.*4 (*PL* 80:474)

Max.*Pyrr.* (*PG* 91:336)

Max.*Opusc.*8 (*PG* 91:109); Serg.*Ep.*3 (Mansi 11:533)

Gr.Naz.*Or.*30.3 (*PG* 36:108); Cyr.H.*Catech.*10.3 (Reischl-Rupp 1:262)

Max.*Opusc.*1 (*PG* 91:33); Max.*Ambig.*7 (*PG* 91:1076)

from potentiality. Sometimes it was closely related to "function [ἀποτέλεσμα]." In the course of the controversy over "one action" in Christ, it became necessary to specify the meaning of the term more precisely and to distinguish between "action [ἐνέργεια]," "activity [ἐνεργητικόν]," which was defined as "the nature from which action proceeds," "act [ἐνέργημα]" defined as "the outcome of action," and "the agent [ἐνεργῶν]," defined as "the one who uses the action, the hypostasis." The confusing relation between these abstractions and christological dogma is suggested by the last of these terms, which would seem to imply that action properly belonged to the hypostasis and that therefore the one hypostasis Jesus Christ had one action; in fact, however, the purpose of the distinction was to argue for two actions in Christ.

Ironically, Monenergism, the notion of one action in Christ, was able to claim the support of both christological extremes, the Nestorian and the Monophysite: the former taught that the two hypostases in Christ concurred in a single action, while the latter taught that there was "a single, individual action of one hypostasis," namely, the divine, because of the union. Repeatedly the opponents of this notion urged that it was a concession to, or rather a relapse into, the theory of one nature as taught by Apollinaris and Severus. But it was no less the adoption of a device by which the descendants of Nestorius attempted to salvage a genuine union between the divine and the human: there was one action shared by Father, Son, and Holy Spirit, hence one action shared by both hypostases in Christ. And so when the advocates of "a single action" charged that the idea of two actions would lead to Nestorianism, one could reply that, on the contrary, Nestorius "teaches the doctrine of one action." From this sort of argumentation one might get the impression that it had been only heretics who had proposed such a doctrine.

Such an impression would, however, be mistaken. For one thing, both sides had to acknowledge that the question whether action belonged to the hypostasis and was therefore single or whether it belonged to the natures and was therefore double had not occurred to the church fathers, who had actually spoken very little about the matter of action at all. Gregory of Nazianzus, for example, as well as Cyril of Jerusalem, had spoken of the "action" of the incarnate Christ in the singular, making it necessary to explain this usage. The two most notorious instances of the term "action" in patristic language about Christ were, however, a passage from the celebrated *Tome* of Pope Leo I and a passage from Dionysius the Areopagite. In a formula that was quoted often during this controversy, Leo had said that "each form [that is, nature in the incarnate Logos] does the acts that belong to it, in communion with the other," the word "form" being in the nominative as the subject of the verb. Without any change in the spelling of the Latin and with at most a very slight change in the spelling of the Greek, Leo's formula could be read to say that the incarnate Logos "does, by means of each form, the acts that belong to it, in communion with the other," with the word "form" now in the ablative or instrumental dative. This was the interpretation of Leo set forth by Sergius, patriarch of Constantinople, an advocate of "one action." Yet if our transmitted texts are reliable, he elsewhere quoted the same passage correctly, ascribing the acting to each of the natures rather than to the single hypostasis of the Logos; and on the other hand, his opponent, Pope Martin I, seems to have quoted it with "form" as the instrument. Whatever may be the state of these texts, it does seem clear that the official formulations coming out of the controversy—the decree of the sixth ecumenical council, the official letter of the pope, and the edict of the emperor— all were careful to use the nominative and to make each nature, rather than the hypostasis of the Logos, the subject of the verb "to act."

Even more significant in the controversy was the statement of Pseudo-Dionysius that Christ had "not done divine things as God and human things as man," but that there had been "a certain new divine-human action of God made man [ἀνδρωθέντος θεοῦ καινήν τινα τὴν θεανδρικὴν ἐνέργειαν]." Even as it stood, this statement was embarrassing to those who said that there were two actions, the divine and the human, for here a writer who had, according to Acts 17:34, been a pupil of the apostle Paul used the word "action" in the singular. But somewhere in the course of its transmission, perhaps as a result of a textual variant, the statement had become "a single divine-human action [μίαν θεανδρικὴν ἐνέργειαν]." So it was that Cyrus of Alexandria read it, declaring that "one and the same Christ does the acts that befit God and the human acts by a single divine-human action, according to Dionysius, one of the saints." Cyrus and his colleagues were accused

Margin references (left column):

Max.*Opusc*.8 (*PG* 91:96)

Leo.M.*Tom*.4 (*ACO* 2–II–1:28)

Serg.*Ep*.3 (Mansi 11:537); *Ep*.1 (Mansi 10:973)

Serg.*Ep*.2 (Mansi 11:525)

Mart.I.ap.CLater.(649)*Act*.2 (Mansi 10:951–52)

Symb.CP(681) (Mansi 11:637); Agath.*Ep*.3 (*PL* 87:1221–22); Const.Pogon.*Edict*. (Mansi 11:708)

Dion.Ar.*Ep*.4 (*PG* 3:1072)

Max.*Ambig*.5 (*PG* 91:1056–60); Max.*Pyrr*. (*PG* 91:345–48); Max.*Opusc*.7 (*PG* 91:84–85); Max.*Schol.Ep.Dion.Ar*.4 (*PG* 4:533); Soph.*Ep.syn*. (*PG* 87:3177)

CCP(681)*Act*.13 (Mansi 11:572)

Cyrus.Al.*Cap*.7 (Mansi 11:565)

Mart.I.ap.CLater.(649)Act. 3; 4 (Mansi 10:979; 1015)
CCP(681)Act.11 (Mansi 11: 489); Joh.D.Volunt.44 (PG 95:184)

Mac.Ant.Symb. (Mansi 11: 353); Them.fr.ap.CLater. (649)Act.3 (Mansi 10:981)

Pyrr.ap.Max.Pyrr. (PG 91:340)

Steph.Dor.Ep. (Mansi 10: 893); CLater.(649)Act.3 (Mansi 10:957)

Max.Opusc.10 (PG 91:136)

Thdr.Phar.fr.11 (Mansi 11:572)

Hon.I.Ep.4 (PL 80:471)

Paul.II.CP.Ep.Thdr. (PL 87:96)

Serg.Ep.3 (Mansi 11:536)

Parente (1953) 243–44

Paul.II.CP.Ep.Thdr. (PL 87:95)

Cyrus.Al.fr.6 (Mansi 11:569)

of having adulterated the text to suit their purposes, and the orthodox made a point of insisting that the word was "new" rather than "single." Yet even without "single," the formula was proof that when "we say that one and the same [hypostasis] was the agent," this could claim eminent patristic authority.

The question was not, of course, merely the grammar in Leo's formula or the textual criticism of Dionysius's formula, but the locus of "action" in the incarnate Logos: Was the action "hypostatic," belonging to the one hypostasis, or "natural," belonging to the two natures? For if, as both sides had to acknowledge, "the agent was one," namely, the hypostasis, it seemed to follow necessarily that "the action was single." The case for this interpretation seems to have been made first by Theodore of Pharan. It was he who "ascribed to the person as person that action which is characteristic of a nature." More specifically, he taught that whatever had been done by the incarnate Logos had been done by him as Creator and God, with his humanity serving as the organ of his divinity, and that "therefore all the things that are said of him either as God or in a human way are the action of the divinity of the Logos." As the Mediator between God and man, Christ had been the subject who "carried out human actions in an ineffable way by means of the flesh that he had assumed." Thus the incarnate Logos was the agent and subject of all action, whether this was appropriate to his divine or to his human nature. The humanity of Christ was the "organ," or, in a more technical term, "that which is moved by God [θεοκίνητος]," as in the formula of Sergius: "In the Lord Christ, his entire humanity was eternally united to the divinity of the Logos and in all things was directed and moved by God." This meant that "the soul of Christ never acted in its movements by its own decision, but was dependent in everything on the Logos who moved it."

As the advocates of a single nature had been quite willing to affirm that there were two natures before the union, but not since the moment of the union, so the proponents of a single action made it clear that they were speaking of the incarnate Logos. It was "all the things that pertain to the saving economy" that were to be predicated of the one Christ. Because he had, "by a divine and wise economy," taken upon himself such human needs as sleep, work, hunger, and thirst, it was necessary to attribute these very things to "the single action of one and the same Christ." To the question whether this single action was divine or human or neither, the reply was that it did not pertain to either of the two natures, but to "the mode of the union." It was no longer permissible "to speak of two actions after the union," but only of a "single dominant action," which directed everything that the incarnate Logos said or did or experienced in mind or body. The alternative position, which ascribed a distinct action to each of the two natures, would be obliged to go on to posit a distinct action for the body of Christ's humanity and another for his soul, which, by a reductio ad absurdum, would lead to three actions in the incarnate Christ. For, it was asked, "what do we attribute to the whole [Christ] if we do not give to the whole the single action through the union?"

The difficulty was that there could easily be a reductio ad absurdum on either side of the question of "action." It became increasingly clear that neither could find very much documentation in biblical or patristic sources for its views. The very term "action" was ambiguous, referring either to the process or to the result; if it meant the latter, everyone had to agree that it was single, but the process or "motion" was in controversy. One way out of the ambiguity was to rule the whole question out of court. No one was to be permitted "any longer to speak either of one action or of two in Christ our God. But rather, as the holy and ecumenical councils have handed down by tradition, [we say] that one and the same only-begotten Son, our Lord Jesus Christ, the true God, was acting." Some fathers had spoken of one action, but this was disturbing to many; the notion of two actions also offended people, although it had not been used by any of the fathers. Therefore both formulas were to be outlawed. Such was the compromise proposal of the *Ecthesis* written by the patriarch Sergius of Constantinople and promulgated by the emperor Heraclius in 638. The proposal was endorsed by Pope Honorius I, who urged that "avoiding . . . the offense of recent innovations, we must not speak either of one or of two actions in our definitions; but instead of the 'one action' of which some speak, we must confess one agent, Christ the Lord, in both natures." It was useless to quarrel about the matter, which belonged more to the grammar school than to the study

Thdr.Phar.*fr*.2 (Mansi 11:568)

Pyrr.ap.Max.*Pyrr*. (*PG* 91:340)

Cyrus.Al.*Ep*.2 (Mansi 11:561)

Pyrr.ap.Max.*Pyrr*. (*PG* 91:336)

ap.Max.*Opusc*.9 (*PG* 91:117)

Max.*Opusc*.20 (*PG* 91:232–33)

Serg.*Ep*.3 (Mansi 11:533)

Heracl.*Ecth*. (Mansi 10: 996; 993)

Hon.I.*Ep*.4 (*PL* 80:475)

Hon.I.*Ep*.4 (*PL* 80:473)

Heracl.*Ecth*. (Mansi 10:996)

Grumel (1930) 18

Hon.I.*Ep*.4 (*PL* 80: 473)

Elert (1957) 243

Paul.II.CP.*Ep.Thdr*. (*PL* 87:98)

Hon.I.*Ep*.4 (*PL* 80:473)

Max.*Opusc*.3 (*PG* 91:48)

Max.*Opusc*.6 (*PG* 91:68)

Joh.D.*Volunt*.41 (*PG* 95: 180); Max.*Opusc*.7 (*PG* 91:81)

CLater.(649)*Act*.2 (Mansi 10:905)

Max.*Pyrr*. (*PG* 91:300); Max.*Opusc*.15 (*PG* 91:169)

of Christian theology. Instead of teaching either one action or two, therefore, "we, following the holy fathers in all things and also in this, confess one will of our Lord Jesus Christ, true God." Thus the discussion was moved from "a single action" to "the source of the action, which is the will." From the term "one will [μόνον θέλημα]" this position came to be called Monotheletism.

"One will" was plainly of another order of magnitude than "one action." For one thing, while the latter could claim "neither the Gospels nor the writings of the apostles nor the decision of a council" for its authority, the will of Christ was near the center of the New Testament message, at the heart of the passion narratives. The passages that "finally proved to be fateful for the entire Monotheletist christology" were Luke 22:42, "Not my will, but thine, be done," and John 6:38, "I have come down from heaven, not to do my own will, but the will of him who sent me." Both sides in the controversy were obliged to deal with these passages. Being a defender of the idea of one will, Pope Honorius interpreted them as referring "not to diverse wills, but to the economy of [Christ's] assumed humanity" and therefore as "spoken for our sake." But Maximus, contending for two wills, saw them as proof that "the Savior, as man, had a will belonging to his human nature," which was characterized by a "sublime conformity to his divine will and to that of his Father." Apparently on the basis of Maximus, John of Damascus explained "not my will" as referring to the human will of the incarnate Logos and "but thine" as referring to his divine will, which was in complete union with the Father. The prominence of these and similar passages in the Gospels meant, moreover, that there were bound to be many references to the will or wills of Christ in earlier Christian writers.

And so indeed there were, not least among those who had been condemned as heretics. It was to be expected that the idea of a single will would be present among those who taught a single nature and that the proponents of the idea would be accused of agreeing with them. Earlier councils had condemned Arius and Apollinaris for teaching one will, and now the teaching was being revived. In fact, false doctrine had even deteriorated; for "if those who confess a single composite nature in Christ and deny two natures still acknowledge the difference between the natures, how is it that you, who confess and

Joh.D.*Volunt*.28 (*PG* 95:164)

Max.*Opusc*.2 (*PG* 91:45)

ap.CLater.(649)*Act*.4 (Mansi 10:1063–64)

CLater.(649)*Act*.5 (Mansi 10:1120)

Tim.I.*Ep*.34 (*CSCO* 75: 127[74:186])

Tim.I.*Ep*.36 (*CSCO* 75: 179[74:258])

Bab.*Un*.3.9 (*CSCO* 80: 74–75[79:106])

Luke 22:42

Bab.*Un*.7; 3.9 (*CSCO* 80: 225; 65[79:278; 81])

CCP(681)*Act*.8 (Mansi 11:365)

Paul.II.CP.*Ep*.*Thdr*. (*PL* 87:98)

Cyr.*Ep*.46 (*ACO* 1–I–6:158); Max.*Opusc*.7 (*PG* 91:81)

Gr.Naz.*Or*.30.12 (*PG* 36:117)

Pyrr.ap.Max.*Pyrr*. (*PG* 91:316)

affirm two natures in Christ, devise a single will in him?" What was striking in the heretical discussions of a single will in Christ was the prominence of the idea of "identity of will [ταὐτοβουλία]" among the Nestorians, who taught not only two natures but two hypostases after the incarnation. The advocates of a single will sought to disengage their position from that of the Nestorians, and quotations from the Nestorians appeared in the collections read and condemned at the Lateran Council in 649. Timothy I, the Nestorian patriarch, taught that the hypostasis of the man assumed by the Logos had "a single will and action with the Logos who had clothed Himself in him." There could not be "one will and another will," for "everything was brought together into an ineffable union." It seems, however, that the christology of Babai was a turning point also in this respect, for he definitely spoke of one will in the Logos and another in the man assumed by Him. "Not my will, but thine, be done" meant that while "there is a single will of the Trinity, . . . one will of [the Logos] with the Father and the Holy Spirit," the humanity assumed by the Logos had to have a free will distinct from that shared between the Logos and the other hypostases of the Trinity. It would seem plausible to suggest that the original Nestorian doctrine of two hypostases with a single will was revised in the direction of greater consistency as a consequence of the debates among the Chalcedonians over this issue.

Because both sides in the controversy over wills in Christ wanted to be identified, not with either Monophysite or Nestorian heresy, but with the tradition of the fathers, it was the previous history of the question in this tradition that was of primary concern to them. The defenders of the doctrine of two wills accused their opponents of quoting the fathers out of context, but the accusation would have been appropriate in either direction. For their part, the protagonists of a single will claimed the support of "all the teachers and heralds of godliness." It had to be acknowledged that some of the fathers had indeed spoken of one single will. Thus Maximus admitted that Cyril had spoken of "one will," corresponding to the "one ousia." The opponent of Maximus, Pyrrhus, also quoted the words of Gregory of Nazianzus that the will of the incarnate Logos "was in no way contrary to that of God, but had been completely deified." Although the comments attributed to Athanasius on the words, "Not

Luke 22:42
Sev.Ant.*Gram*.3.33 (*CSCO*
102:132[101:182])

Ath.*Ar*.3.57 (*PG* 26:441);
Max.*Opusc*.15 (*PG* 91:160)

Max.*Opusc*.2;7 (*PG* 91:
45; 81)

See vol. 1:260–61

Mac.Ant.*Symb*. (Mansi
11:356)

Luke 22:42

ap.Joh.D.*Volunt*.28 (*PG*
95:164)

Pyrr.ap.Max.*Pyrr*. (*PG*
91:293)

Thdr.Phar.*fr*.6 (Mansi
11:569)

Hon.I.*Ep*.4 (*PL* 80:472)

Mac.Ant.ap.CCP(681)*Act*.8
(Mansi 11:365)

Pyrr.ap.Max.*Pyrr*. (*PG*
91:289)

Pyrr.ap.Max.*Pyrr*.
(*PG* 91:292)

Mac.Ant.ap.CCP(681)*Act*.8
(Mansi 11:360)

my will, but thine, be done," had already been cited by Monophysites and now seemed to support the Monothelete position, Maximus laid claim to "the one who has his name from immortality [ἀθανασία]" as an authority for one will in the divine nature and another in the human. He collected additional sayings of Athanasius and Gregory of Nazianzus, as well as of other fathers, to justify his doctrine.

Monotheletism took its start from the position already affirmed at Ephesus in 431, that one should attribute "all the statements in the Gospels to the single person, the one incarnate hypostasis of the Logos." Such a statement as "Not my will, but thine, be done" must therefore also apply to the single hypostasis, and so "the will does not pertain to the nature, but to the hypostasis." That which pertained to a nature was in every respect determined and necessary, not free, since it could not be anything other than what it was; but if the incarnation and other acts were acts of free will, they had to be acts of the hypostasis, not of the human nature. Consequently, "the divine will is the very will of Christ himself, and his will is single, namely, the divine." To confess a single will meant to assert that "our nature was assumed by the divinity . . . , that nature which was created before sin" and which therefore had no will except the will of God. When pressed, Monotheletes thus had to admit that "we do not say that there was a human will in Christ . . . for his will belonged only to his divinity." If Christ was truly one, he must also have willed as one and must therefore have possessed only one will. But if his human nature also had a will of its own because willing belonged to the nature rather than to the hypostasis, it would follow from the statements of "the illustrious fathers, that there is one will both of God and of the saints," that God and the saints would also have a single nature, which was blasphemy. Will, therefore, had to be a function of the single hypostasis of the incarnate Logos and had to be single itself. "I will never," declared Macarius of Antioch at the Third Council of Constantinople in 681, "say two natural wills nor two natural actions in the incarnate economy of our Lord Jesus Christ, even if I were to be torn limb from limb and cast into the sea."

At that council, together with the synod held at the Lateran in Rome in 649 (even though the synod was "completely ignored and not referred to in a single word

Caspar (1932) 135

CCP(681)*Act*.18 (Mansi 11:656)

Harnack (1931) 2:433

Steph.Dor.*Ep*. (Mansi 10:896)

CCP(681)*Act*.1 (Mansi 11:216)

CLater.(649)*Act*.5 (Mansi 10:1071–1108)

CLater.(649)*Act*.3 (Mansi 10:958)

CCP(681)*Act*.10 (Mansi 11:392)

CCP(681)*Act*.10 (Mansi 11:421)

CCP(681)*Act*.12 (Mansi 11:528)

Symb.CP(681) (Mansi 11:636)

CLater.(649)*Act*.5 (Mansi 10:1149–50)

of the *Acts*" of the council), the issues raised by Monenergism and Monotheletism were reviewed and "the faith of the apostles, the faith of the fathers, the faith of the orthodox" was promulgated. To prove their claims to this ancestry for their dogmatic decrees, the Lateran synod and the ecumenical council pored over ancient tomes and patristic manuscripts from various libraries, becoming in effect erudite congresses "of antiquarians and paleographers." Sophronius of Jerusalem, one of the early opponents of Monotheletism, had compiled two books containing six hundred quotations from the fathers in opposition to the idea of a single action or a single will in Christ. At Constantinople the emperor asked that the acts "of the holy and ecumenical councils . . . be brought in by the archivist and be read aloud," and so they were. At the Lateran synod, a collection of quotations from the fathers had been read to the fifth session, and many other passages were also brought to the attention of the bishops, with Theophylact, the papal secretary, producing a manuscript, whether of an orthodox or of a heretical author, and asserting: "In accordance with the command of Your Beatitude, I have the codex in my hands. What is your order?" These patristic authorities, collated at Rome, were forwarded, in a sealed volume, to the council at Constantinople, where their readings were checked against manuscripts available in the library of the patriarchate, for example, a volume of Athanasius covered in silver. Those quotations that were obviously forgeries were ruled out of consideration.

As the controversy had shown, however, the mutual exchange of patristic quotations would not settle anything either way without greater precision in the use of the controverted terms, especially "will." Yet it was necessary to affirm and to demonstrate continuity with the orthodox doctrine of the fathers and the councils. The solution for this dilemma was to declare that the creed of Nicea and Constantinople, "this devout and orthodox symbol of divine grace, was sufficient for the knowledge and confirmation of the orthodox faith," but that new heresies had arisen, requiring that the same orthodox faith be stated in opposition to these challenges. First the Lateran synod and then the Council of Constantinople, therefore, embedded their formulations on two actions and two wills into a recitation of the Chalcedonian creed, declaring that the two natures confessed there required also "two natural wills and two natural actions, without division, without change, without separation, without confusion [ἀδιαιρέτως, ἀτρέπτως, ἀμερίστως, ἀσυγχύτως]." The christology of Leo I, canonized at Chalcedon, required that each nature have its own will and its own action. In opposition to the effort of Monotheletes to be identified with Chalcedon, it was declared that "whoever refuses to believe this way [that is, as the Lateran synod was teaching], despises the holy Council of Chalcedon." This clarification and expansion of Chalcedon in the direction of teaching two wills and two actions was made necessary on the grounds both of theology and of economy.

Like the Nestorian and the Monophysite christologies, this reformulation of the orthodox doctrine about Christ took its start from the doctrine of the Trinity, clarifying its christological terminology on the basis of trinitarian usage. In the Trinity there were three hypostases, but only one divine nature; otherwise there would be three gods. There was also a single will and a single action. Thus will was an attribute of a nature and not of a hypostasis, natural and not hypostatic. Hence, the person of Christ, with a single hypostasis and two natures, had to have two wills, one for each nature. "Nature" was the general or universal, that which was shared by more than one, as for example "humanity," which could also be called "human nature," while "hypostasis" was particular. Some qualities pertained to the nature or the ousia of a being (for example, that man was rational), while others pertained to a particular hypostasis (for example, that a specific man had an aquiline nose); in a real if imprecise sense, this could be applied also to the ousia and the hypostases in the Trinity. Clearly this argumentation was attempting to prove that a contrary position on the two actions and wills in Christ, by confusing what pertained to nature and what pertained to hypostasis, would lead to a similar and a heretical confusion in trinitarian doctrine.

The specific error lay, however, in christological doctrine, in the area of economy. Because of the economy, the incarnate Logos was to be seen as a composite hypostasis, but not as having a composite nature. If he was a complete human being, how could he be devoid of anything that belonged to a human nature, such as human activity or a human will? If he was less than complete

Symb.CP(681) (Mansi 11:637)

Mart.I.ap.CLater. (649)
Act.1 (Mansi 10:875)

Max.Aquil.ap.CLater.(649)
Act.1(Mansi 10:886)

Joh.D.Volunt.24 (PG 95:156)
Const.Pogon.Edict. (Mansi 11:701)

Max.Pyrr. (PG 91:289)

Joh.D.Volunt.4 (PG 95:133)

Max.Opusc.21 (PG 91: 248–49)

Max.Ep.13 (PG 91:517)

Mart.I.Ep.1 (PL 87:125);
Max.Opusc.16 (PG 91:189)

Steph.Dor.*Ep.* (Mansi
10:897)

in either activity or will, whether in his human nature or
in his divine nature, he was not perfect God and man.
As the official documents, both imperial and ecclesiastical,
issuing from the Third Council of Constantinople declared, his perfect humanity had to include a human mind,
the faculty by which "we do our willing and reasoning,"
for the mind was nothing without this capacity; therefore
he must have had a human will. Otherwise the flesh of

Const.Pogon.*Edict.* (Mansi
11:704); *Symb.CP*(681)
(Mansi 11:636)

the incarnate one, his humanity, would have been "will-
less [ἀθέλητον]" and "action-less [ἀνενέργητον]." But both
of these declarations went on to say that the human will

Const.Pogon.*Edict.* (Mansi
11:705); *Symb.CP*(681)
(Mansi 11:637)

of Christ was not only complete as a human will but had
also been completely "deified." This referred partly to the
general rule that all human acting and willing had its
source and derived its power from the Creator; it was also
a special quality of the human nature of Christ as not
merely one man among others but "universal man."

Trinitarian and christological consistency required,
then, that "as we have recognized two natures, so we also
acknowledge two natural wills and two natural actions.
We dare not declare either of the natures in Christ after

CCP(681) *Or.imp.* (Mansi
11:664)

his economy to be without will or action." This was the
answer of the council to the question of the "divine-human
action of God made man" raised by the mooted passage in
Pseudo-Dionysius. A "natural action" was essential to a
human nature, also to the human nature of Christ. Were

Max.*Opusc.*16 (*PG* 91:200)

the Monenergists willing to say that "both the miracles
and the sufferings were carried out by a single action"?

Max.*Pyrr.* (*PG* 91:344)

Because of the union of the divine and the human natures,
"we confess every natural action, so as not to confuse the
natures that have been united without confusion," but
they all "proceed from one and the same Christ and Son."

Soph.*Ep.syn.* (*PG* 87:3172)

Here again it had to be pointed out that there was a single
action in the Trinity, since action belonged to the divine
nature, which was single, rather than to each of the three
hypostases. Wherever there was a nature, divine or human,

Max.*Schol.E.h.*4.10
(*PG* 4:157)
Max.*Pyrr.* (*PG* 91:349)

there also had to be an action appropriate to it. Yet as the
doctrine of two natures had to be interpreted according
to the communication of properties, so the doctrine of two
actions, which appeared to be a necessary corollary of the
doctrine of two natures, also had to be seen in this perspective. With the declaration of two actions, one had to
go on to say that Christ "carried out divine actions in a

Mart.I.ap.CLater.(649)*Act.*1
(Mansi 10:878)

bodily way . . . [and] human actions in a divine way."

Symb.CP(681) (Mansi
11:637)

Agath.Ep.1 (PL 87:1167–68)

Max.Opusc.4 (PG 91:60)

Joh.D.Volunt.26 (PG
95:157)

Max.Opusc.16 (PG 91:
192; 196)

Meyendorff (1969) 104

Joh.D.Volunt.21 (PG 95:
152); Max.Opusc.16 (PG
91:185–88)

Max.Pyrr. (PG 91:292)

Luke 22:42

Const.Pogon.Edict. (Mansi
11:704)

Meyendorff (1969) 120

Gr.Naz.Ep.101 (PG 37:181)

Joh.D.F.o.50 (Kotter 2:121)

The doctrine of two wills was likewise a corollary of the doctrine of two natures. The council at Constantinople, having recited the orthodox Chalcedonian faith, asserted that there were "two natural wills [ϑελήσεις ἤτοι ϑελήματα]" in Christ, but not "two natural wills that are contrary to each other. God forbid!" Rather, the human will of Christ's human nature was completely subject to the direction of the divine and omnipotent will of his divine nature. If there were two natures, there had to be two wills. Specifically, the only difference between the human nature of Christ and our human nature lay in "the novel mode of his genesis," the virginal conception. In every other way it was a nature like ours, hence one that had a will. When Christ was hungry or thirsty, it was his human will that desired food or drink, which his divine nature did not need. To make the doctrine of two natural wills coherent, certain distinctions were necessary. It was helpful to make a distinction in the human nature of Christ between the natural will [τὸ φυσικὸν ϑέλημα], which was ontologically distinct from the divine will, and the deliberative will [τὸ γνωμικὸν ϑέλημα], which was functionally identical with the divine will. In addition to this distinction, which "constitutes one of the most important contributions of [Maximus] the Confessor to the elaboration of the Christian tradition" (although he himself gave credit for it to an unnamed monk), there was a related distinction between the will as a natural psychological faculty and the will as "that which is willed, that which is subject to the will" as faculty. These distinctions enabled the theologian to posit two natural wills without even having to entertain the unthinkable possibility that there would be a conflict between them in their objects. The question of a conflict was in any case "not a matter of number," whether one or two, but of "opposition." The prayer of Christ in Gethsemane meant: "Not my human will [be done], but thy will, that which is common to me the Logos and to thee [the Father]."

The integrity of both natures in this formulation was not, however, dictated by an aesthetic or intellectual symmetry; it was, in fact, "a dissymmetric Christology conceived as soteriological necessity." From Gregory of Nazianzus had come the axiom: "Whatever has not been assumed [by the Logos in the incarnation] has not been healed [τὸ γὰρ ἀπρόσληπτον ἀϑεράπευτον]." Quoting this axiom, Maximus argued that since the will and the action

Max.*Opusc*.15 (*PG* 91:156)

of men both had to be healed, they must also have been assumed in the incarnation. John of Damascus elaborated on this argument, saying that "if he did not assume a human will, that in us which suffered first has not been healed," for it was, after all, specifically the human will

Joh.D.*Volunt*.28 (*PG* 95:161)

that had been guilty of sin. If Christ had not been capable of being sad, he would not have liberated human nature from sadness; so it would have been also if he had not

Mart.I.ap.CLater.(649)*Act*.5 (Mansi 10:1145–46)

possessed a distinct human will. There were fundamental soteriological considerations at work in compelling the idea of two natural actions and two natural wills in one single agent who was committed to one single purpose. Nevertheless, this soteriological consistency seemed to have been achieved by means of a christological abstraction far removed from the figure described in the Gospels, so that "practically the whole of Byzantine religion could have been built without the historical Christ of the Gos-

Fedotov (1966) 1:35

pels." The effort to show that this was not so, and that the "dogma of Christ" had in fact been true to the "picture of

Elert (1957) 12–15

Christ," was the work of the generation that systematized the results of this development.

Christ the Universal Man

The christological abstractions of the several theories that we have been expounding were all concerned with the salvation of man through the God-man. The theory eventually affirmed as orthodox claimed to be defending salvation by a view of the God-man in which he, being fully divine and fully human and altogether one, had within

Joh.D.*F.o*.50 (Kotter 2:121–22)

himself both the universal and the particular. For what he assumed into unity with his divinity was not a particular human being but "universal man [τὸν καθ᾿ ὅλου] or the universal [human] nature, yet a nature that is seen in an

Thdr.Stud.*Antirr*.1.4 (*PG* 99:332–33) Max.*Qu.Thal*.60 (*PG* 90:620)

individual." It was this "mystery of Christ," the doctrine of the two natures with all that it presupposed and implied, that orthodoxy had formulated at Ephesus and Chalcedon and that it was now compelled to reformulate and to clarify in response to a series of attacks from within and from beyond its own boundaries. While it was necessary to insist that this reformulation of dogma was no more than a repetition of the changeless truth that had been confessed since the beginning, the outcome of the debates was, in a very real way, a new development of the doctrine of the person of Christ.

Many of the writers upon whom we have drawn as

sources for our study of the Monenergist and Monothelete doctrines, simply because the written statements of those doctrines have not survived, are at the same time important witnesses to the new interpretation of Chalcedon; this is true above all of Maximus Confessor, upon whom much of the preceding chapter was based, and of John of Damascus, whose theology will be prominent in the next chapter. But there is perhaps no document from the seventh and eighth centuries in which this new christological orthodoxy was more appropriately expressed than a treatise entitled *The Doctrine of the Fathers on the Incarnation of the Logos,* ascribed to a certain Anastasius. It is "the most comprehensive and most valuable dogmatic florilegium handed down to us by the ancient church," valuable not only for the quotations it contains from "93 different writers and ecclesiastical documents," some of them now lost except for these passages, but for its review of the controversies and its adjudication of the issues. In addition to clarifying some of the metaphysical points that had been raised in the course of the debates (such as the problem of universals), and reasserting some of the older polemical positions that had been mooted during the debates (such as the condemnation of Origen by the Second Council of Constantinople), *The Doctrine of the Fathers* assembled familiar and unfamiliar quotations under a series of doctrinal headings. The comprehensiveness of these themes and the subsequent influence of the florilegium itself commend this summary of orthodox christology as a basis for our examination.

The superscription of *The Doctrine* announced its content: "Sayings of the holy fathers, or a selection of authorities by which we are clearly instructed in the entire teaching of the apostolic church, namely, the proclamation of theology and the message of the divine economy and the precise formulation of the other correct dogmas of the church." As we have seen, the distinction here assumed between theology and economy was shared by all the parties in the christological controversies. The Nestorian Babai invoked it to explain the difference between such titles as "Logos" and "Christ." Monophysite theologians took it as a starting point in their argument that the result of the economy was a composite single nature through the assumption of the flesh by God the Logos, who had (by theology) been from eternity. Indeed, the distinction

Diekamp (1907) iii

Diekamp (1907) xiv

*Doct.patr.*26
(Diekamp 188–91)

See vol. 1:277
*Doct.patr.*25
(Diekamp 179–88)

*Doct.patr.*superscr.
(Diekamp 1)

Bab.*Un.*6.20 (*CSCO* 80:
161–84[79:199–227])

See p. 55 above

appeared to be built into the structure of the Nicene Creed, which described God the Father in himself and then as Creator, God the Son from eternity and then as incarnate, God the Holy Spirit as proceeding from the Father eternally and then as speaking by the prophets. As one of the sources of *The Doctrine of the Fathers,* Maximus distinguished between those things in Scripture that dealt with the head of Christ and those that dealt with the feet of Christ; the former pertained to theology, to his divinity, and the latter to the economy through his incarnation.

It was important to maintain this distinction because it put the discussion of christology into a trinitarian context. The opening chapter of *The Doctrine* had as its subject "the doctrine of God [ϑεολογία] as One and Three." So self-evident was the dogma of the Trinity that Maximus, quoting a poem of Gregory of Nazianzus, could indulge in the pleasant conceit of calling "the Holy Trinity the first virgin" because it neither gave birth nor was born. In the course of the debates of the seventh century it became clear that it was no mere traditionalism that made the introduction of "theology" necessary at the beginning of an argument that was to deal with "economy." Technically speaking, it was correct to say, as for example the Nestorian Timothy I said, that the Chalcedonians and the non-Chalcedonians shared the orthodox doctrine of the Trinity, but differed on the doctrine of the incarnate union. But as had become clear in the aftermath of the Council of Chalcedon, any profound consideration of the latter doctrine had to lead to a reconsideration of the former. Hence it was no mere polemical rhetoric when Monotheletism was attacked as "a new tritheism," for the christological problem of wills in the incarnate Logos had led to the question of the relation between the will of the Logos and the will of the Father within the Godhead— a trinitarian question.

The purpose of a trinitarian confession at the beginning of a christological confession was to clarify various concepts and terms. In the Trinity there was one nature, but there were three hypostases; in the person of Christ there were two natures, but there was one hypostasis. In both there was union without any confusion, reciprocal being in one another [περιχώρησις] without any change or loss of identity. The principal implication of trinitarian doc-

See vol. 1:201

Max.*Ambig*.56 (*PG* 91:1380)

Doct.patr.1.1 (Diekamp 1) Gr.Naz.*Carm*.2.1.20 (*PG* 37:523)

Max.*Ambig*.66 (*PG* 91:1396)

Tim.I.*Ep*.1 (*CSCO* 75:6 [74:12])

See vol. 1:269–71

Soph.*Ep.syn*. (*PG* 87:3156)

Max.*Pyrr*. (*PG* 91:289)

Joh.D.*F.o*.49 (Kotter 2:118)

See pp. 183–98 below

Aug.*Trin*.2.10.18
(*CCSL* 50:104)

Joh.D.*Volunt*.24 (*PG* 95:156)

Const.Pogon.*Edict*. (Mansi 11:701)

Meyendorff (1969) 110

See vol. 1:270–71

Joh.D.*Rect.sent*.5 (*PG* 94:1429)

Bab.*Un*.7 (*CSCO* 80:226 [79:269–70])

Jac.Ed.*Hex*.1 (*CSCO* 97:23–24[92:30–31])

trine for the issues under debate lay in the questions of action and will. For it was self-evident, as a direct corollary of monotheism, that "there is one single action of the Holy Trinity"; although the internal relations between the hypostases within the Trinity were a matter of argument between the Eastern and the Western churches, Augustine was speaking for both when he said that toward the outside [ad extra] "the Trinity acts without separation" of hypostases. As there was one action in the Trinity, so there was also a single will, "one natural will of the three hypostases, . . . wherefore the three hypostases are not three gods, but one God." Action and will belonged, then, not to the hypostasis of Father, Son, or Holy Spirit, but to the nature that was common to the three; those who had "one nature also have one will and one action." And where, on the other hand, there were two natures, there had to be two wills and two actions, one for each nature. If there were a single will and a single action in Christ, this would require that will and action belong to the hypostasis; applied to the Trinity, this meant that "three divine hypostases would suppose three deities and three energies."

A special problem in the relation between trinitarian and christological doctrine that had arisen repeatedly was the correct liturgical usage and the orthodox theological interpretation of the Trisagion, the angelic doxology first recorded in Isaiah 6:3 and embodied in Eastern liturgies. Controversy over whether it referred to the Trinity or to the hypostasis of Jesus Christ had erupted around the time of Chalcedon, and it continued for centuries. John of Damascus now affirmed: "I confess that the hymn Trisagion means the three hypostases of the Godhead, and the one ousia and lordship." The addition of the clause, "thou who wast crucified for us," would have implicated this one ousia and lordship in the sufferings of the crucifixion. It is understandable that the Nestorians would reject this addition as blasphemous, for it seemed to obscure the distinction between the divine and the human in Christ. The Jacobites saw in the Trisagion a confession of the Trinity, but insisted that the one divine nature of God the Logos had taken the flesh up into itself in such a way that "thou who wast crucified for us" could be spoken without violence to the impassibility of God.

*Doct.patr.*1.28
(Diekamp 10)

The Doctrine of the Fathers declared "that the Trisagion is spoken about the three hypostases." Of course this did not forbid, in principle or in practice, prayers addressed to Christ rather than explicitly to the Trinity as an entirety, although the dogma meant that such prayer was in fact being spoken to Father, Son, and Holy Spirit even when only one was mentioned by name.

Max.*Qu.Thal.*48 (*PG*
90:433)

Two other ambiguous and controversial formulations also needed to be clarified. One was the phrase "from two natures," which, in Jacobite doctrine, was set in sharp contradistinction to "in two natures": the latter would imply a continuing duality also after the union through the incarnation, while the former made it clear that what had taken place through the incarnation was "a composition and a union without confusion." The Doctrine of the Fathers asserted "that the divinely inspired fathers in orthodox fashion proclaimed Christ to be 'from two natures' and 'in two natures.' " As a historical judgment, this was incontestable, for there was ample documentation for the use of "from two natures" by church fathers claimed as orthodox by Chalcedonian theology. Even though in some cases there may have been a conscious preference for "in two natures" as a less equivocal way of stating that, in the language of Chalcedon, "the difference of the natures [was] by no means taken away because of the union, but rather the distinctive character of each nature [was] preserved," the phrase as it stood did not preclude "from two natures," but actually presupposed it, so long as this phrase was not taken to imply "a single composite nature after the union." Hence it became standard among Chalcedonian theologians to accept "from two natures" and "in two natures" as synonymous, with "in" protecting "from" against the implication that duality was abolished by the union.

See p. 57 above

Sev.Ant.*Gram.*2.29 (*CSCO*
112:177[111:226–27])

*Doct.patr.*2.1
(Diekamp 11)

Joh.D.*F.o.*47 (Kotter 2:112)

Max.*Ep.*12 (*PG* 91:500); Max.
*Ep.*13 (*PG* 91:524–25);
Joh.D.*F.o.*47 (Kotter 2:111);
Nicet.Byz.*Arm.*1 (*PG* 105:
589); Mich.Anch.*Arm.* (*PG*
133:228)

A similar rescue was effected for the phrase "a single incarnate nature of God the Logos," which was the very hallmark of Jacobite, Monophysite doctrine. There was no denying that the phrase had been fundamental to the christology of Cyril of Alexandria, to whose paternity the Chalcedonians no less than the Jacobites laid claim. Maximus took the phrase to mean that Cyril and Nestorius had shared "the statement of two natures up to the point of

Max.*Ep*.12 (*PG* 91:477)

Max.*Ep*.12 (*PG* 91:501)

Joh.D.*F.o*.51 (Kotter 2:125)

Ps.Joh.D.*Trin*.5
(*PG* 95:17)

Doct.*patr*.3.1
(Diekamp 25)

Doct.*patr*.4.1
(Diekamp 29)

Doct.*patr*.5.1
(Diekamp 33)

Philox.*Diss*.1.60 (*PO* 15:483)

Max.*Opusc*.24 (*PG* 91:268)

See p. 48 above

See p. 55 above

acknowledging the difference," but not "the confession of the union." He went on to explain the Cyrillian formula to mean that there were two natures before the union and that there remained two after the union, so that the formula was "a periphrasis . . . according to the union," not a denial of duality. The very use of the term "incarnate" made the phrase "a single incarnate nature of God the Logos" acceptable to the defenders of two natures, for it "means that the flesh has an ousia, according to the blessed Cyril." And therefore when the question was, "In which hypostasis do you worship the Son of God?" the Chalcedonian answer could be: "In the hypostasis of God the Logos, one nature incarnate and worshiped. [We render] one worship, since from the coming together of two there is one worshipful person." Both these formulations, therefore, were taken by the doctrine of two natures as its own.

The union of the two natures, which was the principal emphasis of these formulations, had as its direct corollary, according to *The Doctrine of the Fathers,* "that the name 'Christ' refers to both of the natures, and that Christ is God and the Virgin is the Bearer of God [Theotokos], contrary to [the teaching of] the godless Nestorius." The implications of this were spelled out in the next chapter, which collected passages to prove "that Christ is called 'double' by the fathers on account of the duality of the natures, and again is not called 'double' on account of the singularity of his hypostasis or person." The following chapter of the florilegium reaffirmed the Chalcedonian principle that "the natures which have come together into the union have remained unchanged," with their properties and distinctive characteristics preserved. All three of these propositions were addressed to the relation between duality and singularity in the incarnate Christ and sought to show that the Chalcedonian doctrine of "in two natures" after the incarnation did not signify a relapse into Nestorian ways of thinking, as its Jacobite critics maintained.

Patristic usage did support the axiom stated by Maximus that "the name 'Christ' is indicative not of a nature but of a composite hypostasis." This was, for that matter, the Nestorian view of how the title "Christ" was to be used in precise language; the Jacobites, too, saw that the title belonged, strictly speaking, to the economy of the incarnation. The differences between the three positions lay

Gr.Naz.*Or*.2.23 (*PG* 35:432)

Max.*Ep*.12 (*PG* 91:493)

in the question of singularity and duality. From Gregory of Nazianzus it was possible to quote the epigram: "One from both ... and both through the one." "We proclaim," wrote the patriarch Nicephorus in the context of the debate over images, "the duality of the ousias that have come together in him, ... but we likewise affirm a combination that had taken place ontologically from these into the unity of a person by means of the hypostatic

Niceph.*Imag*.21 (*PG* 100:588)

union." Basic to the Chalcedonian position over against its rivals was the simultaneous insistence on the continuing difference between the natures and on the inseparabil-

Max.*Ep*.12 (*PG* 91:469)

ity of the natures. Although the polemical exchange with so-called Monophysites and the new issues that had arisen within the Chalcedonian camp took the bulk of attention, the Nestorian system of teaching—especially, as *The Doc-*

Thdr.AbuQ.*Opusc*.14 (*PG* 97: 1537–40);Joh.D.*F.o*.56 (Kotter 2:135)

trine of the Fathers also showed, the denial of the title Theotokos to the Virgin Mary—still called for refutation. This made it seem all the more incongruous that Monotheletism, a theory intended to strengthen the case for the unity of the person of Christ in opposition to Nestorianism, should have found itself teaching a Nestorian idea, the union of wills between divine and human [ταὐτοβουλία]—even though it maintained that its teach-

Max.Aquil.ap.CLater.(649) *Act*.4 (Mansi 10:1063–64)

ing was altogether different from this idea. It was, of course, no less necessary for the orthodox to maintain that the Chalcedonian doctrine of two natures after the incarnation was different from Nestorianism, and that Nestorianism, by accepting the first and second ecumenical councils but not the third and fourth, was being arbitrary

Thdr.AbuQ.*Mim*.1.26 (Graf 114–15)

and inconsistent.

In opposition to Nestorian and to Jacobite doctrine, it was also important to clarify the meaning of trinitarian terms and to distinguish among them. The sixth chapter of *The Doctrine of the Fathers* consisted of a group of quotations intended to show "that nature and hypostasis are not the same, but that ousia and nature are the same,

Doct.patr.6.1 (Diekamp 35)

likewise that hypostasis and person are the same." All these terms had been employed in the discussions of the doctrine of the person of Christ. Were they used, or should they be used, the same way in both doctrines? In the Trinity, nature or ousia referred to that which was one, hypostasis or person to that which was more than one; in the person of Christ nature or ousia referred to that which was more than one, hypostasis or person to that which was one. A

See vol. 1:219–20

Bab.*Un*.3.9 (*CSCO* 80: 78[79:97])

Sev.Ant.*Gram*.2.22 (*CSCO* 112:146[111:187])

Joh.D.*F.o*.47 (Kotter 2:112); Joh.D.*Jacob*.6–7 (*PG* 94:1439–40)

Max.*Ep*.13 (*PG* 91:528)

Joh.D.*Volunt*.4 (*PG* 95:133)

Joh.D.*F.o*.48 (Kotter 2:116)

Joh.D.*Volunt*.2 (*PG* 95:129)

Joh.D.*F.o*.46 (Kotter 2:110)

Meyendorff (1969) 121

further complication was the history of previous usage even within the orthodox tradition, where ousia and hypostasis had sometimes been equated. Both the Nestorian and the Jacobite traditions had their own distinctive usages: the former distinguished between hypostasis and person, assigning to Christ one person but two hypostases; the latter tied nature to hypostasis, ascribing to Christ not only a composite hypostasis, as did the Chalcedonians, but a composite nature.

"What causes the error of the heretics," according to John of Damascus, "is their saying that nature and hypostasis are the same." Simply defined, a hypostasis was an ousia together with its properties; but Christ, being a composite hypostasis, had to be defined as a composite ousia together with its properties. Another simple definition was to say that hypostasis was the particular, nature the general. But these two definitions had to be qualified in trinitarian usage, where "ousia is one thing and hypostasis another. . . . Ousia signifies the common and collective form of uniform hypostases." When one nature was compared with another nature, the differences were "natural"; when one hypostasis was compared with another hypostasis of the same kind, the differences were in "the properties characteristic of the several hypostases"; but when a hypostasis of one kind was compared with a hypostasis of another kind (a man with an ox, for example), the differences were differences of nature, not of hypostasis. In the person of Christ, consequently, there could not be two hypostases in one person, as the Nestorians taught; for nature and hypostasis were not the same, and he had one composite hypostasis, but two natures. Nor could there be one nature in one hypostasis, as the Jacobites taught; for nature and hypostasis were not the same, and in the incarnation "the Logos of God himself, standing to the flesh in the relation of subsistence . . . has become the hypostasis of the flesh," so that there was still one hypostasis but two natures. Hence "as the source of existence, and not as the product of natural existence, the hypostasis thus represents the key notion of orthodox Chalcedonian soteriology: the incarnate hypostasis of the Word, by becoming for Jesus' human nature the source of a properly human existence, becomes precisely because of this the fount of salvation."

With the determination of how hypostasis was to be

understood in relation to other trinitarian terms, the subject could move from "theology" to the thesis "that Christ is God and man at the same time and that he is one," which included an examination of "the manner of the economy or of the divine incarnation, his suffering and his descent into hell, as the fathers have handed it down by tradition." This examination required a critical scrutiny of such statements as "the deity suffered by means of flesh" or "God suffered through the flesh," the so-called theopaschitic formulas. Out of the conflict over these formulas orthodoxy had learned to speak more carefully about the communication of properties, by which each nature communicated its characteristic attributes to the concrete hypostasis of the incarnate Logos. On the basis of this communication it was permissible to say that "economy" was beautifully expressed in the statement "that one of the Trinity suffered." One could even heighten the paradox of the communication of properties to say that Christ had "suffered divinely . . . but performed the miracles humanly." It was by "the life-giving sufferings of our God and Savior Christ" that men were "redeemed from the power of darkness." But such statements of the paradox had to be understood to mean "that the eternal Son, begotten of the Father before the ages, died for us not in his divine but in his human nature." For the divine was and remained incapable of suffering or death. The concrete, composite hypostasis of the incarnate Logos had suffered and died, or he who was God had suffered and died; but the deity had not suffered and died. The notion of a Theotokos was not a violation of this principle; it could even be extended, so that David could be called "the ancestor of God [ὁ θεόπατωρ]." But it would have been wrong to call Mary the mother of the divine nature of Christ; for the communication of properties did not mean that the properties of either nature were to be predicated of the other nature as such, but that "when we speak of his hypostasis, whether we give it a name implying both natures, or one that refers to only one of them, we still attribute to it [the hypostasis] the properties of both natures."

The communication of properties may, in a sense, be interpreted as the orthodox Chalcedonian way of achieving what the Jacobites sought to achieve through their idea of "a single composite nature." Replying to that

*Doct.patr.*7.1
(Diekamp 47)

*Doct.patr.*8.1
(Diekamp 55)

Max.*Schol.D.n.*1.3
(*PG* 4:196)

Max.*Ambig.*5 (*PG* 91:1056);
Mart.I.ap.CLater.(649)*Act.*1
(Mansi 10:878)

Max.*Ep.*11 (*PG* 91:456)

Thdr.AbuQ.*Mim.*8.18
(Graf 210)
Max.*Opusc.*9 (*PG* 91:128)

Max.*Opusc.*9 (*PG* 91:113)

Joh.D.*F.o.*48(Kotter 2:117)

*Doct.patr.*9.1
(Diekamp 58)

*Doct.patr.*10.1
(Diekamp 66)

Max.*Ep.*13 (*PG* 91:517)

Max.*Opusc.*5 (*PG* 91:64–65)

Joh.D.*Volunt.*8 (*PG*
95:137)

Max.*Ep.*12 (*PG* 91:488–89);
Joh.D.*F.o.*47 (Kotter 2:111)

*Doct.patr.*11.1
(Diekamp 67)

Thdr.Stud.*Antirr.*1.4
(*PG* 99:332–33)

Joh.D.*F.o.*50 (Kotter 2:122)

idea, *The Doctrine of the Fathers* asserted that it was "impossible to speak of a single composite nature of Christ, synthesized from the uncreated and the created." While having to admit "that some of the fathers did employ the term 'mixture' for the union that follows from the economy," the treatise strove to make clear, by its quotations, that "mixture" here did not refer to a single composite nature but to a composite hypostasis that was "from two natures" but also still "in two natures." The coming of the Logos to men through the flesh had taken place "by the manner of the economy, not by the law of nature"; therefore he had to be a composite hypostasis, of whom a composite nature could not be predicated. The Monenergist theory, with its construct of "a single composite action," had to lead to a composite nature, since action belonged to the natures of Christ rather than to his hypostasis. The clinching argument against any talk of a "composite nature" was, however, the soteriological one: "If his nature is compounded of different natures, it is not homoousios to either of them." Therefore it could not carry out the act of salvation, which only the divine nature could do, and it could not make the act efficacious for men, which only the human nature could do. The idea of a composite nature was therefore to be rejected.

The soteriological argument could be summarized thus: "That the whole of the divine was united to the whole of humanity through the single hypostasis, not a part to a part, . . . and that the Logos assumed everything that is ours." Christ could be universal man only if his entire divine nature, with all its properties, was joined to a complete human nature, with all its properties, in a permanent and indissoluble union. This was all undone if, for example, as the Nestorians taught, the union was achieved by the coming together of a divine hypostasis and a human hypostasis. The Logos had "not assumed some particular human being, but universal man, or the universal [human] nature, yet a nature that is seen in one individual." It was not a denial of the doctrine of the two natures to use such a phrase as "the nature of the Logos"; for by it one was referring to the Logos himself, and "Logos" meant both "the universal of the ousia and the particular of the hypostasis." Although the "particular of the hypostasis" meant in the first instance the divine hypostasis, since the human nature had no hypostasis and hence no particularity of its own, it was this very combination that made the incarnate Logos universal man. He was "the first fruits of the nature that belongs to us . . . and thus a leaven for the entire lump."

As universal man, the incarnate Logos was also "perfect man." Being perfect God, he had now become perfect man, bringing about thereby the greatest of all possible novelties, "the only new thing under the sun." The only difference between his humanity and ours was that his was free of sin in its origin and in its life. This, too, was "for the sake of us men and for the purpose of our salvation," as the Nicene Creed said. He was obedient to his parents, even though as the divine Logos he was their Creator, so that the universal Lawgiver might fulfill the law he had given and so that he might live out a complete and perfect human existence. In the incarnation, said John of Damascus in some of the same words as *The Doctrine of the Fathers,* "we declare that the entire and perfect nature of the divinity in one of its hypostases was united to the entire human nature, not a part to a part." And since, in turn, "man is a microcosm," the incarnation of the Logos in human flesh brought benefit to all, exalting all of human nature—"not as though all the hypostases of human beings had been exalted . . . but because our entire nature has been exalted in the hypostasis of Christ." This definition of Christ as universal man and as perfect man was jeopardized by the denial of a human action and a human will in him.

Therefore *The Doctrine of the Fathers* turned next to these two questions, action and will, with a consideration of the ignorance and the emotions of Christ inserted between them. In so doing it summarized the conciliar settlements of the Monenergist and Monotheletist debates recounted earlier. It began by asserting the thesis "that those who have a single ousia also have undoubtedly a single action." This meant that the hypostases of the Trinity, though three, had a single action. Any such thesis, however, had to clarify the ambiguous term "action [ἐνέργεια]" and its cognates, with a view toward determining "those that are appropriate to each nature," this, of course, on the assumption that action was a function of the nature rather than of the hypostasis, both in trinitarian and in christological thought. *The Doctrine of the Fathers* therefore went on to specify the relation between

1 Cor.5:6; Gal.5:9
Max.*Ambig*.31 (*PG* 91:1280)

Joh.D.*Volunt*.13 (*PG* 95:141)

Joh.D.*F.o*.45 (Kotter 2:108)

Max.*Opusc*.4 (*PG* 91:60)

Thdr.Stud.*Or*.3.6
(*PG* 99:705)

Joh.D.*F.o*.50 (Kotter 2:120)
Joh.D.*Volunt*.15 (*PG* 95:144)

Joh.D.*F.o*.50 (Kotter 2:122)

Mart.I.*Ep*.3 (*PL* 87:142)

Doct.patr.12.1
(Diekamp 73)

Doct.patr.13.1
(Diekamp 78)

Doct.patr.13.1
(Diekamp 78)

Doct.patr.14.1
(Diekamp 87)

Doct.patr.15.1
(Diekamp 91)

Max.Opusc.16 (PG 91:209)

See pp. 64–66 above

Max.Ambig.5 (PG 91:1056);
Doct.patr.15.21
(Diekamp 98)

Max.Pyrr. (PG 91:348)

Max.Opusc.16 (PG 91:200)

Tim.I.Ep.1 (CSCO 75:2
[74:5]); Thdr.CP.Qu.Max.
ap.Max.Opusc.19 (PG 91:
216); Max.Qu.dub.66 (PG
90:837–40)
Gr.M.Ep.10.14; 21 (MGH Ep.
2:248–49; 256–57)

See vol. 1:272

Luke 2:52

Doct.patr.16.1 (Diekamp 104)

Joh.D.Volunt.38 (PG 95:177)

Matt.24:36

"action [ἐνέργεια]" and its synonyms in Greek, all with the point of assigning action to the natures rather than to the hypostasis in Christ. Indeed, "the natures cannot be known otherwise than through their actions, and it is impossible for a nature to be without its action." The actions of Christ belonged to the two natures and were therefore dual. Yet it was necessary to insist that "the one and single Christ carries out the double action in a divine and at the same time in a human manner." These several theses were all intended to support the argument that action belonged to a nature and that Christ would be neither perfect God nor perfect man if he did not share an action with each nature. They meant that one and the same Christ had two actions. The ambiguous and mooted passages from Leo and Pseudo-Dionysius had to be interpreted in the light of this presupposition, as the quotation from Maximus in *The Doctrine of the Fathers* showed. Action, belonging to nature, participated in the nature rather than in the hypostasis. There would not be a genuine human nature in Christ unless there were a human action. In all of this the florilegium was merely reaffirming the councils.

A special difficulty for all parties was the ignorance ascribed to the incarnate Logos. *The Doctrine of the Fathers* explicitly referred to the "Agnoetae," declaring, in response to them and in opposition to the "Aphthartodocetae," who said that Christ's "body was free of corruption from the moment of union," that Christ had in fact passed through all those emotions of a truly human nature that could be experienced in a blameless way, such as fear and ignorance. This was the meaning of the biblical statement that he "increased in wisdom and in stature," which had to be interpreted in the light of the doctrine of the two natures. Christ did not increase in divine wisdom, which was perfect in him from the moment of conception and indeed perfect in the Logos from all eternity, but in human wisdom, which developed as he grew and matured. Thus there was in him a "double knowledge," reflected in his own words: "Of that day and hour no one knows, not even the angels of heaven, nor the Son, but the Father only." Although in some manuscripts of the New Testament the difficulty was resolved by the elimination of the words "nor the Son," the theory of "double knowledge" solved it by distinguishing between the perfect knowledge which the Logos, as eternally homoousios with the Father, had from eternity, and the imperfect knowledge which his human nature had: "the Son" in this passage did not refer to "theology," but to "economy."

Niceph.*Antirr.*1.50
(*PG* 100:328)

Not only the human ignorance spoken of in the Gospels, but also human emotions, such as the fear and dread especially prominent in the passion story, constituted a problem for traditional christology. The device eventually adopted for coping with the problem was a classification of human emotions into those that were sinful and those that were "blameless [ἄγνοια]." To the former category belonged above all the emotions related to sex. It was widely held that procreation through the union of man and woman had not been the original will of God. God would have devised another method of procreation if man had not fallen to the level of the animals, and he would have abolished the difference between male and female. Hence sexual desire was not an emotion that belonged to the essence of human nature, and it was not necessary to attribute it to Christ in order to prove that he was a complete human being. On the other hand, there were natural and blameless pleasures and emotions, "without which it is impossible to live," such as the appetite for food. If Christ was truly human, he must have experienced these emotions and appetites, but not of course any that would have involved him in sin.

Matt.26:38; Heb.5:7–8

*Doct.patr.*16.1
(Diekamp 104)

Max.*Qu.dub.*3 (*PG* 90:
788); Sim.N.Th.*Catech.*15
(*SC* 104: 224)

Max.*Ambig.*31 (*PG* 91:
1276)

Joh.D.*F.o.*27 (Kotter 2:80)

It is characteristic of this period, however, that action and will were more prominent in the controversies than emotion and appetite. Returning to these controverted issues, *The Doctrine of the Fathers* once again summarized the conciliar theology about two wills examined earlier. The will pertained to the nature, not to the hypostasis. The crucial passages such as "Not my will, but thine" were to be explained in the light of the distinction between the human will of Christ and the divine will which he shared with the Father. They were spoken by him "as man . . . and with a view to unity with the will of the Father." As man he wanted to do the will of the Father, which was also his divine will; therefore "he was endowed not only with a will in accordance with his being God and homoousios with the Father, but also [with a will] in accordance with his being man and homoousios with us." This insistence on a distinct human will in Christ was a

*Doct.patr.*17.1
(Diekamp 115)

Luke 22:42

*Doct.patr.*18.1
(Diekamp 117)

Max.*Opusc.*7 (*PG* 91:81)

Max.*Pyrr.* (*PG* 91:324)

Doct.patr.19.1
(Diekamp 121)

Dorner (1853) 255

Doct.patr.20.1
(Diekamp 124)

Doct.patr.15.21
(Diekamp 97)

Doct.patr.20.16
(Diekamp 132)

way of assuring that "his power to make choices shared in our being," since every rational soul had to possess a decision-making capacity that was free of coercion. Even an unsympathetic interpreter of this christology is obliged to admit that "there is noticeable in dyotheletism [the doctrine of two wills] . . . a reaction against the overriding power of the divine nature in favor of a true and free humanity in Christ." The freedom of the human will of Christ was not to be overwhelmed by his divinity, so that even such a patristic notion as "the deified will" was not permitted to obliterate this freedom. The mooted phrase of Pseudo-Dionysius about the "divine-human action" of Christ was quoted in this connection by *The Doctrine of the Fathers,* as it had been earlier in the same treatise, with the explanation that the action of each nature was "divine-human" and that there were two actions and two wills.

Doct.patr.21.1
(Diekamp 133)

Doct.patr.27.1
(Diekamp 191)
Max.Ep.15 (PG 91:556–60);
Doct.patr.21.9 (Diekamp 137–38)

The emphasis on a duality of natures and therefore also of actions and of wills might seem to come dangerously close to the Nestorian theory of a duality of hypostases, in fact if not in terminology. To forestall any such impression, the orthodox Chalcedonianism represented by *The Doctrine of the Fathers* invoked the formula "enhypostaton [το ἐνυπόστατον]" as an interpretation of the hypostatic union. A later chapter was devoted to an explanation of "what enhypostaton is, what anhypostaton is, and what hypostasis is." One of the most productive sources of quotations on this topic was Maximus. Also drawing upon Maximus and upon other authorities, John of Damascus defined the idea of enhypostaton as follows: "The hypostasis of the Logos, who previously was simple, becomes composite . . . , but he keeps the characteristic and distinctive property of the divine Sonship of God the Logos, by which he is distinguished from the Father and the Spirit. He also has, according to the flesh, characteristic and distinctive properties distinguishing him from

Joh.D.F.o.51 (Kotter 2:123)

his mother and from all other human beings." Briefly stated, the term meant "having its being in the hypostasis, and not being real in and of itself"; therefore it could not be thought of apart from the hypostasis.

Max.Opusc.23 (PG 91:261)

In trinitarian usage "enhypostaton" implied that the divine ousia could not be thought of apart from the three hypostases, just as they could not be thought of apart from the ousia and were therefore "enousion." But applied to

Joh.D.Jacob.12 (PG 94:1441–44)

Psell.*Om.doct*.4
(Westerink 18)

Leont.B.*Nest.et
Eut*.1.1(*PG* 86:1277)

D.Evans (1970) 136

Thdr.Stud.*Antirr*.1.4
(*PG* 99:333)

Max.*Opusc*.14 (*PG* 91:149)

Doct.*patr*.22.1 (Diekamp
138)

Doct.*patr*.22.13 (Diekamp
141–44)

Doct.*patr*.23.1
(Diekamp 148)

Max.*Ep*.12 (*PG* 91:472)

Mart.I.ap.CLater.(649)*Act*.3
(Mansi 10:966–67)

Sev.Ant.*Gram*·2.33 (*CSCO*
112:197[111:252])

the God-man, this required that his human nature find its reality in his divine hypostasis. Previously the formula had been used for quite another christological purpose. Starting from this idea of enhypostaton as "having one's being in another," Leontius of Byzantium had concluded that "in their union in Jesus Christ, in which Word and flesh remain distinguished as natures, the nature of Word and flesh are both enhypostasized natures." This understanding of enhypostaton was rejected by the orthodox in favor of the view that the single divine hypostasis of the Logos was constitutive of the union in the God-man, taking up into that union a perfect human nature, which was not a hypostasis on its own but achieved hypostatic and personal reality in the union.

Such a readiness to adapt to orthodox purposes a formula that had been tainted with heresy showed "that true piety does not consist in phrases and sounds, nor in names, but in facts, and that one should not consider terms by themselves but should find the meaning of what has been said." In particular was this necessary for the proper interpretation of Cyril of Alexandria, whose use of the terms "nature" and "hypostasis" apparently as synonyms seemed to support the Monophysites. It was likewise necessary to show by documentary evidence "that Cyril did not forbid speaking of two natures after the union." It had long been a problem to the defenders of Chalcedon that "those who without purpose make war on the holy church" sought to invoke the authority of Cyril. In the proceedings against Monotheletism, therefore, the support of Cyril for what eventually became the teaching of Chalcedon—and even more for what eventually became the official interpretation of the teaching of Chalcedon—was a valuable weapon. The argument was that the Monophysites were using some of the phraseology of Cyril, such as the slogan, "one incarnate nature of God the Logos," but were in fact teaching contrary to Cyril's fundamental intent. The defenders of Chalcedon, on the other hand, were indeed inventing new words, for which the Monophysites attacked them; but in so doing they claimed to be more loyal to the fathers than those who went on reciting patristic formulas in support of heretical doctrine. For example, the use of the union between body and soul as an analogy for the union between human and divine in Christ could claim the support of tradition, but the fathers had not meant by it that the result of the union was a single nature in Christ as it was in the human being. True piety and true orthodoxy did not consist in phraseology, but in content.

In connection with the defense of Cyril against those who cited his authority, *The Doctrine of the Fathers* presented a point-by-point comparison of Cyrillian and Chalcedonian doctrine, proving their congruence on all the points at issue between the Jacobites and the Chalcedonians. The defense of Chalcedon and the defense of Cyril converged in this argument. Theodore Abû Qurra wrote several works in Syriac defending Leo and Chalcedon, and in Greek he also wrote a summary of the teachings promulgated in 451. This campaign to defend Chalcedon was, of course, at the same time a reinterpretation of it as more consistently Cyrillian than it had actually been—and therefore a tacit admission that the criticism of Chalcedon by the Jacobites had some point. Political realism in the light of the Saracen peril coincided with theological inclination and devotional commitment: for all these reasons it seemed desirable to find a form of speaking about the union in Christ that would assign the primary function in the incarnation to the single hypostasis of God the Logos, but would not do so in such a way that the salvation achieved through the incarnation would be sold short. It was indeed ironic that the doctrine of union in Christ should have become the occasion for division of doctrine in the church. But it was this doctrine of union in Christ that provided the basis for the flowering of Eastern Christian thought about mystical theology, as well as for the christological defense of Eastern devotion to the icons. By continuing the debate over christology for many centuries after it had ended in the West, the Eastern theologians of the seventh, eighth, and ninth centuries also gave characteristic doctrinal expression to some of the deepest religious concerns of their tradition.

Thdr.AbuQ.*Mim.*10.16 (Graf 252)

*Doct.patr.*24.10–15 (Diekamp 166–79)
Nicet.Byz.*Arm.*11 (*PG* 105: 617–24); Mich.Anch.*Arm.* (*PG* 133:232)

Thdr.AbuQ.*Mim.*8.21 (Graf 212)
Thdr.AbuQ.*Opusc.*4 (*PG* 97:1504–21)

3

Images of
the Invisible

Although the christological debates after Chalcedon
(described in the preceding chapter), when taken in
continuity with those leading up to Chalcedon (described
in the preceding volume), probably constitute the longest
sustained doctrinal controversy in Christian history, Eastern or Western, the most vigorous polemics in the doctrinal history of Eastern Christendom did not—or, at least,
did not at first—deal with the problem of the person of
Christ. During the eighth and ninth centuries, Eastern
theologians and churchmen, monks and simple believers,
and not least emperors and empresses—all were engaged
in a dispute over the propriety of the use of images in
Christian worship and devotion. Before it was over, this
dispute had become a new version of the christological
debates. It had also opened up the problem of tradition
in a new way, for both sides claimed to be following the
authority of the fathers even though both sides also had
to acknowledge that there was some contrary evidence in
the tradition. The impending schism of East and West
figured in the iconoclastic controversy as well; for "during
the entire Middle Ages in the West there was never as
lively a theological examination of the relations between
religion and art as there was among the Greek theolo-

Ladner (1931) 14

Niceph.*Antirr*.3.84 (*PG*
100:528–33)

gians." The inspiration for the arguments against images
was traced by the defenders of images to Jewish and
Muslim influence, and many modern historians have concurred in this judgment. In this way the attacks upon
images and the defense of them managed to touch upon
most of the doctrinal issues with which this volume is
dealing.

Jones (1959)

Grégoire (1961) 105

Ladner (1940) 127

Joh.D.*Imag*.2.12 (*PG* 94:1296)

Florovsky (1950) 79

Dvornik (1958) 168

Kitzinger (1954) 149–50

Niceph.*Antirr*.2.5 (*PG* 100:344); Thdr.Stud.*Or*. 9.12 (*PG* 99:788)

More even than most of these other doctrinal issues, the conflict over icons can be interpreted as a "social movement in disguise" and as a power struggle that used doctrinal vocabulary to rationalize an essentially political conflict. One can go so far as to maintain that "the controversies of the ancient [theological] schools count for nothing in Iconoclasm and in the defence of the icons, even though their champions employ *a posteriori* Christological arguments and hurl against each other charges of Nestorianism and Eutychianism. The disturbances which we must now recount are concerned with anything but philosophical speculation." The debate was in fact "one of the greatest political and cultural crises of Byzantium," reaching as it did into every aspect of East Roman civilization, not only into the church but into the court, the academy, the monastery, the artist's studio, and the private home. Inasmuch as the locus of authority in the church was itself a doctrinal question, the power struggle between emperor and patriarch does belong to our narrative of the development of doctrine; for "all doctrinal movements in the Early Church (and possibly, all doctrinal and philosophical movements) were, in some sense, 'politically involved' and had political and social implications," and, besides, the iconoclasts "were inclined to exalt the position of the emperor in religious matters, at the expense of the priests." The political and the doctrinal did often coalesce in this period, but we shall not be concerning ourselves directly with the exigencies of ecclesiastical and imperial politics.

Nor shall we deal explicitly with the aesthetic theories at work on both sides, except as these also affected, and were affected by, doctrinal positions. "For the art historian these facts [of the iconoclastic controversy] are of the greatest interest, [for] .... here is an instance where the chances for a successful integration of art-historical studies with social and intellectual history are unusually bright." These two aspects of the controversy, the political and the art-historical, have dominated the secondary literature, at the expense of the doctrinal or even the religious aspects. They are also involved in the sorry state of the primary sources about the controversy: the iconoclasts destroyed all the icons they could, so that "throughout this time the churches that were built were dedicated without sacred relics," leaving very little for later historians of art to investigate; on the other hand, the Second Council of Nicea in 787 ordered the confiscation of all the icono- clastic literature, with the result that "not a single one of these writings has been transmitted to us today in its original form." By a twist of fate not entirely unique in Christian history, both sides thus made sure that historical justice would be difficult to achieve for their opponents —and hence also for themselves.

Images Graven and Ungraven

The iconoclastic controversy was the eruption into open conflict of deep-seated differences that went back to the earliest stages of patristic theology, perhaps back to the Jewish origins of Christianity. But it was also the expres- sion of divergent implications that were drawn from a body of assumptions shared by both sides. These assump- tions pertained to what was believed in the devotional and sacramental life of the church, to what was taught in the preaching and theology of the church, and to what was confessed in the creeds and dogmas of the church. The debates over images do not make sense unless we docu- ment these shared assumptions and trace the development of the differences that proceeded from them.

If, as has been suggested, there is a consensus among modern historians that "at the root of image worship lay the concept that material objects can be the seat of divine power and that this power can be secured through physical contact with a sacred object," this was in fact a concept held in common by the opponents and by the supporters of images; for it was the root of the universal belief of Christians in the East about the sacraments, or, as they were usually termed there, "mysteries." "About these," said an iconoclast, referring to the mysteries, and specifically to the Eucharist, "everyone is in agreement." The iconoclastic emperor, Constantine V, asserted that "the bread which we receive is an image of his [Christ's] body, taking the form of his flesh and having become a type of his body." For their part, the defenders of the images affirmed the true presence of the body of Christ in the Eucharist, held in human hands and distributed to those who were worthy of it. When the priest an- nounced, in *The Liturgy of the Presanctified,* "The holy things that have been presanctified to those who are holy," the orthodox took this to mean that the "mystical sacri-

CNic.(787)*Can.*9 (Mansi 13:378)

Ostrogorsky (1929) 1

Alexander (1958) 5

ap.Thdr.Stud.*Antirr.*2.33 (*PG* 99:376)

Const.V.ap.Niceph.*Antirr.* 2.3 (*PG* 100:337)

Niceph.*Antirr.*2.19 (*PG* 100:373)

Lit.Praesanct. (Brightman 351)

Thdr.Stud.*Praesanct.* (*PG* 99:1689)

Lit.Bas. (Brightman 341)

ap.Thdr.Stud.*Antirr.*2.31–33 (*PG* 99:373–76)

Lit.Bas. (Brightman 329)

Niceph.*Imag.*27 (*PG* 100:605)

Kitzinger (1954) 136

Niceph.*Antirr.*3.35 (*PG* 100:429)
Joh.D.*Imag.*1 (*PG* 94:1268);
Thdr.AbuQ.*Imag.*12 (Arendzen 27)

Joh.D.*Imag.*3.9 (*PG* 94:1332)

Niceph.*Imag.*62 (*PG* 100:749)

Arnob.*Nat.*6.4 (*CSEL* 4:217)

fice" carried out in the eucharistic celebration was an offering of the "holy blood" of Christ. When, in *The Liturgy of Basil,* the priest proclaimed, "Holy things to those who are holy," this meant to the iconoclasts that the sanctified elements in the Eucharist deserved to be called "holy" and that they were therefore "worthy of worship." Iconoclasts and iconophiles in their common liturgy both called the elements "the true and present signs [τὰ ἀντίτυπα] of the body and blood of Christ." The orthodox were obliged to acknowledge that the iconoclasts did teach the real presence of the body and blood of Christ in the Eucharist, but they claimed that this was inconsistent with their general theological position. Therefore the question between them regarding the Eucharist was not, in the first instance, the nature of the eucharistic presence, but its implications for the definition of "image" and for the use of images. Was the eucharistic presence to be extended to a general principle about the sacramental mediation of divine power through material objects, or was it an exclusive principle that precluded any such extension to other means of grace, such as images?

Closely related to this agreement and disagreement over what was believed about the Eucharist was a shared concern about the unsophisticated members of the church. "The original Christian defense of the visual arts," it has been noted, "was based on their usefulness as educational tools. Imagery was . . . a means of instruction or edification, especially for the illiterate." Images were preferable to the plain cross as symbols of the passion, because they communicated its meaning more effectively to the simple rustics. The images were "books for the illiterate," instructing them about the Christian message. As such, they could be worshiped, kissed, and embraced with the heart, instead of being read. The crude and uninstructed masses often failed to pay attention to the readings from Scripture in the public services of the church, but even they could have their attention drawn by images and could thus learn from them what was in the lessons. All these asseverations of concern for simple believers, which echoed the pagan defenses attacked by earlier Christians, came from the advocates of the images; but the same concern was also at work in the campaign against the images. This campaign was animated by the fear "lest some of the more simple and rustic, being uninstructed and hence

ap.Niceph.*Imag*.65 (*PG* 100:756)

ignorant of what is proper . . . be deceived by lifeless matter" and worship it as though it were divine. More sophisticated believers might be able to make appropriate distinctions between the image and the divine, but the simple faithful could not. It is significant that the very treatise in support of images where these words against images are quoted contains, in the same paragraph, the counterargument that the images were necessary precisely for those pious and uninstructed folk, to instruct them. Thus the same pastoral and devotional premise could lead to diametrically opposite conclusions.

The iconoclasts and their opponents shared not only these premises, on which the theology and official dogma of the church had not yet articulated a position, but also the theology and the official dogma, in both of which the notion of "image" was prominent. For example, the Old Testament was a "shadow," but the New was an "image." Again, "the gospel possesses the things that are true." Although there had been no dogma regarding its meaning, the testimony of the creation story that man was made "in the image of God" had probably done as much to determine the content of the term "image" as anything else in Christian thought. In the liturgy which both parties used, man was said to be created "in thy image." Both sides in the iconoclastic debates were agreed that the term was to be applied with special appropriateness to the distinctive character of the original human creation. Both could have said that "man, created according to the image of God, is the image of God, especially because he is chosen by the Holy Spirit as His habitation," even though the orthodox author of these words went on to say that "it is fitting, then, that I honor and worship the image of the servants of God, the habitation of the Holy Spirit." Both could have asked, and answered, the rhetorical question: "Who can circumscribe man created according to the image of God? No one." The story of man's creation in the image of God was proof to both sides that the term "image" was an ancient category of Christian teaching. It would be agreed by both sides that "because man has been created according to the image and likeness of God, it is necessary for human nature . . . as the image to bear within itself the representations of its archetype." But from this common assumption it was possible to conclude either that therefore man could be portrayed in his divine

Max.*Schol.E.h*.3.2 (*PG* 4:137)

Max.*Ambig*.21 (*PG* 91:1253)

Gen.1:27

Lit.Bas.(Brightman 324)

Thdr.AbuQ.*Imag*.21 (Arendzen 46)

Leont.N.*Serm*.3 (*PG* 93:1604)

Joh.H.*Const*.4 (*PG* 95:317–20)

Niceph.*Antirr*.3.58 (*PG* 100:481)

Thdr.Stud.*Ep*.1.13 (*PG* 99:952)

Steph.Bostr.*fr.* (*ST* 76:204)

imagehood or that this was the very quality of human existence that was beyond the grasp of pictorial representation. Thus the idea of the image of God in man compelled the question: Was it the noumenon or only the phenomenon of this image that could be described and circumscribed in a picture?

Joh.H.*Const.*4 (*PG* 95:320)

Although "image of God" was a familiar term in the Christian doctrine of man, it was more familiar, and had become more precise, in christology than in anthropology. As passages such as 2 Corinthians 4:4 asserted, Christ was "the image of the invisible God," and icon-worshipers

Niceph.*Antirr.*3.58 (*PG* 100:484)

hailed him as such. They applied the same passage to their opponents, declaring that "the god of this world has blinded their minds so that they do not see the light of the gospel of the glory of Christ, who is the image of

Joh.H.*Icon.*1 (*PG* 96:1349)

God." The Son of God was, in the words of Colossians 1:15, "the living, natural, and exact image of the invisible

Joh.D.*Imag.*1.9 (*PG* 94:1240)

God." Using the very same term, however, the iconoclasts argued that "if the Son is the exact image of the Father . . . in accordance with the words, 'He who has seen me

John 14:9

has seen the Father,'" it had to follow that no pictorial representation of Christ could do justice to him as the

ap.Thdr.Stud.*Antirr.*3.1.39 (*PG* 99:408)

image of God. They insisted that, by contrast with other so-called images, the Son was called "the image of God

ap.Niceph.*Antirr.*3.18 (*PG* 100:404)
CCP(754) ap.CNic.(787) (Mansi 13:252)

and the Father" in a special sense by Scripture; Christ was "the image both of God and of man." Without denying that the creation story conferred on man a special character as one made in the image of God, the christological tradition had come to identify Christ even with the image

Thdr.Stud.*Antirr.*1.16 (*PG* 99:348)

in this story. There was "one Lord . . . the stamp and image of the Godhead . . . the visible [representation] of the

Ps.Joh.D.*Trin.*2 (*PG* 95:12)

invisible one." In response to the iconoclasts' univocal assignment of the title "image of God" to Christ, to the exclusion of other so-called images, the orthodox maintained that "we, too, concur . . . that the Son is . . . the

Niceph.*Antirr.*3.19 (*PG* 100:405)

image of God and the Father." The word of God had given the Son the prerogative of being the image and stamp of

Niceph.*Antirr.*3.31 (*PG* 100:424)

the Father. Yet from this common premise that Christ, as the Son of God, was the image of God in a unique sense, it was possible either to conclude that therefore he must not be portrayed in a pictorial representation or that therefore he could be portrayed this way. "Concerning the person and the hypostasis, whom they [the iconoclasts] also seem to confess, . . . they are in agreement and of like mind with us." The controversy was over the implication of this premise for images.

Overarching all of this disagreement-within-agreement was the acceptance of the formal authority of the tradition of the church, combined with a fundamental dispute over the material content of the tradition on the question of images. "In view of the sharpness with which Christianity originally directed itself against the idols," it has been observed, "it always remains surprising that later, without being blocked and almost without being observed, the pagan practice was able to establish itself even within the church." Such a comment begs many of the questions at stake in the controversy, above all the question of whether the Christian worship of images was indeed "the pagan practice" that had originally been attacked by Christians and that had now crept back into the church, but also the question of how much "later" this had happened. For to the opponents and to the defenders of the images alike, it mattered a great deal whether images were a recent innovation or a traditional part of Christian usage.

"The main authority of the Iconoclasts . . . was an appeal to antiquity, and this was possibly the strongest point both of their attack and of their self-defense." They insisted that the veneration "of the falsely named images does not come from the tradition either of Christ or of the apostles or of the fathers." In their attack on the worship of images, they felt able to "produce additional testimonies from the holy fathers [which] . . . completely prohibit the erection of the image of the Lord and of the Theotokos and of any of the saints." When the orthodox hurled at them such a question as, "Do you confess that the Son and Logos of the Father was made flesh?" they would reply: "I agree. How should I not agree, since that is what the theologians and fathers declare?" It was from the tradition of the theologians and fathers, as represented by Asterius of Amasea, that they drew the prohibition of images: "Do not portray Christ!" They themselves claimed that they were deriving their arguments "from various patristic testimonies," by which such arguments would be confirmed for their hearers. When the defenders of the images tried to make a case for the practice of

Niceph.*Antirr.*1.20 (*PG* 100:237)

Holl (1928) 2:388

Florovsky (1950) 81

CCP(754) ap.CNic.(787) (Mansi 13:268)

ap.Thdr.Stud.*Antirr.*2.47 (*PG* 99:388)

ap.Thdr.Stud.*Antirr.*2.1 (*PG* 99:353)

ap.Niceph.*Antirr.*2.16 (*PG* 100:364)

ap.Thdr.Stud.*Antirr.*2.28 (*PG* 99:373); CCP(754) ap. CNic.(787) (Mansi 13:333)

worshiping them, the iconoclasts would reply: "Where did

ap.Thdr.Stud.*Antirr*.2.10
(*PG* 99:357)

you get this? I will not accept you as a new lawgiver." So
uncompromising were they in their loyalty to the ancient
tradition of the fathers that their opponents, comparing
them to men who had just been released from prison
into the sunlight, objected that "like men who have no-

Niceph.*Antirr*.3.1 (*PG*
100:376)

where else to escape . . . they run away to the tradition."
This was a criticism which the iconoclasts would have
taken as praise.

Yet the friends of the icons could not let the iconoclasts lay claim to the tradition—not if "orthodoxy" was
to mean support of the icons. For "orthodoxy" meant above
all loyalty to the tradition of the fathers. The images in the
church could not be "a recent invention," but had to have
the authority of Christian antiquity, patristic and even

Niceph.*Antirr*.3.3(*PG*
100:380)

apostolic, behind them. From the same Asterius of
Amasea on whom the iconoclasts depended, the orthodox

Niceph.*Antirr*.2.16 (*PG*
100:364)

quoted evidence to show that "Asterius [is] on our side."
The authorities quoted by the iconoclasts were not "the

Thdr.Stud.*Antirr*.2.48 (*PG*
99:388)

authorities of saints, but . . . of heretics." The church, they
maintained, had been worshiping images "ever since the
time of Christ's descent to earth"; appealing to the authority of the councils, held in reverence by both sides,
they added that there had been six ecumenical councils
since the fourth century and that none of these had con-

Joh.H.*Const*.5 (*PG* 95:320)

demned images. It was characteristic of every heresy, and
especially of the iconoclastic heresy, that it sought to
dissociate itself from the heresies that had preceded it and
that it laid claim to the apostolic and patristic doctrines

Thdr.Stud.*Ref*.18
(*PG* 99:465)

and to the authority of the councils. But this traditional
authority belonged to the images, which had been "from
the beginning, from the tradition of the apostles and
fathers," as could be seen from the practice of the most
ancient churches and from the multitude of the images

Niceph.*Apol*.2 (*PG* 100:836)

themselves. The very history of the church over so long a
period of time was evidence for the antiquity and ortho-

Niceph.*Imag*.71 (*PG*
100:781–84)

doxy of the practice. It was a disparagement of the fathers
and teachers of the church to seek to abolish this practice
after so long. Or were the iconoclasts willing, despite the
promise of Christ that the gates of hell would not prevail

Matt.16:18

against the church, to claim that the church had been in

Joh.H.*Icon*.16 (*PG*
96:1361)

error for seven hundred years until they came along?

When they were not simply scoring debating points on
behalf of the case for images, the orthodox were obliged

to admit that, for a practice that was supposed to be based on the tradition of the apostles and of the church fathers, this one had very little written testimony, either in Scripture or in ancient Christian writers, to support it. Indeed, "no literary statement from the period prior to the year 300 would make one suspect the existence of any Christian images other than the most laconic and hieroglyphic of symbols." The partisans of images maintained that they were "supported by the simple faith and the unwritten tradition of the catholic church," but argued that "unwritten tradition is the most powerful of all." In substantiation of this idea they often drew upon such passages as that in the treatise *On the Holy Spirit* by Basil of Caesarea, which attributed various practices—for example, the sign of the cross, trine immersion at baptism, and facing east at prayer—to the authority of a tradition that was unwritten in form but apostolic in origin. Of course Christ had not commanded images in Scripture, but then he had not commanded prayer to the East or the crowning of wedding couples either. Terms such as "Trinity" were not biblical, and yet they were authoritative as formulations of traditional doctrine. One of the earliest apologists for images, Leontius of Neapolis, argued that even Solomon, in adorning the temple, had "made many graven and molded objects which God had not commanded" and yet had not been condemned for this, because "he made these forms to the glory of God just as we do." The liturgy also contained elements that had been transmitted "ἀγράφως," which meant either "apart from Scripture" or even "without being written down anywhere." And so, "just as throughout the universe the gospel has been proclaimed without being written, so throughout the universe there has been handed down, without being written, the tradition that images are to be made of Christ the incarnate God and of the saints, as well as the tradition that one should worship the cross and pray in a standing position facing the East." For after all, law was only custom that had been put down in writing, and it was not the writing that made it normative.

Because the partisans of both positions affirmed the authority of this apostolic and patristic tradition, they both ransacked the writings of the church fathers for evidence in support of their teaching. At times the conflict appeared to end in a stalemate, with one side asserting

Kitzinger (1954) 86

Niceph.*Antirr*.3.7 (*PG* 100:385)

Bas.*Spir*.27.66 (*PG* 32:188); Max.*Schol.E.h*.1.4 (*PG* 4:121)

Joh.D.*Imag*.1.23 (*PG* 94:1256); Niceph.*Antirr*.3.8 (*PG* 100:389)

Joh.H.*Const*.5 (*PG* 95:320)

Joh.D.*Imag*.3.11 (*PG* 94:1333)

Leont.N.*fr*.ap.Joh.D.*Imag*.1 (*PG* 94:1273)

Niceph.*Antirr*.3.7 (*PG* 100:388)

Joh.D.*Imag*.2.16 (*PG* 94:1304)

Niceph.*Antirr*.3.8 (*PG* 100:388)

Thdr.Stud.*Antirr*.2.40 (*PG* 99:381)

Niceph.*Imag*.71 (*PG* 100: 681–84)

Thos.Ed.*Nat*.4 (Carr 20[18])

Ex.20:4

Clem.*Prot*.4.51.6 (*GCS* 12:40)

Clem.*Paed*.3.11 (*GCS* 1:270)
ap.Niceph.*Antirr*.3.26 (*PG* 100:416)

Clem.*Pasch.fr*.33 (*GCS* 17:218)

Or.*Cels*.4.31 (*GCS* 2:301)

that it had "a multitude of authorities, both ancient and modern" and the other declaring that "I, too, have a multitude of authorities." Was there any way out of this cul-de-sac, and could the devout practice of "all Christians," their words and deeds, be cited as testimony for one or the other of the contending theologies? A survey of the surviving evidence available to us, incomplete though such evidence is, may serve simultaneously as a background for the debates and as a partial answer to this important issue in the debates. It is not always possible to date this evidence with any accuracy, since some of it has been preserved for us only by the very partisans in this debate who made use of it; therefore it may be best to consider it more or less in the chronological order which they attributed to it, and then to look at some of the critical problems.

From its Jewish origins early Christianity had inherited a profound aversion to the worship of idols. Although branded as heretical, *The Treatise on the Nativity* of Thomas of Edessa spoke for all theological parties in describing paganism as a state in which "dumb idols were adored, Satan was worshiped, evil spirits rejoiced, and demons were happy." This attitude was based on the divine prohibition, "You shall not make for yourself a graven image, or any likeness of anything that is in heaven above, or that is in the earth beneath, or that is in the water under the earth." To Clement of Alexandria this prohibition meant that graven images of anything were a deception; for "the image is only dead matter shaped by the hand of the artisan. But we [Christians] have no tangible image made of tangible material, but an image that is perceived by the mind alone, the God who alone is truly God." In other passages, however, Clement spoke more positively about the plastic arts, even providing a list of subjects that could properly be portrayed on seals. If a quotation attributed to him during the iconoclastic controversy is accurate, Clement even said, in a lost treatise *On the Passover,* that the image of an absent person was to be accorded the honor that was due the person himself. Clement's disciple, Origen, used the absence of images and of image makers among the Jews to prove the superiority of Jewish to pagan worship, and he characterized as madness the idea that any images fashioned by human hands could confer honor upon

Or.*Cels*.3.76 (*GCS* 2:268)

beings that were truly divine. Another early apology for Christianity, the *Octavius* of Minucius Felix, boasted of the lack of images and temples among Christians: "Do you suppose that because we have neither temples nor altars, we are hiding the object of our worship? And yet what image shall I make of God, when, if you think correctly, man himself is the image of God?"

Min.Fel.*Oct*.32.1–3 (*CSEL* 2:45–46)

Lib.*Car*.4.10(*MGH Conc.Sup.* 2:189–90)

Probably the most celebrated of early references to "Christian images" appears in an apocryphal account in Syriac of negotiations between Jesus Christ and Abgar V, king of Edessa, relating that Christ cured the king and that Hannan, an artist in the service of the king, painted a portrait of Christ. During the Persian siege in 544, this image was said to have repelled the invaders. For such a supporter of images as John of Damascus, the legend of Abgar provided evidence that an image made during the lifetime of Jesus "has been preserved until the present time." This story was proof to Andrew of Crete that "the use of the holy images is a matter of ancient tradition." In his defense against the iconoclasts, the patriarch Nicephorus also referred to the story, first without mentioning Abgar by name and later with an explicit reference to him. The legend of Abgar, complete with a letter from Christ to the king (which does not appear in the Syriac version), was transmitted to Greek-speaking audiences by Eusebius and to Latin-speaking audiences by his translator, Rufinus. Eusebius claimed to have translated the account directly from the Syriac archives in Edessa. Yet in his version of the legend there is no reference whatever to any image. His reference to a statue of Christ healing the woman with a hemorrhage (a miracle also celebrated in poetry), although claimed as support by the iconophiles, seems in fact to have been a criticism of the statue as a vestigial remnant of paganism. It is also from Eusebius, in another context, that there came one of the most explicit rejections of the very idea of images. In response to a letter from the empress Constantia, requesting an image of Christ, he wrote: "I do not know what has impelled you to command that an image of our Savior be drawn. Which image of Christ do you want? Is it a true and unchangeable one, portraying his countenance truly, or the one which he assumed on our behalf when he took on the appearance of the form of a slave?" This position made Eusebius "the coryphaeus and acropolis" of the iconoclasts,

Doct.*Ad*. (Phillips 1–5)
Evagr.*H.e*.4.27 (Bidez-Parmentier 174)

Thdr.AbuQ.*Imag*.23 (Arendzen 48); Joh.D.*Imag*.1 (*PG* 94:1261)

Andr.Cr.*Imag*. (*PG* 97:1301)

Niceph.*Antirr*.1.24; 3.42 (*PG* 100:260; 461)

Eus.*H.e*.1.13.5 (*GCS* 9: 84–86)

Matt.9:20–22
Rom.Mel.*Hymn*.23 (*SC* 114:86–100)
Thdr.AbuQ.*Imag*.8 (Arendzen 13–14)
Eus.*H.e*.7.18 (*GCS* 9:672)

Eus.*Ep.Constant*. (*PG* 20: 1545)

Niceph.*Imag*.12 (*PG* 100: 561); Niceph.*Antirr*.3.30 (*PG* 100:421); Niceph.*Apol*. 11 (*PG* 100:848)

whom they would quote, together with some church fathers who seemed to be supporters of their position. Eusebius's account of the legend of Abgar is earlier than any Syriac version now in existence, although it was based on Syriac sources; therefore it seems sensible to regard the story of the image as a later accretion. Yet one cannot ignore the slight possibility that this story was present in the sources used by Eusebius but was omitted by him because of his strong antipathy against the very idea of portraying Christ in an image.

Lib.Car.4.25 (*MGH Conc. Sup*.2:223–25)

That antipathy appeared also in another fourth-century writer who figured prominently in the debates of the eighth and ninth centuries, Epiphanius of Salamis. He maintained that "the devil . . . . has now again drawn away

Epiph.*fr*.10 (Holl 360)

. . . the faithful into ancient idolatry." He opposed the introduction of images into Christian places of worship,

Epiph.*Haer*.27.6.10 (*GCS* 25:311)

for he was sure that "when images are erected, the customs of the pagans do the rest." Anticipating an argument that was to be used in support of the images much later, Epiphanius declared in his last will and testament: "If anyone should dare, using the incarnation as an excuse, to look at the divine image of God the Logos painted with earthly colors, let him be anathema." So strong and explicit was the rejection of images by Epiphanius, "that

Epiph.*fr*.34 (Holl 363)

CCP(754) ap.CNic.(787) (Mansi 13:292)

famous standard-bearer" of orthodoxy, that the iconoclasts were able to make good use of these writings to support their case from patristic tradition. Citing their use of Epiphanius, John of Damascus suggested that these writings might not be genuine; but even if they were, they did not of themselves constitute normative tradition,

Joh.D.*Imag*.1.25 (*PG* 94: 1257)

which was on the side of the images. Nicephorus, too, sought to show that Epiphanius was not the true author of the works attributed to him by the iconoclasts. He also

Niceph.*Apol*.4 (*PG* 100:837)

composed a work *Against Epiphanius,* refuting, and, inci-

Niceph.*Epiph*. (Pitra 4:294–380)

dentally, preserving fragments from, these early treatises against images. Even in modern times the authenticity of these treatises has been questioned, but they are now regarded as probably genuine. The debate over their authenticity, both ancient and modern, illustrates the ambiguity of the tradition and hence of the argument from tradition.

In some ways the quotations from the fathers which the

Niceph.*Antirr*.3.26 (*PG* 100:416); *Lib.Car*.3.15 (*MGH Conc.Sup*.2:133–36); Ps.Anast. S.*Jud.dial*.1 (*PG* 89:1224)

orthodox found most useful did not deal with images of Christ and the saints, but with images of Roman em-

Thdr.Stud.*Antirr*.2.18 (*PG* 99:361)

Ath.*Ar*.3.5 (*PG* 26:332)
Lib.Car.2.14 (*MGH Conc. Sup*.2:73–74); Thdr.Stud.*Antirr*.1.8 (*PG* 99:337); Thdr.AbuQ.*Imag*.8 (Arendzen 12–13)
Thdr.Stud.*Antirr*.1.8 (*PG* 99:337)

Bas.*Hom*.24.4 (*PG* 31:608)

Bas.*Spir*.9.23 (*PG* 32:109)

Joh.D.*Imag*.1.21 (*PG* 94:1252–53)

Bas.*Spir*.18.45 (*PG* 32:1249)

ap.Niceph.*Antirr*.3.18 (*PG* 100:404)

Bab.*Un*.4.17 (*CSCO* 80:133[79:165])

Niceph.*Antirr*.3.12 (*PG* 100:393)

Joh.D.*Parall*.8.4 (*PG* 96:17)

CCP(754)ap.CNic.(787) (Mansi 13:300)

perors. Thus Athanasius, praised by the supporters of the images as "a man of many trials," had declared that "the likeness of the emperor in the image is exact. . . . Accordingly he who worships the image, in it worships the emperor also; for the image is his form and appearance." Other works attributed to Athanasius also served as authorities in support of this interpretation. Even more important was the testimony of "the divine Basil" of Caesarea, who had said "that the image of the emperor is also called 'emperor' and yet there are not two emperors." Elsewhere, too, Basil had used the concept of the "imperial image" in speaking about the Holy Spirit. Above all, one passage was cited frequently by John of Damascus, in an extended discussion of "image" applied to Christ, to the Theotokos, and to the other saints. In his own interpretation of "image" Basil had said: "The honor that is paid to the image passes over to the prototype." Precisely this, it was argued, took place when Christians paid honor to an image. In reply the iconoclasts argued that this was spoken "in relation to theology," to the inner life of the Godhead, and did not apply to the images now being used in churches. Technically they were right, for "image" here meant Christ himself, not a man-made portrait; but taken as a proof text out of context—which is how such passages were often taken by both sides—it seemed a strong support for the orthodox. The Nestorians used the relation between the emperor and his image to support their distinction between hypostasis and person. The reverence paid to the emperor's image and the legal precedent of "taking refuge at the statues" of the emperor for asylum, supported by an apposite quotation from Chrysostom, gave further support. For if these practices were permissible also under the Christian emperor, who was temporal, then a fortiori it was permissible to give similar honor to the image of the eternal King. Significantly, the iconoclasts found passages in these very three fathers—Athanasius, Basil, and Chrysostom—as well as in others, to support their stand.

In spite of all this evidence, however, it must be admitted that the case for images or against them was not based initially on considerations of doctrine. In the usage of a church opposed to idolatry, images arose on the basis of other factors, which lay more in what was believed implicitly than in what was explicitly taught and confessed.

Ps.45:3

Dobschütz (1899) 29

When "instead of Isaiah 53 the word of the psalm about 'the fairest among the children of men' was made the guide for the appearance of Christ," this meant a change of attitude with which the official teaching of the church eventually had to come to terms. This change coincided with the growth of devotion to the relics of the saints and martyrs. One of the most suggestive formulations of such devotion appears in Gregory of Nyssa: "Those who behold them [relics] embrace, as it were, the living body itself in its full flower. They bring eye, mouth, ear, all their senses into play. And then, shedding tears of reverence and passion, they address to the martyr their prayer of inter-

Gr.Nyss.Thdr. (PG 46:740)

cession as though he were alive and present." It is not a long step from this veneration of relics to the veneration of images; Gregory also described his feelings at viewing

Gr.Nyss.Deit. (PG 46:572)

an image portraying Abraham's sacrifice of Isaac. A younger contemporary of Gregory's, Paulinus of Nola, gives evidence that images of Christian saints were already being set up in Christian churches. Although he had refused to allow his own image to be used this way, arguing that "the only representation of me which can be necessary for you is that in which you yourself are fash-

Paulin.N.Ep.30.2 (CSEL 29:262–63)

ioned, by which you love your neighbor as yourself," he did consent to the installation of an image of Martin of Tours in a baptistery. The reason was that "he bore the image of the heavenly man by his perfect imitation of Christ," and therefore this "portrait of a heavenly soul worthy of imitation" was an appropriate subject for men to look at when, in baptism, they were laying aside their

Paulin.N.Ep.32.2 (CSEL 29:276)

own earthly image. At about the same time, the devotees of Simeon Stylites were putting up images of him at the entrances of their workshops for protection—and this

Thdt.H.r.26.11 (Lietzmann 8)
Jac.Ed.Can.21 (Kayser 18)

apparently while he was still alive. The non-Chalcedonians too, paid devotion to relics. Scattered and meager though they are, these bits of evidence suggest that, beginning with the fourth and fifth centuries, there grew among Christians the belief that in relics and images there was available some special form of divine presence and help. The doctrinal tradition was sufficiently equivocal to lead to inconclusive results, and it was only when the problem of images became a matter of open and sustained controversy that the implications of this tradition could be drawn.

Images as Idols

Kitzinger (1954) 133

As the belief in the power of images developed, so did the resistance to them, and "there is ... no century between the fourth and the eighth in which there is not some evidence of opposition to images even within the Church." Yet it was in the eighth and ninth centuries that the doctrinal case against images was articulated more fully than ever before or since: in the eighth century by the emperor Constantine V and by the iconoclast synod held at Constantinople in 754, in the ninth century by the synod of 815 and its exponents. Of the treatise of Constantine it has been said: "There is hardly another monument that gives us such a deep insight into the essence of the iconoclast heresy, that expounds its philosophical and theological foundations so clearly, as do these writings of the emperor." Even his opponents, by the violence of their polemics, paid grudging tribute to the force of his ideas. Politically and ecclesiastically, the eighth- and ninth-century stages of the iconoclast movement do need to be distinguished; but for our purposes the doctrinal presuppositions of the movement can be treated together, even though the first of the two main accusations, that of idolatry, was more prominent in the eighth century, "while the christological formulation of the problem stands even more in the foreground" in the ninth century than it had in the eighth. It also bears repeating that for our reconstruction of the case against images we are forced to rely on the accounts (always ex parte) and quotations (often verbatim) supplied by the orthodox victors in the controversy.

Ostrogorsky (1929) 2–3

Thdr.Stud.*Or.*11.3.17 (*PG* 99:820)

H.G.Beck (1959) 303

The allowances that must be made in handling partisan accounts apply also to the different versions they give of the origins and sources of iconoclasm. According to one such story, the eighth-century campaign against images originated in the plot of a Jew with the sobriquet "Forty Cubits Tall [Τεσσαρακοντάπηχυς]," who conspired with the caliph Yazid II to ban images from Christian churches; thus it was "the Jewish mind," in unholy alliance with the Muslim mind, that made Christian emperors serve its iconoclastic purposes. It does seem clear that Yazid ordered the destruction of Christian images, but the Jewish influence on him is less evident; above all, the influence

Niceph.*Antirr.*3.84 (*PG* 100:528–33)

Thdr.AbuQ.*Imag*.1 (Arendzen 1–2)

See vol. 1:54–55

Florovsky (1950) 82–83

of either Muslim or Jewish ideas on the thought of Christian iconoclasts seems to have been highly exaggerated, both by contemporaries and by modern scholars. Attractive though it is as evidence of reaction against the "hellenization of Christianity" through images and dogmas, this explanation has little more "than a parallelism and 'analogy'" to support it. On the other hand, there were explicit foundations in Christian thought for the iconoclastic position. In presenting their case, the opponents of images cited these as their authority, giving voice to the long-standing suspicion of many Christians that it was unseemly for the church to permit, even to encourage, a recrudescence of the worship of idols.

ap.Niceph.*Antirr*.3.9 (PG 100:389)

CCP(754) ap.CNic.(787) (Mansi 13:268)

This argument from authority expressed itself in such a question as: "What is the source for this, and what kind of law commands us to worship an image of Christ?" There was no such authority for the worship of images; it did not come "from the tradition either of Christ or of the apostles or of the fathers." The tradition of the fathers did not condone the practice; in fact, if it was read aright, it contained many undeniable prohibitions of it. Still less could the veneration of images appeal to the tradition of the apostles or of the prophets, upon whom the fathers had drawn. The biblical passages quoted by the iconoclasts in opposition to the worship of images were a prominent part of their argument, prominent enough to warrant special attention from their orthodox opponents. These latter, forced to admit the affinities between the iconoclast case and the attack of the Old Testament prophets upon the idolatrous propensities of the people of Israel, criticized the iconoclasts as "half-baked wiseacres [νεόσοφοι]," who perverted to their own purposes "the statements that have been beautifully expressed by the prophets." The iconoclasts were, in other words, applying to Christian images and their veneration in the churches the biblical passages that had originally been written against pagan idolatry; but the idolatrous abuse of images by the Greeks did not imply, according to the iconodules, that "our practice, which arose out of [proper] devotion," was to be abolished. Nevertheless, the biblical authorities cited by the iconoclasts could not be dismissed so summarily as all that.

ap.Thdr.AbuQ.*Imag*.7 (Arendzen 11–12)

Joh.H.*Icon*.2 (PG 96:1349)

Joh.D.*Imag*.1.24 (PG 94:1256–57)

From the existing evidence it seems that a very prominent weapon in this biblical arsenal was the prohibition

Joh.D.*Imag*.2.7 (*PG* 94:
1288); Joh.H.*Const*.7 (*PG*
95:324); CCP(754) ap.
CNic.(787) (Mansi 13:284);
Thdr.Stud.*Antirr*.1.5 (*PG*
99:333); Niceph.*Antirr*.3.40
(*PG* 100:445)

Gr.Pal.*Dec*. (*PG* 150:
1092–93); *Conf.Petr.Mog*.
3.53 (Karmirēs 760)
Aug.*Quaest.Ex*.71.1–2
(*CCSL* 33:102–3)

ap.Joh.D.*Imag*.2.7 (*PG*
94:1288)

Ps.97:7
ap.Joh.D.*Imag*.2.7
(*PG* 94:1288)

Is.42:8

ap.Thdr.Stud.*Antirr*.3.3.14
(*PG* 99:425)

Mal.1:12

ap.Niceph.*Imag*.27
(*PG* 100:604)

of graven images in Exodus 20:4. Each of our five major orthodox sources from the eighth and ninth centuries— John of Damascus, John of Jerusalem, the Second Council of Nicea, Theodore of Studios, and Nicephorus—took the trouble to note the iconoclast exegesis of this disturbing passage and to refute it. Here was a part of the Decalogue itself that could be used against the images; for in Eastern Christendom (and later in Calvinism) this prohibition was counted as the second of the ten commandments, while in Latin Christendom (and later in Lutheranism) it was regarded as only an appendix to the first commandment. Its strictures against depicting not merely God, but even his creatures, had served some Christian fathers as a basis for their specification of the distinction between pagan and Christian worship. The iconoclasts apparently saw in it a major resource also for their case. It had been promulgated "through Moses the lawgiver" and thus had a special status also in the Christian law. Other passages directed against idols also seemed apposite, for example, the curse of the psalmist: "All worshipers of images are put to shame." In addition, there seemed to be a special appropriateness in the word of God through the prophet: "I am the Lord, that is my name; my glory I give to no other, nor my praise to graven images." This seemed to prove that the reverence appropriately paid to God could not be transferred to images, even if this were done on the pretext of Christian devotion to so-called images of Christ and the saints. Also from the Old Testament abhorrence of idolatry came the iconoclasts' application to the orthodox of such passages as the first chapter of the Book of Malachi, with its discussion of how the table of the Lord had been polluted: this the worshipers of images had done by paying to these idols the reverence that properly belonged only to the Lord.

Yet it would be a mistake to conclude from the reliance of the iconoclasts on the Old Testament, as some interpreters have, that whereas the cult of images was an acute hellenization of Christian worship and a revival of pagan practices, the iconoclast challenge to this cult was a reassertion of the Semitic elements in the Christian heritage. For not only were the iconoclasts as vigorous as their opponents in the denunciation of Judaism, but some of their most important arguments were based on biblical passages of a decidedly "Greek" and "non-Semitic" cast.

ap.Niceph.*Antirr*.3.13 (*PG* 100:396)

Two such passages from the Gospel of John may serve as illustrations. One was John 18:36: "My kingship is not of this world." In view of the authoritative role assigned to the king and emperor by the iconoclasts, this might seem strange; but they appear to have used the passage to emphasize the transcendence of Christ over this physical and material world, which was the world of images. Even more explicit a proof text for this transcendence was the saying of Jesus in John 4:24: "God is spirit, and those who worship him must worship in spirit and truth." This was cited as "the first passage" and as a "statement chosen

CCP(754) ap.CNic.(787) (Mansi 13:280)

by the Lord." As the context in the Gospel shows, it was directed against Jews and Samaritans and was intended to emphasize that with the coming of Christ worship was to become even more spiritual, therefore less bound to physical places and objects, than it had been in Judaism. It followed, then, that Christians had to go even beyond the Old Testament strictures on images.

In addition to the authority of Scripture and the fathers, the iconoclasts asserted also the authority of the Byzantine emperor. To be sure, all parties throughout most of Byzantine history had a high view of his authority. It had long been customary to speak of him with honorific titles. But

See vol. 1:341

it seems clear that iconoclasm raised this authority to a higher level than was customary. This is evident from the attacks of the orthodox, who declared that "emperors do not have the authority to legislate for the church." According to the New Testament, God had instituted apostles, prophets, pastors and teachers—but not emperors—to govern the church. "The business of emperors is political administration; ecclesiastical governance pertains to pas-

Joh.D.*Imag*.2.12 (*PG* 94:1296)

tors and teachers." That iconoclasm did involve an elevation of imperial authority can be seen also from the decrees of the iconoclast synod of 754, which declared that as Christ had originally sent out the apostles, "so also now he has raised up his servants, the peers of the apostles, our faithful emperors," to drive out the diabolical delusion of

CCP(754) ap.CNic.(787) (Mansi 13:225)

the images. Although it may be saying too much to maintain that the issue of the imperial authority was the fundamental religious question in the iconoclastic controversy, it does seem clear that this issue was not exclusively political but did involve the very structure of religious authority as it was interpreted by the iconoclasts.

On the basis of these authorities—and of these interpretations of the authorities—iconoclasm articulated certain presuppositions which determined its attitude toward images. Fundamental to its position was an understanding of the nature of an image; and even though this was not always formally set forth in a logical definition, it did shape iconoclastic doctrine. The orthodox based their definition on the relation between the original or prototype [πρωτότυπος] and the copy that was derived from it [παράγωγον]; the iconoclasts also taught that "every image is known to be a copy of some original." But Constantine V developed this definition further by asserting that a genuine image was "identical in essence with that which it portrays." The term used here, "identical in essence [ὁμοούσιος]," came from the trinitarian language of orthodox dogma, where it had been used to define the deity of the Son in relation to that of the Father; it was in this sense that the Son was "the image of the Father." This definition of the relation between the image and the thing or person imaged, which "undoubtedly was characteristic not only of Constantine but of all the leading minds of iconoclasm," meant that an image of Christ being used in worship was in fact "the falsely so-called image of Christ," since it obviously could not be "identical in essence" with the person of Jesus Christ himself; not even the most vigorous defenders of the images maintained that it was. The very definition of a true image necessarily implied for the iconoclasts that no painting or statue could ever be an image of Christ.

But the Eucharist could be, and in fact was, a true image, for only it was identical in essence with Christ. In spite of the assurance that everyone was in agreement about the sacraments, the controversy over images did bring out some differences. To the iconoclasts, the Eucharist was the only true image. "It had been laid down for us," they said, "that Christ is to be portrayed in an image, but only as the holy teaching transmitted by divine tradition says: 'Do this in remembrance of me.' Therefore it is obviously not permitted to portray him in an image or to carry out a remembrance of him in any other way, since this portrayal [the Eucharist] is true and this way of portraying is sacred." When Constantine V said that "the bread which we take is an image of his [Christ's] body, taking the form of his flesh and having become a type of his body," he meant not merely "*an* image" but "*the*

Joh.D.*F.o*.89 (Kotter 2:206)
ap.Niceph.*Antirr*.1.13 (*PG* 100:224)

ap.Niceph.*Antirr*.1.15 (*PG* 100:225)

See vol. 1:200–210

Ostrogorsky (1929) 41
CCP(754)ap.CNic.(787)
(Mansi 13:257)

See pp. 93–94 above

1 Cor.11:24–25

ap.Thdr.Stud.*Antirr*.1.10
(*PG* 99:340)

Const.V.ap.Niceph.*Antirr*.
2.3 (*PG* 100:337)

Const.V.ap.Niceph.*Antirr.* 2.2 (*PG* 100:333)

image." By "image" and "type," moreover, he did not mean an empty sign, but that which was "precisely and truly" the very body of Christ. Nor was he speaking for himself alone. At their council in 754, he and his fellow believers declared that apart from the Eucharist there was "not any other form or type capable of representing his incarnation in an image." Only the sacrament was "the image of his life-giving body," and nothing else could set forth for men the mystery of the salvation wrought by the dispensa-

CCP(754)ap.CNic.(787) (Mansi 13:261)

tion of God. These ordinances had come down from heaven, and through them it was possible to know the grace of the dispensation that had been achieved through

ap.Niceph.*Imag*.9 (*PG* 100: 553)
ap.Niceph.*Antirr*.3.28 (*PG* 100:420)

the humiliation of Christ. What could be more deserving of honor and reverence than the very body of the Lord? The sanctified eucharistic elements, as the body and blood of Christ, were to be called "holy" and were to be ac-

ap.Thdr.Stud.*Antirr*.2.31–33 (*PG* 99:373–76)

knowledged as worthy of worship. For that very reason holy pictures could not lay claim to such reverence.

Iconoclastic doctrine does appear to have made at least one exception to this rule against images and symbols: the holy cross. Quoting the words of the apostle Paul in

Leo III.*Ep*. (Jeffery 322)

praise of the cross as the only thing in which he was will-ing to glory, the iconoclasts asked: "Where is there any-thing written about the image to compare with what is

Gal.6:14; 1 Cor.1:18

written here about the cross?" When they were challenged

ap.Thdr.Stud.*Antirr*.1.8; 1.15 (*PG* 99:337; 345)

for their inconsistency in being willing to worship the symbol of the cross but not the images of Christ, they replied that "we worship the symbol [τύπος] of the cross

ap.Niceph.*Antirr*.3.34 (*PG* 100:425)

on account of him who was fastened to it." Although they were accused not only of inconsistency but also of pre-

Niceph.*Imag*.61 (*PG* 100:748)

tense for their reverence toward the cross, it is quite clear that the reverence was an authentic part of their teaching and practice. An acrostic hymn of iconoclastic provenance hailed the cross as "support of the faithful and worship of God, [which the Logos had] given to us for our salvation, the life-giving symbol" of the sufferings of Christ, by con-trast with "the wickedly graven image and deception"

ap.Thdr.Stud.*Ref*. (*PG* 99:437)

that had come into the church. At least part of the expla-nation for this inconsistency should perhaps be found in the widespread worship of the symbol of the cross (also,

Bab.*Un*.5.18 (*CSCO* 80: 146[79:180])

for example, among the Nestorians) and in the universal use of the sign of the cross throughout all periods of the church's history. As the champions of the images also

Joh.D.*Imag*.2.16 (*PG* 94:
1301)

acknowledged, the custom of worshiping the cross was an unwritten tradition but an apostolic one. Unlike other so-called unwritten traditions, this one could claim to have the support of a patristic consensus.

In spite of this loyalty to patristic consensus, the iconoclasts—or, at any rate, some of them—did diverge from the implications of the orthodox development in their attitude toward the saints, which naturally affected their attitude also toward the images of the saints. The defenders of the images went so far as to charge the entire iconoclastic movement with disrespect for the saints: as they did not hesitate to do violence to the history of the Gospels, which was set forth in images of Christ, so they also debased the history of the saints, which was told in

Niceph.*Imag*.38 (*PG*
100:645)

other sacred books and portrayed in other images. This blanket accusation seems, however, to have been unjust to many adherents of the movement. There is at least some indication that the party of the iconoclasts included some who objected to the images of the saints but were prepared to accept images of Christ and of Mary. Such a position was, then, directed not against images but against the saints, and it was on this ground that the orthodox re-

Joh.D.*Imag*.1.19 (*PG*
94:1249)

sponded to it.

It does appear, moreover, that some spokesmen for the movement, notably the emperor Constantine V, based their rejection of the images of the saints partly on a heterodox view of the saints and even of the Virgin. According to the report of Nicephorus, Constantine "dares to do away with the term 'Theotokos' and to remove it completely from the tongue of Christians." He was charged with having expunged references to Mary from the

Niceph.*Antirr*.2.4 (*PG*
100:341)

litanies and canticles used in worship. As part of this campaign, he was even said to have denied that Mary could intercede for the church; much less, therefore, would the intercessory prayers of the other saints have any efficacy. In fact, not only the title "Theotokos" but

Niceph.*Antirr*.1.9 (*PG*
100:216)

even the title "saint" was to be proscribed. Although some of this was an expression of Constantine's private opinions, others joined him in the opposition to the devotional extravagances connected with the cult of the Theotokos and the saints. Mary was, to most of the iconoclasts no less than to the orthodox, "the utterly immaculate and superglorious truly Theotokos"; but she was only human,

CCP(754)ap.CNic.(787)
(Mansi 13:272; 277)

as were the prophets, apostles, and martyrs. Amid all their high praise for her and for other saints, however, the iconoclasts made clear that this did not mean that they were to be "portrayed by the art of [pagan] Greece." It was one thing to pay the proper respect [τιμή] to the saints, quite another to address worship [προσκύνησις] to them, and yet another to portray them in worshipful images.

ap.Thdr.Stud.*Antirr.*2.26
(*PG* 99:369)

If portraits of Christ, of Mary, and of the saints were to be rejected on these grounds, the portraits of angels in Christian images were suspect on additional grounds as well. For at least the former had once lived on earth as human beings and had possessed faces and features of which a contemporary artist could presumably have made a picture. But "no one has ever seen an angel. How do they make a picture of an angel?" And by what right, specifically, "do they make and depict angels as though they had the form of a human being and were equipped with two wings?" Angels were spirits and could not be touched; therefore they could not be circumscribed in a picture, for they did not have bodies. Philoxenus of Mabbug, a Monophysite, had objected to the anthropomorphic images of angels, and even the orthodox thought that it was going too far when some artists drew images of angels as crucified. For although "angel" had once been a title for the divine in Christ, acceptable in orthodox usage, it was a dangerous violation of the distinction between spirit and matter to make such images; and the practice was condemned. The distinction between spirit and matter seems to have meant even more to the iconoclasts than to the orthodox, who accused the iconoclasts of "defaming matter and calling it dishonorable." "It is," the iconoclasts said, "degrading and demeaning to depict Christ with material representations. For one should confine oneself to the mental observation [of him] . . . through sanctification and righteousness." Images were made of "inglorious and lifeless matter." But passages like "God is spirit" commanded that worship be "in spirit and truth" and that it therefore be carried on "only mentally [νοερῶς μόνον]." Pagan temples may have claimed to be holy on account of their images made of wood, metal, or stone, but Christian churches were holy on account of the prayer, thanksgiving, and sacrifice that were offered up in them. The spirituality of this worship had been violated

ap.Joh.H.*Const.*11; 12 (*PG* 95:328)

ap.Thdr.Stud.*Antirr.*3.1.47
(*PG* 99:412)

ap.CNic.(787) (Mansi 13:180–81)

See vol. 1:182–84

Thdr.Stud.*Ep.*1.15 (*PG* 99:957)

Joh.D.*Imag.*2.13 (*PG* 94:1297)

ap.Thdr.Stud.*Antirr.*1.7 (*PG* 99:336)

CCP(754)ap.CNic.(787)
(Mansi 13:277; 261)

John 4:24

ap.Joh.D.*Imag.*1 (*PG* 94:1264)

ap.Niceph.*Antirr.*3.54 (*PG* 100:477)

when the pagan materialism of images was smuggled back into Christian churches.

That is what the iconoclasts accused the churches of having done. This generation, they charged, had deified images. In this charge they included themselves, acknowledging that they, too, had bowed down before false gods and had committed idolatry. It was their confession and their accusation that "we Christians have worshiped idols, and have been doing so until the time of the reign of Constantine [V]." Therefore they called the image-worshipers "idolaters." So pervasive had this idolatry been that "if Constantine had not rescued us from our madness for idols, Christ could not have been of benefit to us in any way." Underlying this accusation was an explanation of how the worship of images had established itself in the church. Citing John 4:23, they interpreted the work of Christ as that of delivering men "from the corrupting doctrine of demons and the deception of idols" and of replacing this with "worship in spirit and truth." But the devil, who was dedicated to the promotion of a worship addressed to the creature rather than to the Creator, refused to accept defeat at the hands of Christ and "surreptitiously reintroduced idolatry under the outward appearance of Christianity." All of this had been done as an expression of Christian devotion and with the connivance of Christian theologians, monks, and prelates.

Worship in spirit, achieved by the coming of Christ, had now been forced to yield to the adoration of matter; and worship in truth had been superseded by the lies and deception of idolatry. For the Christian images that were being worshiped in the churches were not authentic images. An authentic image had to be "identical in essence" with that which it portrayed, and only the Eucharist could fully satisfy this definition. All other images of Christ were "falsely so-called," because they were a poor and unfaithful imitation. In formulating this accusation of idolatry against Christian image-worship, the iconoclasts revived the earlier criticism of images as a form of deception, attacking "the deception of the likenesses done by the painters, which drag one from a worship that is sublime and pleasing to God, down to the degraded worship of creatures practiced by men nowadays." The worship of God in spirit and truth adored him in his real nature, but images had to be artificial and therefore decep-

Margin notes:

ap.Joh.H.*Const*.13 (*PG* 95:329)

ap.Niceph.*Imag*.65 (*PG* 100:756)

ap.Niceph.*Imag*.17 (*PG* 100:577)
ap.Joh.H.*Const*.3 (*PG* 95:313)

ap.Niceph.*Imag*.27 (*PG* 100:601)

CCP(754) ap.CNic.(787) (Mansi 13:216)

Rom.1:25

CCP(754) ap.CNic.(787) (Mansi 13:212; 221)

ap.Niceph.*Antirr*.1.15 (*PG* 100:225)

CCP(754) ap.CNic.(787) (Mansi 13:257)

CCP(754) ap.CNic.(787) (Mansi 13:229)

tive. In short, "they saw the images drawing the spirit of man from the lofty adoration of God to the low and material adoration of the creature," which was the essence of the idolatry condemned in the second commandment.

It was obvious to everyone, according to the iconoclasts, that "portraying Christ in an image is an invention of the idolatrous mentality." By their images pagan Greeks glorified and celebrated what was theirs, but this sort of behavior was not permissible for Christians. The argument of the orthodox that there was a fundamental distinction to be drawn between the image-worship of the pagan Greeks and that of the Christian Greeks was dismissed as sophistry, for there was no real difference between them. The patristic defense of the doctrine of the Trinity had justified it by maintaining that it did not imply three systems of worship, but a single worship addressed to the one triune God. That defense, which was also under attack from other directions, came into jeopardy with the adoption of images by the church, for this showed that the worship of the orthodox was addressed to a plurality of objects. The proliferation of icons and of worship addressed to them meant that there were now "many Lords" and "many Christs," and that amounted to polytheism. For if the worship of God alone was the duty of men and of angels, how could the single worship of an image be addressed to Christ? Or were there not in fact two kinds of worship, one addressed to Christ and the other to the image? If such was the case, this was blasphemy and idolatry. In formulating this equation of image and idol, the iconoclasts were drawing their argumentation from a respectable lineage of orthodox theologians, who had sought to demonstrate the superiority of the gospel to paganism on the grounds that worship was now being rendered to the Creator rather than to the creature.

Less evident in this lineage, but not completely absent, was another line of accusation against Christian images, the christological argument stated in the fourth century by Eusebius and Epiphanius. After the first defeat of iconoclasm by the seventh ecumenical council held at Nicea in 787, this argument became increasingly prominent in iconoclastic polemics, hence also in orthodox responses; and eventually it came to provide the orthodox with their own most effective doctrinal (as distinguished from political) weapon. It was a seemingly obvious inference from

Martin (1930) 115

Ex.20:4

ap.Thdr.Stud.*Antirr*.3.1.55 (*PG* 99:413)

ap.Niceph.*Antirr*.3.28 (*PG* 100:420)

ap.Thdr.Stud.*Antirr*.1.16 (*PG* 99:345)

See vol. 1:239, 223

See pp. 203–4, 230–33 below

ap.Thdr.Stud.*Antirr*.1.2 (*PG* 99:329)

1 Cor.8:5
ap.Thdr.Stud.*Antirr*.1.9 (*PG* 99:337)

ap.Thdr.Stud.*Antirr*.3.39 (*PG* 99:424)

See pp. 101–2 above

See vol. 1:157–60

See vol. 1:344–47

Dion.Ar.*D.n.*3.1 (*PG* 3:680)

Dion.Ar.*C.h.*3.2 (*PG* 3:165); Max.*Myst.*24 (*PG* 91:705)

ap.Niceph.*Antirr.*1.42 (*PG* 100:308)

CCP(754)ap.CNic.(787) (Mansi 13:252)

ap.Joh.H.*Const.*4 (*PG* 95:317)

ap.Thdr.Stud.*Antirr.*3.1.39 (*PG* 99:408)

ap.Niceph.*Antirr.*3.38 (*PG* 100:437)

the christological development when theologians used the relation between the human and the divine in Christ as an epitome of the dialectic between finite and infinite, as this dialectic manifested itself, for example, in the relation of the earthly and the heavenly elements in the Eucharist. Such an application of the christological analogy to other doctrines became all the more congenial to Eastern Christians when the thought of Dionysius the Areopagite interpreted the relation between time and eternity, between the ecclesiastical hierarchy and the celestial, as part of a great ontological "chain." For the present discussion it was a matter of great historical significance that one of the favorite technical terms in the Dionysian tradition for this chain of being between the various levels of reality was "image." Hence it was altogether natural for the combatants in the struggle over images to introduce in evidence the doctrine of the person of Christ.

The taxonomy of christological heresies since the fourth century and the proliferation of dogmatic vocabulary about the person of the God-man supplied the iconoclasts with a variety of proofs that the champions of the images were being heterodox in their doctrine of Christ. These proofs could be summarized in a disjunctive syllogism: Either an image of Christ essayed to picture him in both his divine nature and his human nature, or it contented itself with picturing him only in his humanity. If it were to claim to be doing the former, it would be maintaining that the divine nature was susceptible of being circumscribed in a portrait [περιγραπτός]. Anyone who said anything of this sort was guilty of foolishly supposing that "with the circumscription of the created flesh he has also circumscribed the deity, which cannot be circumscribed." But this violated the orthodox doctrine of the deity of Christ, which, according to the iconoclasts, was "incapable either of being circumscribed or of being comprehended or of suffering or of being grasped." This total person in his two natures was the only image of God, and the image shared with the prototype this quality of incomprehensibility. Some of the iconoclasts appear to have taught that it was permissible to draw a portrait of Christ before his suffering, death, and resurrection, but that after the resurrection even his body had inherited immortality and could not be circumscribed in a portrait. But the iconoclasts seem usually to have maintained that

ap.Joh.D.*Imag.*2.4; 3.2 (*PG* 94:1285; 1320)

Thdr.Stud.*Antirr.*3.1.40 (*PG* 99:408)

ap.Niceph.*Antirr.*1.42 (*PG* 100:308)

ap.Thdr.Stud.*Antirr.*3.1.22 (*PG* 99:400)

ap.Niceph.*Antirr.*2.1 (*PG* 100:329)

CCP(754)ap.CNic.(787) (Mansi 13:252)

See vol. 1:263–66

ap.Niceph.*Antirr.*1.9 (*PG* 100:216)

ap.Niceph.*Antirr.*1.19 (*PG* 100:232)

CCP(754)ap.CNic.(787) (Mansi 13:257)

ap.Niceph.*Antirr.*1.23 (*PG* 100:253)

"the saving miracles and sufferings of Christ" even before his resurrection were not to be represented in images, for these had also been the deeds of the one divine-human person. In response the orthodox had to agree, of course, that "as the image of the Father, [Christ] cannot be circumscribed," but they urged that the incarnation had made this image portrayable. This, according to iconoclasm, amounted to running from the error of teaching that the deity could be portrayed to the error of dividing the two natures of Christ.

For if the Logos had taken up the human nature into his own divine hypostasis, which was invisible and without outward form, an artist who claimed to be drawing an image of this human nature was separating it from the person of Christ. As Constantine V put it, "if someone makes an image of Christ, . . . he has not really penetrated the depths of the dogma of the inseparable union of the two natures of Christ." Anyone who defended images by saying that "we are drawing the image . . . only of the flesh" of Christ had lapsed into Nestorianism. At Chalcedon in 451 the orthodox church had defined the doctrine of the person of Christ as "acknowledged in two natures without confusion, without change, without division, without separation." Employing this same technical vocabulary, the iconoclasts could now charge the champions of the images with christological heresy. The union of the natures was "without confusion . . . , that is, dual in one person, even though every image is known to be derived from some prototype"; hence the only proper use of the term "image" in the case of Christ was to describe his relation to the Father. It was impossible to draw a portrait of this one person without confusion of the natures —unless, that is, one went to the opposite extreme and violated the second pair of prohibitions in the Chalcedonian decree. If the divine nature "remains without separation [from the human] even in the suffering" of Christ, it followed that one could not draw a picture either of the suffering or of any other incident or aspect of the life of Christ unless one could draw a picture of the divine as well, which was by definition impossible. To draw an image without the divine nature was to make Christ a mere creature, as though there were only a human nature in him. Because the two natures were inseparable, such a portrayal, in effect, made the man Jesus a fourth person

ap.Niceph.*Antirr*.1.22 (*PG* 100:248–49); CCP(754)ap. CNic.(787) (Mansi 13:257)

in the Trinity by claiming to be able to deal with him apart from the Logos. Orthodox christology had come to the position that there was no separate person of the man Jesus. If, then, his human nature was "man in the universal," how could he possibly be portrayed in a tangible and polychrome image?

ap.Thdr.Stud.*Antirr*.3.1.15 (*PG* 99:396)

Thus "on the iconoclastic side the strongest weapons were the prohibitions of the Old Testament, the essential concept of the image and the christological dilemma first

Alexander (1958) 53

proposed by Constantine V." But the extrapolation of principles from christology for new areas of doctrinal concern was a game at which two could play. By accepting the iconoclasts' definition of the issue as a christological one, the defenders of the images were able to say that the two parties appeared to be in agreement about the hypostasis of Christ but appeared to disagree about the natures and the relation between them; but by the time this dispute was over, the iconoclasts, who had introduced the christological argument, stood accused of not having a

Niceph.*Antirr*.1.20 (*PG* 100:237)

proper view of the hypostasis either. They were not able to resist the demands of popular and monastic piety, especially when these were reinforced with imperial authority, and this was what defeated them; but the doctrinal form that these demands took was, in its most decisive formulation, the application of the orthodox dogma of the incarnation to the controversy about images.

Images as Icons

The reverence for images was deeply seated in the piety of Eastern faithful and was passionately defended by the monks, but it remained for John of Damascus, Theodore of Studios, and the patriarch Nicephorus to provide it with an elaborate theological defense. Like the thought of the iconoclasts, iconophile theology has been divided into several periods: the "traditional," the "christological," and the "scholastic." For our purposes, however, the loyalty

Alexander (1958) 189

to the images expressed in what was believed by the people, the defense of the images expressed in what was taught by the theologians, and the victory of the images expressed in what was confessed by the orthodox councils should all be treated together. Whether one calls the system of Theodore an "iconosophy compounded of super-

Harnack (1931) 2:490

stition, magic, and scholasticism," or whether one regards Nicephorus as "perhaps the most penetrating among the

Ehrhard (1897) 150

defenders of the cult of images," the doctrinal definition of images as icons won out over the doctrinal definition of images as idols largely through the theological clarification provided by these three thinkers of the eighth and ninth centuries and by some of their lesser-known associates. It was under their leadership that orthodoxy decreed "that the venerable and holy icons be erected, just as the form of the revered and life-giving cross is . . . in the holy churches of God . . . , namely, the icon of our God and Savior Jesus Christ, as well as that of our immaculate Lady, the Holy Mother of God, and those of the revered

CNic.(787)Act.7 (Mansi 13:378)

angels and of all the saints and holy men." In reflecting on the relation between this formulation and the previous history of the church, the iconophiles saw themselves as the legitimate heirs of ancient orthodoxy and saw the iconoclasts as standing in continuity with ancient enemies of the true faith. Older heresies had erred on the hu-

Joh.H.Const.18 (PG 95:336)

Niceph.Antirr.2.6 (PG 100:344–45)

manity of Christ, iconoclasm on his deity; older persecutors had warred against the living saints, these men even against the dead saints. While such persecutors had been guilty of evil deeds, heretics had until now been content with evil words, but the iconoclasts had resorted to deeds

Niceph.Imag.60 (PG 100:245)

as well as to words in their campaign against the images. So it was that the devil led the enemies of the church from one extreme to the other, from worshiping the images of men and animals in paganism to destroying the images of

Joh.D.Imag.2.4 (PG 94:1285)

Christ and the saints in iconoclasm.

As the iconoclastic identification of images as idols rested on a particular definition of what an authentic image ought to be, so the iconophile defense of the images as icons proceeded from its own and quite different definition. This definition took various verbal and logical forms.

1 Cor.13:12

On the basis of the apostle Paul, John of Damascus defined an image as "a mirror and a figurative type, appropriate to

Joh.D.Imag.2.5; 3.2 (PG 94: 1288; 1320)
Dion.Ar.E.h.2.8.2 (PG 3:397)

the dullness of our body." On the basis of Dionysius the Areopagite, Theodore of Studios defined it as "a likeness of that of which it is the image, in itself showing by imitation the character of its archetype . . . the true in the

Thdr.Stud.Ep.imag. (PG 99:500–501); Steph.Bostr.fr. (ST 76:203)

likeness, the archetype in the image." Other definitions, some of them by these same thinkers, appeared without explicit reference to the supporting authority of Scripture or tradition. Theodore of Studios called the image "a kind of seal and representation, bearing within itself the au-

Thdr.Stud.Antirr.1.8 (PG 99:337)

thentic form of that from which it also gets its name." Apparently drawing upon pre-Christian usage, John of

Joh.D.*Imag*.2.11; 3.10 (*PG* 94:1296; 1333)

Joh.D.*Imag*.3.16 (*PG* 94:1337)

Damascus defined an image as "a triumph, a manifestation, and a monument in commemoration of a victory," in this case the victory of Christ and his followers over the demons. Again, he defined it as "a likeness, an illustration, and a representation of something, showing forth in itself that which is imaged." One of the most complete and abstract of such definitions was provided by Nicephorus, who itemized the component elements of the image as: "a likeness of an archetype, having impressed upon it the form of what it represents by similarity, differing from it only by the difference of essence in accordance with the materials [of which they are made]; or an imitation and similitude of the archetype, differing [from it] in essence and substance; or a product of some technical skill, shaped in accordance with the imitation of the archetype, but differing from it in essence and substance."

Niceph.*Antirr*.1.28 (*PG* 100:277)

Niceph.*Antirr*.1.30 (*PG* 100:280)

Underlying all these definitions, even the most abstract ones, was the idea that an image had to be understood and defined on the basis of that to which it was related, its "to what [πρός τι]." This idea implied, on the one hand, a close relation and, on the other hand, a precise distinction, between the image and that which was imaged. "By nature," then, "Christ is one thing, and the image of Christ is another, and yet there is an identity because they are called the same." The identity was not, as iconoclast theory had maintained, an identity of essence between the image and the prototype. On the contrary, an image had to be "a likeness that characterizes the prototype in such a way that it also maintains some distinction from it." Even before the controversy over the images, such definitions had been formulated by Maximus, who had noted that "although an image bears an immutable and, in a sense, a perfect likeness to its archetype, nevertheless it is different from it in essence," especially because, in the case of Christian images, the original was living and the image was not; hence it was essential to distinguish between likeness and identity. Artistic skill could imitate the true nature of that which it represented, but this did not make the original and its image identical in essence. From all of this it followed that when one paid worship to an image, one was thereby worshiping not the essence of the image, but rather the imprint of the prototype that had been stamped as a seal onto the image.

Thdr.Stud.*Antirr*.1.11 (*PG* 99:341)

Niceph.*Antirr*.1.30 (*PG* 100:280)

Joh.D.*Imag*.1.9 (*PG* 94:1240)

Max.*Schol*.*E*.*h*.4.1 (*PG* 4:152–53)

Niceph.*Antirr*.1.16 (*PG* 100:225)

Thdr.Stud.*Antirr*.3.3.2 (*PG* 99:421)

By clarifying the nature of the image and of its relation

to its prototype, the iconophile theologians were able to put their defense of the icons into the framework of a much more comprehensive classification of images. On the basis of Pseudo-Dionysius, they could interpret the universe as a graduated hierarchy of images, in which there existed a close relation and a creative involvement between the image and its prototype, but not an identity of essence. In various developments of this stratification of images, John of Damascus identified several senses of the term "image" in Christian language about God: the Son of God as the image of the Father; the Father's eternal will to create images and paradigms for the visible world; the visible things that acted as physical types of the invisible prototypes; man as a creature "in the image of God" and therefore "called into being by God as an imitation"; the Old Testament "types," which foreshadowed what was to come in the New; images erected as memorials, whether in books or in pictures, in words or in objects, in commemoration of glorious deeds in the past, pointing backward as the Old Testament shadows had pointed forward. As a special example of the last category, the icons could justify themselves in opposition to the attempt to see them as Christian idols. Despite the obviously Neoplatonic implications of speaking about preexistent images on the basis of which God had created the particular realities of this visible world, such a classification provided a general setting in support of the case being made by the iconophiles.

Joh.D.*Imag*.1.9–13; 3.18–23 (*PG* 94:1240–44; 1340–44)

Nicet.Steth.*Jud*.20 (*SC* 81:436)

The case was strengthened, in their judgment, by their ability to appeal to what must be called "psychological" arguments for the icons. Such arguments began quite early in the campaign for Christian images. Writing in the first or second decade of the seventh century, Leontius of Neapolis asked his readers whether one would not, for example, kiss the clothing of his departed wife in her memory, and maintained that Christian icons were no more than especially vivid examples of such memorials. Similarly, John of Damascus noted: "I have often seen those with a sense of longing, who, having caught sight of the garment of their beloved, embrace the garment as though it were the beloved person himself." Christian worship of the icons was an instance of this same devotion, in which respect and affection were being paid to the garment, but were in fact addressed to the person of the

Leont.N.*Serm*.3 (*PG* 93:1600)

Joh.D.*Imag*.3.10 (*PG* 94:1333)

departed, be it Christ or his mother or some other saint. It was in this sense that he saw an image as a mirror appropriate to the dullness of the human physical constitution. Because such was the human condition, the use of such props as images was quite appropriate. If, for example, a pagan were to say to a Christian, "Show me your faith, so that I too may believe," the Christian would begin at the point where his hearer stood, leading him from the data of sense experience to things invisible. Specifically, he would take his friend to church and show him the icons there, so that the pagan would ask about these figures and in this way open himself to the Christian message. Such arguments suggested that the use of icons in Christian worship was not a relapse into paganism, but a concession to the psychology of all normal men, whether Christian or pagan.

One feature of this psychology that had special relevance to Christian images was the role of sight among the senses. In classical antiquity various authors had attempted to identify this role by considering the several senses and their special functions. Christian thought inherited the interest in "the distinct senses," specifying that "hearing is one thing, sight another, and the others likewise." As Photius said in a discussion of an icon of the Virgin, "sight, having touched and encompassed the object through the effusion of optical rays, transmits to the mind the essence of what has been seen." This was reinforced by the language of Scripture about sight. When Christ said, "Blessed are your eyes . . . and ears," he gave his endorsement to the quest for beatitude through seeing, and therefore for the use of icons as a present-day substitute for the miracles and other deeds which his disciples were privileged to behold. When the prophet Isaiah, in his inaugural vision, saw the Lord upon his throne in the temple, this was proof that sight took precedence over hearing "by its local position and by the nature of its sense experience." Originally, sight and hearing had been co-ordinated, for the message contained in the Gospels came by word of mouth to those who had seen the events it described. Now the icons could act as a substitute for such seeing. "The eye comes first," Theodore argued, and Nicephorus pointed out that in many cases sight proved to be more effective than hearing. Being able today to see the life-giving tree of the cross made up for the fateful

Marginal source citations (left column):

Joh.D.*Imag.*2.5;3.2 (*PG* 94:1288; 1320)

Joh.H.*Const.*10 (*PG* 95:325)

Arist.*An.*2.7–11; 3.1–2; Herodot.*Hist.*1.8; Hor.*A.p.* 180–82
Max.*Schol.D.n.*7.2 (*PG* 4:345); Psell.*Cant.*2.2 (*PG* 122:573)

Phot.*Hom.*17.5 (Laourdas 170–71)

Matt.13:16–17

Joh.D.*Imag.*3.12 (*PG* 94:1333)
Is.6:1

Thdr.Stud.*Antirr.*3.1.2 (*PG* 99:392)

Niceph.*Antirr.*3.4 (*PG* 100:381)
Thdr.Stud.*Or.*9.8 (*PG* 99:781)

Niceph.*Antirr.*3.3; 3.5 (*PG* 100:380; 384)

Gen.3:6

Thdr.Stud.*Or*.2.4 (*PG* 99:696)

Joh.D.*Imag*.1.17 (*PG* 94:1248)

Joh.D.*Imag*.3.3 (*PG* 94:1320)

Joh.H.*Const*.9 (*PG* 95:325)

Joh.D.*Imag*.2.23 (*PG* 94:1309)

Joh.D.*Imag*.3.12 (*PG* 94:1336)

Joh.D.*Imag*.1 (*PG* 94:1264)

Thdr.Stud.*Ref*.4; 8 (*PG* 99: 445; 452)

Thdr.Stud.*Ref*.2 (*PG* 99:444)

"seeing" of the tree of the knowledge of good and evil in Paradise. Hence each of the senses was hallowed by the saving action of God. Sight, as the primary sense, was hallowed through the visible appearing of God in Christ, just as hearing was hallowed through the word of God. The icon served as a means for this hallowing of sight, combined as it was with the hearing of the word.

When they put such an emphasis on the role of the senses in worship, the iconophiles were affirming the role of the body in salvation—of the physical body of Christ as the means of achieving it and of the physical body of man as a participant in it together with the soul. The iconoclasts claimed to worship the invisible God in a purely spiritual and mental way, disdaining the use of visual aids such as images. But "how do you, as someone who is visible, worship the things that are invisible?" Of course the soul could adore the one God, invisible and immaterial, but to do so it required the aid of visible means. Only through such means could one proceed to the worship in spirit and truth. The biblical law and the patterns of Christian worship were material things, but "they lead us through matter to the God who is beyond matter." Man was body as well as soul, and the means of grace were accommodated to this condition; therefore there was a baptism in water as well as in the Spirit, and therefore man also needed to see the divine represented in images. Or, as it was put by John of Damascus, from whom much of this argumentation came, "Perhaps you are sublime and able to transcend what is material . . . , but I, since I am a human being and bear a body, want to deal with holy things and behold them in a bodily manner." The spiritualism of the iconoclasts seemed to put them into the same class with the ancient Gnostics, who claimed that the body of Christ was not physical but heavenly, and who despised the physically minded believers as less spiritual than they. Such statements accorded with the interest of the iconophiles in the use of images as a substitute for books in the instruction of illiterate believers.

On the basis of these convictions about doctrine and worship, iconophiles replied indignantly to the charge of idolatry: "The truth is not error, nor are we running back to idolatry." The accusation against them was based on a

Niceph.*Imag*.73 (*PG* 00:789)

Thdr.Stud.*Antirr*.1.7 (*PG* 100:337)

Niceph.*Antirr*.1.29 (*PG* 100:277)

Thdr.Stud.*Ref.* (*PG* 99:440); Petr.Sic.*Hist*.7 (*PG* 104:1249)

Niceph.*Antirr*.3.40 (*PG* 100:453)

Niceph.*Imag*.47; 82 (*PG* 100:696; 809) Leont.N.*Serm*.3 (*PG* 93:1601)

Thdr.Stud.*Icon*.1 (*PG* 99:485)

Niceph.*Imag*.48 (*PG* 100:700)

Niceph.*Antirr*.1.42 (*PG* 100:308)

Niceph.*Imag*.41 (*PG* 100:661)

Thdr.Stud.*Antirr*.2.6 (*PG* 99:356)

Niceph.*Antirr*.3.17 (*PG* 100:401)

failure to make some fundamental distinctions. Because the iconoclasts did not distinguish between the sacred and the profane, they did not understand that there could not be any relation between the temple of the true God and the worship of idols. "What person with any sense does not comprehend the distinction between an idol and an icon?" An idol was the representation of persons or things that were devoid of reality or substance, while an icon represented real persons; those who failed to observe this distinction were the ones who should be charged with idolatry. Ultimately, the distinction between the two was this: the images of heathen worship were devoted to the service of the devil, but the icons of Christian worship were dedicated to the glory of the true God. As Theodore of Studios said in one of his acrostic poems, the representation of Christ in an icon was a way of dispelling idolatry, not of reinstating it. The tree of the cross had replaced the wood of pagan worship, and the eucharistic sacrifice had come in place of heathen rituals; so also the holy memorials of the Savior had overthrown the various unclean monuments of the Gentiles. Was it fair to accuse the entire church, including the faithful departed, of a shameful complicity in idolatry? For "if I worshiped idols, why would I honor the martyrs, who destroyed idols?" It was not accurate to describe the worship of icons as idolatry, for "to make a god" meant to worship something that was not divine as though it were. The true worshipers of the Holy Trinity had excluded and put aside all idolatry in the service of the true God. Their orthodoxy was a via media between the false spiritualism of the iconoclasts and the false materialism of the idolaters. Every remnant of the "heathen and mortal mind" had been set aside in their orthodox confession and purified worship.

Because such was the true state of orthodox worship, it was a distortion of Scripture for the iconoclasts to apply to it the biblical passages that prohibited making and worshiping false gods, or for them to ask, "Where is it written [in Scripture] that the icon of Christ is to be worshiped?" The answer to this rhetorical question was: "Wherever it is written that Christ is to be worshiped." In support of their attack on the icons, the iconoclasts were falsely interpreting the statements of Scripture and the "sayings of the mystagogues of the church," the fathers.

Thdr.Stud.*Antirr*.1.7 (*PG* 99:337)

Is.19:1

Matt.2:13–15
Thdr.Stud.*Or*.3.4 (*PG* 99:704)

See vol. 1:377

Niceph.*Imag*.78 (*PG* 100:801)

Col.1:15

Gen.1.27
Joh.D.*Imag*.3.26 (*PG* 94:1345)

Ex.20:4

Ex.36:8; 35
Joh.D.*Imag*.3.9 (*PG* 94:1329)

Heb.9:5

Niceph.*Antirr*.2.8 (*PG* 100:348)
Niceph.*Imag*.70 (*PG* 100:769); Thdr.AbuQ.*Imag*.10 (Arendzen 19); Steph. Bostr.*fr.* (*ST* 76:204); Ps.Anast.S.*Jud.dial*.2 (*PG* 89:1233); *Troph.Dam.* 3.6.3 (*PO* 15:246)
Heb.9:13
Joh.D.*Imag*.1.20 (*PG* 94:1252)

Matt.22:16–21

Joh.D.*Imag*.3.11 (*PG* 94:1333); Joh.H.*Const*.5 (*PG* 95:321)

Heb.10:1
Joh.D.*Imag*.1.15 (*PG* 94:1245)

Gen.19:1

Heb.2:16
Joh.D.*Imag*.3.26 (*PG* 94:1348)

By "applying to the icon of Christ" those "scriptural statements directed against the idolatrous representations of the Greeks," they were misconstruing the intent of Scripture. The coming of Christ, whose image the orthodox church worshiped, had put an end to idolatry; when Scripture prophesied that "the idols of Egypt will tremble at his presence," this was a prediction of the flight of the Christ child to Egypt. Passages such as Isaiah 63:7–14 (LXX), which had been used by earlier defenders of the faith to prove the identity of essence between the Father and the Son, were useful to the orthodox as proof that they were not guilty of idolatry. In fact, according to Scripture, God himself had been the first to have images of himself. First was the eternal Son of God as "the image of the invisible God"; then came Adam, made in the image of God.

The most important proof text in the iconoclast arsenal was the prohibition of graven images in the Decalogue, delivered to Israel through Moses. Yet the same Second Book of Moses that contained this prohibition also contained, a few chapters later, the account of his building the tabernacle, complete with images of cherubim. When one made images of cherubim, these could not be, as were the cherubim themselves, incorporeal, but, as the language also of the New Testament showed, had to be "holy images of them," which were nevertheless referred to as "cherubim." It was evident, then, that the cherubim were depicted in human form. In addition to the cherubim, there also were in the temple the blood and ashes of sacrificed animals; these had now been replaced by the images of the saints, as the rational took the place of the irrational. The saying of Jesus about giving to Caesar what was Caesar's and to God what was God's meant, as the context made clear, that one gave the image of Caesar to Caesar; so also one was to give the image of God to God. The very law that prohibited images was, according to the New Testament, itself only a "shadow" and not yet the "image" of the things to come. In the account of Abraham on the plain of Mamre, he was said to have worshiped an angel. But if God had taken on himself not the form of an angel but that of man in Christ, was not this human form to be worshiped even more? By reading the biblical evidence differently and, in effect, reinterpreting the law of the Old Testament in the light of the incarnation taught in the New Testament, the iconophiles rejected the argumentation of the iconoclasts from Scripture and laid claim to the authority of Scripture for themselves.

In a similar way they laid claim to the authority of the practice of Christian worship—indeed, even to that of Jewish worship. To the Jewish attack on icons, the orthodox replied: "As you, in worshiping the Book of the Law, are not worshiping the nature of the parchment or of the ink, but the words of God in them; so I, when I worship the image of God, am not worshiping the nature of the wood and the colors (God forbid!), but, holding the lifeless portrait of Christ, I hope through it to hold and worship Christ himself." Such argumentation was even more pertinent in the discussion between Christian and Christian. If icons were not to be worshiped because they were products of human skill, what, if anything, could be worshiped? Specifically, could the altar or the Gospels or even the cross be the object of proper worship? The worship of the symbol of the cross appears to have been of special concern to the iconoclasts. While maintaining that there should be no distinction, the iconophiles, if pressed, would have to say that "the image of Christ is more deserving of honor and reverence than the symbol of the cross." If, as both iconoclasts and iconophiles taught, there was a special power in the symbol of the cross of Christ, how much more power must there be in the symbol of the Crucified himself, that is, in his icon? A demonstration of such power had come repeatedly in miraculous deeds ascribed to the icons. It was a general axiom that "no reasonable man dare accept any religion that is not founded on divine miracles, which are a proof that their worker truly comes from God." Precisely this was true of the icons, for by the relics and icons of the saints demons had been exorcised, miraculous appearances had been effected, and sinners had been converted. Defending the icons and attaching their arguments to the iconoclasts' assertion of the real presence in the Eucharist, the iconophiles maintained that the doctrine of the real presence, which the faith and practice of the people appears to have validated beyond any refutation, led inescapably to a justification of the icons and of their worship.

Yet such worship had to be squared with the demand of the divine law: "You shall worship the Lord your God, and him only shall you serve." How was it possible for

Thdr.AbuQ.*Imag*.5
(Arendzen 7–9)

Leont.N.*Serm*.3 (*PG*
93:1600)

Joh.H.*Icon*.3 (*PG*
96:1352)

Niceph.*Antirr*.3.35 (*PG*
100:428)

Thdr.Stud.*Or*.2.5 (*PG*
99:697)

Thdr.AbuQ.*Mim*.1.2 (Graf
90); Thdr.AbuQ.*Imag*.6
(Arendzen 9–10)

Leont.N.*Serm*.3 (*PG*
93:1601)

Deut.6:13;Matt.4:10

Christians to pay worship to icons in the light of so exclusive a demand? To reply to this troubling question, the orthodox were obliged to set forth a theory of worship that would protect the uniqueness of the worship of the true God and yet permit other acts of reverence. When iconoclasts argued that "there is only one kind of worship, not many kinds," the orthodox replied that "this is true of the worship of adoration [ἡ λατρευτική]" but that the worship of mortals, for example of kings, was nevertheless permissible by analogy and derivation from the single worship of God. If this was permissible in the case of kings and other earthly rulers, it was even more appropriate in the Christian attitude to the saints and to their icons. There was a "worship of adoration, which we pay only to the God who is by nature adorable." But there was also a worship paid to "the friends and worshipers of God" for his sake, because of their derivative divine nature; this included both angels and saints. Adoration pertained only to God, but either by love or by reverence or by law one was also bound to others to whom one paid worshipful respect. The distinction was grounded in biblical evidence about worship paid to creatures by men whose adoration of the one true God was beyond reproach. When such men worshiped the places and objects associated with Christ, "it is not the place nor the house nor the location nor the city nor the stones that we honor," but Christ, the incarnate one who made himself manifest through them.

Thdr.Stud.*Antirr.*1.19 (*PG* 99:348);Thdr.AbuQ.*Imag.*9 (Arendzen 18)

Joh.D.*Imag.*1.14 (*PG* 94:1244)

Niceph.*Antirr.*3.10 (*PG* 100:392)

Joh.D.*Imag.*1.8 (*PG* 94:1240)

Leont.N.*Serm.*3 (*PG* 93:1600)

Of course it was not only Christ whose image the iconophiles wanted to worship but also the saints and angels, and, second only to Christ himself, his mother, the Theotokos. "Who has ever seen death worshiped or suffering revered?" asked John of Damascus. "Yet we worship the bodily death of my God and his saving suffering. We worship thine icon. We worship all that is thine, thy ministers, thy friends, and above all thy mother, the Theotokos." Christ was the natural image of the mother who gave birth to him [εἰκὼν φυσικὴ τῆς τεκούσης αὐτὸν μητρός], which apparently was intended to mean that reverence paid to her and to her image was paid to his image and to him. In her case, therefore, the worship of her icon was not a revival of the pagan custom of adoring earth mothers and maternal deities, because she was the

Joh.D.*Imag.*1.conc. 94:1281)

Thdr.Stud.*Antirr.*3.2.1 (*PG* 99:417)

Thdr.Stud.*Icon*.1 (*PG* 99:489)

Thdr.Stud.*Or*.5.2 (*PG* 99:721)

Joh.D.*Imag*.2.11 (*PG* 94:1293–96)

Joh.D.*Imag*.2.15 (*PG* 94:1301)

Thdr.Stud.*Or*.8.8 (*PG* 99:768)

Joh.D.*Imag*.1.21 (*PG* 94:1253)

Luke 1:11

Thdr.Stud.*Or*.7.5 (*PG* 99:752)

Theotokos—not a goddess, but the bearer of one who was God. In a sermon on the "dormition [κοίμησις]" of the Virgin, Theodore of Studios paid respect to her "shaded icon," with its sunlike representation of her appearance. The fathers of the church had torn down the temples of demons and had replaced them with temples named for the saints; so also they had thrust aside the images of the demons and had put in their place the icons of Christ, of the Theotokos, and of the saints. The worship of the saints did not conflict with, but supported, the worship of Christ. It was characteristic of orthodox worship that "we portray Christ as King and Lord in such a way that we do not deprive him of his army. Now the army of the Lord are the saints." The study of the icons of the saints was a way of appropriating their history, as was evident, for example, in the case of John the Baptist. The real choice before the iconoclasts was not between the retention and the abolition of the icons; it was between the abolition of the icons and the retention of the memory of the saints at all, for this memory was inseparable from the icons. Considering the role played by angels in the lives of the saints, and of course also in the life of Christ, the icons of the angels also had a legitimate place; for when the Gospel said that an angel of the Lord appeared to Zechariah, the father of John the Baptist, this meant that he must have assumed a visible form, hence one that could be represented in an image. The orthodox defended the images of Christ, but also the images of his mother, of the other saints, and of the angels against the accusation that idolatry had been surreptitiously reintroduced into Christendom by the patrons of the icons.

The accusation of idolatry and the response to it struck at a deep and sensitive point in Christian belief. Nevertheless, the most elaborate and significant arguments over icons were not those that dealt, either pro or con, with this accusation, but those that took up the later and more specifically Christian charge that representations of Christ in images were inadmissible because he was simultaneously divine and human. This charge had not been prominent in early stages of iconoclasm, though it had been present in the arguments of Epiphanius and Eusebius. Its revival in the more sophisticated forms of iconoclasm was at least partly responsible for the prominence of the christological defense in the definitive forms of iconophile theology. The connection between the argument over idolatry and the christological argument becomes clear, for example, in the contention of John of Damascus that the prohibition of images and likenesses was based on the absence of any "form on the day that the Lord spoke" in the Old Testament. But now, with the incarnation of the divine Logos in Jesus Christ, the situation had changed and there was a "likeness [ὁμοίωμα]" of God available; therefore the prohibition was superseded, since "the lawgiver interprets it." Not every piece of Old Testament law was automatically binding on the church, which had now received "more divine and more sacred legislation." Before the incarnation in Christ a representation of the Logos in an image would indeed have been "inappropriate and alien." The prohibition had been addressed to those who lived before the age of grace and who needed to be led to a recognition of the divine "monarchy," that is, of monotheism. All of that had been reversed; now it was not the use, but the prohibition, of icons that was "inappropriate and alien."

Because of this reversal, "iconoclasm, according to [John of Damascus], is a species of docetism, a disrespect for the mystery of God-manhood." The reality of the incarnation of the Logos provided the authorization for Christians to make icons. To deny this was to diminish the genuineness of the humanity of Christ, for "man has no characteristic more fundamental than this, that he can be represented in an image; that which cannot be represented this way is not a human being, but an abortion." Moreover, the incarnation was not a debasement for Christ but an honor, so that it was not true loyalty to him to seek to protect him from the limitation and circumscription of a genuinely human body. According to a classic proof text for the incarnation, Philippians 2:5–11, Christ had two "forms [μορφαί]," the form of God and the form of a slave. Certainly according to the latter he could be represented in an image. While it was true that by its union with the divine Logos the body of Jesus had been made divine, yet even after the resurrection it had not been transformed or transplanted into the ousia of the Godhead. The complex structure of christological and trinitarian metaphysics and the precise technical terminology of the debates before and after Chalcedon were

Ex.20:4
Deut.4:15–18

Joh.D.Imag.3.7 (PG 94:1325)

Niceph.Antirr.3.40 (PG 100:456)

Thdr.Stud.Ref.13 (PG 99:457)

Thdr.Stud.Antirr.1.5 (PG 99:333)

Florovskij (1933) 250

Joh.D.Imag.2.16 (PG 94:1304)

Thdr.Stud.Ref.3 (PG 99:444–45)

Thdr.Stud.Antirr.1.7 (PG 99:336)
See vol. 1:255–58

Niceph.Antirr.1.38 (PG 100:293–96)

Niceph.Antirr.3.39 (PG 100:444)

Thdr.Stud.*Prob*.13
(*PG* 99:484)

Thdr.Stud.*Ep.imag.*
(*PG* 99:502)

See pp. 88–89 above

Thdr.Stud.*Antirr*.3.1.17
(*PG* 99:397); Niceph.*Antirr.*
2.17 (*PG* 100:365)

See p. 73 above

Niceph.*Antirr*.1.48 (*PG*
100:325)

Niceph.*Antirr*.1.44 (*PG*
100:312)

Martin (1930) 187

ap.Phot.*Ep*.2.102
(*PG* 102:925)

now put into the service of a theological validation for the worship of icons.

Working in this framework, Theodore of Studios drew a parallel between the eternal relations within the Trinity and the relations between the two natures in the economy of the incarnation: as in the Trinity that which was distinctive of each hypostasis did not divide the unity, so in the incarnation that which was distinctive of each nature "does not divide the one hypostasis of God the Logos"; from this it followed that Christ could be represented in an image. Again, the Father and the Son were one in nature but two in hypostasis, while Christ and the image of Christ were one in hypostasis but two in nature; from this it followed that there was only one mode of worship, whether addressed to the entire Trinity because of the unity of nature or to the icon of Christ because of the unity of hypostasis. In the christological debates it had been concluded that the Logos had taken on a universal human nature, which found its hypostasis in him; this, too, proved that it was appropriate to draw an image of the incarnate one. The orthodox teaching that there were two actions in the incarnate Logos, not one, was likewise taken to prove that an icon of the person of Christ was permissible. Anyone who read Scripture would find it speaking of "Christ crucified" or calling Jesus of Nazareth "Son of God"; the iconoclasts ignored this "mode of communication," by which the properties of one nature were attributed to the entire God-man. In all these arguments "Theodore [as well as his colleagues] uses the words . . . as they are used in Trinitarian theology. . . . He adopts the phraseology of Dionysius and identifies it with the phraseology of the Trinitarian formula."

The adaptation of trinitarian and christological technical vocabulary to the defense of the icons was made necessary by the christological argument of the iconoclasts, that it was impossible to draw a picture of one who was both God and man without either claiming to represent the divine nature (which was blasphemy) or attempting to divide the natures and to portray only the human (which was heresy). The central issue in the christological argument over the icons, therefore, was the question whether it was possible or permissible to "circumscribe [περιγραφεῖν]" Jesus Christ—a question that was to recur long after the controversy. To this the first response was

Joh.D.*Imag*.2.5; 3.2 (*PG* 94:1288; 1320)

Niceph.*Imag*.71 (*PG* 100:781)

Niceph.*Antirr*.2.18 (*PG* 100:367)

Thdr.Stud.*Prob*.5 (*PG* 99:480)

Niceph.*Antirr*.1.20 (*PG* 100:233–36)

Thdr.Stud.*Antirr*.3.1.6 (*PG* 99:392)

Niceph.*Antirr*.2.13 (*PG* 100:360)

Niceph.*Antirr*.2.19 (*PG* 100:369)

Niceph.*Antirr*.3.49 (*PG* 100:468)

See vol. 1:250

Joh.D.*Imag*.3.8 (*PG* 94:1329)

to make clear that it would be a sin to make an image of the invisible and uncircumscribed God, or to make an image of a man and call it a god. Neither of these, however, was what the icons were claimed to be. They were representations of "Christ, our God, who took upon himself our poverty and . . . body. . . . Why should he not be portrayed or circumscribed?" When Christ was in the temple in Judea, he was not at the same time bodily in Galilee, even though he was "everywhere and above all things as God" and was therefore uncircumscribed. For if Christ was both God and man, he was, obviously, uncircumscribed according to his divine nature, but, equally obviously, circumscribed according to his human nature. Otherwise the distinction between the two natures was eliminated. If Christ could not be circumscribed, he could not suffer either, for both of these attributes were corollaries of his deity; yet Scripture said that he did suffer, and therefore he could also be circumscribed. To be completely precise, however, "a picture does not circumscribe a man, even though he is circumscribed; nor does circumscription depict him, even though he is capable of being depicted." What was going on in the making of icons was not circumscription, since Christ was not bodily present, but depiction. The issue of circumscription was in fact a false issue. It did not apply to the icons of the Theotokos and the saints, who had only a human nature; yet the iconoclasts objected to these as well.

The real issue, as the iconophiles saw it, was the reality of the history of Christ, which the icons sought to portray. As the christology of Cyril of Alexandria had been preoccupied with "the concrete scenes of the Gospel," so the iconophile argument hinged on the identity of content between the verbal and the pictorial descriptions of such scenes. John of Damascus enumerated the deeds of Christ —his descent from heaven for the incarnation, his birth from the Virgin, his baptism in the Jordan, his transfiguration on Mount Tabor, his sufferings, his miracles, his burial, resurrection, and ascension. "Describe all of these," he declared, "both in speech and in colors, both in books and in pictures." John of Jerusalem was even more detailed in cataloguing the events and even the tangible physical objects of Gospel history, such as the swaddling cloths in the Christmas story, the palms on the road at Christ's entry into Jerusalem, the sponge and the lance at the crucifixion.

Joh.H.*Const*.3 (*PG* 95:313–16)

1 John 1:1

John 4:6; 6:19; 2:12

Thdr.Stud.*Ref*.1 (*PG* 99:441–44)

Joh.Maur.*Carm*.10.16–17 (Lagarde 8)

Niceph.*Antirr*.1.23 (*PG* 100:256)

Joh.H.*Const*.8 (*PG* 95:324–25)

Niceph.*Imag*.61 (*PG* 100:748)

Joh.H.*Const*.3 (*PG* 95:316)

Niceph.*Antirr*.1.37 (*PG* 100:292)

Thdr.Stud.*Antirr*.3.3.15 (*PG* 99:428)

Thdr.Stud.*Ep.imag*. (*PG* 99:505)

"This beautiful exposition and beneficial description, how do you dare to call it idolatry!" Theodore of Studios, quoting the opening verse of the First Epistle of John, "That which . . . we have seen with our eyes, which we have looked upon and touched with our hands," proceeded to identify specific scenes from the life of Christ, primarily from the Gospel of the same apostle John: Christ seated at the well, walking on the water, visiting Capernaum. As the Gospel writers had been able to "write of Christ in words [λογογραφεῖν]," so it was also possible to "write in gold [χρυσογραφεῖν]" by depicting these scenes in icons. The genuineness of the incarnation meant that these scenes and these objects were to be portrayed as "graphically" as possible, whether in words or in icons.

For despite the differences between the two means, the same content was being set forth in the icons and in the accounts of the Gospels, and "the same history" was to be seen in both. As in the Gospels, so in the icons one could see "the noble deeds of the pious and the wicked deeds of the impious." The iconoclasts were making a both/and into an either/or, requiring a choice between the Gospels and the icons. But if the Gospels and the cross were to be revered, the icons were also: "If the one is worthy of honor, the other is worthy of honor also." Since the content of Scripture and that of the icon were identical, "why do you worship the book and spit upon the picture?" Consistently carried out, the opposition of the iconoclasts to the use of pictures ought to lead to a similar hostility toward the Gospels as well. "Either accept these [icons]," Nicephorus demanded, "or get rid of those [Gospels]." With such argumentation as this, iconophile theology attempted to prove that the use of the icons not only accorded with the orthodox teaching of the church about the Trinity and the person of Christ, but also was a practice implied in the picture of the person of Christ handed down in the New Testament.

The work of Christ, no less than his person, was at issue in this debate, according to the iconophiles. To make this point, Theodore of Studios invoked the traditional distinction between "theology" and "economy." He went so far as to argue that if "the worship of the icon of Christ" were to be abolished, "the economy in Christ" would also have to be abolished. By this he apparently meant that the theological assumptions underlying iconoclasm implied a view of Christ that would have made salvation through him impossible, for such a Christ as it taught could not have assumed and transformed genuine humanity. If, as the iconoclasts said, Christ had come in a body that could not be portrayed in a picture, then the salvation attributed to him was invalidated. Only a truly human Christ could save, and it belonged to true humanity to be susceptible of portrayal. In "theology" as distinct from "economy," there could not be any discussion or consideration of a similitude or picture, and it was to this that the Mosaic prohibition applied. But in "economy," similitude was entirely in place. In this way the doctrine of the icons and the doctrine of salvation supported each other, through the doctrine of the incarnation. Arguing in a similar fashion, Nicephorus accused the iconoclasts of teaching, in effect, that Christ either did not know how or did not want or was not able to achieve the salvation of mankind. Far from representing either a relapse into idolatry or a distortion of orthodox christology, the practice of icon-worship was the only permissible corollary of the one holy and catholic faith. "There is," Theodore asserted at the beginning of his polemical treatise against the iconoclasts, "one faith and one adoration and one worship among us Christians, namely, that of the Father and the Son and the Holy Spirit," and this one faith and worship not only permitted, but required, the worship of icons.

It would, of course, be altogether fatuous to imagine that the nuances of this christological defense of icons were intelligible to the illiterate believer on whose behalf both sides claimed to be speaking. Yet it was his faith that was ultimately at stake in these debates. It does seem clear that for the hoi polloi of the church the icons were a cherished object of religious devotion and a valued source of religious instruction, "books for the illiterate." At the same time, the recurrence of objections to their presence in Christian worship is cogent evidence that, even as they were using them in their devotional life, many Christians continued to have misgivings about their propriety in the light of the biblical strictures against image-worship. The refutation of the iconoclast accusation of idolatry partially allayed these misgivings, but they could not be laid to rest until the theologians had made their case that, as worship paid to Jesus Christ, the second person of the Trinity, did not militate against biblical

Thdr.Stud.*Ref*.3–4 (*PG* 99:444–45)

Ex.20:4
Thdr.Stud.*Antirr*.2.4 (*PG* 99:353)

Niceph.*Imag*.75 (*PG* 100:793)

Thdr.Stud.*Antirr*. 1.1 (*PG* 99:329)

Joh.D.*Imag*.1 (*PG* 94:1268)

faith in the oneness of God, so worship paid to the image of Jesus Christ, and to the images of his mother and of the saints, was not inconsistent with this faith either. In this sense what was believed by the people in their devotion to the icons was taught by the theologians in their subtle application of christology to the icons and was eventually confessed by the seventh ecumenical council of the church in its reinstatement of the icons and in its anathema upon those who fought the icons.

The Melody of Theology

The doctrine that triumphed over iconoclasm was not merely a justification of the place of icons in Christian liturgy and devotion. It was a liturgical doctrine, or, as one of its most articulate proponents termed it, "the melody of theology." Speaking of the role of the icons in worship, Nicephorus asserted that they conveyed "theological knowledge" about a divine reality that transcended all being. "They are," he continued, "expressive of the silence of God, exhibiting in themselves the ineffability of a mystery that transcends being. Without ceasing and without silence, they praise the goodness of God, in that venerable and thrice-illumined melody of theology."

Niceph.*Imag*.70 (*PG* 100:773)

The liturgical argument in support of the icons took various forms. In response to the charge that images were idols and that the iconophiles had reintroduced idolatry into the church by their worship, Nicephorus quoted from *The Liturgy of Basil,* which both the iconophiles and the iconoclasts used in their services. After the singing of the Trisagion, the prayer of the priest went on to praise Christ because he had "delivered us from the error of idols and introduced us to the knowledge of thee, our true God and Father." If the iconophiles also recited this prayer in *The Liturgy of Basil,* he twice retorted, they could not be accused of idolatry in their veneration of the icons. In the same *Liturgy of Basil* the priest offered up the sacrifice of the body and blood of Christ. From this Nicephorus concluded that, to be sacrificed, the body of Christ had to be a real and tangible body. The interpretation of the Eucharist as a sacrifice had long stood in close relation to the doctrine of the real presence in the Eucharist, and Nicephorus also related the two ideas to each other. What he added to them in his eucharistic thought was the argument that the body of Christ, tangible and real enough in

Lit.Bas. (Brightman 326)

Niceph.*Imag*.26; 27 (*PG* 100:601; 604)

Lit.Bas. (Brightman 329)

See vol. 1:167–69

Niceph.*Antirr.*2.19 (*PG* 100:373)

its presence to be a sacrifice, therefore also had to be the kind of body that could properly be represented in an image. "How," he asked in a peroration, "can that which is uncircumscribed be sacrificed?" The doctrine of the real presence became the most clinching of proofs for the iconophile solution to the inconoclast dilemma of the "circumscription" of the body of the God-man. Circumscription in the icon became another instance of the circumscription whose reality in the incarnate Christ and in the eucharistic Christ all orthodox theologians were obliged to acknowledge.

Niceph.*Antirr.*3.59 (*PG* 100:484)

Elsewhere Nicephorus formulated this generalization explicitly. Speaking of the liturgical action of "our priests," he asserted that "they express the form of the orders of being that transcend this world." This they did "both in the divine liturgies and in the other forms of worship which they celebrate." Among such forms of worship were also the icons; for once it was admitted that the real presence in the eucharistic liturgy could be generalized, the holy images were the most obvious instances of "other forms of worship" in the churches. In a parallel passage, Theodore of Studios demanded of his opponents: "What do you call the things that are spoken in cultic language and sung in hymns by the priest?" He went on to enumerate various parts of the liturgy, in which the mysteries of salvation through Christ were depicted. Those same mysteries were also depicted in the icons. Like the liturgy, the practice of image-worship was binding on the church by the authority of tradition. "The law," Theodore said in another place, "is utterly sacred, namely, the ancient customs which the great Basil commands us to keep. It has been established by the tradition of the church, as the church under heaven proclaims by her deeds in her sacred temples and offerings, that since the beginning, from the outset of the divine proclamation [of the gospel], the holy images were erected, those which you now condemn. Behold, then, the legislation of the church on this issue!" Liturgical law, coming from custom and tradition, extended not only to the celebration of the Eucharist, but to the icons as well. By such argumentation as this, "the triumph of the venerators of images under Irene and Theodora restored the union between liturgy and art," but also the union between liturgy and doctrine in official

Thdr.Stud.*Antirr.*1.10 (*PG* 99:340)

Thdr.Stud.*Ref.*29 (*PG* 99:469)

Dalton (1911) 648

Byzantine theology, which became once more, as it had been before iconoclasm, a liturgical theology.

A liturgical theology, by Byzantine definition, would be one in which the praise and worship of the church, as expressed in its liturgy, simultaneously determined and was determined by the church's doctrinal confession. When the liturgy spoke of praising God in "ceaseless theologies," this specified the content of theology as doxology. The Trisagion of the liturgy, derived from Isaiah 6:3, could be called "theology," and the "gold" spoken of in 1 Corinthians 3:13 was "theological mystagogy." The Gospel story of the boy Jesus in the temple was a source for "theology." Clearly the word did not refer only to the reflection and systematization carried on by the erudite, but to the doctrine set forth in worship and instruction. Worship had a special function in such a "theology," for it could convey the knowledge of the unknowable. To the question, "Who can understand the incarnation?" Maximus replied: "This only faith can grasp, as in silence it reveres the Logos." Faith could be defined as "an assent devoid of rationalization and of undue curiosity"; by means of such faith one went on to grace, which conveyed a special kind of knowledge by the Holy Spirit, and by this knowledge one accepted "the things that have been handed down by tradition to the catholic church." Faith did not require logical demonstrations and did not indulge in logomachies, but simply and spontaneously assented to revealed truth, which was accepted by "faith alone."

The definition of faith in relation to doctrine and liturgical practice could be elaborated. When the iconoclasts asked to be shown where Christians were commanded to worship icons, Nicephorus replied by pointing to "faith, as well as the inward and spontaneous impulse of believers toward divine things." To this was added "the practice that has been handed down by tradition to the church, confirmed by the passage of a long period of time and still prevailing." All of this was consistent with "the natural law within us" and with "the law set down in letters." Traditional liturgical practice took its place within this pattern of authority, where it was coordinated with the orthodox confession of the church. *The Liturgy of Basil* spoke of "rendering the appointed worship and doxology"

Lit.Bas. (Brightman 323)

Max.*Schol.E.h*.4.5 (*PG* 4:156)

Max.*Qu.dub*.73 (*PG* 90:845)
Luke 2:41–52
Thdr.Stud.*Or*.3.5 (*PG* 99:704)

Max.*Ambig*.5 (*PG* 91:1057)

Niceph.*Antirr*.3.2 (*PG* 100:377)

Niceph.*Imag*.82 (*PG* 100:813)

Niceph.*Antirr*.3.10 (*PG* 100:392)

Lit.Bas. (Brightman 313; 322)

and of "praising, hymning, blessing, and worshiping thee." Doctrine was based on this doxology, which was in turn conformed to true doctrine; for "as the word of the gospel" had been spread over all the earth, so also had "the proper mode of doxology and worship." The church was holy, apostolic, and orthodox if it "accepts all divine things obediently, and adores, worships, and reveres them all faithfully and unquestioningly." Theodore of Studios spoke of the harmony between "praise and confession" in the exhibition of the holy cross, which was the content of both. The remembrance of the history of Christ "in every ritual" of worship was a way of illumination for the mind, for by sharing in the hymns of the angels at the birth of Christ the church was able to "behold the ineffable" and to know the unknowable. What the church did in the Eucharist "in remembrance of me" was simultaneously "completely manifest knowledge," "participation in the divine mysteries," and obedience to "the things that have been commanded by divine tradition."

Niceph.*Imag.*36 (*PG* 100:632)

Joh.H.*Icon.*8 (*PG* 96:1356)

Thdr.Stud.*Or.*2.1 (*PG* 99:692)

Luke 2:14
Thdr.Stud.*Or.*3.3 (*PG* 99:701)

1 Cor.11:24-25

Thdr.Stud.*Ref.*6 (*PG* 99:448)

Divine tradition found its characteristic expression in the writings of John of Damascus. His *Fountain of Knowledge* presented the philosophical presuppositions, the polemical and historical development, and the orthodox articulation of characteristically Eastern religious tenets. "Like a bee," he said, "I shall gather all that conforms to the truth, even deriving help from the writings of our enemies. . . . I am not offering you my own conclusions, but those which were laboriously arrived at by the most eminent theologians, while I have merely collected them and summarized them, as far as was possible, into one treatise." With the aid of philosophy he was able to incorporate into his system the results of the christological debates, the Eastern attitude toward angels, saints, and icons, and the solution of ethical and practical problems on the basis of the tradition. His writings became the classic exposition of Eastern dogmatics, destined to influence most major theologians of both East and West until the Reformation, although it should be noted "that the influence of the Damascene was in fact probably greater in the West than in the East, thanks to a circumstance that was, to be sure, in some sense accidental, namely, that his *Exposition* was translated relatively early and thus constituted one of the few bridges by which scholasticism had access to the literary deposit of the

Joh.D.*Dialect.*pr. (Kotter 1:52-53)

Hoeck (1951) 59

Greek fathers." Of particular importance was the way this system, together with other expositions that followed it, correlated icon and incarnation, worship and dogma, piety and theology.

As a traditional system, liturgical theology was bound to the doctrines and practices of the orthodox past. For example, the practice of genuflexion was affirmed because it had come down "from the fathers." Loyalty to the fathers and to their tradition implied that a distinction had to be drawn between an idea that had "the confirmation of dogmatic formulation" and an idea that was merely "a theory, albeit one that is set forth by a saint," even though the latter also had some force because it had been handed down. It was likewise important to distinguish the formulations set down in the language of technical theology from the simple beliefs of the faithful, but this distinction was one chiefly of form rather than of content. The same Scripture that was a weapon against heretics was also the foundation of lay piety, as Theodore's mother showed when she memorized and recited the psalms of "the divine David" amid her household duties. The place that brought together the scholarly exegesis of Scripture and the devotional recitation of Scripture, the technical dogmatic vocabulary of the erudite and the inarticulate affirmation of the simple, was the "melody of theology" in the liturgy. Every doctrine of the orthodox creed was a liturgical doctrine, for the creed was recited in the liturgy. Nevertheless, some doctrines were liturgical in a special sense, because they had been articulated more satisfactorily in worship than in dogma. Even though some of them would eventually be defined as orthodox by a council, they were at this time, and in a way would always remain, liturgical rather than dogmatic in their fundamental character.

Such a doctrine, preeminently, was the atonement. Maximus had spoken of "a remedy from all these evils" and "a shortcut to salvation, the true love of God in accordance with a knowledge of him," but then he went on: "For this is the true worship, genuinely pleasing to God, the strict discipline of the soul by means of the virtues." It was in moral discipline and in liturgical worship that the meaning of salvation was enunciated. *The Liturgy of Basil,* at its very beginning, saluted Christ as "our Lord and God, Jesus Christ, Savior and Redeemer and Ben-

Thdr.Stud.*Or*.11.3.16
(*PG* 99:817)

Thdr.Stud.*Antirr*.2.18–19
(*PG* 99:365)

Thdr.Stud.*Or*.11.4.24
(*PG* 99:828)

Thdr.Stud.*Or*.13.3 (*PG* 99:885)

See vol. 1:141–52

Max.*Qu.Thal*.pr. (*PG* 90:260)

Lit.Bas. (Brightman 309)

efactor." The specification of what this meant and of how the salvation had been achieved came especially in the liturgical apostrophes to the holy cross. Christ had "given himself over to death as an exchange" and had "come by the cross into Hades, in order that he might fulfill in himself the pangs of death and, by arising on the third day, open the way for all flesh to the resurrection of the

Lit.Bas. (Brightman 327)

dead." The centrality of the resurrection of Christ to the atonement was emphasized even further when the very words of institution were amplified to include the command: "For as often as you eat this bread and drink this cup, you proclaim my [Christ's] death and you confess

Lit.Bas. (Brightman 328)

my resurrection." This amplification not only put the words of the apostle Paul in 1 Corinthians 11:26 into the mouth of Christ, but added the words, "You confess my resurrection" even to those of Paul. The resurrection was no mere declaration that an atonement achieved by the crucifixion was acceptable to God, but an integral and decisive part of an atonement that consisted in Christ's victory, through both crucifixion and resurrection, over the powers of death and Hades.

The thought of the liturgical theologians developed the themes of the liturgy. They did speak of the crucifixion as a sacrifice and describe Christ as simultaneously the priest

Niceph.Imag.52;68 (PG 100:724; 764)

of the sacrifice and the victim. But when they came to speak in more detail about the cross, it was the imagery of battle and victory that seemed to serve them best. The same treatise in which the idea of sacrifice appeared developed this imagery at greater length, affirming that "our Lord and God Jesus Christ" had achieved "victory over

Niceph.Imag.27; 36 (PG 100:608; 628)

death" by his resurrection on the third day. The apostrophe to the cross celebrated "this tree, on which the Lord, like

Thdr.Stud.Or.2.1 (PG 99:693)

a prince, was wounded in battle . . . by the wicked dragon." Death was often represented as the insatiable dragon which had devoured all men and sought now to devour

Niceph.Imag.50 (PG 100:705)

Christ on the cross. But while other men had been helpless before the dragon, Christ had prevailed over him by his death and resurrection. "Christ has arisen from the dead, and the whole cosmos has cause for rejoicing. By his life-giving death he has killed death, and all those who were

Thdr.Stud.Or.4.1 (PG 99:709)

in the bonds of Hades have been set free." The blood of Christ was a "ransom" for sin, as theologians quoted from the New Testament; but then they went on to quote, also from the New Testament: "When he ascended on high he

Eph.4:8
Niceph.*Imag*.44 (*PG*
100:680)

Max.*Schol.E.h*.3.11 (*PG*
4:149)

led a host of captives," which meant that he led a tri-
umphal procession after his victory. The victory over
Satan, moreover, had not been won by deception, but
fairly, "in judgment and in justice." Nothing was further
from their minds than any disjunction between the crucifixion and the resurrection of Christ as means of atonement, but the language of the liturgy made the themes of
battle and victory a natural way of describing the way of
salvation.

The praise of the life-giving cross was, moreover, a
theme of the liturgy and of the icons on its own. Both
The Liturgy of Basil and *The Liturgy of Chrysostom*
prayed: "King and Lord, God of hosts, save thy people
and grant them peace by the power of thy Holy Spirit,
through the symbol [τύπος] of the precious cross of thine
only-begotten Son, who is blessed with thee forever and

Lit.*Bas*.; Lit.*Chrys*. (Brightman 314)

ever." In the invocations of both liturgies, the church
prayed for the sake of "thy saving sufferings, thy life-
giving cross, thy three-day burial, thy resurrection from
the dead, thy ascension into heaven, thy sitting at the
right hand of God and the Father, and thy glorious and

Lit.*Bas*.; Lit.*Chrys*. (Brightman 328–29)

awesome second coming." Not only on Easter, but even on
the Sunday of Mid-Lent, "on this day the all-holy cross is
worshiped and the resurrection of Christ is proclaimed.
Today the life-giving tree is worshiped, and the entire

Thdr.Stud.*Or*.2.3 (*PG*
99:693)

cosmos is reawakened to praise." The symbol of the cross
had been prefigured in the Old Testament, but was being fulfilled also in the present, through conquests over
the barbarians, through the expulsion of demons, and

Thdr.Stud.*Or*.2.4–5
(*PG* 99:696–97)

through miraculous cures. The iconoclasts had also been
devotees of the symbol of the cross and had given it preference over the icons, ascribing to it the power that the
iconophiles claimed for the images. Now the iconophiles
connected the cross to the icons, in which it played an
important role, and through it developed their interpretations of the doctrine of the atonement.

Another doctrine whose principal locus was liturgical
was the doctrine of the Virgin Mary. To be sure, dogma
had also spoken of her and had defined her as "Theotokos."

See vol. 1:261

Yet even this dogmatic formula had been derived from

Rom.Mel.*Hymn*.1.24
(*SC* 99:92)

devotion and liturgy, which continued to be a seedbed of
ideas and titles; for "to introduce the name of Mary and
hymns to Mary into all possible pieces of ancient liturgical
treasure was one of the predominant concerns of the

Fedotov (1966) 1:54

Lit.Bas. (Brightman 314)

Lit.Chrys. (Brightman 314)

Lit.Bas.; Lit.Chrys.
(Brightman 330; 331)

Rom. Mel.*Akath.Oik*.46
(Eustratiades 55)

Rom.Mel.*Akath.Kont*.1
(Eustratiades 52)

Psell.*Salut*.5 (PO 16:522);
Psell. *Com.Sim.Met*.5 (PG
114:204)

Lazarev (1960) 27–30

Leont.N.*Serm*.3 (PG
93:1601)

Germ.I.*Dorm*.2
(PG 98:356–57)

Thdr.AbuQ.*Mim*.1.2 (Graf
90); CCP(681)*Act*.15
(Mansi 11:608–9)

Theoph.Nic.*Theot*.7.15
(Jugie 82–84)

Thdr.Stud.*Ref*. (PG
99:437–40)

Thdr.Stud.*Or*.6.9
(PG 99:741)

Niceph.*Antirr*.2.4
(PG 100:341)

Thdr.Stud.*Or*.5.1; 5.4
(PG 99:720; 725)
Joh.Maur.*Carm*.27
(Lagarde 12–13)
Germ.I.*Dorm*.3
(PG 98:468–69)
Thdr.Stud.*Or*.5.3
(PG 99:724)

Gen.5:24; 2 Kings 2:11

Byzantine liturgists." *The Liturgy of Basil* spoke of "the intercessions of the Holy Theotokos," and the same phrase appeared also in *The Liturgy of Chrysostom*. Later in the service she was acclaimed in both these liturgies as "our all-holy, immaculate, supremely blessed Queen [Δέσποινα], the Theotokos and ever-Virgin Mary." Byzantine hymnody had developed the praise of the Virgin Mary even further, most notably in the hymn *Akathistos*, often ascribed to Romanus the Melodist, where she was called "unwed bride" and, in some versions, "the invincible general" who delivered Constantinople from invaders by her miraculous intervention. She was "the guard of the channel, and . . . the fortress . . . for defense against hostile forces," as well as "temple, throne, and ark of God, who is the King of all." One more title for Mary in Eastern devotion was "the unshaken wall [nerušimaja stena]," represented in the eleventh-century mosaic of her in the Cathedral of Saint Sophia in Kiev. Innumerable miracles were credited to the icons of the Theotokos, and the lives of Byzantine saints are replete with accounts of conversions and cures effected by her—all presumptive evidence, by commonly accepted standards, for the validity of the iconophile position.

Byzantine theologians took up these liturgical and devotional motifs into their expositions of the faith. Most of these theological expositions, of course, were written in prose, but Theodore of Studios, for one, composed an acrostic poem in praise of the Theotokos and in refutation of the iconoclasts. She was, he said elsewhere, the only one in all history who, participating in an angelic nature, which transcended human nature, nevertheless chose to have a family and to share in ordinary human existence. The iconoclasts had erred gravely in their attacks on the saints, and especially on the very first among the saints, the supreme among all the creatures, "our most holy Queen, the Mother of God." She was "the Empress and the Lady of the entire universe . . . , the throne of mercy for mortals throughout the universe." At her "dormition," a favorite subject of painters, she was surrounded by apostles, martyrs, and saints, as well as by Enoch and Elijah (both of whom were assumed into heaven at the end of their earthly lives). "We confess and proclaim," Nicephorus wrote, "that she has been appointed as [our]

mediator and secure patron in relation to him [her Son],
on account of the confidence she has as his mother." A
special object of her interest as mediator and patron was
the welfare and purity of the church: "granting peace to
the church, strengthening orthodoxy, protecting the empire, driving away the barbarian tribes, maintaining the
entire Christian people."

Many of these mariological ideas were to be developed
much more fully as theological concepts, and eventually
also as ecclesiastical dogmas, in later centuries. But before
they were confessed by the church or even taught by the
theologians, they had already been believed and celebrated
by the liturgy and devotion of the people. The defense of
mariology also lent support to the cult of the other saints,
as they were portrayed in their own icons. Directly after
her name, *The Liturgy of Basil* and *The Liturgy of
Chrysostom* cited that of "Saint John, the Forerunner and
Baptizer," followed by the name of the particular saint
whose feast day was being celebrated, and then by the
commemoration "of all the saints, by whose intercessions
do thou look down upon us, O God." Opposition to the
icons had sometimes been a form of hostility to the cult
of the saints, so that the revival of liturgical theology included a reassertion of the prerogatives of the saints. Citing
the person of John the Baptist, Theodore spoke of the
activities of all the saints, who rewarded from heaven those
who sang their praises. In fact, "the saints performed the
same miracles as the apostles did." In this way the re-
habilitation of the icons was also a reaffirmation of the
role of the saints in the church—above all of the Virgin,
but also of all the other saints—as participants in the life
and service, but especially in the liturgy, of the worshiping
community, which located itself within the continuity of
"all the saints who from all ages have been well-pleasing
to thee, the forefathers, fathers, patriarchs, prophets,
apostles, preachers, evangelists, martyrs, confessors, disciples," and all the faithful.

Although the cult of the saints and that of the angels
were in fact linked in the decrees of the Council of Nicea
in 787, the doctrine of angels followed its own path of
development in theology as well as in liturgy. Certainly
one factor in this development was the role assigned to the
angels in the speculations of Dionysius the Areopagite, for

Dion.Ar.*C.h*.6.2 (*PG* 3:200–201)

Rom.Mel.*Hymn*.24.1; 28.2 (*SC* 114:110; 236)

Lit.*Chrys*. (Brightman 313)

Lit.*Bas*. (Brightman 312)

Lit.*Bas*. (Brightman 323)

Thdr.Stud.*Or*.6.1 (*PG* 99:729)

Thdr.Stud.*Or*.2.2 (*PG* 99:693)

Thdr.Stud.*Or*.6.1 (*PG* 99:732)

Joh.Maur.*Carm*.24.7–8 (Lagarde 12)

Joh.Maur.*Carm*.pr. (Lagarde 2)

whom the angels formed the missing ontological link between the visible world and the invisible world. But interacting with this philosophical and theological angelology was the liturgical sense that when the church worshiped God, it was doing so in the company of the angelic host. The liturgies gave repeated expression to this sense. Thus *The Liturgy of Chrysostom,* in its extended paraphrase of the Trisagion, sang: "Holy is God, who is worshiped and glorified by a multitude of holy angels and archangels invisibly trembling before him. Holy is God, who looks with unsleeping sight upon the many-eyed cherubim and ceaseless sound . . . and mounted upon the six-winged seraphim." *The Liturgy of Basil* likewise invoked God as the one who had "established brigades and armies of angels and archangels for the service of thy glory." Later it prayed: "Thee the angels, archangels, thrones, lordships, principalities, authorities, and powers, together with the many-eyed cherubim, do praise." Theodore of Studios was echoing these liturgical doctrines when he spoke, especially in his preaching, of the angels as a "precosmic cosmos before this cosmos, who announce to this cosmos a cosmos that is above the cosmos, namely, Christ." When the liturgy of the church praised God, it did so in the company of the angels, together with apostles, prophets, martyrs, and all the righteous. The hymns of the angels had been incessantly praising God in an ineffable chorus before the divine tabernacle, either heaven or the church or both. The doctrine of angels is a preeminent example of liturgical doctrine; for the icons and the liturgy were far more explicit in describing the angels—not as they were by nature, but as they became visible—than the dogma of the church ever became, and in their angelology the theologians were following the orthodoxy of proper worship rather than that of proper teaching.

These several themes taken together—Christ as Savior through his cross and resurrection, Mary the Mother of God and the other saints, and the angels as fellow worshipers—were the subjects of most of the icons. Therefore the incorporation of their message into the "melody of theology" was a way of defending the icons and at the same time of articulating Christian doctrine even in areas where the dogmatic legislation of the church had not yet spoken. But the effort to systematize this liturgical theology must treat one more doctrine, not necessarily included as a theme for iconographic portrayal but presuppposed by the icons, namely, church and sacraments. Some aspects of it even appeared in icons; for example, the doctrine of baptism was never absent from icons of the baptism of Christ at the hands of John the Baptist. Yet the doctrine of the church, including the doctrine of the sacraments, was actually being articulated also in those icons that did not deal with pictorial representations of incidents in the Bible or in the lives of the saints, where these doctrines were the primary subject matter in the mind of the painter.

Joh.Maur.*Carm*.3.33–36
(Lagarde 3–4)

The doctrine of the church and the sacraments, although a matter of debate from time to time in the early centuries of Christian history, has in fact been more implicit than explicit through most of the centuries of doctrinal development, becoming an overt subject of discussion only when circumstances absolutely required it. Even when the theologians were not devoting special chapters of their dogmatics to it, however, this doctrine was a powerful element in their thought. How powerful it was can be seen best from the liturgy. *The Liturgy of Basil* prayed that God would "unite all of us who have shared in the one bread and in the cup into one fellowship of the Holy Spirit . . . with all the saints who from the ages have blessed thee." The church was gathered "in the sacred ritual of thy divine mysteries," as it said at the beginning of the service, "in the participation of thy holy, undefiled, immortal, and heavenly mysteries," as it said at the end. Through the sacramental mystery of baptism, believers became "members of thy holy church," who were deemed "worthy of the washing of regeneration, the forgiveness of sins, and the garment of incorruptibility"; they were united "to thy holy catholic and apostolic church" and included "in thy chosen flock." A special feature of the prayers for the church was the invocation of divine blessing upon "our most devout and most faithful emperor, whom thou hast endowed with justice to hold imperial sway on earth; crown him with the weapon of truth, with the weapon of thy good pleasure, cover his head in the day of battle; . . . subjugate to him the barbarian tribes which plot war."

See vol. 1:155–71

Rom.Mel.*Hymn*.2.3
(*SC* 99:106)

Lit.*Bas*. (Brightman 330)

Lit.*Bas*. (Brightman 310)

Lit.*Bas*. (Brightman 342)

Lit.*Bas*. (Brightman 315)
Titus 3:5

Lit.*Chrys*. (Brightman 315)

Lit.*Bas*. (Brightman 333)

During the debate over the icons, the doctrine of the church—its apostolic character, its worship, its orthodoxy, its sacraments, its relation to the empire—had been seriously at issue. The defenders of the icons saw themselves as simultaneously the defenders of that church which worshiped as it did in these prayers. This church might be coextensive with the empire, but it did not have to be; for "even if very few continue in orthodoxy and true religion, these few are the church, and the authority and the protection of the laws of the church reside in them." Recalling some of the scenes and symbols that appeared on the icons, Theodore depicted the church as the new Paradise, in which the cross was the tree of life and no demon could ever seduce an Eve again, because the angel of the Lord was standing on guard. Later he spoke of "the ineffable mystery" of baptism, "through which you have received a new birth in the Spirit and the right to be called a child of light." The one who was baptized, Nicephorus declared in the course of his defense of icons, confessed the orthodox doctrine of the Trinity, came to share in the salvation wrought by Christ, and was purified by the fire of the Holy Spirit. The prayers of the liturgy on behalf of the emperor found their echo in the liturgical theologians. On the one hand, they refused to concede to the emperor any right to interfere with the orthodoxy of the church. On the other hand, when an emperor—or an empress—did intervene to preserve or to restore orthodoxy, this was an act of obedience to the divine vocation of the imperial office. Writing to the emperor, Theodore asserted that God had given Christians "two gifts, the priesthood and the empire, by which affairs on earth are healed and ordered as they are in heaven." The controversies of the eighth and ninth centuries had compelled greater precision in the understanding of the relation between these two gifts, with the result that "with the end of iconoclasm caesaropapism was replaced by a dyarchy of emperor and patriarch."

For the development of Christian doctrine in the East, as distinguished from the development of relations between church and empire, this meant that the church, which had called itself orthodox all along, felt obliged to define its orthodoxy in a manner that would protect it from interference. Not the will of the majority, nor the ukase of the emperor, nor the subtlety of the learned could determine what was orthodox. The church was orthodox when it prayed and taught aright, in accordance with apostolic Scripture and apostolic tradition. It prayed aright when it asked God "to remember the en-

Niceph.*Apol*.8 (*PG* 100:844)

Thdr.Stud.*Or*.2.3 (*PG* 99:693)

Thdr.Stud.*Or*.3.2 (*PG* 99:701)
Niceph.*Imag*.36 (*PG* 100:628)

Joh.D.*Imag*.2.6 (*PG* 94:1288)

Thdr.Stud.*Ep*.1.16 (*PG* 99:961)

Ladner (1940) 142

2 Tim.2:15
Lit.Chrys. (Brightman 332)
Thdr.Stud.*Can.imag.*1
(*PG* 99:1769)

tire episcopacy of those who are orthodox, those who rightly handle the word of truth." The icons were "symbols of orthodoxy," for in them correct teaching and correct worship were united. It was a recognition of this role of the icons when the anniversary of the restoration of the icons, on the first Sunday in Lent, 11 March 843, came to be designated as the Feast of Orthodoxy. On this occasion, a document entitled *Synodicon* was promulgated; with various editorial additions, it has been read as part of the liturgy for the feast ever since. In it the orthodox church celebrated its restoration to "the reaffirmation of true devotion, the security of the worship of icons, and the

Meth.CP.*Syn.* (Gouillard 47)

festival which brings us everything that saves." Summing up the victory of the icons, the *Synodicon* declared: "As the prophets have seen, as the apostles have taught, as the church has received, as the theologians have taught, as the ecumene has agreed with one mind . . . so we believe, so we say, so we proclaim, honoring Christ, our true God, and his saints, in our words, writings, ideas, sacrifices, temples, and images." "This," it concluded, "is the faith of the apostles, this is the faith of the fathers, this is the faith of the orthodox, this is the faith that has sustained the

Meth.CP.*Syn.* (Gouillard 51)

ecumene."

4

The Challenge of the Latin Church

It has been almost possible to recount the history of the development of doctrine in Eastern Christendom to this point without explicit reference to the West—almost possible, but not quite, for as a matter of fact the Western church was a participant, from near or far, in every one of the doctrinal debates that we have examined. And from the ninth century to the eleventh, the schism between the Eastern and the Western parts of the orthodox and catholic church was itself a central issue of doctrinal debate and of doctrinal development.

There had, to be sure, been schisms before. The Gnostics and Montanists judged to be "outside the mainstream"; the Arians condemned as heretics at Nicea; the Nestorians and "Monophysites" who had maintained, and still maintain, a distinct existence after the christological conflicts of the fifth century; the iconoclasts and iconodules—all these and others had been involved in schism and division during century after century of Christian history. In some ways the most fundamental and far-reaching schism of all had been the early break between Christianity and its parent Judaism, a schism whose implications were to assert themselves repeatedly in Christian thought. Although these events make it impossible to claim that the church was a "seamless robe" until the conflict between Rome and Byzantium, the fact remains that "the schism between Eastern and Western Christians is one of the greatest calamities in the history of the Church." For "on the one hand, it seriously undermined the powers of resistance of the Christian East to the advance of Islam," and on the

John 19:23–24;
Cypr.*Unit.eccl.*7
(*CSEL* 3:215)

Zernov (1942) 6

Gibbon (1896) 6:370

Southern (1970) 67–68

See vol. 1:340

See vol. 1:354

See p. 37 above

Phot.*Ep*.2.90 (*PG* 102:900)

Cerul.*Sem*. (Will 157); Aen.
Par.*Graec*.pr. (*PL* 121:686)

Verg.*Aen*.2.65
Liut.*Leg*.30 (*MGH Scrip*.
3:353)

other hand, it hastened the centralization of Western Christendom, which "resulted in many abuses and provoked widespread discontent," so that "the Reformation itself, which split the West into two hostile camps, was one of its consequences."

We cannot—and for our purposes here, we need not—date the schism with any precision. Traditionally, the excommunication of the patriarch of Constantinople, Michael Cerularius, by the legates of the pope of Rome in 1054 has been identified as the "thunderbolt [from which] we may date the consummation of the schism." Although this excommunication did not, in the precise and technical sense, effect the institutional break between the two churches, still "it was in 1054 that all the elements of disunity which had come to light over the centuries were first concentrated into a single event." The formal severance of communion came later, but the loss of community had been there earlier. In many ways it seems correct to look for the religious and doctrinal origins of the split in the fourth, fifth, and sixth centuries, even though there was only occasional explicit acknowledgment of the widening gulf. For such acknowledgment we need to look at the "Photian schism" of the ninth century, when the doctrinal differences over questions ranging from the Trinity to the nature of the church came out into open controversy. As in the conflicts over the person of Christ, so in these controversies, the institutional and the doctrinal schism did not coincide chronologically, but acted reciprocally as cause and effect. "The church of God," lamented the patriarch Photius, was "divided. What divides it is the fear of God, as well as human fear." The rancor and snobbery—which expressed themselves in such judgments as the suggestion of Cerularius and other Greeks that those who lived in the direction of the sunset dwelt in darkness, or in the reminder of Liutprand that Vergil had already warned Latins against "the wiles of the Greeks"—were deeply felt and mutually expressed. Beyond their cultural significance, which is not our direct concern here, such statements also indicated a theological gap between East and West that must claim our attention. Yet it should not be forgotten that "from the eleventh to the fifteenth century, the union was the 'great ambition' of the Popes and Emperors" in both East

Bréhier (1936) 594

ap.Mich.Anch.*Dial.*
1 (Loparev 344)

and West. Emperor Manuel Comnenus was speaking for both sides when he said: "I yearn for peace, and I urge the union of those who have been called by Christ." That yearning remained unfulfilled for a variety of reasons, some of which had little or nothing to do with Christian doctrine, but others of which were fundamentally doctrinal; it is to these latter that we now turn.

The Orthodoxy of Old Rome

Dominating the jurisdictional and theological conflict between East and West was the massive fact of Rome's spotless (or nearly spotless) record for doctrinal orthodoxy. Amid all the vicissitudes of the centuries, when, as the Byzantine emperor, Constantine IV, wrote to Pope Leo II, "the hierarchs have become heresiarchs," it was the hierarch of Rome who had held firm, so that those "agree-

Const.Pogon.*Sacr*.2
(Mansi 11:721–22)

ing in theology with the ecumenical chief shepherd in spirit and in letter" were saved from error. The popes, too, made a point of this record. Quoting the promises and commands of Christ to Peter in Matthew 16:18–19 and in John 21:15–17, Pope Agatho declared, probably in Greek: "Relying on his [Peter's] protection, this apostolic church of his has never been deflected from the way of truth in the direction of any error whatsoever. The entire catholic church of Christ and the ecumenical councils have always embraced his authority as that of the

Agath.*Ep*.1 (*PL* 87:1169–70)

prince of all the apostles." Such absolutes as "never" and "always" meant, of course, that evidence of even one historically documented instance of deviation from orthodoxy would be sufficient to refute the claim.

The positive evidence of history was certainly cogent. The supreme example of the orthodoxy of Rome in the period covered by volume 1 of this work was the role played by Pope Leo I at the Council of Chalcedon, which was then cited over and over during the conflicts between East and West. The East had to admit that Leo had been

Mich.Anch.*Dial*.35
(Loparev 357)

hailed at Chalcedon as "pillar of orthodoxy" and had been remembered as such ever since. The christology of preexistence, kenosis, and exaltation espoused by Leo's *Tome* to Flavian attempted to accept what was correct about both extremes and to achieve an evangelical moderation on which most Christians could unite, and it carried the day. The fathers assembled at the council exclaimed: "Peter has spoken through the mouth of Leo!"

CChalc.*Act*.3 (*ACO*
2–I–2:81)

In the period with which we are dealing in this volume, East and West agreed that Leo had indeed been the spokesman for Peter and for the Holy Spirit at Chalcedon. "The divinely given and divinely inspired epistle of the great and brilliant and divinely minded Leo, of the most holy church of the Romans" was, according to Sophronius of Jerusalem, sacred and worthy of honor as a "producer of orthodoxy." The Council of Constantinople of 681 declared that "the letter of Leo [the *Tome* to Flavian], like the powerful [ῥωμαλέον] roar of a lion sounding from Rome," had frightened away the hunters. In the course of this very council, the christology of Leo and of Chalcedon was not only restated, but reinterpreted in a direction that brought it closer to that of Cyril of Alexandria; the meaning of some of Leo's formulas was also a factor in the debates. But all those who laid claim to Chalcedonian orthodoxy also thereby repudiated what Leo had called the "robber synod" of 449 in Ephesus and joined themselves to Chalcedon's encomium of the pope.

By the period we are considering here, this papal prerogative had been extended backward from Chalcedon to the three councils that had preceded it and forward from Chalcedon to all subsequent councils. For without Rome, so Nicholas I, the pope of Old Rome, wrote to Photius, the patriarch of New Rome, in 862, all the councils would have been "robber synods"—if, that is, "Leo the Great had not been an imitator of that lion of whom it is written, 'the lion of the tribe of Judah has conquered,' and if he, called of God, had not opened his mouth and struck terror into the hearts of the whole world, even of the emperors." Chalcedon proved, according to a Western theologian of this same century, that "the pontiff of the Roman see" had precedence over Constantinople and hence authority over councils. In fact, this theologian maintained that "every council, whether it was held in the Orient or in Africa, always either had presiding officers appointed by the Roman pontiff or had its decrees validated by the authority of letters from him. . . . Whichever councils were ratified by his declaration have remained in force, while those that he condemned have been regarded as null and void and have been unable to claim any authority at all." Therefore it was urged even by Theodore Abû Qurra, who also lived in the ninth century but wrote chiefly in Arabic and in Syriac, "that we should

Soph.*Ep.syn.* (*PG* 87:3188)

CCP(681) *Or.imp.* (Mansi 11:661)

See p. 65 above

See vol. 1:262–63

Ans.Hav.*Dial.*3.12 (*PL* 188:1226–28)

Rev.5:5

Nicol.I.*Ep.*88 (*MGH Ep.* 6:473)

Ratr.*Graec.*4.8 (*PL* 121:341)

Ratr. *Graec.*4.8 (*PL* 121:337)

Thdr.AbuQ.*Mim*.8.32
(Graf 222)

Phot.*Syn*.1 (*PG* 104:1220)

ap.*Avell*.195.3 (*CSEL*
35–II:652–53)

Lib.Car.1.6 (*MGH
Conc.Sup*.2:21)

Butler (1962) 370

build on the foundation of Mar Peter, who directed the six holy councils, which were assembled at the command of the bishop of Rome, capital of the world." On the other hand, Patriarch Photius argued both historically and theologically against "the canon that says that the bishop of Rome has the authority in every council." But one of his predecessors in the see of Constantinople, the sixth-century patriarch Epiphanius, had declared it to be his "prayer to unite myself to you [the pope] and to embrace the divine dogmas that had been handed down by tradition from the blessed and holy disciples and apostles of God, especially from Peter the chief of the apostles, to your holy see."

So it was that the authority of the fathers and the achievements of the councils came to be seen by most spokesmen for the West and even by some for the East as a corollary of the orthodoxy of Rome: Rome had been on the side that emerged victorious from one controversy after another, and eventually it became clear that the side which Rome chose was the one that would emerge victorious. In the two dogmatic issues that we have examined thus far, the doctrine of the person of Christ and the question of images in the church, the orthodoxy of Rome was a prominent element, in the first of these perhaps the decisive element, so that when the relation of East and West itself became a matter of debate, the Latin case could draw support from the record established not only in the early centuries but in the immediate past. Those who argued against the Latin case were not entirely bereft of documentation for their counterclaim that Rome had not been absolutely right every single time, but the weight of the evidence for the astonishingly high average accumulated by the see of Peter sometimes proved to be all but overwhelming.

The charge that Rome had sometimes erred and the claim that it had never erred could both find substantiation in the debate over wills and actions in Christ. In fact, the language used by Pope Honorius I in this debate was to be acknowledged even at the time of the First Vatican Council in 1870 as "the strongest obstacle from the side of Church History to the definition of papal infallibility." A thousand years earlier, in the controversy between East and West with which we are dealing here, the case of Honorius served as proof to Photius that the popes not only lacked authority over church councils, but were fallible in matters of dogma; for Honorius had embraced the heresy of the Monotheletes. The proponents of that heresy likewise cited the case of Honorius, not in opposition to the authority of the pope but in support of their own doctrine, urging that all the teachers of the true faith had confessed it, including Sergius, the bishop of New Rome, and Honorius, the bishop of Old Rome. Although this argument, addressed by Paul II, the successor of Sergius, to Theodore, the successor of Honorius, did not prevail, it does suggest the significance of Honorius's espousal of a theological position that cannot be labeled anything but "Monothelete," in fact if not in intention.

If we distinguish between Monenergism, the doctrine of one action [ἐνέργεια] in Christ, and Monotheletism, the doctrine of one will [θέλημα] in Christ, Honorius must be identified with the latter but not with the former, while many, perhaps most, who held to either doctrine held to both. When faced with the question of one action or two, he had stressed that there was one agent, the Lord Jesus Christ, who carried out divine as well as human actions through the humanity that was united to the Logos. Therefore the question of one action or two actions was declared to be insoluble on the basis of dogmatic authority and was ruled out of discussion. "The scandal of recently discovered novelty" was to be avoided, and "one agent" rather than "one action" was the proper christological formula. But Honorius's avoidance of Monenergism had as its corollary an explicit avowal of Monotheletism. "We confess," he wrote, "a single will of our Lord Jesus Christ, because our nature has truly been assumed by the divinity." It is evident, as Maximus noted in exoneration of Honorius, that his opposition to the idea of "two wills" was based on the interpretation of "two wills" as "two contrary wills." He did not mean that Christ was an incomplete human being, devoid of a human will, but that as a human being he did not have any action in his body nor any will in his soul that could be contrary to the action and will of God, that is, to the action and will of his own divine nature. "But this makes it possible to explain why Honorius was a Monothelete, not to deny that he was one."

The Council of Constantinople in 681 condemned the letter of Honorius, together with the letters of Sergius, as

Phot.*Syn*.1 (*PG* 104: 1220–21)

Paul.II.CP.*Ep.Thdr.* (*PL* 87:98)

Hon.I.*Ep*.4 (*PL* 80:471)

Hon.I.*Ep*.4 (*PL* 80:473)

Hon.I.*Ep*.5 (*PL* 80:475)

Hon.I.*Ep*.4 (*PL* 80:472)

Max.*Opusc*.20 (*PG* 91:244)

Max.*Opusc*.20 (*PG* 91:241)

Elert (1957) 239

"altogether alien to the apostolic doctrines, to the definitions of the holy councils, and to all the accepted fathers." After enumerating the false teachers who were to be posthumously excommunicated for their Monotheletism, the decree went on specifically to declare: "And with these we define that there shall be expelled from the holy church of God and anathematized Honorius, who was at one time pope of Old Rome, because of what we found written by him to Sergius, where he in all respects followed the latter's view and confirmed his impious doctrines." In his accompanying edict the emperor anathematized Honorius as "a companion in heresy with these men in every respect, a fellow traveler [σύνδρομος], and an affirmer of their heresy." That was also how the action of the council was understood in the West. Paraphrasing the decree, Pope Leo II listed the founders of Monotheletism and then added: "And along with them Honorius of Rome, who consented to the pollution of the unpolluted rule of the apostolic tradition, which he received from his predecessors [qui immaculatam apostolicae traditionis regulam, quam a praedecessoribus suis accepit, maculari consensit]." In another letter, Leo even charged Honorius with "having tried to subvert the immaculate faith by his utter treachery" instead of "bringing luster to this apostolic church by the doctrine of the apostolic tradition"; so, at any rate, the Latin recension of the letter reads. The Greek recension moderates the accusation to that of "having yielded," which would conform to the version of the charge in another Latin letter, where Honorius was blamed for "not extinguishing the flame of heretical dogma from its inception, as was the duty of apostolic authority, but fostering it by his negligence." *The Diary of the Roman Pontiffs,* of uncertain date, likewise acknowledged that Pope Honorius had "helped to foment the erroneous assertions" of Monotheletism. Even in our period, in the ninth and in the eleventh century, Honorius was listed by Western polemicists against the East among those condemned for Monotheletism.

During the Middle Ages in the West, a mythical "monk Honorius" was discovered to be the one condemned at Constantinople, to spare Old Rome the embarrassment of having had an incumbent of its see denounced as a

CCP(681)*Act*.13
(Mansi 11:554–56)

Const.Pogon.*Edict*.
(Mansi 11:709)

Leo II.*Ep*.7 (*PL* 96:419)

Leo II.*Ep*.3 (*PL* 96:408)

Leo II.*Ep*.3 (*PL* 96:410)

Leo II.*Ep*.4 (*PL* 96:414)

Lib.diurn. (Foerster 155)

Hinc.R.*Opusc*.20 (*PL*
126:359); Humb.*Resp.Nicet.*
17 (Will 142)

Ans.Hav.*Dial*.3.12 (*PL* 188:122)

heretic. More commonly perhaps, the embarrassment was relieved by simply omitting Honorius from the catalogue of heretics anathematized for Monotheletism. This began already with Pope Martin I, whose encyclical on Monotheletism condemned Theodore of Pharan, Pyrrhus of Constantinople, and other heretics, but did not even

Mart.I.*Ep*.1; *Ep*.3; *Ep*.5 (*PL* 87:121; 142; 159)

mention Honorius. When the successor of Martin and of Honorius, Agatho, forwarded a catalogue of heretics to the Council of Constantinople, the name of Honorius did not appear on it, but only the phrase, "and those who agree

Agath.*Ep*.3 (*PL* 87:1224)

with these men." In his own catalogue of Monotheletist heretics, Photius did, of course, include Honorius, as well as Sergius, the patriarch of New Rome, but not Pyrrhus,

Phot.*Ep*.1.1 (*PG* 102:593)

Sergius's successor. The irenic patriarch of Antioch in the eleventh century, Peter III, managed to have it both ways: in his enthronement letter to his colleague at Jerusalem he condemned "Sergius and Pyrrhus and Paul and Ho-

Petr.Ant.*Ep.H*.8.2 (Michel 2:444)
Petr.Ant.*Ep.Leo* IX.8.2 (Michel 2:456)

norius, of Old Rome, asinine in mind," while in a similar letter to the pope, he mentioned only the first three. The inclusion of the name of Honorius or its omission was, obviously, important not on account of the man, but on account of the see. Claims of impeccable orthodoxy for Old Rome would have to be squared with historical facts

Nil.Cab.*Prim*. (*PG* 149:705; 708–9)

if it was acknowledged that Honorius had been a heretic. Therefore Martin was able to condemn "all those without exception who vainly affirm one nature or will or action of the divinity and humanity of Christ or who confess none" as "enemies and adversaries [of] the catholic and

Mart.I.*Ep*.12 (*PL* 87:192)

apostolic church of God"; yet at the same time, by not including Honorius in his list of those who had done so, even though he undoubtedly had, Martin could declare that "we, that is, the pontiffs of this apostolic see, have not permitted them to spread this [error], or to steal the

Mart.I.*Ep*.11 (*PL* 87:176)

treasure of the faith."

The case of Honorius apart, Pope Martin's claim for Old Rome was borne out by the record. It had been, in the christological controversy of the seventh century as in that of the fifth, the "pillar of orthodoxy," and non-West-

Mich.Anch.*Dial*.35 (Loparev 357)

ern spokesmen hailed it as such. Even Maurus, the archbishop of Ravenna who contended for the independence of his see from Rome, declared that "on the points now under discussion, which are being proposed contrary to the decrees of the orthodox fathers, I do not believe other-

Maur.Rav.*Ep.* (*PL* 87: 104–5)

ap.CLater.(649)*Act*.2 (Mansi 10:905)

ap.Steph.Dor.*Ep.* (Mansi 10:896)

Const.Pogon.*Sacr*.2 (Mansi 11:716)

CCP(681)*Act*.18 (Mansi 11:684)

CCP(681) *Or.imp.* (Mansi 11:665) Serg.Cyp.*Ep.Thdr.* (Mansi 10:913–16); Col.Afr.*Ep.Thdr.* (*PL* 87:82–86)

Symb.CP(681) (Mansi 11:636)

Niceph.*Imag*.25 (*PG* 100:597)

Dobroklonskij (1913) 1:824–25 Thdr.Stud.*Ep*.1.28; 1.38 (*PG* 99:1001; 1041–44)

wise than as your holy apostolic doctrine and orthodox church [of Rome] teaches," over against the doctrine "defended by Pyrrhus, bishop of Constantinople." The Greek abbots and priests who remained loyal to orthodox doctrine in opposition to Monotheletism appealed to Old Rome as "the apostolic and chief see." Sophronius of Jerusalem said that one could "wander from the edge of the earth to its outer limits until you come to the apostolic see, where the foundations of orthodox dogmas stand." After the Third Council of Constantinople, the Byzantine emperor, Constantine Pogonatus, voiced his admiration for "the director of the apostolic chorus, Peter, the occupant of the prime see, who teaches the theology about the mystery of salvation with understanding eyes." That council itself, in an official epistle to Agatho, acknowledged his primacy, and specifically his direction as "the wise . . . physician" who had cured the illness of the church with his "orthodox medicines." The council gave the same testimony about Old Rome in its epistle to the emperor of New Rome. The testimony was corroborated by other Eastern prelates and theologians. What Rome decided in opposition to Monotheletism, in 649 and again in 680, was what the orthodox, catholic, and ecumenical church decided, in council assembled, in 681. Peter was still speaking through the mouth of the pope.

The appeal to Old Rome likewise became a factor in the iconoclastic controversy. It would be possible to assemble statements from all the principal defenders of the images in which the primacy and the orthodoxy of Rome were affirmed, as, for example, when Nicephorus, in his defense of icons, asserted that a dogma "cannot have approval nor a practice gain acceptance" without Rome. The most explicit such assertions came, for reasons that are related no less to his biography than to his theology, from Theodore of Studios; but it is essential to keep in mind that while "in Theodore's consciousness the Roman see possessed a preeminent importance among the patriarchates," nevertheless "in this respect Theodore and his party do not offer anything new and peculiar for the Eastern church." For although Theodore did at times disparage the universal authority of Rome, especially before the conflict over the icons, the outbreak of that conflict gave him the occasion to cite as his authority the written and unwritten tradition of the church, as assured by "that

Matt.16:18
Thdr.Stud.*Ep*.2.1
(*PG* 99:1117)

Luke 22:32

Thdr.Stud.*Ep*.2.12 (*PG*
99:1153)

Thdr.Stud.*Ep*.2.13
(*PG* 99:1156)

Gr.M.*Ep*.9.208; 11.10 (*MGH
Ep*.2:195; 270–71)
Lib.Car.2.23 (*MGH
Conc.Sup*.2:82)

Haendler (1958) 26

CNic.(787)*Act*.2
(Mansi 12:1059)

Hadr.*Ep*.2 (*MGH Ep*.5:5–57)

see of which Christ said, 'You are Peter, and on this rock I will build my church, and the gates of hell shall not prevail against it.' " Writing directly to the pope, he appealed: "Christ, our God, has said to you: 'And you, when you have been converted [Latin: conversus], confirm your brethren.' Behold, this is the time and this is the place. . . . Because you are the first in rank of all, you have strength from God, who has placed you into this rank." The see of Rome, he wrote later to the pope, had been, "from the beginning until now, by the very providence of God, the one and only help in recurrent crises . . . the pure and genuine source of orthodoxy . . . the distinct calm harbor for the whole church from every heretical storm."

Theodore's appeal to Rome for its help in the iconoclast crisis was not without some curious aspects, for the stand of the Latin church on the question of images had by no means kept pace with the situation in the Byzantine Empire. For example, the utterances of Gregory I on the subject, while defending the propriety of images in the churches, had been content to stress the didactic value of the images. Gregory's statements about images remained normative in the West for centuries. Relying on the authority of Gregory and of others, the incumbent of the see of Peter during the iconoclastic controversy rejected the accusation that the worship of images was idolatry; "but in Byzantium things had come to the point that iconoclasts as well as iconodules were basing their theories on christology." So striking was the disparity between East and West that the Greek translator of the pope's epistle took it upon himself to add the words: "And through [the images] they [who look at them] are elevated to faith and to the remembrances of the economy of our Lord Jesus Christ." The theological gap did not lead in this case, as it had in the case of Honorius, to doctrinal statements in which naïveté became the source of heresy. But the epistle of Pope Hadrian to Charlemagne on images shows that it would be gross historical exaggeration to maintain that during the conflict over images, particularly during the christological stage of that conflict, the church of Rome had in fact evinced the sort of doctrinal leadership which in theory—in the theory of Theodore, and in her own—was hers to provide. The reaction of the Carolingian theologians (to whom we shall return in the next volume) to the cult of images showed a profound difference of spirit between the Greek East and the Latin West. Coming from Charlemagne himself were such comments as "Perfect!" on the statement of *The Caroline Books* that "we do not reject . . . images, but their . . . superstitious adoration."

By the time of the conflict between Old Rome and New Rome in the last third of the ninth century, therefore, the pattern of Eastern deference to Rome (made even more expressive by the courtly language of the Byzantines) had been set. Conditions in both East and West encouraged further development of Western claims, but also encouraged Eastern resistance to such claims. The contrast between the record of the two sees for dogmatic orthodoxy became a dogmatic question. One of the earliest of the innumerable Western treatises "against the errors of the Greeks" prefaced its compilation of patristic quotations, otherwise an "extremely feeble" production, with the observation that it had been from the areas subject to Byzantine hegemony "rather than from those who live under Roman jurisdiction that there will be found to have sprung up the generations of vipers, that is, very many originators of perverse dogmas." It was, the author said, lamentable that Constantinople, the very see which was now attempting to assert its superiority over others, had once had heretics as its incumbents; by contrast, "thanks to the direction of God, never has any disgrace of this sort happened in the Roman see, that some heresiarch should have presided over it."

This identification of Constantinople as the source of heresies went back at least as far as Gregory the Great, but beginning with the ninth century it acquired a new value in the Western arsenal. In his defense of the West, the legate Liutprand of Cremona in the tenth century told the Byzantine emperor that "all the heresies have taken their rise from you and have flourished among you, but it was by us, that is by the Occidentals, that they were swallowed up and killed." In the eleventh century, when the controversy came to a head, Humbert drew the same contrast between Rome, which, "founded by the first among the apostles on the cornerstone itself, on Christ Jesus, has never yielded to any heresies," and Constantinople, "that church, which Arius corrupted, which Macedonius prostituted, which gave birth to and nourished generations of

---

ap.Freeman (1971) 610

*Lib.Car.*2.9 (*MGH Conc.Sup.* 2:70)

Dvornik (1970) 280

Matt.23:33
Aen.Par.*Graec*.pr. (*PL* 121:686)

Aen.Par.*Graec*.pr. (*PL* 121:687)

See vol. 1:354

Liut.*Leg.*22 (*MGH Scrip.* 3:351); Ans.Hav.*Dial.*3.6 (*PL* 188:1215)

Humb.*Resp.Nicet.*33–34
(Will 149–50)

Ans.Hav.*Dial.*3.6
(*PL* 188:1216–17)

Matt.16:18–19

Max.*Opusc.*11 (*PG* 91:140)

Ludwig (1952) 103

See vol. 1:108–20

vipers, namely, Nestorius, Eutyches, the Monotheletes, the Theopaschites, and the rest of the pestilential heretics." Other sees had suffered shipwreck; "only the bark of Peter" had not.

The explanation for this record of Old Rome as "fountain of orthodoxy" was not difficult to find. It lay in the promise and the commission of Christ to Peter, and through him to his successors: "And I tell you, you are Peter, and on this rock I will build my church, and the gates of hell shall not prevail against it. I will give you the keys to the kingdom of heaven, and whatever you bind on earth shall be bound in heaven, and whatever you loose on earth shall be loosed in heaven." At the very least the commission and promise meant, as Maximus had said, that the see of Peter had "the keys of the orthodox faith and confession of [Christ]." Together with much of the Eastern tradition, Maximus thus "looks only at the power of the keys and gives it the sense of the confession of faith. By virtue of this power the pope decides about orthodoxy and heresy, opens the gates of the church to true believers, but closes them to the apostates. It is in this sense that he looses and binds." Yet such an acknowledgment of Roman orthodoxy, fundamental though it was, was not an adequate exegesis of the promise of Christ, according to the spokesmen of the Latin church. That promise laid down certain conditions that would guarantee the church against the gates of hell: the church, the entire church, had to be built on the rock.

The Foundation of Apostolic Polity

That rock was Peter. To be built on the rock, the church must show that it stood in the succession of Peter and that it was an heir of the promises given to him. It was agreed on all sides, moreover, that this succession pertained to the church as an institution. Right believing and correct teaching could be achieved and maintained only within a proper structure: for the church to be apostolic in doctrine, it had to be apostolic in polity. From very early times an episcopal polity, presumed to stand in unbroken succession from the apostles, had been taken to be one of the criteria of apostolic continuity, in conjunction with the authoritative canon of Scripture and the creedal rule of faith. There was, of course, a pragmatic and even a political aspect to the administrative structure of the church, but questions of jurisdiction became (or were) questions of theology because Christ had built his church on Peter the rock and had vouchsafed his protection against the gates of hell only to that church which could legitimately claim this foundation of apostolic polity.

In the ninth century, therefore, the struggle between Rome and Constantinople over the Christianization of Moravia and of Bulgaria was not only a question of jurisdiction, but simultaneously a question of theology. "It was impossible for Constantinople not to recognize that the political alliance of [the Bulgarian czar] Boris with [the Frankish emperor] Louis could have as its probable consequence the baptizing of the Bulgarian nation by the Roman church, and not to foresee the consequences of this for the Eastern empire and especially for the church of Constantinople in its conflict with the pope of Rome, who already in his first letter to [the Byzantine emperor] Michael III proclaimed his ecclesiastical authority over all the provinces of the Balkan peninsula."

Zlatarski (1935) 283

When the pope, Nicholas I, addressed himself to Michael III in assertion of this ecclesiastical authority, he opened his letter with the claim that Christ, by his words to Peter,

Nicol.I.Ep.82 (MGH
Ep.6:433)

had conferred primacy on the see of Rome. It was not obvious, particularly to Constantinople, that this primacy automatically carried with it a Roman jurisdiction over the Slavic tribes. In the event, Moravia, after being converted by missionaries from Constantinople (Cyril and Methodius), became Western in jurisdiction, while Bulgaria, after negotiating with Rome, nevertheless remained Eastern in its polity. But this arbitration of the jurisdictional dispute by history did nothing to settle the doctrinal controversy. Although the pope's claim upon Bulgaria failed of recognition, the basis of that claim still stood in the charter of the Roman see, the words of Christ to Peter.

The exegesis of those words and their application to the polity of Christendom, Eastern as well as Western, was an unavoidable question for theologians of every tradition. Even the Monophysites and the Nestorians, who anathematized not only each other but Rome and Constantinople as well, had to explain what these words meant. The Monophysite Timothy Aelurus, in his refutation of Chalcedon, explained them to mean that the faith once delivered to the saints would not decay with age or change

Tim.Ael.*Chalc*.4 (*PO*
13:222)

Jac.Bar.*Ep.Thds*.
(*CSCO* 103:63[17:91])

Episc.Or.*Ep*. (*CSCO* 103:
134[17:192-93])

Tim.I.*Ep*.1 (*CSCO*
75:11[74:20])

Bab.*Un*.1.1; 1.2 (*CSCO*
80:3-4; 6[79:4; 7])

Bab.*Un*.3.10 (*CSCO*
80:84[79:91])

Bab.*Un*.6.21 (*CSCO*
80:199[79:245-46])

with time because it was "built upon an unshakable foundation, that is to say, upon Christ, and the gates of hell shall not prevail against it." Another Monophysite theologian likewise quoted the words without reference to Rome, in fact without reference to Peter, with perhaps some application to Antioch. A group of Monophysite bishops, also perhaps with Antioch in mind, drew the line of succession "from Peter, the chief of the divine company of apostles, all the way to Severus." On this point, as on relatively few others, the Nestorians agreed with the Monophysites, identifying the "rock" not with the person of Peter, much less with that of his successors at Rome, but with his confession. Timothy I spoke of "the rock of our affirmation, on which the Lord promised to build his church." Babai spoke of the church as "built on the faith . . . the rock," and then quoted the words to Peter. He declared that "the church of Christ, whose foundation is built on the rock of Peter, confesses thus," and followed this with a definition of the union between divine and human in Christ as one neither of nature nor of hypostasis, but of will and person. He even identified Theodore of Mopsuestia as one "who builds solidly . . . and correctly on the foundation of Peter."

The greatest importance of the exegesis of Matthew 16:18 for the history of Eastern Christianity lies in the Greek interpretation of the passage over against the Latin claims that were being based upon it. The Latin exegesis, represented in this period by Nicholas I, drew from the words of Christ authorization for the unique place of the Roman see. After quoting the passage and describing the succession of his see from Peter, Nicholas declared, writing to Photius, that "the entire company of believers looks for its doctrine to this holy Roman church, which is the head of all the churches," and that therefore it was the special responsibility of the Roman pope to be solicitous for the doctrinal orthodoxy and the general welfare of all the other sees in Christendom, including Constantinople. Two other proof texts that were often cited in conjunction with Matthew 16:18 in support of Roman claims were Luke 22:32 and John 21:17, also words of Christ to Peter: "I have prayed for you that your faith may not fail; and you, when you have been converted, confirm your brethren"; "Feed my sheep." These texts served to explain the passage in Matthew, so that taken together the

Nicol.I.*Ep*.86 (*MGH
Ep*.6:447)

Hadr.*Ep*.2 (*MGH Ep*.5:6)

Nicol.I.Ep.87; 88
(MGH Ep.6:452; 476)

Nicet.Nicom.ap.Ans.
Hav.Dial.3.9 (PL
188:1221)

sayings meant that "he who receives those who agree with us receives us, and through us the chief of the apostles, and through him Christ. Therefore it is up to us to convert those who err, since the lot has fallen upon us to occupy the place of the first shepherd," to whom Christ had said these words, as well as the words about the rock.

Max.Ep.13 (PG 91:512)

Thdr.AbuQ.Mim.1.24 (Graf
113); Cosm.Sl.19
(Popruženko 36)

Greek theologians tended to apply these sayings less specifically. Maximus called himself "a genuine child of the holy catholic and apostolic church of God, one who is founded on the pious confession, against which the wicked mouths of the heretics, opened up like the gates of hell, will never prevail." The identification of the gates of hell with the great heresies of the second, third, and fourth centuries was generally accepted. Against these gates of hell not only the apostle Peter, but all the apostles, especially John, had successfully contended with the authority of the word of God. Indeed, the power of the keys conferred upon Peter by Christ in Matthew 16:19 was not restricted either to him or to his successors on the throne of Old Rome; all the faithful bishops of the church were imitators and successors of Peter. They had this status as orthodox adherents of the confession of Peter in Matthew 16:16: "You are the Christ, the Son of the living God." By attaching the promise in the following verses to that confession it was possible to admonish orthodox believers to "run to the faith . . . of this immovable rock . . . and let us believe that Christ is both God and man." The unshakable foundation of the church was the rock that was Christ, but at the same time Peter could be called "the foundation and support of our faith." He was this, however, principally because of his confession, which was repeated by all true believers. It was a polemical extension of this general Greek tendency when a later treatise, falsely ascribed to Photius, stated flatly that the rock in Christ's promise was the confession of Peter rather than his person.

Thdr.Stud.Or.9.9 (PG
99:784)

Max.Schol.E.h.7.7 (PG
4:181)

Thdr.AbuQ.Opusc.4
(PG 97:1504–5)

Niceph.Imag.36 (PG
100:621)

Ps.Phot.Rom.5
(Gordillo 12)

Yet the primacy of Peter among the apostles and the identification of his primacy with Rome's were too well established in the orthodox tradition of East and West to be controverted very easily. The opening words of *The Doctrine of the Fathers* were: "The words of Saint Peter, the coryphaeus of the apostles, from the *Clementines*" (which were, to be sure, apocryphal). To Maximus,

Doct.patr.1.1 (Diekamp 1);
Psell.Cant.5.15 (PG
122:652)

Peter was the head of the apostles, the great foundation of the church. When a conflict had arisen between the apostle Paul and the church at Jerusalem, it was settled not by either Paul or Barnabas, but by "the council of the apostles, of which Mar Peter was the head and chief." Thus Peter was the foundation of the church, so that whoever believed as he believed would not go astray. But for most Greek theologians Peter was above all "the chief of the theologians" because of his confession. All the titles of primacy, such as foundation and basis and "president of the disciples," pertained to him as trinitarian theologian. The church was to be built on the rock, on Christ the cornerstone, on which Peter, as coryphaeus of the disciples of the Logos, had also been built—"built, that is, by the holy and divine dogmas." Primacy belonged to Peter on account of his confession, and those who confessed Christ to be the Son of the living God, as he had, were the beneficiaries of the promise that the gates of hell would not prevail against the church built on the rock.

The primacy of Rome was likewise a gift of that promise and a corollary of that confession. All men, Maximus wrote, acknowledged "her confession and her faith . . . in the holy dogmas of the fathers" and in the ecumenical councils. Such sayings of Christ to Peter as Luke 22:32 "do not refer to Mar Peter and the apostles themselves, but to those who occupy the official position of Mar Peter, which is in Rome, and the official positions of the apostles." Everyone paid tribute to the achievements of the see of Peter in defending and in defining the orthodox faith, and everyone affirmed the desirability of "agreeing in theology with the ecumenical chief shepherd," the bishop of Rome. At the risk of oversimplification, one might say that to the East the pope was chief bishop because he was orthodox, while to the West he was and always would be orthodox because he was chief bishop. Defenders of the Western position cited Rome's support of orthodoxy in the East when the rulers of the East, ecclesiastical and secular, had opposed the true faith, as in the days of Athanasius, of Chrysostom, and of Flavian. Nicholas asserted that "the holy Roman church, through blessed Peter, the chief of the apostles who earned the right by the mouth of the Lord to assume primacy over the church, is the head of all the churches." They were to

Max.*Qu.Thal.*61; 27 (*PG* 90:637; 356)

Thdr.AbuQ.*Mim.*1.22–23 (Graf 111–12)

Niceph.*Antirr.*1.47 (*PG* 100:320)

Niceph.*Imag.*17 (*PG* 100:576)

Niceph.*Imag.*3 (*PG* 100:537–40)

Nicet.Byz.*Arm.*2 (*PG* 105:592); Ps.Anast.S.*Jud. dial.*1 (*PG* 89:1221)

Max.*Opusc.*11 (*PG* 91:137)

Thdr.AbuQ.*Mim.*1.24 (Graf 112)

Const.Pogon.*Sacr.*2 (Mansi 11:722)

Gelas.I.*Ep.*13 (*PL* 59:67)

seek and follow the guidance of Rome in doctrine and practice. The defenders of Rome against the Greeks made the case that its authority had preeminence over all the churches, so that the Roman pontiff was the head of all the bishops and his judgment determined whatever was to be settled in the affairs of all the churches. For this reason, all the churches throughout the world had to look to Rome, which it had become customary to call the "apostolic see" in a special sense.

Through much of their early history, Eastern theologians had "applied the title 'apostolic' sparingly to their own sees," for the very "idea of apostolicity had, in general, not yet achieved prominence among them" until the latter part of the fifth century or even later. The argument for Roman primacy on the basis of Petrine foundation had only a limited force. As Gregory the Great himself had acknowledged, Peter had been in Alexandria and in Antioch as well. Eastern polemicists sometimes referred to this circumstance, recalling that Peter had been in Antioch before coming to Rome, so that Antioch could claim priority as well as primacy. Peter had been bishop of Antioch for eight years before coming to Rome; and so if Rome claimed the primacy because of the chief of the apostles, Antioch had a better claim, as, for that matter, did Jerusalem. It was perhaps an expression of some such claim when an eleventh-century patriarch of Antioch spoke of his concern about "why the great successor of the great Peter, the shepherd of Old Rome, has come into schism and division from the divine body of the churches."

The real rival to Old Rome, as that very title suggests, was not Antioch, but New Rome. In addition to the political, legal, and cultural sources of the rivalry, the doctrinal disagreement had to do with the original grounds for the primacy of Rome. Had Rome achieved this position because it was founded by the apostle Peter or because it was the capital city of the Roman Empire? In what came to be known as the twenty-eighth canon of the Council of Chalcedon of 451, "Constantinople, which is New Rome," was granted special privileges, alongside those of Old Rome, on the grounds that Old Rome had received its position in the church because it was the imperial city. On the basis of this canon, later Byzantine advocates, such as the twelfth-century theologian and canonist Nilus Dox-

Marginal notes:

Nicol.I.*Ep*.86 (*MGH Ep*.6:448)

Ratr.*Graec*.4.8 (*PL* 121:336)

Aen.Par.*Graec*.195 (*PL* 121:752)

Dvornik (1958) 67

See vol. 1:353

Mich.Anch.*Dial*.21 (Loparev 350)

Ps.Phot.*Rom*. 1; 3 (Gordillo 11)

Petr.Ant.*Ep*.*Leo* IX.1.2 (Michel 2:446)

CChalc.*Can*.28 (*ACO* 2–I–3:88)

opatres, maintained "that they argue wrongly who say that Rome acquired its position of honor on account of Saint Peter. You see, this canon of the holy council says that because Rome has the imperial authority, it has the position of first honor." Therefore Constantinople, as New Rome, was second only to Old Rome. Peter, he maintained, had come "to Rome, which at that time was the imperial city among all the cities," but which did not hold that position now. Sometimes the later Byzantines would argue that it was a vestigial remnant of Judaism to restrict the grace of God to any particular place, and that therefore the application of Matthew 16:18 to Rome was mistaken. But the sharper form of the Byzantine attack was the thesis that "the patriarch of Constantinople is called archbishop of New Rome because he has taken over the privileges and prerogatives of Rome."

It is not clear just when this form of attack made its appearance in Byzantine theology and canon law. The first unequivocal reference to such a notion is not found in Greek sources, but in a papal response to Eastern accusations. The Greeks, Pope Nicholas charged, "even maintain and boast that when the emperors moved from the city of Rome to Constantinople, the primacy of the Roman see was also transferred to the church of Constantinople, and that the privileges of the church of Rome changed hands together with the imperial honors." Although this was aimed at Photius and his anti-Roman epistles and treatises, there seems to be no documentary evidence that he maintained any such thing. Hence "the interpretation of this canon [of Chalcedon] which the Pope fathers on the Greeks seems somewhat far-fetched, since before Nicholas no Greek had ever read into it such a radical meaning." Earlier in the same century Nicephorus had asserted that those who had inherited the new name of "Romans" were built on one and the same foundation of the faith as the representatives of Old Rome, for in the church of God there was to be no "numbering by precedence." For him, Constantinople, New Rome, was "the city that now presides and bears the primacy because of its imperial prerogatives." It had long been customary to speak of Constantinople in such terms as "this holy city of Christ our God" and of its patriarch as "the one who directs the eye of the universe"; but it was apparently in the conflicts of the eleventh and twelfth centuries that some spokesmen

Nil.Dox.*Not.* (*PG* 132:1100)

Nil.Dox.*Not.* (*PG* 132:1085)

Ps.Phot.*Rom*.5 (Gordillo 11–12)

Nil.Dox.*Not.* (*PG* 132:1101); *Metrop.* (Darrouzès 130)

Nicol.I.*Ep*.100 (*MGH Ep*.6:605)

Dvornik (1970) 125

Niceph.*Ep.Leo III* (*PG* 100:181)

Niceph.*Imag*.25 (*PG* 100:597); Nicet. Nicom.ap.Ans.Hav. *Dial*.3.7 (*PL* 188:1218)

Soph.*Ep.syn.* (*PG* 87:3149) Nicet. Amas.*Patr.* (Darrouzès 170)

for New Rome seriously advanced the theory that Old Rome had lost its primacy to the new capital.

The spokesmen for the Old Rome refused to accept any such theory. The florilegium of patristic quotations compiled in the ninth century by Aeneas of Paris against the Greeks quoted the statement of an earlier pope that Constantinople, which did not even have metropolitan rank in the church, could not claim a higher position on the grounds of its being the imperial city, for "the power of the kingdom of the world is one thing and the distribution of ranks in the church is quite another." Pope Nicholas pointed out to Photius that the church of Constantinople had customarily been dependent on Rome for its doctrinal stability and firmness. It was on this basis that he took it upon himself to prohibit and to nullify the patriarchal election of Photius as invalid, using the authority that had always been held by his predecessors. As Liutprand declared during his visit to Constantinople a century later, Constantine had indeed founded New Rome, but he had given many territories, both western and eastern, to Old Rome. Therefore the church of Constantinople was still subject to the church of Rome, as was shown by the fact that the bishop of Constantinople did not wear the pallium except by the permission of the pope of Rome. The Western version of apostolic polity, by contrast with the Eastern, had definitely become a form of monarchy by the time of the collision between Old Rome and New Rome in the ninth century.

The Eastern version, despite some of the extreme statements we have been examining, was not the monarchy of New Rome in place of the monarchy of Old Rome, but the doctrine of pentarchy. This doctrine came to its focus in the schism of the eleventh century, but its basic elements had been present earlier. Pentarchy was the theory that the apostolic polity of Christendom would be maintained through the cooperation between the five patriarchal sees: Rome, Constantinople, Jerusalem, Antioch, and Alexandria. Citing the words of Christ in Matthew 16: 18–19, Theodore of Studios asked: "Who are the men to whom this order is given? The apostles and their successors. And who are their successors? He who occupies the throne of Rome, which is the first; he who occupies the throne of Constantinople, which is the second; and after them those who occupy the thrones of Alexandria, Antioch, and Jerusalem. This is the pentarchic

Gel.I.*Ep*.13 (*PL* 59:82)

Aen.Par.*Graec*.201 (*PL* 121:754)

Nicol.I.*Ep*.86 (*MGH Ep*.6:450)

Nicol.I.*Ep*.82 (*MGH Ep*.6:435)

Liut.*Leg*.17 (*MGH Scrip*.3:350)

Liut.*Leg*.62 (*MGH Scrip*.3:361)

Thdr.Stud.*Ep*.124 (*PG* 99:1417); *Metrop.* (Darrouzès 140)

Corp.iur.civ.*Nov.* 109.pr. (Schoell-Kroll 518)

CCP(681)*Act*.18 (Mansi 11:681)

Petr.Ant.*Ep.Dom. Ven*.3 (Will 211)

Petr.Ant.*Ep.Dom. Ven*.5 (Will 212)

Thdr.H.ap.CCP(869) *Act*.1 (Mansi 16:35)

Phot.*Ep*.1.24.3 (*PG* 102:797)

Niceph.*Imag*.25 (*PG* 100:597)

Max.*Pyrr.* (*PG* 91:352)

Joh.Diac.ap.CNic. (787)*Act*.6 (Mansi 13:208–9)

Max.*Ep*.12 (*PG* 91:464)

Phot.*Ep*.1.24.6 (*PG* 102:800)

Petr.Ant.*Ep.Dom. Ven*.4 (Will 211)

Nil.Dox.*Not.* (*PG* 132:1007)

[πεντακόρυφος] authority in the church; these [patriarchs] have jurisdiction over divine dogmas." Even earlier the *Code of Justinian* had referred to the five patriarchs "of the whole universe," and the Third Council of Constantinople in 680–81 had sent its dogmatic definition "to the five patriarchal thrones."

Underlying the doctrine of pentarchy was the Eastern view of the patriarchate. In the strict sense of the title "patriarch," it was pointed out by a patriarch of Antioch, the title "pope" was the more appropriate one for the patriarch of Rome, as well as for those of Alexandria and Jerusalem, while the patriarch of Constantinople bore the title "archbishop." Of the five, only the incumbent of the see of Antioch was strictly to be called "patriarch." But even at that one had to note that there was a "patriarch" of Venice also, although he was not a patriarch in the same sense as the five. Patriarchal authority was fitted into the structure of apostolic and patristic authority by the thesis that the Holy Spirit, having spoken by the prophets and then by the apostles and then by the church fathers, had now "instituted the patriarchs as heads of the world." This structure of authority, past and present, constituted "the universally valid tradition and doctrine of the great and patriarchal sees," which no one, not even an incumbent of the most prestigious among these sees, had the right to contradict. Hence Nicephorus, after his tribute to the special position of Rome, immediately went on to assert the common authority of the patriarchs. Their consent and representation were necessary for a council to be legitimate. The iconoclastic council of 754, for example, could not be called ecumenical or even legitimate because, despite the involvement of the patriarch of Constantinople, the patriarchs of Rome, Alexandria, Antioch, and Jerusalem had not been represented and had not given their consent to its decrees. Apart from councils or between councils, disputes were to be referred "to our most devout emperor and to the most holy patriarchs, the one at Rome and the one at Constantinople." Photius accepted a primacy for Rome, but insisted that Rome had to "harmonize and agree with the other four high-priestly sees."

A nice theory arose that there were five patriarchs because there were five senses. But in expounding this theory one could either decline to say "which patriarchs occupy the place of which senses" and by this device avoid the issue of primacy; or one could maintain, as the West did, that while the health of the body required all five to be functioning, still the patriarch of Rome was to be compared to sight, on the grounds that sight "is the first among all the senses, is more vigilant than [the others], and is in communion with all of them to a greater degree than they

Anast.Bibl.CCP(869) pr. (Mansi 16:7)

are with each other." To the East, this definition of the primacy of Rome was a negation of the principle of pentarchy, which meant that no patriarch was to intrude

Nil.Dox.Not. (PG 132:1092)

upon the internal affairs of any other patriarchate. This was, of course, precisely what the patriarch of Rome claimed the right, indeed the duty, to do, as when Nicholas, addressing himself to the patriarchs of Alexandria, Antioch, and Jerusalem in the matter of Constantinople, declared that "by apostolic authority we charge and com-

Nicol.I.Ep.84 (MGH Ep.6:442)

mand you" to agree with the stand of Rome. For the Latin church, then, there were also five patriarchs; but among these the pope was different from the others in kind and not only in degree, for he could act for the entire church without them but they could not act without him. This was what the words of Christ in Matthew 16: 18–19 meant. For the Greek church, by contrast, those words meant, as the Latinophile emperor, Basil the Macedonian, said, that "God has established his church on the foundation of the five patriarchs, and he has defined in his holy Gospels that they would never fail altogether, because

Bas.I.Mac.ap.CCP(869)Act.8 (Mansi 16:140)

they are the heads of the church."

One especially sensitive point was the relation between the pope and the ecumenical council as arbiter of doctrine and practice. In the light of the historical record, no one could claim that New Rome had been as consistent as Old Rome in upholding the standards of orthodoxy, nor even that these standards had been upheld by the five patriarchs acting in concert. But it was possible to maintain that when there had been need in the first century for the adjudication of a dispute, no one apostle had determined the right answer, but the matter had been referred to an apostolic council, over which Peter had

Thdr.AbuQ.Mim.1.22 (Graf 111)

presided. So it was to be throughout the history of the church: Rome did not legislate unilaterally on matters affecting the church as a whole, but did preside over an apostolic council. This conciliar principle implied a

Niceph.Imag.25 (PG 100:597)

consensus among the apostolic patriarchs, analogous to that achieved by the apostles themselves at the council described in the fifteenth chapter of the Book of Acts. The stipulation that no council had an a priori title to

See vol. 1:354-55

legitimacy or ecumenicity precluded any simplistic definition of a proper council as one that had been either convoked or validated by the see of Rome—or by any other see. Much less did it allow for the arrogation to the see of Rome or to any other see of the legislative function that had historically been exercised by councils. Otherwise, as Nicetas of Nicomedia said ironically, "Why do we need a knowledge of the Scriptures or a study of literature or the doctrinal discipline of the masters or the noblest achievements of the wise Greeks? All by itself, the authority of the Roman pontiff nullifies all of these. . . . Let him alone be bishop, master, and preceptor, let him alone, as the only good shepherd, be responsible to God for everything that has been committed to him!"

Nicet.Nicom.ap.Ans.
Hav.*Dial*.3.8 (*PL*
188:1219)

Conflict erupted in the ninth century between East and West over the relation of pope and council because of the disputed status of the so-called seventh ecumenical council, the Second Council of Nicea of 787, which had concluded the first stage of the iconoclastic controversy. Partly because of the garbled transmission of the Latin translation of its proceedings and partly because of the political situation in the West, this council had not been acknowledged by Rome. It was "the pseudocouncil on images, called the seventh universal council among the Greeks," in which neither party had been right; it had, moreover, been held "without the authority of the apostolic see not

Hinc.R.*Opusc.Hinc.L*.20
(*PL* 126:360)

long before our own times." The iconoclasts had been wrong in rejecting all cult of images, and the iconodules had been wrong in ascribing too much to the images;

Lib.*Car*.pr. (*MGH
Conc.Sup*.2:6)

but both had been wrong in ignoring Rome. Although there had not been a formal act of approval in the East either, the council was generally acknowledged as official. Therefore Photius was expressing a common Eastern view when he defended the authority and the ecumenicity

Phot.*Enc*.40-42 (*PG*
102:740)

of the "seventh" ecumenical council. The West asserted the rule that "universal councils are especially convoked by the authority of the apostolic see," and argued that

Hinc.R.*Opusc.Hinc.L*.20
(*PL* 126:362)

without the controlling discipline of Rome a council could not preserve the integrity of the apostolic tradition. An

Nicol.I.*Ep*.82 (*MGH
Ep*.6:434)

earlier pope had already claimed that "the apostolic see has frequently exercised the power, . . . without any preceding council," to affirm what a false council had condemned and to anathematize false doctrine whether or not

Gelas.I.*Ep*.13.18
(*CSEL* 35:780)
Aen.Par.*Graec*.199
(*PL* 121:753)

it had been denounced by a council; this declaration, too, was now quoted against Photius.

In point of historical fact, the councils had usually not been convoked by the bishop of Old Rome, but by the emperor of New Rome. Everyone remembered that this had been true of Constantine I at the First Council of Nicea and of Justinian at the Second Council of Constantinople, and that both emperors had also taken part in the deliberations of the councils; but the other councils had also been imperial as well as ecumenical. Although the West and its representatives had gone along with this arrangement, it did represent an understanding of church polity with which they fundamentally disagreed. The very appointment of Photius as patriarch and the deposition of his predecessor was an intolerable interference by the Byzantine emperor in the administration of the church. It was not surprising if other attacks on the church, and specifically on the Roman see, came "from men . . . supported by the secular power." Yet "it is not the business of emperors, but of bishops, to dispute about sacred dogmas and about the liturgy of the church." The Eastern bishops were venal because this arrangement had made their churches "tributary" and servile in their dependence on the emperor. Eastern theologians, especially during the conflict over images, had had their own occasion for lamenting the arrangement, but they also had reason to remember that in both cases when the images were restored, it was thanks to the authority of the emperor, more precisely, of the empress. Long before the iconoclastic debates, the authority of the emperor had been celebrated in Byzantine ritual and literature. He was, to cite only one statement among many, "similar to God, who is over all, for he does not have anyone higher than himself anywhere on earth." Important as such statements are for Byzantine political thought, they also became in this context formulations of Christian doctrine and issues of doctrinal conflict with the West.

Yet the deepest issues in the doctrinal conflict over the foundation of church polity were the issues of the catholic and apostolic character of the church. The affirmation that the church was catholic and apostolic—as well as one and holy—belonged to the faith originally delivered to the saints and transmitted to the generations that followed; whatever the differences over the words that shortly preceded these in the Nicene Creed, everyone was agreed on the confession of faith in "one holy catholic and apostolic

Phot.*Syn*.7 (*PG* 104: 1225–28)

Ratr.*Graec*.1.2 (*PL* 121:228)

Liut.*Leg*.63 (*MGH Scrip*.3:362)

Agap.*Cap*.21; 63 (*PG* 86:1172; 1184)

church." Everyone was also agreed that the church was to be catholic and apostolic in its institutional structure. But in what sense, and by what means, was the church "built upon the foundation of the apostles and prophets, Christ Jesus himself being the cornerstone"? For although this predicate of apostolicity was applied to the church from the beginning, "it must be stressed that the early Church found a model for its organization in the political organization of the Roman Empire rather than in the apostolic tradition." The New Testament had also required continuance in the doctrine of the apostles as fundamental, and this emphasis had been maintained in the church from the beginning. But when Old Rome, which could point to an all but unspotted record of having continued in the doctrine of the apostles, cited its apostolic foundation as the cause of its orthodoxy and proceeded to draw organizational implications from this foundation, it behooved New Rome, despite its spotty record of orthodoxy, to do the same.

This it did by calling itself "the great and apostolic see of Constantinople." For if Peter, who according to tradition was the apostolic founder of Rome, was "first bishop [πρωτόθρονος]," then his brother Andrew, who according to legend was the apostolic founder of Byzantium, was "first to be called [πρωτόκλητος] among the disciples," since it had been through him that Peter was brought to Christ. According to the most far-reaching of Byzantine polemics, this meant that "if Rome seeks the primacy on account of Peter, then Byzantium is first on account of Andrew, the first to be called and the brother senior in birth." But even when polemics did not go to the extreme of claiming that the position of Peter's Old Rome properly belonged to Andrew's New Rome, the demand that the church be catholic and apostolic could be seen as the doctrinal core of the jurisdictional disputes. It was not merely a rhetorical peroration, but a theological declaration when a treatise against the Latins (and against the Armenians) closed with the exhortation to be loyal to "the orthodox faith, which has today been confirmed by the Holy Spirit, who spoke through the prophets and apostles and ecumenical teachers to the one holy catholic and apostolic church, [the faith] which this same ecumenical church of Christ, embraced in various provinces of bishops, maintains from the beginning until now." It

Eph.2:20

Dvornik (1958) 4

Acts 2:42

See vol. 1:108–20

Bas.Ochr.*Ep.*1 (*PG* 119:932)

Thdr.Stud.*Or*.9.10 (*PG* 99:784)

John 1:40–42

Ps.Phot.*Rom*.4 (Gordillo 11)

Nicet.Steth.*Arm.et Lat*.14 (Hergenröther 153)

was a similar theological declaration from the Latin side when a treatise against the Greeks urged them "not to attribute to themselves what had been conferred on all nations," but to "consider the catholic church of Christ scattered through the breadth of the entire world, extending from the East to the West."

Ratr.*Graec.*3.1 (*PL* 121:272)

Latins and Greeks would both have been able to declare, in the words of a sixth-century pope, who had himself been involved in an earlier schism between East and West, that "the first [condition of] salvation is to preserve the rule of the true faith, and not to deviate in any way from the constitution of the fathers." But when he went on to quote the words of Matthew 16:18-19 and to argue that "these words have been proved true by events, for in the apostolic see the catholic religion has always been kept immaculate," the ideological conflict over the foundation of apostolic polity became visible.

Horm.*Ep.*9 (*PL* 63:393; *CSEL* 35:520-21)

The Theological Origins of the Schism

While the East-West schism stemmed largely from political and ecclesiastical discord, this discord also reflected basic theological differences, whose importance must be neither exaggerated (as it was by the antagonists) nor minimized (as it has been by modern historians). It may be excessive to say that "from the intellectual point of view, the breach between the Latins and Greeks arose from the fact that each side came to regard as absolute and irreconcilable certain differing representations, differing mental images, of the Truth," but the documents of the schism do show the depths of the intellectual alienation that had developed between the two sections of Christendom. In the precise sense of the patristic distinction between "schism" and "heresy," the two sides could properly accuse each other of the former more than of the latter. Yet the accusation of heresy was in fact the one frequently voiced. Although the reference of Pope Paul I to "Greek heretics who meditate and scheme how to humiliate and crush the holy catholic and apostolic church" was probably aimed at the iconoclasts, eventually such epithets were being applied to the two churches. When Photius called Constantinople the place where the fountains of orthodoxy flowed, he may have been implying that Rome was not such a place. Whether he was or not, Michael Cerularius went much further than he, ad-

Sherrard (1959) 50

See vol. 1:69

Paul.I.*Ep.*27 (*PL* 98:183; *MGH Ep.*3:539)

Phot.*Enc.*2 (*PG* 102:721)

Cerul.*Panop*.26.1 (Michel 2:244)
Cerul.*Panop*.36.2 (Michel 2:254)

monishing: "O you who are orthodox, flee the fellowship of those who have accepted the heretical Latins and who regard them as the first Christians in the catholic and holy church of God!" For, as he said a little later, "the pope is a heretic." Not only schism, then, but heresy was the charge: the differences between the churches were matters of doctrine.

Admittedly, not all the differences were matters of doctrine. Both sides recognized, as a Greek spokesman put it, that "the fathers have permitted the use of [some] things as adiaphorous," neither right nor wrong but neutral.

Petr. Ant.*Ep.Cerul.* 7 (Will 194)

Aen.Par.*Graec*.pr. (*PL* 121:689)

Humb.*Dial*.22 (Will 105)

From the Latin side, many of the Greek objections were dismissed as "useless questions pertaining more to secular than to spiritual affairs" or as "frivolous matters." Much of the debate and rebuttal in both directions dealt with regional differences in usages and customs, which offended those who had been taught that one particular way of observance was the right way, as the early church had discovered with regard to Jewish dietary laws. In principle it

See vol. 1:13–14

was easy to assert that there were such adiaphora, but in practice it was more difficult to identify which customs were purely adiaphorous and which carried implications

Ans.Hav.*Dial*.2.pr. (*PL* 188:1161)

for doctrine, especially in a cultural ambience where liturgical actions were constantly being interpreted as fraught with symbolic meaning. Photius asserted that "where there is no denial of faith nor abandonment of a general and catholic decree," those who observed the custom were not acting unjustly and those who failed to observe it were not breaking the law; for there were different customs and regulations among different groups. In response, Nicholas,

Phot.*Ep*.1.2 (*PG* 102:605)

Nicol.I.*Ep*.86 (*MGH Ep*.6:451)

too, allowed for "different customs in different churches, so long as they are not opposed by a canonical authority on account of which we ought to avoid them." This latter was, of course, the difficulty in the concrete application of the principle. But when a Latin dismissed the conflict

Ratr.*Graec*.4.5 (*PL* 121:322)

Petr.Ant.*Ep.Cerul.* 6 (Will 193)

over the proper tonsure of monks as inconsequential or a Greek identified the wearing of beards by the clergy as a matter of indifference, this expressed the recognition by both sides of nondoctrinal differences, that is, those which

Ratr.*Graec*.4.1 (*PL* 121:303–4)

"contain nothing of the dogma of faith, in which the fullness of Christianity consists."

Sometimes one side falsely accused the other of denying such a dogma of faith, perhaps on the basis of rumor or from the account of a traveler or because of distortion through translation. Whatever the source of the accusations, they came in both directions. For some reason, the doctrine of Mary was singled out as a subject of such accusations on both sides. Already in the fifth century "those who have endeavored to becloud Latin purity with a Greek thunderstorm" were attacked for teaching incorrectly about the proper titles for her. A ninth-century treatise on the assumption of the Virgin Mary, written in the pseudonymous form of a letter of Jerome, attacked the Easterners for "beclouding you with the darkness of their smooth talk or bemusing [your] Latin purity with [their] Greek confusion"; as an antidote, it urged its Latin readers to "imitate the blessed and glorious Virgin whom you love and whose festival you are celebrating today." In the East, on the other hand, it was the Franks who were accused of "not calling the mother of our Lord Jesus Christ Theotokos, but only Saint Mary." Among other such accusations by the Greeks was also the charge that the Latins "refuse to worship the relics of the saints" —this in the eleventh century, during which a zeal for relics was one of the factors that impelled Western Christians to undertake the Crusades.

More prominent and more important than such false accusations was the acknowledgment by both sides of their common faith and of their shared loyalty to the orthodox catholic tradition. Of all the forms of fellowship, the noblest was the fellowship of faith and of true love, represented by "the faith that is ours and yours." The conflict was one that was being carried on within the circle of those who wanted to be "orthodox Christians, abiding unshakably in the dogmas of piety and rightly in the ancient usages and in the decrees laid down as law by the holy fathers." Enumerating the authorities for this orthodox faith—Scripture, the councils, the fathers, the "common ideas" shared by all rational men, and the unwritten and mystical tradition of the church—the East accused the West of violating a standard that was accepted, at least in theory, by both. The response of the West to such accusations was to affirm loyalty to the same standard. A favorite passage, quoted over and over again in statements of the Latin case, was Proverbs 22:28: "Do not cross the boundaries which your fathers have set." The promises and the commands of Scripture applied alike to East and West. This implied to the West, and also

Petr.Chrys.*Serm.* 145 (*PL* 52:590)

Radb.*Cog.*13 (*PL* 30:136)

Ps.Phot. *Franc.*10 (Hergenröther 65)

Cerul.*Ep.Petr.Ant.* 1.14 (Will 183)

Phot.*Ep.*1.1 (*PG* 102:589)

Cerul.*Panop.*37.2 (Michel 2:254)

Nicet.Byz.*Lat.*24 (Hergenröther 126)

Episc.Ger.*Graec.* (*PL* 119: 1211); Ratr.*Graec.*3.1 (*PL* 121:271); Leo IX.*Ep.Petr.Ant.* 5 (Michel 2:464)

Ratr. *Graec.*3.1 (*PL* 121:272)

though less obviously to the East, that there could be variety of local emphasis within the single large tradition, so that some idiosyncratic idea set forth by one or another church father would not cost him his standing within the total company of the fathers. Yet loyalty to the fathers meant, as Eastern theologians continued to argue, that the words of Paul, "Even if we, or an angel from heaven, should preach to you a gospel contrary to that which we preach to you, let him be accursed," forbade the church and its theologians to add anything to the received deposit of faith.

The antipathy to doctrinal novelty, so characteristic of Eastern theology, was shared by Western theology. For example, the *Caroline Books* based their opposition to what they supposed to be Eastern teaching about the "adoration" of icons on the premise that "we—being content with the prophetic, evangelical, and apostolic Scriptures; being imbued with the ordinances of the holy orthodox fathers, who have never deviated in their dogmas from Him who is the way, the truth, and the life; and being loyal to the six holy and universal councils—reject all novelties of phraseology and all foolish inventions of new ways of speaking." Therefore even the Western addition to the text of the Nicene Creed had to be defended as a teaching that had been "most diligently ventilated by the holy fathers," but had been "lying neglected for a long time," so that it appeared to be new. It was not the Western church, but the Eastern church which, by separating itself from Rome and adopting its own rules, was "attempting something novel and singular." Quoting what he claimed were the words of Chrysostom, Cerularius blamed the differences between East and West on "the innovation of the Italians." If "a turning away from dogma and an innovation" was the cause of the separation, this was not to be found in the East, where "the apostolic and patristic forms of orthodox doctrine are preserved." Both sides accepted a common faith and claimed to eschew any innovation or addition as a deviation from it.

Most of the controversy that went on within this common faith had to do in one way or another with questions of ecclesiology, with the structures or with the practices of the church. The controversy over apostolic polity, as that polity was set forth in the charter of Petrine primacy,

Ans.Hav.*Dial*.1.2 (*PL* 188:1143); Phot.*Ep*.1.24.20 (*PG* 102:813)

Gal.1:8

Phot.*Myst*.69 (*PG* 102: 348); Cerul. *Panop*.7.2; 24.2 (Michel 214; 242)

Lib.Car.pr. (*MGH Conc.Sup*.2:4)

Smarag.*Spir*. (*PL* 98:924)

Ans.Hav.*Dial*.3.3 (*PL* 188:1211)

Cerul.*Panop*.14.3 (Michel 2:228)

Petr.Ant.*Ep.Leo* IX.1.2.2 (Michel 2:448)

Cerul.*Panop*.8.1–2 (Michel 2:216–18)

Matthew 16:18–19, was, of course, a matter of ecclesiology, too. So completely did it dominate the writings of the polemical theologians on both sides that the other ecclesiological differences could be overshadowed by it. Perhaps it would be true to say that if the doctrinal basis of the jurisdictional dispute could have been settled, all these other differences could have been negotiated—or overlooked. Nevertheless, there was a real divergence of teaching between East and West on items of structure and on items of practice that did involve doctrinal considerations, even though at least some of the items themselves were not strictly doctrinal.

As the relation between the patriarch of Rome and the four other patriarchs of Christendom concerned church doctrine no less than church administration, so the relation between bishops and clergy could not be treated as simply the responsibility for the orderly management of the church's affairs, but had to affect, and to be affected by, doctrinal judgments. It was management and ecclesiastical politics, rather than doctrine, when East and West collided on the propriety of the elevation of Photius from layman to patriarch with unseemly haste. Photius was able to cite in his own defense the case of Ambrose, who had also passed directly through the intervening

Phot.Ep.1.2 (PG 102:609)

stages. Pope Nicholas retorted that the two instances were not truly analogous, partly because miracles had attended the promotion of Ambrose but not that of Photius, but also because the appointment of Ambrose as bishop of Milan had not involved the condemnation and deposition of an incumbent, while the elevation of Photius as patriarch of Constantinople had been accomplished at the

Nicol.I.Ep.85; 86 (MGH Ep.6:444–45; 449)

expense of Ignatius. Central though the matter of Photius's patriarchate was to the "Photian schism," it did not of itself reflect the doctrinal differences that did exist between East and West in the definition of the episcopal office and of its powers, as well as in the understanding of the priestly office itself.

The differences made themselves evident in connection with two other administrative questions, the question of the proper minister for the sacrament of confirmation and the question of the compulsory celibacy of the clergy. In the East it was customary for the local parish priest to administer confirmation, but in the West this was ordinarily reserved to the bishop. In support of this episcopal prerogative, Western theologians quoted John 20:22, which was spoken to the apostles and through them to their successors, who were not all the priests of the church but, strictly speaking, only the bishops. "And in fact there is a difference between priests and bishops that is not trivial, namely, that the priests, together with the other ranks in the church, are consecrated through the ministry of the bishops, but the bishops are not blessed by the priests." Hence it was fitting that confirmation, by which the baptized layman was inducted into his own special rank in the church, be administered by the bishop. The other practical issue in the management of the church and its ministry that became a doctrinal issue was the Western insistence on celibacy. There was special resistance to this insistence in the East when it went so far as to dissolve marriages into which priests had entered; this was a violation of the absolute teaching of Christ. But also the law of celibacy itself exceeded the authority of the church. "Who is it," asked an Eastern theologian, "who has handed on to you the tradition that you should both prohibit and dissolve the marriage of priests? What kind of teacher of the church was it who handed on such an absurd tradition to you?" Although celibacy was a matter of discipline and of canon law, rather than of doctrine, it became a doctrinal issue.

The same was true of other differences in the area of church life, especially of differences in liturgy and piety. In spite of the acknowledgment on both sides that there were permissible local variations in custom, these could easily move into the area of doctrine. As early as the time of Augustine it had been known in the Latin church that there were those "who, most of them being in Eastern parts, do not partake of the Lord's Supper daily" as Western clergy tended to do; but this difference was "without offense." Now other such differences of usage had developed. For example, the West criticized the East for failing to mix water with the wine in the celebration of the Eucharist. When the Greeks claimed that their practice was the authentic one, the Westerners replied: "Then how is it that there was no mention at Nicea and at the other four ecumenical councils of such necessary matters? Why is it that all the way to the sixth council the Greeks and the Latins ignored the question of the Mass and of fasting and were in error on such issues for six hundred years

Ratr.Graec.4.7 (PL 121:333)

Cerul.Sem. (Will 159)
Matt.19:6; Mark 10:9

Nicet.Steth.Antidial.15.1 (Michel 2:338)

Aug.Serm.Dom.2.7.26 (CCSL 35:114–15)

Ans.Hav.Dial.3.20 (PL 188:1241–45)

Humb.*Resp.Nicet*.20
(Will 143)

Aen.Par.*Graec*.175
(*PL* 121:741)

Episc.Ger.*Graec*. (*PL*
119:1201–12)

Thds.Peč.*Lat*.11
(Popov 75) ; Niceph.Kiev.
Posl. (Makarij 2:343)

Vernadsky (1943) 2:270
Cerul.*Ep.Petr.Ant*.1.14
(Will 183)

Ps.Phot.*Franc*.8
(Hergenröther 65)

Lib.Car.pr. (*MGH
Conc.Sup*.2:6)

after the passion of Christ? Or is it perhaps possible that the Greeks knew these things and the Romans were ignorant of them?" Except for its basis in the special authority of the pope, the canon law regulating fasting could not claim divine sanction, "for in diverse regions," even within the Western church itself, "various practices of abstinence are observed." Hence these were "superfluous" issues; yet they could easily merge with the more obviously doctrinal issues, even in Western polemics, as when a Latin treatise entitled *On the Faith of the Holy Trinity, against the Heresy of the Greeks* turned out to be in fact a catena of quotations from Augustine about Lenten fasting.

In a special category, for reasons described earlier, were the differences between East and West over the use of images. As far away as the Pečerskaja Lavra, the monastery of Kiev, it was charged that the Latins did not pay respect to the icons. In this, as in other polemics against the Latins, Kiev was echoing Constantinople; for "it is significant that all the anti-Catholic polemic treatises which circulated in Russia in the Kievan period were either translations from the Greek or written by Greeks in Russia." Sometimes the West was accused of disrespect not only for icons but also for relics, and at least one Eastern writer went so far as to maintain that the Latins "do not set up representations of the saints, except for the crucifixion, in their churches" and would not even portray the crucifixion except in sculpture. Underlying such criticism was the Western misunderstanding of the icons, as articulated in the formula of the *Caroline Books* over against both the iconoclasts and the iconodules: "We do not smash [images] with the former, nor adore them with the latter." Although the devotion to holy pictures in the West soon went beyond the limits temporarily imposed by Carolingian theology, images never played the role in the public liturgy of the Latin church that they held in the East. In this sense, despite the polemical exaggeration and misinformation, there was a fundamental difference between the two churches, and a difference which, because of the theology of icons being articulated in the East during the eighth and ninth centuries, was bound to have repercussions in the area of doctrine.

Yet the liturgical practice that played the largest part in the East-West debates was not the devotion to images, but the seemingly secondary difference between the Western use of azymes (unleavened bread) in the Eucharist and the Eastern insistence on leavened bread. As one Eastern ecclesiastic put it, "the principal cause of the division between them and us is in the matter of azymes. . . . The matter of azymes involves in summary form the whole question of true piety; if it is not cured, the disease of the church cannot be cured." Although a treatise on the subject was eventually fathered upon Athanasius, the issue did not arise in the controversies between Photius and Nicholas during the ninth century, but only in the conflicts of the eleventh century. When it did arise, the relations of the two communions were already strained by other problems, so that there is some plausibility to the interpretation that azymes became so important in the controversy as a justification for the "real differences." But these "real differences" are usually taken to have been based on anything but faith and dogma, whereas a less reductionist interpretation would be that azymes became both a useful pretext for the political and personal conflict and at the same time an appropriate expression for the religious and doctrinal differences. This was not the first time, nor yet the last, that questions of ritual became decisive, ecclesiastically and even doctrinally, in Eastern thought.

Azymes became divisive by bringing to light divergent attitudes toward the relation between the Old Testament and the New. Partly as a result of the intense and continuing controversy that they were having with Jewish thought, Byzantine theologians stressed the distinctiveness of Christian teaching and practice. Even before the eleventh century they had accused the West of following Jewish practice in sacrificing a lamb on the altar along with the body and blood of Christ in the Eucharist—an accusation that may have been based on too literal an interpretation of the Agnus Dei in the Latin liturgy of the Mass. But Eastern critics in the eleventh century fastened upon azymes as proof that the Latins were acting "Mosaically" in their observance of the Eucharist, contrary to the statement of the apostle that Christ was the Passover of Christians. Those who used unleavened bread were still under the shadow of the law and were still "eating at the tables of the Jews." As Archbishop Leo of Ochrida in Bulgaria put it, "those who keep the Sab-

Joh.Ant.*Az*.2 (Leib 113)
Ps.Ath.*Az*. (*PG* 26:1328-32)

See pp. 200–215 below

ap.Episc.Ger.*Graec*. (*PL* 119:1212)

Leo Ochr.*Enc*.3 (Will 56)

1 Cor.5:7

Cerul.*Ep.Petr.Ant*.1.12 (Will 180); Nicet.Steth.*Antidial*.2.4 (Michel 2:324)

Leo Ochr.*Enc*.3 (Will 59);
Cerul.*Panop*.20.4 (Michel 2:236)

Petr.Ant.*Ep.Dom.Ven.*
111 (Will 217)

Cerul.*Panop*.17.2–3 (Michel 2:232)

Humb.*Dial*.5 (Will 96)

Humb.*Dial*.43 (Will 116)

Nicet.Steth.*Arm.et Lat*.7 (Hergenröther 145–46); Nicet.Steth.*Antidial*.7 (Michel 2:330–31)

Humb.*Resp.Nicet*.11 (Will 140)

Matt.13:33; Luke 13:21

Humb.*Dial*.30 (Will 107)

Humb.*Dial*.12 (Will 99) Nicet.Steth.*Arm.et Lat*.5 (Hergenröther 143); Nicet.Steth.*Antidial*.4.4 (Michel 2:326); Petr.Ant. *Ep.Dom.Ven*.8–9 (Will 214–16)

Dom.Ven.*Ep.Petr. Ant*.3 (Will 207)

Nicet.Nicom.ap.Ans. Hav.*Dial*.3.14 (*PL* 188:1230)

Nicet.Steth.*Arm. et Lat*.13 (Hergenröther 151)

Leo Per.*Lat*. (Pavlov 127)

bath and the azymes and say that they are Christians are neither genuine Jews nor genuine Christians." And therefore, paraphrasing Galatians 5:2–3, it was possible to argue that anyone who kept azymes was bound to keep the whole law, so that "if you eat unleavened bread, Christ will be of no advantage to you." The anathema of the apostle upon circumcision and upon the compulsory observance of the Sabbath applied also to the azymes. The Westerners replied, in rebuttal, that retention of the azymes did not mean any relapse into the old Jewish ways, which were altogether alien to Christians. For "to us and to all who are concerned to walk in the newness of the Spirit, all things have become new, whether temples or altars" or azymes.

In the course of the debate over azymes various exegetical questions were also aired. Some Easterners sought to prove, partly from the chronology of the passion narratives in the Gospels, that Christ had instituted the Lord's Supper with leavened bread; to this the Latins replied that, despite the difficulty of determining the chronology with any precision, it was clear that on whatever day Christ instituted the Lord's Supper "there was no leavened bread available anywhere in all the territory of Israel." If biblical usage were to be consulted, moreover, it would be evident that almost every reference to "leaven" in the New Testament was pejorative, except for the one saying in the Gospels where it was a symbol for the kingdom of God and the doctrine of the apostles. It was clear, in addition, that throughout Scripture the term "bread" was applied indifferently to leavened and to unleavened bread, so that the East had no right to claim that only leavened bread was the "living" bread of the New Testament. Both leavened and unleavened bread were acceptable, the former being a manifestation of the ousia of the incarnate Logos and the latter being a symbol of the purity of his human nature. At least some Eastern theologians agreed, since it seemed that the apostles themselves had used both sorts of bread and that the East and the West each had taken over part of apostolic usage. It is not surprising, in the light of the direction taken by earlier controversies, that the Greeks soon interpreted the azymes in christological terms as an Apollinarist denial of the full humanity of Christ or as a Nestorian effort to divide the two natures. Such argumentation suggests that the azymes became an issue that went far beyond variations in liturgical usage to the underlying differences of spirit and of doctrine between East and West, and that "by emphasizing this intimate connection between Christology, ecclesiology, and the Eucharist, the Byzantines differ from their Latin contemporaries," even though "most of the differences are implied rather than expressly stated."

Erickson (1970) 23

It was, indeed, characteristic of all the deepest theological differences between East and West that they were usually implied rather than expressly stated. Not simply this or that theological idea of the Greeks, but their very method of theologizing, was foreign to the Latins. There had been an unmistakable lag in the development of theology in the West behind that of the East, a lag that was, of course, related to the cultural differences between East and West. In an exchange between the Byzantine emperor and Liutprand of Cremona during the latter's visit to Constantinople in 968, the emperor remarked that the "Saxons" had a naïve faith, implying that they were therefore immature in their attitude to matters of doctrine and theology. Liutprand replied: "I, too, agree with you when you say that the faith of the Saxons is young; for faith in Christ is always young, and never old, among those for whom works follow faith. But here [in Byzantium] faith is not young but old, here where works do not accompany faith, but where [faith] is despised on account of its age, like a worn-out garment." The valid point behind these charges of naïveté and of decadence was the difference between a more sophisticated theology which by the end of the tenth century had worked out a modus vivendi with its past and with philosophy and a more rudimentary theology which was not to undertake that assignment at the same depth until the twelfth and thirteenth centuries. Although the two were existing side by side within one undivided Christendom, it was only with increased contact between them that the contrast became obvious and eventually divisive.

Liut.*Leg*.22 (*MGH Scrip*.3:352)

With the increased contact came also a growing awareness of how linguistic peculiarities affected theological positions, and hence of how the ignorance of each other's languages had helped to bring about the theological lag. Maximus had noted that some of the peculiarities of Roman teaching were due to their "not being able to ex-

Max.*Opusc*.10 (*PG* 91:136)

Petr. Ant. *Ep.Cerul.*14
(Will 198) ; Thphyl.Ochr.*Lat.*
5 (*PG* 126:228–29)

Phot.*Myst*.87 (*PG*
102:376)

Petr.Ant.*Ep.Cerul*.24
(Will 204)

Hussey (1937) 56

Nicol.I.*Ep*.88 (*MGH
Ep*.6:459)

Aen.Par.*Graec*.pr.
(*PL* 121:689)

Ratr.*Graec*.3.1 (*PL*
121:273)

press their mind in another language and way of speaking as they do in their own." By the eighth century or so, the duchy of Benevento was almost the only place in Italy where the study of Greek was still being fostered. It became a commonplace of Byzantine polemics to observe that Latin-speaking barbarians did not have the same capacity for theological precision that Greek writers had acquired. Photius recalled that Pope Leo III, who played an important role in the history of the Filioque, had ordered the creed to be recited in Greek at Rome because he recognized the poverty of Latin as a medium for expressing Christian doctrine. But the poverty was not all on the Western side. The Byzantines, who called themselves "Romans ['Ρωμαῖοι]," often could not read Latin. A Latin polemical treatise in the eleventh century had remained unanswered because "we were not able to find anyone who could accurately translate this message into Greek." In fact, "by the eleventh century knowledge of Latin was unusual." Even in the ninth century the pope pointed out that the man who called himself the Roman emperor despised Latin as a "barbaric and Scythian" tongue. Despite its admitted superiority as a sophisticated medium for expressing abstract ideas, Greek had also been a medium for formulating heresy, so that "if iron is sharpened by iron, it would be fitting for the Greek tongue not to diverge from that truth in which Latin maintains the norm of the catholic faith unshakably." When the Holy Spirit descended at Pentecost, he had not come only on those who spoke Greek; therefore it behooved the Greeks to accept with humility whatever instruction they could receive, even if it came in Latin.

The mutual ignorance between East and West extended not only to each other's languages, but also to each other's theological literatures. In the dialogue between Anselm of Havelberg and Nicetas of Nicomedia, held in 1135, the latter asked "whether you accept the authority of those whom you have named [Chrysostom, Athanasius, and other Greek fathers] and of others of our teachers, since you are a Latin." To this Anselm replied that he did not "despise or reject the gift of the Holy Spirit conferred on any faithful Christian, whether he be a Greek or a Latin or a member of any other nation." "It seems to me," said Nicetas, "that I have found a Latin man who is truly

Ans.Hav.*Dial*.2.24
(*PL* 188:1204)
Petr.Dam.*Proc*.5 (*PL* 145:639)

Cerul.*Ep.Petr.Ant*.
1.14 (Will 183)

Aen.Par.*Graec*.166
(*PL* 121:738)

Ps.Alc.*Proc*.1 (*PL* 101:66)

Hussey (1937) 203

Pos.*V.Aug*.11 (Weiskotten 62)

Rackl (1924) 9

Max.Plan.*Aug*.
(*PG* 147:1113–30)

catholic. Would that such Latins had come to us at other times!" The Latins could, and did, voice similar sentiments about the Greeks, for on both sides there was a lack of acquaintance with, and of respect for, the church fathers of the other side. It was a polemical extravagance when Michael Cerularius charged that the Latins "do not count our saintly and great fathers, theologians, and high priests —I mean Gregory the Theologian and Basil the Great and Chrysostom the Divine—among the other saints." Basil, for example, was cited in translation by Latin theologians to support their theory of celibacy. But when it came to Gregory, they sometimes had to refer to "Gregory of Nazianzus, or perhaps it is Gregory of Nyssa." More important and more grave than such an individual lapse of memory or knowledge was the prevailing tendency of both Latins and Greeks to read and to cite only the fathers of their own tradition, at least partly because so few in either tradition had been translated. Individual fathers were quoted across the boundary, but they were an exception.

This was perhaps the reason why the doctrinal and theological issues that separated the two communions most profoundly and most decisively hardly ever were voiced in the polemical treatises being directed back and forth between them. Those issues had been there for centuries before the two communions ever came into open conflict; for "as far as it is possible to assign or discover a watershed, this is found at the end of the fourth century: on the one side is Augustine, whose writings form the basis of the Latin tradition; on the other the Greeks who followed the Cappadocian school." Although some works of Augustine were translated into Greek during his lifetime, "centuries had to pass before there was an awareness in the Orient of the overwhelming significance of Augustine." The first Greek translations of so prominent a monument of Western theology as Augustine's *On the Trinity* did not come until the end of the thirteenth century, with the work of Maximus Planudes. The importance of Augustine for the bifurcation of Christian trinitarianism into Eastern and Western doctrines should not obscure the even more fundamental way in which his thought simultaneously expressed and advanced distinctively Latin styles of interpreting the Christian faith.

It is instructive at this point to contrast the Augustinian system with that of Maximus. For example, Maximus said that "we were freed by holy baptism from ancestral sin [προγονικὴ ἁμαρτία]," which sounds very much like the Augustinian doctrine of a sinfulness passed on from Adam to his descendants for all generations. Human nature lost "the grace of impassibility and became sin." In other passages, too, Maximus spoke of sin and the fall in an apparently Augustinian fashion. But Maximus's doctrine, while referring of course to the sin of Adam, did not have in it the idea of the transmission of sin through physical conception and birth. Rather, Maximus saw Adam not as the individual from whom all subsequent human beings sprang by lineal descent, but as the entire human race embodied in one concrete but universal person. In spite of the superficial parallels between the two, therefore, Augustine's doctrine of man and Maximus's doctrine were really quite different. Photius recognized that the church fathers had had a twofold anthropology, one praising and the other reviling human nature. In the Eastern tradition this did not lead to the Western view of sin through the fall of Adam, but to a view of death through the fall of Adam, a death that each man merited through his own sin. Thus the hardening of Pharaoh, which Augustine had interpreted as at one and the same time a result of the secret predestination of God and an act of Pharaoh's own free will, was to Photius a proof that "God, who never does violence to the power of free will, permitted [Pharaoh] to be carried away by his own will when he refused to change his behavior on the basis of better counsel."

No less striking was the contrast between the Augustinian tradition and the Greek tradition in the understanding of grace and salvation. An epitome of the contrast is the formula of Maximus: "Our salvation finally depends on our own will." For "one could not conceive a system of thought more different from Western Augustinianism; and yet Maximus is in no way a Pelagian." This is because the dichotomy represented by the antithesis between Pelagianism and Augustinianism was not a part of Maximus's thought. Instead, "his doctrine of salvation is based on the idea of participation and of communion that excludes neither grace nor freedom but supposes their union

Max.*Ascet.*44 (PG 90:956)

Max.*Qu.Thal.*42 (PG 90:405)

Max.*Qu.Thal.*5; 21 (PG 90:277; 312–13)

Phot.*Amph.*9 (PG 101:116)

Aug.*Grat.*23.45 (PL 44:911)

Phot.*Amph.*1.24 (PG 101:80)

Max.*Ascet.*42 (PG 90:953)

Meyendorff (1969) 114

See vol.1:318–31

and collaboration, which were re-established once and for all in the incarnate Word and his two wills." Even though the century following the death of Augustine saw his predestinarianism attacked by his critics and mollified by his disciples, the Augustinian understanding of original sin and of grace continued to shape Western theology. Eastern theology, on the other hand, continued to emphasize, with Maximus, that divine sonship was a gift of God and an achievement of man, and neither of these without the other. Such diametrically opposed interpretations of the very heart of the Christian gospel would almost inevitably come to blows when the ecclesiastical situation had shifted and all the other doctrinal differences that we have been examining became matters of open controversy. Nevertheless, over the centuries of the controversy, it was neither in the doctrine of grace nor even in the doctrine of the church that East and West came into dogmatic conflict most frequently, but in a doctrine on which, supposedly, not only East and West, but even Nestorians and Monophysites, were all agreed: the dogma of the Trinity.

Phot.*Amph*.8 (*PG* 101:113)

The Filioque

The principal clash between East and West in the realm of pure dogma was the question whether the Holy Spirit proceeded from the Son as well as from the Father, "ex Patre Filioque," as the Latin church had come to teach, or only from the Father, as the Greek church maintained. It had come to the attention of the patriarch of Constantinople, he wrote in about 883, "that some of those from the West are introducing the idea that the divine and Holy Spirit proceeds not only from God and the Father, but also from the Son." Actually, the theologians of the East—or at least some of them—were aware of this long before 883. During the pontificate of Leo III, who died in 816, a group of Latin monks on the Mount of Olives reported that a Greek monk named John, from the monastery of Saint Sabas, had accused the Franks of heresy for teaching the Filioque. "Prostrate on the ground and in tears," they appealed to the pope "to deign to investigate in the holy fathers, both Greek and Latin, who composed the creed, where it is said [that the Spirit] 'proceeds from the Father and the Son.'" Several chronicles recount that

Phot.*Ep*.1.24.3 (*PG* 102:797)

Ep.Oliv. (*MGH Ep*.5: 64–65)

Ep.Oliv. (*MGH Ep*.5:66)

Reg.*Chron.* (*MGH Scrip.*1:557); Ado.*Chron.* (*MGH Scrip.*2:319); Ein.*Ann.* (*MGH Scrip.*1:145)

as early as "the year of our Lord's incarnation 767 the king [Pepin the Short] . . . held a great council between the Romans and the Greeks about the Holy Trinity and about the images of the saints."

It was sometime later, in 796, that a local synod held in Fréjus under the presidency of Paulinus of Aquileia set down what appears to be the earliest documentation for the Western recension of the Nicene Creed; its pertinent section read: "And in the Holy Spirit, the Lord and giver of life, who proceeds from the Father and the Son; who with the Father and at the same time with the Son is adored and glorified together; who spoke through the prophets. And one holy catholic and apostolic church. I confess one baptism into the remission of sins. And I expect the resurrection of the dead, and the life of the future age. Amen." Over this text the spokesmen for both sides were to do battle for centuries; and although it is probably an exaggeration to say that "nothing can surpass the monotony of these erudite treatises on the Procession of the Holy Ghost, of these dialogues and contradictory debates, which repeat over and over again the same arguments and appeal continually to the same authorities," the persistence of the arguments on both sides does make possible a summary of the two positions on the several theological issues as they were debated in the period under consideration in this chapter, from the ninth through the eleventh century. Several of the other debates that we have been examining also came to focus in the Filioque: the right of the Roman see to fix and to revise the norm of orthodoxy, the Eastern definition of antiquity as the criterion of tradition, the dominance of Augustine in Latin theology, the "theological lag" of the West behind the East. All of this, and more, was seen by both sides as lying at the basis of the dispute over the Filioque. For both sides, therefore, it was a matter of grave importance whether the Holy Spirit proceeded only from the Father or from the Father and the Son.

Paulin.Aquil.CFor.(796) (*MGH Conc.*2:187)

Bréhier (1936) 595

To Eastern theologians, the gravity of the Filioque was a persistent issue. After listing various Western errors in doctrine and abuses in practice, Photius declared that their "excess with regard to the Spirit, or rather with regard to the entire Trinity, is not the least among their blasphemies" and was indeed second to none

Phot.*Enc*.33 (*PG* 102:736)

Laourdas (1959) 85

Cerul.*Ep.Petr.Ant*.1.12 (Will 181)

Petr.Ant.*Ep.Cerul*.11 (Will 196)

Petr.Ant.*Ep.Cerul*. 18 (Will 200–201)

Leo IX.*Ep.Petr.Ant*. 10 (Michel 2:470)

Geo.Kiev.*Lat*.5 (Popov 84); Niceph.Kiev.*Posl*. (Makarij 2:342)

See vol.1:175–76

Paulin.Aquil.*Fel*.1.24 (*PL* 99:377)

of them in deserving a thousand anathemas. While it is noteworthy that "the reference to the addition of the Filioque to dogma by the Western church . . . occurs only in his eighteenth homily and in no other one," he evidently did regard the Filioque as more than a trivial question. Michael Cerularius likewise attacked it as "wicked and dangerous." Peter of Antioch, to whom Cerularius wrote these words, sought to mediate between the extremes of the Eastern and the Western positions on many of the controverted practices, such as fasting and shaving; but when it came to the Filioque, he had to identify it as "a wicked thing, and among the wicked things the most wicked." Other matters were to be treated with understanding and even to be handled by compromise, but on the Filioque (and on the Western refusal to accept the sacraments from the hands of a married priest) the East must be adamant. His irenicism did go so far as to prompt an omission of any reference to Filioque in his letter to the pope, but the pope included it in his response. So fundamental was the heresy of the Filioque to the Eastern brief of argument against the West that even in the Russian treatises against the Latins, which were mainly preoccupied with differences of custom and observance, this one dogmatic difference did play a role. It would seem to have been the widespread contention of Eastern theologians that this difference by itself was enough to divide the two communions.

For the theologians of the West, the inclusion of the Filioque was also a matter of gravity, but for other reasons of their own. The orthodox dogma of the homoousia of the Son with the Father seemed to be jeopardized by the efforts of two Spanish bishops, Elipandus of Toledo and Felix of Urgel, to reintroduce the idea of "adoption" as an explanation of the divine in Christ. Writing in response to Felix, Paulinus of Aquileia asserted: "If you believed correctly concerning the Son, you would surely believe correctly also about the Holy Spirit." From Paulinus's espousal of the Filioque in the setting of an antiadoptionist synod it would appear that an important way of asserting the homoousia and full equality of the Son with the Father in the Trinity was to teach that the Holy Spirit proceeded from both equally. "Let every Christian," he said at that synod, "know the creed [including the Filioque] and the Lord's Prayer by heart . . . because without this blessing no one will be able to receive a portion in the kingdom of heaven." Charlemagne, by whose commission Paulinus had spoken out against adoptionism and in support of the Filioque, applauded as "catholic" the assertion of the *Caroline Books* that the Holy Spirit proceeded "from the Father and the Son . . . not from the Father through the Son." He also commissioned the preparation of a florilegium of patristic quotations in defense of the Filioque by Theodulph of Orléans, who dedicated the compilation to the emperor in 809.

Another of the theological controversies of the Carolingian period (to which we shall be returning in the next volume) also touched on the Filioque. Gottschalk of Orbais, who was the subject of the most severe controversy on predestination between the sixth century and the sixteenth, also became involved in a controversy on the doctrine of the Trinity, contending that it was proper to speak of the Trinity as "trine Deity [trina Deitas]." As part of his defense he used the teaching that "the Holy Spirit alone is God in such a way that he proceeds simultaneously from the unbegotten and from the begotten God" to prove the propriety of the term "trine Deity." His opponent, Hincmar of Reims, also taught the Filioque and even quoted Paulinus of Aquileia in support of it, but refused to accept it as a justification for "trine Deity." These two trinitarian controversies within Latin thought helped to make the issue of Filioque a serious one. A denial of the Filioque was what Christ had meant by the sin of blasphemy against the Holy Spirit, which could not be forgiven. When, therefore, Nicholas and Photius clashed on the Filioque and on other questions, the pope was able to state that "illustrious men, especially Latins, have written some things about the procession of the Holy Spirit" which provided an authoritative support that could refute the Greek position. Or had perhaps "the truth come only to you [Greeks]," and did it abide only there?

The polemic of Nicholas against Photius should not, however, lead to the supposition that the Filioque had been a papal dogma. The Frankish monks accused of heresy by the Greeks were correct in remembering that they had heard the Filioque sung as part of the creed at Mass in the chapel of Charlemagne. The emperor had

Paulin.Aquil.CFor.(796) (MGH Conc.2:189)

ap.Freeman (1971) 611 Lib.Car.3.3 (MGH Conc.Sup.2:110)

Theod.Aur.Spir.pr. (PL 105:239–41)

See vol.1:330

Goth.Deit.1 (Lambot 83)

Hinc.R.Deit.5 (PL 125:535)

Mark 3:29 Ratr.Graec.1.1 (PL 121:227)

Nicol.I.Ep.100 (MGH Ep.6:605)

Ratr.Graec.2.1 (PL 121:244)

Ep.Oliv. (MGH Ep.5:65)

Ado.*Chron*.6 (*MGH Scrip*.2:320)

also convoked a council in 809 to affirm the doctrine over against the East. Yet when he requested the pope to include the Filioque in the text of the Nicene Creed as it was sung in the Mass, Leo III declined. He did indeed accept the Filioque as a doctrine, and in the creed which he composed he confessed his faith in "the Holy Spirit, who proceeds equally from the Father and the Son. . . . In the Father there is eternity, in the Son equality, in the Holy Spirit the connection between eternity and equality." But

Symb.Leo III (*PL* 129:1260)

he was not willing to impose an addition to the creed, although he did permit it to be taught. "We ourselves," the pope said, "do not chant this, but we do speak it [legimus] and by speaking teach it; yet we do not presume by our speaking and teaching to insert anything into the

Smarag.*Acta* (*PL* 102: 971, 975)

creed."

Pope Leo did, of course, claim the authority to do just that. When the representatives of the emperor asked him, "Does not the permission to chant this very creed in the

Smarag.*Acta* (*PL* 102: 975)

church come from you?" he replied that it did. Eventually the question whether the Filioque was orthodox and the question whether Rome had the authority to impose it on the entire church as an addition to the Nicene Creed were closely identified. If, as the defenders of papal primacy maintained, all the councils had been convoked by the authority of the pope and their dogmatic decrees had become valid only through the pope's endorsement, the pope must also have the authority to determine what the valid text of the creed should be. Basing his defense of the Filioque on the words in Matthew 16:18, Peter Damian laid down the principle that "whoever wishes to know anything divine and profound, let him have re-

Petr.Dam.*Proc*.1 (*PL* 145:633–34)

course to the oracle and the doctrine of this preceptor." Since the doctrine of Filioque was both divine and profound, the teaching office of the papacy was the seat of authority for learning about it. Photius sought to stand this argument on its head, on the basis of the principle that "a refutation derived from one's own sources arouses

Phot.*Myst*.85 (*PG* 102:373)

shame even in the most shameless," and proceeded to show that the most eminent among the incumbents of the see of Peter—Leo I, Gregory I, and others—had not taught the Filioque. This was the authentic succession of orthodoxy in Old Rome; and if a later pope taught such

Phot.*Myst*.86 (*PG* 102:373)

a notion, he was betraying his heritage.

Despite such quotations from Leo and Gregory, most

of which were in fact an argument from silence rather than positive proof, the weight of the authentic succession in Old Rome and in Western theology as a whole was on the side of the Filioque. The founder of Western theology and the creator of Latin as a theological language, Tertullian, had spoken of the Spirit as "from nowhere else than from the Father through the Son" and had spoken elsewhere of "the Spirit from God and the Son," in a manner for which "there seem to be no precedents." More influential in the evolution of the idea of double procession was Hilary of Poitiers. During the Carolingian period his treatise on the Trinity was widely used as an authority; for example, during the adoptionist controversy Felix of Urgel and Paulinus of Aquileia both cited him in support of their (mutually contradictory) opinions. As on trinitarian questions generally, so on the Filioque, Hilary was an important source for Western theologians during the Carolingian period and in the later defenses of Latin theology against Greek attacks. There was good reason for this use of Hilary. For although he was still somewhat equivocal in his doctrine of the full deity of the Holy Spirit, he was more explicit in his doctrine of the Holy Spirit as "proceeding from Father and Son [(a) Patre et Filio auctoribus]." The Holy Spirit, he wrote, "receives from the Son; he is also sent by [the Son] and proceeds from the Father," and he added that "to receive from the Son is the same as to receive from the Father," which seems to imply that the Spirit also proceeded from the Son as well as from the Father. Such language, inchoate though it was because the relation of the Holy Spirit to the Trinity had yet to be clarified, did nevertheless help to buttress the doctrine of Filioque.

The importance of Hilary lay also in his unique place as the only church father whose name was mentioned in Augustine's *On the Trinity,* where he was called a "man of no mean authority in treating the Scriptures and in asserting the faith." Augustine was more overt than Hilary in his statements about the Filioque. Although there were in the Trinity "no intervals of time," according to which the procession of the Holy Spirit would come after the begetting of the Son, the procession of the Holy Spirit from both was taught by Scripture when it

Tert.*Prax*.4.1 (*CCSL* 2:1162)
Tert.*Prax*.8.7 (*CCSL* 2:1168)

E.Evans (1948) 203

Paulin.Aquil.*Fel.* 3.19–20 (*PL* 99:452–54)
Ps.Alc.*Proc.*1(*PL* 101:73–74); Theod. Aur.*Spir.* (*PL* 105: 248-49)
Ans.Hav.*Dial*.2.7 (*PL* 188:1174)

Hil.*Trin*.2.29 (*PL* 10:69)

Hil.*Trin*.8.20 (*PL* 10:251)

Aug.*Trin*.6.10.11 (*CCSL* 50:241)

spoke of him as the Spirit of the Son and as the Spirit of the Father. Therefore one should speak of "the procession of the Holy Spirit from both apart from time." The Father and the Son were one "principle [prinicipium]" in relation to the Holy Spirit. "Why then," he asked elsewhere, "should we not believe that the Holy Spirit proceeds also from the Son, since he is the Spirit of the Son as well?" These three passages from Augustine, especially the first of them, became the arsenal for Western defenses of the Filioque. Many other quotations from Augustine's treatise *On the Trinity* were also prominent in the patristic florilegia compiled as proofs for the Latin doctrine. It was the purpose of such florilegia "to learn the reasons which Father Augustine in his books on the Holy Trinity regarded as of primary importance" in arguing for this doctrine. Those reasons are to be found in the very structure of Augustinian trinitarianism; for "since according to Augustine the three persons, to whose common essence it also belongs to be 'person,' are distinguished from one another solely through the functions that pertain to each in relation to the other two, the 'procession from the Father and the Son' is regarded by him as the specific property of the Holy Spirit within the immanent essence of God."

Although the compilers of the florilegia quoted other Latin fathers—notably Ambrose, whose influence upon Augustinian theology extended to this doctrine as well —they took special pains to draw in evidence from Greek theologians too. Many of their writings were not available in Latin, but the treatise *On the Holy Spirit* of Didymus the Blind had been translated by Jerome; in fact, the Latin version is all that has survived of the work. Didymus could thus serve as a support for Latin theologians in their writings against the Greeks. The most abundant source of support was probably the corpus of writings mistakenly attributed to Athanasius. The *Five Dialogues on the Holy Trinity* in that corpus, which were perhaps written by Didymus, were taken as evidence that the father of trinitarian orthodoxy had taught the Filioque. No "Athanasian" writing was more direct in its contribution to the Western cause than the Athanasian Creed, which had been composed in the West, probably during the century after the death of Augustine. Here it was confessed, in

Gal.4:6; Matt.10:20
Aug.*Trin*.15.26.45–47
(*CCSL* 50:524–29)

Aug.*Trin*.5.14.15 (*CCSL* 50:222)

Aug.*Ev.Joh*.99.7 (*CCSL* 36:586)
Ps.Alc.*Proc*.1 (*PL* 101: 690); Theod.Aur.*Spir*. (*PL* 105:261); Ratr.*Graec*.3.3 (*PL* 121:283); Humb.*Proc*. 2; 6–8 (Michel 1:98–99; 102–8)

Theod.Aur.*Spir*. (*PL* 105: 259–63); Aen.Par.*Graec*. 35–55 (*PL* 121:706–11); Ratr.*Graec*.3.2–4 (*PL* 121: 273–94)

Alc.*Trin*.pr.(*MGH Ep*.4:415)

Noesgen (1899) 87

Ratr.*Graec*.2.4 (*PL* 121: 253–59)

See vol.1:289–90

Didym.*Spir*. (*PG* 39: 1031–86)

Ratr.*Graec*.2.5 (*PL* 121: 266)

Theod.Aur.*Spir*. (*PL* 105: 242); Smarag.*Spir*. (*PL* 98:928); Ratr.*Graec*.3.6 (*PL* 121:297–302); Petr. Dam.*Proc*.5 (*PL* 145:640)

See vol.1:351

characteristically Augustinian language, that "the Holy Spirit is from the Father and from the Son, neither made nor created nor begotten, but proceeding"; and to this clause, as to the rest of the Creed, the warning applied: "He therefore who wants to be saved, must think this way about the Trinity." It was quoted as "the faith of Saint Athanasius" in support of the Filioque by the Western monks who clashed with Eastern monks on the question, and as "the faith which from these times . . . until our own times has been held by the Western church and which the catholic church of the Greeks has not abdicated either." Other ninth-century Latin theologians also used it to prove their case. In later Western treatises and dialogues it continued to be prominent. When Anselm of Havelberg quoted it as a creed that was "venerable throughout the entire church," there was, according to his report, no objection from the Greeks present. Cardinal Humbert carried the Western point to its logical conclusion when he declared that "even the holy and great Athanasius would never have found acceptance among the Romans if he had not affirmed in his confession that the Holy Spirit proceeds from the Son."

All of this was used to show that the spokesmen for the West were "not explaining this dogma on their own, but confessing it on the basis of the doctrine of the holy fathers." From the days of Athanasius, the Cappadocians, and Augustine many centuries had passed, and no authoritative doctor of the church had denied the procession of the Holy Spirit from the Son, which had in fact been "the perpetual and constant confession of faith both of the Oriental and of the Occidental church about the Holy Spirit." The *Mystagogy Concerning the Doctrine of the Holy Spirit* by Photius may be taken as a representative statement of the Eastern contention that "the perpetual and constant confession both of the Oriental and of the Occidental church" did not support the case for the Filioque. "Which of our holy and renowned fathers," it demanded, "said that the Spirit proceeds from the Son?" Citing various fathers, including Dionysius and the writings attributed to Clement, Photius went on to "add to them also those from the West," Irenaeus and Hippolytus, neither of whom had taught the Filioque. No Western theologian had been more eminent than Leo I—"pillar of the fourth council," author of "divinely inspired epistles

Symb.Ath.23 (Schaff 2:68)

Symb.Ath.28 (Schaff 2:68)

Ep.Oliv. (MGH Ep. 5:66)

Ratr.Graec.2.3 (PL 121: 247)
Ps.Alc.Proc.1 (PL 101: 73); Theod.Aur.Spir. (PL 105:247); Aen.Par.Graec. 19 (PL 121:701)

Ans.Hav.Dial.2.3; 2.24 (PL 188:1169; 1202)

Humb.Proc.3.2 (Michel 1:99)

Hadr.Ep.2 (MGH Ep. 5:7); Humb.Proc.1.2 (Michel 1:97–98)

Ratr.Graec.2.3 (PL 121:253)

Phot.Myst.5 (PG 102:284)

Phot.Myst.75 (PG 102:356–57)

on dogma," and authority of "orthodoxy shedding light not only over the West but also over the boundaries of the East." He, too, taught that the Spirit proceeded from the Father. As for "those fathers of yours. . . . Ambrose or Augustine or whoever," who did assert a procession also from the Son, it was necessary to remember that they, too, were human, and therefore to cover their shame, as the sons of Noah had done for their father. Photius was quite willing to acknowledge that Augustine and other Western theologians were entitled to the name "fathers," but their authority was superseded by that of "the fathers of the fathers," such as Pope Leo I. Above all, it had to yield to the authority of the Lord himself, who had taught that the Holy Spirit proceeded from the Father.

Within the hierarchy of authority, the testimony of some fathers was clearly superior to that of others, but above them all stood the ecumenical councils of the church. The dogma of the Holy Spirit had been defined for the church by the second council, repeated by the third, confirmed by the fourth, established by the fifth, proclaimed by the sixth, and sealed by the seventh. Among these councils, those of Nicea and Constantinople were the most decisive, for they had formulated the creed in which the dogma of the Holy Spirit was confessed. It was therefore an act of "extreme effrontery" for the West to take it upon itself "to adulterate the holy and sacred symbol" which had been affirmed by so many ecumenical councils. Such an adulteration was nothing less than a "debasement [διαστροφή]" of the sacred coinage of the creed. The spokesmen for the East maintained that for their part they refused to tamper with the authoritative text of the creed. That text, as laid down by the First Council of Constantinople, taught that the Holy Spirit "proceeds from the Father" and did not mention any procession from the Son. The advocates of the Filioque, by deliberately going beyond the received text of the creed, were guilty of innovation. A charitable construction that could be put on this innovation was to suggest that the Latins must have lost their copies of the acts of the Council of Nicea at the time of the Vandal invasions and that they did not know the real text of the creed. Most Greek theologians made no such excuses for the addition of the Filioque, but simply drew the line between the orthodox tradition of a procession from the Father only and the heterodox novelty

Phot.*Myst*.79 (*PG* 102:361)

Phot.*Myst*.68 (*PG* 102:345)
Phot.*Myst*.70 (*PG* 102:352)

Gen.9:21–27

Phot.*Myst*.81; 69 (*PG* 102:365; 348)

Phot.*Myst*.76 (*PG* 102:357)

Phot.*Myst*.5 (*PG* 102:285)

Niceph.Kiev.*Posl.* (Makarij 2:342–43)

Phot.*Enc*.8 (*PG* 102: 725)

Cerul.*Ep.Petr.Ant.* 2.5 (Will 187)

Cerul.*Sem.* (Will 158)

Cerul.*Panop*.7.1 (Michel 2:214)

Phot.*Myst*.34 (*PG* 102:313)

Petr.Ant.*Ep.Cerul*.12 (Will 197)

Phot.*Enc*.16 (*PG* 102:729);
Cerul.*Ep.Petr.Ant*.2.3
(Will 185–86)

Ratr.*Graec*.1.2 (*PL* 121:228)

Aen.Par.*Graec*.93 (*PL* 121:721)

Petr.Dam.*Proc*.2 (*PL* 145:636)

Humb.*Proc*.4.1 (Michel 1:100–101)

Ans.Hav.*Dial*.2.22 (*PL* 188:1197–98)

Paulin.Aquil.*Carm*. 1.119–22 (*MGH Poet*.1:129)

Paulin.Aquil.*Fel*. 1.17 (*PL* 99:369)

Paulin.Aquil.CFor. (796) 7 (*MGH Conc*.2:181)

Ratr.*Graec*.2.2 (*PL* 121:245)

Nicet.Nicom.ap.Ans.Hav.*Dial*. 2.27 (*PL* 188:1209–10)

of a procession also from the Son. Such an addition to the text of the creed was unwarranted and heretical.

It was no such thing, the West replied. There was no new form of worship or of doctrine, no new religion in the Roman church, which "has remained in the same faith as the Eastern church." Although there were some Latins who argued on the basis of the usage in some of the churches of the West that the creed with the Filioque was "the catholic faith," most of them recognized that the phrase had been added to the creed after Nicea and Constantinople. One answer to the objection was to argue that "from the Father" did not in principle exclude "and from the Son," that when the fathers at Nicea "failed to include this, it was not because they did not believe firmly and perfectly that it was so, but because they thought that it was plain and manifest to all the faithful" and did not think it necessary to mention it explicitly. If now it was mentioned, this was in no way contrary to the true meaning of the text of the creed. The Latins would not concede the councils and the creeds to the Greeks. "I embrace the 318 catholic and holy men, the blessed fathers, all of them," said Paulinus in one of his hymns, and elsewhere he declared that the symbol of Nicea was "inviolable." The addition of the Filioque was not a violation of it, but the same thing that the 150 fathers of the Council of Constantinople had done when they expanded the simple phrase of Nicea, "And in the Holy Spirit," to the form now used in the East and in the West. If this addition was legitimate, why was the Filioque illegitimate? This Western argumentation missed at least part of the point in the Eastern critique. For even if an irenic Easterner were persuaded by Western logic to acknowledge the theological correctness of the Filioque, the unilateral insertion of the formula into the creed remained a grave scandal, one that could be set straight only if "a general council of the Western and Eastern church," convoked by papal and imperial authority, were to legislate the addition. It was up to a council to expand a creed that had been formulated by a council.

Thus the formal and procedural objection to the Filioque was a decisive one for the Greeks all by itself. Yet their objection applied no less to the material and substantive issue. The Filioque was not only illegitimate, it was also mistaken. It was based on certain theological premises which the East found to be inadequate or erroneous and which became visible in the course of the debates. Several of these lay in the area of what must be called "theological method," for they involved differences over the way trinitarian doctrine was to be arrived at. Beyond such methodological differences lay some ultimate, metaphysical differences in the doctrine of God itself; but before these can be identified, it is necessary to describe the divergent ways in which the two theologies proceeded in their thought about the doctrine of the Trinity and to specify the distinctions which, while fundamental to one side, were not shared by the other side.

The most far-reaching of these distinctions was that between "economy" and "theology" in the doctrine of the Trinity. It was a part of Western as well as of Eastern trinitarianism, but it was in the East that it was more fully developed. Maintaining that Latin as a theological language was incapable of the precision necessary for such distinctions, some Eastern theologians laid the blame for the Filioque on the absence of a proper distinction in the doctrine of the Holy Spirit between his economic "being sent" and his theological "proceeding." Because of this the Latins "suppose that proceeding [ἐκπορεύεσθαι] is identical with being imparted [χορηγεῖσθαι] and with being conferred [μεταδίδοσθαι], because the Spirit is discovered to have been sent and imparted and conferred from the Son." The Spirit, according to the Greeks, "proceeds from the Father, but is given through the Son and shared by all creation"; the proceeding from the Father was within the Godhead, the giving and sharing was outside the Godhead in the world. For a "Filioque" in the latter sense there was ample patristic precedent, and the Greek theologians readily affirmed it, but the confusion between the theological and the economic was a heresy reminiscent of Marcellus of Ancyra.

An examination of the Latin interpretations of the Filioque shows that many of them did equate the proceeding of the Spirit with his being sent. Pope Gregory I had said that the Spirit's "being sent [missio] is the very procession by which he proceeds from the Father and from the Son," and these words were quoted in support of the doctrine of the Filioque. In addition to this quotation from Gregory, Ratramnus made a point of insisting that the "sending" in John 15:26 (which the East took

Max.*Pyrr.* (*PG* 91:348)

Ps.Phot.*Franc.*1
(Hergenröther 63)

Thphyl.Ochr.*Lat.*
(*PG* 126:228–29)

Nicet.Byz.*Lat.*2
(Hergenröther 91);
Psell.*Om.doct.*2
(Westerink 17)

Gr.Pal.*Conf.* (*PG* 151:765)

See vol.1:208

Gr.M.*Ev.*2.26.2 (*PL* 76:1198)

Ps.Alc.*Proc.*1 (*PL* 101:76);
Ratr.*Graec.*3.2 (*PL* 121:274)

to be economic) and the "proceeding" in the same passage (which the East took to be theological) were identical. The sending of the Holy Spirit, he said, "does not signify subjection, but procession." The equation of the two became the dominant theme of his treatise. Other economic terms, such as the "pouring out" or the "conferring" of the Holy Spirit, were said to be applied to the Son in the New Testament because the Holy Spirit proceeded from both Father and Son; in this way, the economic was read back into the theological, which was then taken to be the basis of the economic. The Western tendency to move from the economic to the theological and back again can be seen in such a formulation as: "The Holy Spirit does not proceed from the Father to the Son, and proceed from the Son for the sanctification of the creation; but he proceeds simultaneously from both." Other passages about "sending," such as John 14:26 and John 20:22, could then become proof texts for the eternal procession from Father and Son. Even when there appeared to be some distinction operative between "sending" and "proceeding," it served finally to reinforce the teaching that both of them were from the Father and the Son.

Another distinction which the Greeks accused the Latins of violating or ignoring was that between the one divine nature and the three hypostases in the Trinity. Photius put the argument this way: "If something is in God, but is not seen in the unity and oneness of nature [ὁμοφυΐα] of the omnipotent Trinity, this obviously belongs to one of the Three. The procession of the Spirit does not pertain to the supernatural unity which is seen in the Trinity. Therefore it pertains to one single [hypostasis] of the Three." According to ousia, there was not separation in the Trinity, but there was a separation according to the properties characteristic of each hypostasis. The eternal spiration of the Holy Spirit was not a matter of the divine nature shared by the Three, but of the specific hypostasis of the Father; therefore there could be no procession also from the Son, for whatever was common to two hypostases had to be common to all three, and then the Holy Spirit would proceed also from himself. The doctrine of Filioque was, in short, failing to note the difference between what was distinct and what was common in the Trinity.

Ratr.*Graec*.1.3 (*PL* 121:229)

Ratr.*Graec*.2.3 (*PL* 121:252)
Ratr.*Graec*.1.7; 3.2
(*PL* 121:241; 274)

Ratr.*Graec*.1.5 (*PL* 121:235–36)

Smarag.*Spir*. (*PL* 98:929)

Alc.*Trin*.3.5 (*PL* 101:40);
Ans.Hav.*Dial*.2.15 (*PL* 188:1184)

Petr.Dam.*Proc*.3 (*PL* 145:637)

Nicet.Byz.*Lat*.15
(Hergenröther 119–20)

Phot.*Myst*.64 (*PG* 102:341)

Petr.Ant.*Ep.Al*.4.2
(Michel 2:434)

Phot.*Myst*.47 (*PG* 102:325);
Phot.*Enc*.22 (*PG* 102:732)

Phot.*Myst*.6; 17 (*PG* 102:288; 296–97)

Cerul.*Panop*.63.4
(Michel 2:276)

Episc.Ger.*Graec.*
(*PL* 119:1201)

Alc.*Trin.*1.4 (*PL* 101:16)

Paulin.Aquil.CFor.
(*MGH Conc.*2:182)

Ratr.*Graec.*2.3 (*PL* 121:252)

Petr.Dam.*Proc.*2 (*PL* 145:636)

Ans.Hav.*Dial.*2.10
(*PL* 188:1178–79)

Gal.4:6
Hil.*Trin.*2.29 (*PL* 10:69)

Aug.*Trin.*15.26.45
(*CCSL* 50:524–25)

Ratr.*Graec.*1.4 (*PL* 121:232);
Smarag.*Spir.* (*PL* 98:926)

Phot.*Myst.*48–52 (*PG*
102:328–29)

Phot.*Myst.*20–23 (*PG*
102:297–304)

Just this difference was the object of one of the earliest Western apologias, which requested that it "be shown what Father, Son, and Holy Spirit have each as his own, and what they have in common within the undivided Trinity; and how the Holy Spirit truly and eternally proceeds from both; and how the Holy Trinity itself exists inseparably." Other Western theologians of the time also distinguished between what was said about the Trinity "according to its ousia [substantialiter]" and what was said "according to the relations between the hypostases [relative]." Yet when they came to the procession of the Holy Spirit, many Western theologians, arguing that the actions of the Trinity "to the outside [ad extra]" were undivided, insisted that the procession was a matter of the divine nature as a whole, hence of the ousia not of the hypostases. And so, "when the Holy Spirit is said to proceed from the Father, it is necessary that he proceed also from the Son, because Father and Son are undoubtedly of the same ousia." In an effort to circumvent the problem, some attempted to locate the procession "neither in the ousia, which is common [to all three persons], nor in the person, which is spoken of in itself, but in the relation [between persons]," which really did not clarify the issue or meet the basic Greek objection. This effort, and others like it, came later in the controversy than the main body of the materials with which we have been dealing, and were a recognition by the West of the need for a more sophisticated defense of the Filioque.

Another area where this need manifested itself was in exegesis. For example, the New Testament title, "the Spirit of his Son," had been interpreted, perhaps by Hilary and certainly by Augustine, to be an indication or even a proof for the procession of the Spirit from the Son. "Is the Spirit of the Son someone other than the Spirit of the Father?" asked Ratramnus, and continued the argument: "If he is the Spirit of both, then he certainly proceeds from both." From the phrase, "into our hearts," in the same passage, Eastern theology argued that "the Spirit of his Son" did not refer to the eternal and theological procession of the Holy Spirit at all, but to his "being sent," which was temporal and economic. Nor could such a passage as John 16:14 be used to support the Filioque, for it did not say "from me [ἐξ ἐμοῦ]," but "from what is mine [ἐκ τοῦ ἐμοῦ]." Such exegetical argumentation led to the principle that when the Holy Spirit was called "the Spirit of the Father," this was to be taken theologically, to refer to his procession from the Father only, but that when he was called "the Spirit of the Son," this was to be taken economically, to refer to his being sent to the creation or the church or the believer. The disengagement of economy from theology in the exegesis of passages about the Spirit went so far that Photius even suggested, contrary to most of the tradition, that "spirit of God [πνεῦμα θεοῦ]" in the creation story did not mean the Holy Spirit, but only a wind that came from God. Whether this exegesis was the source of the East's doctrine of the Holy Spirit or its result, it did show that the Filioque was a question not only of procedure but also of substance.

There are some indications that the question of the Filioque went even deeper. Opposed to each other were not only two systems of dogmatic authority and two conceptions of tradition and two methods of formulating theological distinctions, but, beyond and beneath all of these, two conceptions of the Godhead. In Western trinitarianism, the Holy Spirit was the guarantee of the unity of the Godhead. Describing the Holy Spirit as being "referred both to the Father and to the Son, because the Holy Spirit is the Spirit both of the Father and of the Son," Augustine assigned to the Spirit the function of serving as "a certain ineffable communion of the Father and the Son" and suggested that this was why he shared the name "Spirit" with both. When the apostle admonished the church "to maintain the unity of the Spirit in the bond of peace," he was, in effect, commanding that believers imitate God the Trinity, in whom the Holy Spirit was the personal unity, holiness, and love "by whom the two [Father and Son] are joined." The ninth-century Augustinians who defended the Filioque against the East reiterated this theme. The creed of Leo III declared: "In the Father is eternity, in the Son equality, in the Holy Spirit the connection between eternity and equality." In this matter as in others, Alcuin quoted the very words of Augustine about "ineffable communion," while Hincmar quoted what he thought were the words of Athanasius about the Holy Spirit as "the conjunction of the Deity" and as "the power and the unity of the Trinity." No Latin theologian would have maintained that without the Filioque the unity of God would be forfeit; but Western

Nicet.Byz.*Lat*.4
(Hergenröther 99)

Joh.D.*F.o*.23 (Kotter 2:66)
Gen.1:2

Phot.*Amph*.16 (*PG*
101:137–40)

Aug.*Trin*.5.11.12
(*CCSL* 50:219)

Eph.4:3

Aug.*Trin*.6.5.7 (*CCSL*
50:235–36)

Symb.*Leo III* (*PL* 129:1260)

Alc.*Trin*.1.5 (*PL* 101:16)

Hinc.R.*Deit*.7 (*PL* 125:539)

trinitarianism, which took the unity of God as its starting point, was then able to go to some such view of the Spirit as the bond between Father and Son. And so, "while this theory in its first beginnings tended to rend the Trinity into three disjunct entities, in this its last phase it contributed to the strengthening of the sense of the divine unity by binding into a coherent and organic relation the conceptions entertained of the three divine Persons."

Prestige (1956) 254

Eastern trinitarianism, by contrast, continued to begin with Father, Son, and Holy Spirit, and it needed to formulate the relation between them in such a way as to assure their unity. This way was the identification of the Father—and only the Father—as the source [πηγή], the principle [ἀρχή], and the cause [αἰτία] within the Trinity. The Trinity was a unity only if "both the Son and the Spirit are led forth from one cause, the Father"; any other theory was "blasphemy" and a "resurgence of the godlessness of polytheism . . . in the guise of Christianity." Although the Son and the Spirit, as well as the Father, were without beginning, they did nevertheless have a single cause within the Godhead, namely, the Father, who had no cause distinct from himself. Dionysius the Areopagite had taught that "the Father is the only source of the supersubstantial Godhead." This was what was meant by the enigmatic statement of Christ, "My Father is greater than I," that is, as cause within the Godhead. But the Father was such a cause not according to his nature or essence (which was common to all three hypostases), but according to his hypostasis as Father. Any other theory was not only a denial of the biblical doctrine of "monarchy" and a debasement of the conciliar declaration that the Spirit proceeded from the Father; it was likewise a violation of the rational doctrine that in an ultimate sense there could not be a "multiplicity of principles [πολυαρχία]," but only one principle. The Trinity could be compared to a balance scale, in which there was a single operation and center (the Father), upon which the two arms (Son and Holy Spirit) both depended. And so the Greeks appealed: "O Latin, cease and desist from saying that there are many principles and many causes, and acknowledge that the Father is the one cause."

Nicet.Byz.*Lat*.2
(Hergenröther 91–92);
Gr.Pal.*Conf.* (*PG* 151:765)

Phot.*Myst*.3 (*PG* 102:281)

Phot.*Myst*.11 (*PG* 102:292);
Phot.*Enc*.9 (*PG* 102:725–28)

Petr.Ant.*Ep.Leo* IX.1.4.3
(Michel 2:450); Petr.Ant.*Ep.
H*.4.3 (Michel 2:442)

Dion.Ar.*D.n*.2.5 (*PG* 3:641);
Cerul.*Panop*.10.1 (Michel
2:220)

John 14:28

Phot.*Myst*.41 (*PG* 102:320)

Phot.*Myst*.15 (*PG* 102:293)

Nicet.Nicom.ap.Ans.Hav.
Dial.2.1 (*PL* 188:1165)

Phot.*Amph*. (*PG* 101:896)

Cerul.*Panop*.62.1 (Michel
2:274)

Both sides appealed to tradition to support their positions, and neither without some justification. If a theology may be identified by the heresy into which it all but falls,

Western theology did show signs of coming closer to the modalist than to the subordinationist extreme. Felix, Elipandus, and Gottschalk all appeared to the catholic theologians of the ninth century to be threatening the unity of the Godhead by their excursions into adoptionism or such ideas as "trine Deity." The Eastern refusal to accept the Filioque was taken to be a similar weakening of the unity. Father, Son, and Holy Spirit were a single "principle [principium]," not three. Yet the Father was "principle from no principle," the Son "principle, but from the Father as principle," and the Holy Spirit "principle... from both"; nevertheless, there were not three principles, but one. In this usage, as in its source, Augustine, "'principle' can apply to the Father both within the Trinity and outside the Trinity." It seemed unthinkable to this Augustinian theology that the Filioque should threaten the unity of the Godhead; rather, it confirmed it and was, in fact, a necessary corollary of it.

Paulin.Aquil.CFor.(796) 11 (MGH Conc.2:186)

Ratr.*Graec*.3.4 (PL 121:294)

Schindler (1965) 158

Coming to trinitarian theology as it did from the legacy of Basil, Gregory of Nyssa, and Gregory of Nazianzus—and, behind them, the legacy of Origen—the Greek doctrine of the Trinity could only see such speculation as simultaneously novel and dangerous. If Old Rome had been the champion of orthodoxy at Chalcedon, it was this no longer. Alongside the disputes over dogmatic authority and primacy, the dispute over the Filioque was a sign that issues of doctrine and of doctrinal unity could not be disposed of simply by settling issues of jurisdiction and of organizational unity. When the *Annals* of Einhard reported that "a question arose about the Holy Trinity and about the images of the saints," it summarized the schism between East and West more simply than the theological differences warranted, but also more precisely than the conventional political interpretation of the schism would suggest. As we shall see, the schism was to demand attention again in the thirteenth century, around the time of the Council of Lyons in 1274, and again in the fifteenth century, especially at Florence in 1439. But the doctrines that divided East and West from the ninth century to the eleventh century continued to be the ones that those councils were obliged to consider—and on which those councils, like their predecessors, were destined to founder.

Ein.*Ann.*(MGH Scrip. 1:145)

See pp. 270–80 below

5

The Vindication of Trinitarian Monotheism

Thds.Al.Or.1 (CSCO 103:29 [17:44])

Deut.6:4
Joh.D.Imag.3.6 (PG 94:1324)

Gr.Pal.Theoph.(PG 150:916); Gr.Pal.Tr.2.3.4 (Meyendorff 393–95)

Joh.D.Imag.1.4 (PG 94:1236)

Nicet.Byz.Lat.7 (Hergenröther 106)

The hidden agenda in many of the developments described thus far was the question of the oneness of God. In principle, of course, it was no question at all: Christians of every party could say with John of Damascus that they "know the one who has said infallibly, 'Hear, O Israel, the Lord our God is one Lord.' " Yet the very context of that statement by John of Damascus in his apologia for the icons shows that the wholehearted adherence of all Christians to the monotheism of the Shema in Deuteronomy 6:4 could not be taken for granted, or at any rate was not taken for granted, by all other Christians, even though it was widely held that its content was self-validating [αὐτόπιστον]. John began his apologia with the monotheistic confession, "I believe in one God, the single origin of all things. . . . I worship one God." But he was obliged to begin this way because the iconoclasts had accused the church, past and present, of reintroducing polytheism into Christian worship through the cult of icons. Similarly, the debates between Chalcedonian orthodoxy and the Jacobite and Nestorian christologies had to relate the issue of the unity of Christ to the issue of the unity of God. In the differing theologies of East and West, as articulated in their respective attitudes toward the Filioque, the place of the oneness of God in Christian teaching became, despite a theoretical unanimity, the underlying assumption over which the two sides were disputing and to which the disputants returned over and over. Evidently the repetition of the Shema was no guarantee of a common monotheism.

The church of the fourth century had supposed that it was vindicating monotheism when, in opposition to the

See vol.1:201

Epiph.M.*V.Serg.*(Leonid 40)

Thdr.AbuQ.*Mim.*3.11–12
(Graf 143–45)

Max.*Qu.Thal.*13 (PG 90:296)

See vol.1:347–48
Max.*Schol.D.n.*9.2;
13.2 (PG 4:369–72; 408)

polytheism implicit in the Arian doctrine that Christ was less than God and was nevertheless deserving of adoration as divine, it formulated the dogma of the Trinity. The creed adopted at Nicea did open with the words: "We believe in one God, the Father Almighty, maker of all things visible and invisible." Neither East nor West had questioned this phraseology. When Sergius of Radonež determined "with my whole soul to erect and dedicate this chapel to the Blessed Trinity," thus creating the celebrated Trojickaja Lavra near Moscow, this, too, was a recognition of the centrality of the dogma of the Trinity in Eastern Christianity. Interpreters of church doctrine could recite the arguments for the Trinity as a response to critics, with the supposition that not only all orthodox Christians, but all reasonable men were able to understand. For to those who could hear with their mind, "the creation cries out . . . and as it were proclaims its cause, who is praised in a trinitarian way." The oneness of this God, as Dionysius the Areopagite had taught Eastern theology to say, transcended the number one, and indeed all numbers, being beyond measure and beyond counting. To those who shared the assumptions of Areopagitic theology, such a definition of oneness may have been enough. But during these same centuries, Christian theology in the East was once more compelled to take up the vindication of trinitarian monotheism in response to several challenges, some old and some new.

Trinity and Shema

From its founding, Christianity had been obliged to come to terms with Judaism; and even after it had supposedly settled the nature of its relation to the synagogue, the church could not ignore the continuing presence of the Jewish community. One index of such awareness is the frequency with which Judaism and matters Jewish were referred to in the various doctrinal controversies of the church, even in those having nothing to do with Judaism directly. It had been the theological practice of such thinkers as Gregory of Nazianzus to label as "Judaizing" especially those heresies, such as Arianism, in which the logical consequences of a Christian position seemed to be a relapse into Judaism: by denying the divinity of Christ in order to preserve monotheism, the Arians were treating

Gr.Naz.*Or*.38.8 (*PG* 36:320)

Sev.Ant.*Gram*.1.11 (*CSCO*
112:41 [111:51]); Sev.Ant.*Ep.*
Thds. (*CSCO* 103:13
[17:22])

Max.*Ep*.13 (*PG* 91:524)

Const.Pogon.*Sacr*.2
(Mansi 11:721)

See pp. 105–6 above

Joh.H.*Const*.3 (*PG* 95:313);
Petr.Ant.*Ep.Alex*.8.3 (Michel
2:436)

Niceph.*Imag*.7 (*PG* 100:549);
Joh.H.*Const*.17 (*PG* 95:
333–36)
Niceph.*Antirr*.3.41 (*PG*
100:460)

Thdr.Stud.*Ref*.2 (*PG* 99:443)

Joh.H.*Icon*.2 (*PG* 96:1349)
Thdr.Stud.*Ref*.9; 10; 16 (*PG*
99:453; 456; 465)
Niceph.*Antirr*.1.pr.; 3.1
(*PG* 100:208; 377)

Leo.Ochr.*Enc*.1 (Will 56)
Nicet.Steth.*Antidial.*
2.1 (Michel 2:322)
Cerul.*Ep.Petr.Ant*.1.12
(Will 180)

See vol.1:26–27

Doct.*Jac*.1 (Bonwetsch 1)

him as his Jewish adversaries had treated him. In the controversies with which we have been dealing in this volume, the Nestorian division of Christ into two distinct hypostases could easily be attacked the same way. Jacobite theology was not alone in accusing the Nestorians of crypto-Judaism; Chalcedonian christology made the same accusation. It is less clear why, during the Monothelete controversy, Macarius of Antioch, who refused to predicate two wills of Christ, would have been charged with reintroducing "the Jewish apostasy."

The iconoclastic controversy was an especially appropriate context for the use of such epithets as "Judaizer." Not only was the campaign against icons attributed to Jewish instigation, but the Christian worship of the icons was evidently one of the subjects to which the Jewish interlocutors in the Jewish-Christian dialogues recurred most often. To the orthodox, therefore, an iconoclast was simply "one with a Jewish mind ['Ιουδαιόφρων]," and an iconoclastic synod was not a church council but "Caiphas's Sanhedrin." The iconoclasts were "armor-bearers of a neo-Judaism," men who bore the name of Christian but were actually Judaizers, Pharisees who in effect denied that Christ had come in the flesh; if anything, they were even worse than Jews in their blasphemy. In short, iconoclasm could be dismissed as "Jewish unbelief." Even in the East-West debates, Byzantine theologians found a way to apply the Jewish epithet to their opponents. The Latin use of azymes in the Eucharist was a "sharing in fellowship with the Jews," an "eating at the tables of the Jews," in brief, a way of "Judaizing." It was an indirect and involuntary tribute to the synagogue that the theologians of the church found the Jewish tradition to be so convenient a frame of reference for the labeling of various Christian heresies.

Such labeling could be taken as evidence that Christian theology was continuing the neglect of Judaism that had followed the encounters between the two traditions in the early church. But in our period there came a new series of encounters between Judaism and Christianity. These took their start in the seventh century with "the command of Emperor Heraclius that Jews everywhere should be baptized," partly because of instances during the Persian and then the Arab wars when Jews were accused of having supported the enemies of the Byzantine Empire. A century or two later, the khan (or "khagan") and much of the nobility of the Khazars, a tribe whose territory bordered both the Byzantine Empire and the Slavic lands, were converted to Judaism. This made the relation between Judaism and Christianity a vital issue for the authors of the earliest Christian literature in Russia.

Hil.Kiev.*Sl*.22–54 (Müller 57–143)

The most important work of Hilarion of Kiev, who is "unanimously acknowledged the best theologian and preacher of all ancient Russia, the Muscovite period included," may have been "called forth by the necessity of

Fedotov (1966) 1:84

Ždanov (1904) 1:75

providing a refutation of the propaganda of Judaism." Among Greek-speaking theologians, several wrote treatises against Judaism, including Anastasius of Sinai (al-

Anast.S.*Hex*.6 (PG 89:933)

though the book attributed to him in the editions did

Ps.Anast.S.*Jud.dial.* (PG 89:1203–72)

not come from his hand). Behind the treatises, at least in many cases, were actual disputations between Christian theologians and Jewish rabbis, disputations in which

Gregent.*Herb*.1 (PG 86:621)

the Jews were commanded to participate. There seems to have been an effort to establish rules of procedure for such debates, as in the admonition that neither party should ridicule or blaspheme the faith of the other or

Troph.Dam.2.1.3 (PO 15:216)

tread upon consciences or conceal the truth. Although fairness may have made such rules necessary, the purpose of the encounter was undeniable: to convert the Jews to Christianity. When a Jew suggested that there should be a mutual recognition of one another's faith, with no attempt to proselytize, his Christian opponent rejected the suggestion, arguing that it was to the Jew's benefit to surrender his vain and empty creed in favor of Christian

Gregent.*Herb*.3 (PG 86:740)

belief.

The literary accounts of the disputations must not be read as verbatim transcripts of what was actually said, for these accounts continued to follow the conceits of the anti-Jewish literature of earlier centuries. As in that literature, so here, the climax of the disputation usually

Doct.Jac.2.1 (Bonwetsch 44)

Troph.Dam.4.7.1–2 (PO 15:274–75); Gregent.*Herb*. (PG 86:781)

came when the members of the Jewish party capitulated —or even requested baptism. In some of them the Jew repeated the conventional argument for the use of icons

See p. 124 above
ap.Ps.Andron.Comn.*Jud*.44 (PG 133:874)

on the basis of the cherubim in the Jewish temple. Because so much of the debating concerned itself with Scripture, that is, with the proper interpretation of the Old Testament and with the authority of the New Testament,

ap.*Troph.Dam.*1.8.2 (*PO* 15:214); ap.Gregent.*Herb.*2 (*PG* 86:665)
ap.Gregent.*Herb.*4 (*PG* 86:765)

the Jews were frequently represented as either acknowledging the superior erudition of the Christians as scholars of the Old Testament writings or recognizing the superiority of the New Testament Gospels to the Torah. Of special interest in the development of such literary conceits is the role played by miracles and visions in the treatises. When his former coreligionists objected to the term "Son of God" as applied to Jesus, Jacob, a converted

*Doct.Jac.*2.1 (Bonwetsch 43)

Jew, appealed to a vision that he had had. In the debate between the Jew Herbanus and the Christian Gregentius, the Jew said that in the night he had seen "Moses the

ap.Gregent.*Herb.*3 (*PG* 86:749)

prophet and Jesus the crucified . . . in the temple, standing and discoursing. I saw Moses worshiping Jesus." Then he went on as though he had not said this, calling the

ap.Gregent.*Herb.*4 (*PG* 86:761)

doctrine of the incarnation absurd. At the conclusion of the next inning, he asked Gregentius to pray Christ to come down and promised that if this happened, he would

Gregent.*Herb.*4 (*PG* 86:773–77)

become a Christian. Thereupon Christ appeared and summoned the Jews to believe in him, and they did.

One element of the dispute that undoubtedly did play a part in the face-to-face encounters as well as in the literature was the need to vindicate Christian monotheism in the light of the dogma of the Trinity. If this dogma was correct, the Jews asked, why had God revealed

Gregent.*Herb.*1 (*PG* 86:625)

the Shema? Quoting the Shema, the rabbi declared: "It seems fearful to me to say that God has 'begotten' at some time." The Shema and other passages proved "that God is one, and not two or three, as you say." When the Old Testament spoke of "sons of God," it did not mean "that they are from the ousia of God or on his throne, but that those whom he loves as sons take their refuge in God as in a father." Why had God not said: "Hear, O Israel. I

ap.*Troph.Dam.*1.23 (*PO* 15:196–97)

and my Son and my Spirit am the Lord your God"? The Christian response to these accusations was to affirm that Christian monotheism, despite the Trinity, was as unqualified as Jewish monotheism. Objections based on Old Testament passages about the oneness of God "would be in place if I were asserting a Son who has a nature dif-

Ps.Andron.Comn.*Jud.*3 (*PG* 133:804)

ferent" from that of the Father. The Christians saw no difficulty in quoting the Shema to prove that there were

Thds.Al.*Or.*1 (*CSCO* 103:29[17:44])

Gen.1:26

not three gods, but one, in the Trinity. When, in the creation story, God said, "Let us make man," this could not mean, as the Jews said, that God was addressing the

Ps.Anast.S.*Jud.dial.*1 (*PG* 89:1205)

*Troph.Dam.*1.3.1 (*PO* 15:197)

Ps.Andron.Comn.*Jud.*3 (*PG* 113:803–4)

Ps.Anast.S.*Jud.dial.*1 (*PG* 89:1205)

Deut.6:4

Euth.Zig.*Panop.*8 (*PG* 130:264)

angels; for then it would be the Jews, not the Christians, who would be compromising monotheism by "introducing myriads" of angelic beings into the act of the Creator. Nor was it a plural of majesty as employed by kings and other men. These words were not spoken to the angels, but "God the Father shared this . . . architectonic saying with his associate in the creation, namely, his Son." In fact, the text was a direct reference to the dogma of the Trinity: in opposition to Judaism it said "Let us make," in the plural; and in opposition to Hellenism it said "And he made," in the singular. Properly understood, the Shema itself was a reference to the Trinity. When it said, "Hear, O Israel, the Lord our God is one Lord," this meant that "the terms, 'Lord,' 'God,' and 'Lord' refer to the three hypostases, while the phrase 'is one' refers to the one Godhead and nature in the three."

ap.Gregent.*Herb.*1 (*PG* 86:625)

ap.Ps.Andron.Comn.*Jud.*pr. (*PG* 133:800)

Ex.3:14

Ex.3:6
*Doct.Jac.*2.3 (Bonwetsch 45)

Gregent.*Herb.*1 (*PG* 86:628)

Ps.Anast.S.*Jud.al.* (*PG* 89:1277)

Max.*Or.dom.* (*PG* 90:892)

Max.*Qu.Thal.*28 (*PG* 90:360)

The importance of monotheism as an issue between Jews and Christians is made clear by the prominence of the Jewish objections to the Trinity in the written versions of the dialogues. In one of them, the first question to originate with the Jewish disputant was: "Where did you get the idea of believing in the Father and in the Son and in the Spirit, and of introducing three gods alien to one another?" Elsewhere, the first doctrinal question of the Jewish participant was: "Who are the three gods who are honored and known by you Christians? The law of Moses does not permit this, since it clearly proclaims: 'I am who I am.'" The word to Moses from the burning bush could become, in Christian hands, yet another trinitarian passage, referring as it did in an earlier verse to "the God of Abraham and the God of Isaac and the God of Jacob." When the Jewish disputant asked, "What is the need for proliferating the Godhead and trebling it?" the Christian replied: "It is not I who am trebling it, but David in the Psalms." The Jewish objection that "Scripture proclaims God to be one" did not apply to the dogma of the Trinity, which was the confession of God as one. Neither in a plurality of natures as taught by paganism nor in a unity of hypostasis as taught by Judaism, but in a unity of nature with a plurality of hypostases lay the true meaning of monotheism. Hence it was correct to interpret Abraham as one who knew the doctrine of the Trinity. This was the true worship of the true God.

In Jewish eyes, the Christian claim to be worshiping

the true God was vitiated also by the cult of icons. In some of the dialogues, this rather than the Trinity was the first question raised by the Jewish participants: "Why is it, when God has commanded that one should not worship stone or wood, that you adore and worship them, making crosses and icons out of them?" From the frequency with which this Jewish objection was singled out for response by Christian theologians it seems safe to conclude that it figured prominently in Jewish polemics. Jewish theology did find it puzzling and offensive that Christians, whose Bible contained the same prohibitions of idolatry that appeared in the Jewish law, made "icons and images of animals and crosses" and, relapsing into heathenism, paid worship to them. Another evidence of such a relapse was the Christian practice of prayer toward the East, which came from the heathen worship of the sun. In their responses to such objections, the Christians rehearsed many of the arguments that they were using at the same time against the Christian iconoclasts. "When I worship the cross," a Christian explained to a Jew, "I do not say, 'Glory be to thee, O wood.' God forbid! But I say, 'Glory be to thee, O cross, all-powerful sign of Christ.'" Another Christian said to his Jewish adversary: "Oh, that you would make images of Moses and the prophets, and worship their God and Lord every day!" The worship of icons was not idolatry, as the Jews charged; for the coming of Christ had brought about the destruction of idolatry, and Christians were the ones who daily did battle against idols. In their defense against Judaism, as in their arguments against iconoclasm, Christians used Jewish reverence for the Torah as proof that it was not antibiblical to pay homage to the means of God's revelation. As for prayer facing east, this was not sun-worship, but obedience to the biblical command: "Sing praises to God, who ascends above the heaven toward the east." Whatever the role of the Jews may have been in provoking such iconoclasts as Emperor Leo the Isaurian into action, their objections to the icons added a new issue to those featured in the earlier disputes.

In their format, the disputes and treatises continued to be exchanges of learned opinion about the exegesis of important proof texts from Scripture, especially from the Old Testament. The old proof texts were repeated, and some new ones were added. Genesis 49:10 (LXX) had promised

---

ap.*Dial.Papisc*.1 (McGiffert 51)

Niceph.*Antirr*.1.24 (*PG* 100:261); Ps. Anast.S.*Jud. dial*.2 (*PG* 89:1233); Nicet. Steth.*Jud*.20 (*SC* 81:436)

ap.*Troph.Dam*.3.6.1 (*PO* 15:245)

ap.Gregent.*Herb*.2 (*PG* 86:669); ap.*Troph.Dam*.3.7.1 (*PO* 15:250)

Nicet. Steth.*Jud*.20 (*SC* 81:436)

Dial.Papisc.13 (McGiffert 75).

Leont.N.*Serm*.3 (*PG* 93:1608)

Ps.Andron.Comn.*Jud*.43 (*PG* 133:871); *Doct.Jac*.1.27 (Bonwetsch 26)

Leont.N.*Serm*.3 (*PG* 93:1604)

See p. 125 above

Ps.Anast.S.*Jud.dial*.2 (*PG* 89:1233); *Troph.Dam*.3.6.3–4 (*PO* 15:246–47)

Ps.68:32–33 (LXX)

Joh.H.*Const*.19 (*PG* 95:336)

See vol.1:55–56
Gregent.*Herb*.1 (*PG* 86:633);
Dial.Papisc.9 (McGiffert
58–59); *Doct.Jac*.4.5–6
(Bonwetsch 66–67); Joh.Cant.
Apol.1.3 (*PG* 154:388–89);
Leo III. *Ep*. (Jeffery 285)

Ps.Anast.S.*Jud.dial*.1 (*PG*
89:1220); *Troph.Dam*.3.3.1
(*PO* 15:240–41)

See vol.1:62
Ps.Anast.S.*Jud.dial*.3 (*PG*
89:1248); Joh.Cant.*Apol*.
2.21 (*PG* 154:480); Man.II.
Pal.*Dial*.13 (Trapp 158)

ap.Gregent.*Herb*.1 (*PG*
86:631)

Troph.Dam.2.7.2 (*PO* 15:232)
Ps.Anast.S.*Jud*.1 (*PG*
89:1216)

Thdr.AbuQ.*Mim*.3.9 (Graf
140); Gregent.*Herb*.2 (*PG*
86:653); Ps.Anast.S.*Jud.
dial*.1 (*PG* 89:1216)

See vol.1:177
Niceph.*Imag*.36 (*PG*
100:625); *Doct.Jac*.1.10
(Bonwetsch 8); *Dial.Papisc*.
12 (McGiffert 66); Ps.Anast.
S.*Jud.dial*.2 (*PG* 89:1228–29)
Troph.Dam.1.5.4 (*PO*
15:207)

ap.*Troph.Dam*.1.5.3 (*PO*
15:206)
Just.*Dial*.67.1 (Goodspeed
174)

that "a leader shall not fail from Judah, nor a ruler from his thighs, until that which has been laid up for him shall come; and he shall be the expectation of the nations," and the church fathers had seen the fulfillment of the promise in Christ. Now that even more of the nations had found their hope and expectation in him, it was "in vain that the Jews expect the one whom they expect. For Christ, whom the nations expect, has come. Therefore the prince and leader has already departed from Judah." The Septuagint version of Deuteronomy 28:66, "You shall see your life hanging before your eyes," had also been a part of the ancient Christian arsenal. Christians continued to apply it to the crucifixion, but the Jews claimed that it spoke of the captivity of Israel. The textual variant which added "on the tree" also continued to appear, and according to a Christian treatise was accepted by Jewish scholars. Psalm 2 had been spoken "concerning the incarnate economy of the Son of God," while Psalm 110 in the Septuagint served as proof against the Jews that "the Lord" had addressed "the Lord" and that therefore there was a distinction within the Godhead. Another text unique to the Septuagint was Isaiah 63:9: "Not an intercessor, nor an angel, but the Lord himself has saved them." This, too, continued to appear frequently in Christian apologetics; for "Isaiah was a Jew, and whom does he mean when he says 'them' . . . except the Gentiles?"

Since most of the treatises were written in Greek, it is not surprising to find the Old Testament quoted according to the Septuagint version. What is surprising is that the rabbis were represented as having accepted the Septuagint text even in passages where it contained mistranslations of the original or additions to it. Sometimes —as, above all, in the mooted use of "virgin [παρθένος]" in Isaiah 7:14, as this had been sanctioned by the quotation of the passage in this form in Matthew 1:23—the rendition of the Hebrew in the Greek version continued to be the basis of objections from the Jewish side, as it had been as early as the second century. But in the several passages just cited that were peculiar to the Septuagint, sometimes even with such Christian additions as "from the tree" in an already free adaptation of Deuteronomy 28:66, the dialogues seemed to have the Jews acquiescing in the Christian version without any reference to the original Hebrew. At other times, however, the dialogues gave an indication of a more critical attitude. Herbanus criticized his own Jewish forebears for translating the Hebrew Bible into Greek, because this had made it too easy for Christians to score debating points against Jews in their disputes. In another dialogue, a Jewish convert to Christianity declared that since his baptism he "had not ceased examining the law and the prophets in the Greek tongue, having obtained a Bible from the church through some dear Christians from a monastery." The Septuagint, not the Hebrew text, was the Old Testament of Greek-speaking Christians. If they attempted to show a grasp of the Hebrew text in proving a point against Jewish opponents, they usually proved to be mistaken. But there would seem to be reason to surmise that the Jewish participants in the actual dialogues were less docile in accepting the Septuagint and the "Christian midrashim" than the printed accounts might indicate.

It was not primarily the text or the translation of the Old Testament, but its interpretation, over which Jews and Christians clashed. The Jews accused the Christians of taking passages from the Jewish Bible and of interpreting them "as you please" or of "appropriating whatever David said . . . and [applying it] to your Christ." To such charges of arbitrary exegesis the Christians would respond: "I am not quibbling over etymologies, but from your own Scriptures I am attempting to persuade you of the truth." Not the Christians, but the Jews, were arbitrary in their quotations from the Bible. Although Christians were willing to call the Old Testament "your Scriptures and your prophets" instead of calling them exclusively Christian, their practice denied to Judaism any legitimate claim upon the interpretation of the Bible. It was necessary to interpret it "anagogically," not literally; for if someone maintained that it was enough to agree on the authority of the Bible but not on its spiritual interpretation, "he is making the Christians Jewish" by clinging to the letter rather than to the spirit. Nor were the Christians willing to concede to the Jews that "the prophets are found to be inconsistent in most places," favoring the Jews in some passages and the Gentiles in others. Properly understood, that is, understood according to the spiritual and anagogical sense, "Moses and the prophets speak of the coming of Christ," even though the literal sense seemed to refer to Israel.

Marginal references (left column):

ap.Gregent.*Herb*.1 (*PG* 86:624); Man.II.Pal.*Dial*.1 (Trapp 9)

Doct.Jac.1.7 (Bonwetsch 5)

Tim.I.*Ep*.36 (*CSCO* 75:116 [74:241]); Max.*Qu.Thal*.54 (*PG* 90:508–9)

ap. *Troph.Dam*.1.6.1 (*PO* 15:208)
ap.Gregent.*Herb*.1 (*PG* 86:648)

Gregent.*Herb*.1 (*PG* 86:637)

Gregent.*Herb*.2 (*PG* 86:692)

Dial.Papisc.4 (McGiffert 53); Ps.Anast.S.*Jud.dial*.1 (*PG* 89:1205)
See vol.1:19
Troph.Dam.2.4.1 (*PO* 15:223); Gregent.*Herb*.2 (*PG* 86:653)

Thdr.AbuQ.*Mim*.1.18; 1.32 (Graf 104;121)

Gregent.*Herb*.2 (*PG* 86:713)

Hil.Kiev.*Sl*.23 (Müller 61–62)

That Jesus was the Christ and the one promised in the Old Testament was the central conviction with which Christianity had arisen out of Judaism. The conviction had been worked out in early Jewish-Christian debates, but Byzantine theology expanded the case for this identification of the Christ. The first question addressed by Gregentius to his Jewish opponent was: "Now that the night is over and the Sun of righteousness has risen, why do you stubbornly resist his light and oppose him by refusing to believe in him?" It was the theme and purpose of Christian writings against Judaism to show "from the Scriptures and from the truth itself [that various passages of the Old Testament] speak about the incarnate economy of the Son of God." These passages had been fulfilled before the eyes of the entire cosmos, proving that Jesus was the promised one. The Jews must recognize that while they themselves were the most despised among all the nations of the earth, these same nations had "turned away from their own religions and had decided in favor of a Jew when his message had appeared, and were following him." Therefore it was appropriate to refer to Jesus Christ as "the second Israel" and to contrast the exodus of Israel from Egypt and its victory over Pharaoh with the exodus achieved by Christ and his victory over the devil. Jewish theology was willing to call the Christ "the anointed one" or "Savior" or even "Redeemer"; what it found unacceptable was the term "Son of God." Which of the Jewish fathers had ever said such a thing as this, that God had begotten a Son, that God had in fact been abiding in the womb of a human mother? The Christian assertion that Jesus was the Christ promised in the Old Testament had special difficulty with this Jewish objection. By this time it had also become increasingly clear that Christianity, no less than Judaism, was a religion of expectation, not only one of fulfillment. Christians had to admit that Christ had not yet come in the full and final sense; and they had to listen to the Jewish objection that the word of Psalm 118:26, "Blessed is he who comes in the name of the Lord," quoted in the Gospels and used in the liturgy of the Eucharist, implied that at least some of the "signs of his coming" had not yet appeared.

An important part of the Christian argument for the identification of Jesus as the promised one of the Old Testament prophecy was the continuing search of Chris-

Gregent.*Herb*.1 (*PG* 86:621)

Ps.Anast.S.*Jud.dial*.1 (*PG* 89:1216)

Dial.Papisc.12 (McGiffert 70)

Thdr.AbuQ.*Mim*.2.2 (Graf 129)
Ps.Andron.Comn.*Jud*.31 (*PG* 133:844)

Troph.Dam.2.2.3 (*PO* 15:219–20)

ap.*Doct.Jac*.2.1 (Bonwetsch 43)
ap.Ps.Andr.Comn.*Jud.dial*.5 (*PG* 133:807)

ap.*Troph.Dam*.2.5.1–2 (*PO* 15:225–26)

Ps.Anast.S.*Jud.dial*.1 (*PG* 89:1216)

Matt.21:9
Lit.Chrys. (Brightman 324)
ap.*Troph.Dam*.1.6.1 (*PO* 15:207)

tian exegesis for "types of Christ" in the Old Testament. The Christian conviction that Jesus was the Christ had made it possible for the early fathers to lay the foundations for this tendency, and in our period it was systematized. The name "Jesus" itself was such an Old Testament type; for it was, at least in some Greek versions of the Old Testament, the translation of the name "Joshua" and had been so used in the New Testament more than once. The

Acts 7:45; Heb.4:8

parallelism had become for Origen the basis of an elab-

Or.*Jos*.1.1 (*SC* 71:94–96)

orate spiritual exegesis of the Book of Joshua. The Byzantines continued to develop extended parallels between the two in their anti-Judaic polemics, with the intent of

Gregent.*Herb*.1 (*PG* 86:637)
Euth.Zig.*Panop*.8 (*PG* 130:260)
Gen.22:1–19
Ps.Andron.Comn.*Jud*.15–18 (*PG* 133:819–22); *Doct.Jac*. 5.13 (Bonwetsch 82–83) Rom.Mel.*Hymn*.3:16 (*SC* 99:154)

showing that "Jesus the son of Nun . . . is not the promised prophet," but that Jesus the son of Mary was. Another such type of Christ and of the sacrifice on the cross was the "binding of Isaac," which had been used since the early days of Christianity. A favorite form of parallelism in these disputes was the discovery of types

Ps.Andron.Comn.*Jud*.20 (*PG* 133:824–26); Rom.Mel. *Hymn*.4.19 (*SC* 99:192)

for the relation between synagogue and church: Esau was the first son, but Jacob obtained the promise; Leah was

Doct.Jac.1.38 (Bonwetsch 37)

the first wife, but Rachel was the more beloved wife. Old

Troph.Dam.1.1.3 (*PO* 15:194); Ps.Andron.Comn. *Jud*.45 (*PG* 133:874–75)

Testament circumcision had been a type for New Testament baptism, which had also been prophesied in such

Gregent.*Herb*.3 (*PG* 86:728)

Old Testament passages as Isaiah 1:16. The bread and

Gen.14:18

wine offered by Melchizedek were types of the Eucharist,

Dial.Papisc.5 (McGiffert 55)

"as Christ our high priest has given it over to us." The

Nicet.Steth.*Jud*.22 (*SC* 81:438); *Troph.Dam*.2.2.3 (*PO* 15:220)

manna from heaven, given to Israel in the wilderness, likewise was a type of the Christian Eucharist. In its case against Judaism, as in its thought generally, Byzantine theology was intent on preserving and transmitting the patristic legacy, not on inventing new ideas; and its argument from "types" was a part of that legacy.

The case against Judaism as well as the case against Islam brought into new prominence a topic that had long been present in the Christian interpretation of prophecy in relation to Jesus, the designation of the Messiah as "more than a prophet." "We say that he is a man, that he is like one of the prophets," the Jews were represented

ap.*Dial.Papisc*.6 (McGiffert 56); ap.Ps.Anast.S.*Jud*. *dial*.1 (*PG* 89:1217)

as arguing, "and not God; for there is only one God, and not two, as you [Christians] suppose." Jewish messianism included the expectation of "a great and mighty prophet, one anointed by God," but this did not mean that he would be called the Son of God and would be said to have come

ap.Ps.Andron.Comn.*Jud*.30 (*PG* 133:842)

down from heaven. For the Christian understanding of

Christ, it was not enough to regard him as a great prophet; nor had the Old Testament prophets themselves regarded it as enough. "About whom are you speaking, prophet?" the Christian theologian asked. "Tell us, do you

*Troph.Dam.*1.7.4 (*PO* 15:211)

say that he who is to come is a man, or is he God?" From the prophets of Israel the Christians sought to prove that "whether he has already come or is still coming, in any case [David] says that he who is coming is God and is

*Troph.Dam.*1.6.2 (*PO* 15:208)

very wondrous as God and Lord." And so, in Christian judgment, a prophet was no longer necessary; for Christ was the righteousness of God, taking away all sin, and no

*Doct.Jac.*1.21 (Bonwetsch 19)

prophet could ever go beyond what he had done. Prophetism had had a valid ministry, but a temporary one. When Jewish spokesmen identified as the chief source of their "wonder and doubt" the claim that God had begotten a

ap.Ps.Andron.Comn.*Jud.*5 (*PG* 133:807)

Son, and demanded to know "which of our forebears" had even suggested such a notion, the Christian response was an interpretation of the Old Testament in which "prophet" was simply an inadequate category to carry what God had promised to do. He had promised nothing less than a kingdom that was to abide forever. "But except for Christ, no king has ever lived forever, or rules forever"; therefore the promise must apply to Jesus Christ, but also to the

Ps.Andron.Comn.*Jud.*35 (*PG* 133:854)

Christian empire founded by him.

The Christian claim that the promises of the Old Testament applied not only to Christ, but to Christian history, made the Byzantine form of the Christian argument against Judaism especially significant. In Byzantium, the evolution of the Christian empire had reached the point where it had become possible to repossess in the Christian name various Old Testament themes that had previously been alien and unavailable to Christians. The process had begun already with Eusebius, whose "imperial theology" drew a parallel between the victory of Constantine over Maxentius and the victory of the Israelites over the hosts

Eus.*H.e.*9.9.5–9 (*GCS* 9:828–32)

of Pharaoh in the Red Sea. Now this parallel was carried still further. The "fourth kingdom" in Daniel 2:40 was taken to be the Roman Empire, which had now become

*Doct.Jac.*3.9 (Bonwetsch 60–62); *Troph.Dam.*4.4.3–5 (*PO* 15:267–69)

Christian. Other kingdoms had fallen, including the kingdom of Israel, some of them conquered "by these barbarian Turks." Yet "the kingdom of the Romans, or rather of the Christians, whose coregent is our Lord Jesus Christ,

Ps.Anast.S.*Jud.dial.*1 (*PG* 89:1212)

will not be dissolved until the end of the world." Therefore the prophecies of a kingdom that would not end could not refer to the kingdom of David, which had ended, but must refer to the Christian Roman Empire, in whose realm the kingship of Christ himself was being exercised. Even here, however, the eschatological promises of a world in which swords would be beaten into plowshares and the wolf and the lamb would lie down together had not yet been fulfilled, and Judaism could ask Christianity whether this did not refute Christian claims. "What other people is as involved in war as are the Christians?" the Jew would ask. "How is it, if [the Old Testament prophecies of peace] have not been fulfilled and if instead you engage in war, that you can say that the Christ of God has come?" To this the Christian replied that "our kingship" had in fact enjoyed "a profound peace" for all of fifty years.

Among the this-worldly prophecies which Christian spokesmen were appropriating were those that dealt with the promised land. The treatise ascribed to Gregentius of Taphar in Yemen made much of the argument that Jerusalem was now in Christian hands, not in Jewish hands, proving that the prophecies applied to the Christians. This was, of course, before the Muslim conquest of Jerusalem. The prophecy that many nations would come to Zion, the mountain of the Lord, had not come true in the days of the Jewish temple, but was coming true through the churches built in Jerusalem by Helena, the mother of Constantine I. The prophecies of conquest in the Old Testament had not become reality through the military action of Joshua or Gideon, but through the missionary work of the Christian apostles, who had conquered the world for Christ. Even the prophecy that "the desert shall rejoice and blossom" was carried out only under Christianity, when the hermits and monks went out into the desert. When the Jew declared, "I am the son of Israel, and the promises pertain to me," the Christian replied, "No, but I am the son of Israel. . . . I take over your promises." The name "Israel" properly belonged to the one who manifested the character of the faith of Abraham, Isaac, and Jacob, therefore to the Christian rather than to the Jew. God had taken the kingdom, then the law and the prophets, then worship and sacrifice, and finally the city and the temple away from the Jews and had transferred them to the Christians. The "enemies" who were to become the footstool of the Lord were the Jews, who had been subjected "under the feet of the Christian tribe until the hour of consummation." So complete was the

Mic.4:3

Is.11:6

ap.Leont.N.*Serm*.3 (*PG*
93:1609)

ap.*Troph.Dam*.2.3.1 (*PO*
15:220–21)

Troph.Dam.2.3.2 (*PO*
15:221)

Gregent.*Herb*.2 (*PG* 86:700)

Is.2:3

Gregent.*Herb*.3 (*PG* 86:729)

Gregent.*Herb*.3 (*PG* 86:748)

Is.35:1

Euth.Zig.*Panop*.8 (*PG*
130:272)

Thdr.AbuQ.*Opusc*.10 (*PG*
97:1533)

Max.*Qu.Thal*.23 (*PG* 90:325)

Gregent.*Herb*.1 (*PG* 86:629)

Ps.110:1

Ps.Anast.S.*Jud.dial*.1 (*PG*
89:1216)

identification of the church as the heir of the prophecies that even the curses of the Old Testament "befell thy former people as type and figure, but now they are actually being fulfilled in us."

Where did that leave Judaism in relation to prophecy? The prophecy could not apply to Judaism, for its authority and its freedom had proved to be short-lived. "Where now is their kingdom, their celebrated city, their far-famed temple?" Which of the places granted to the Jews by God in the conquest of Palestine still belonged to them, the Christians would ask. Even Jordan was remembered not because of the way the first Jesus (Joshua the son of Nun) had crossed it, but because of the way the second Jesus (the son of Mary) had been baptized in it. It was not Jerusalem that was called "the great city of God" in Scripture, but the church. The prophecy that the house of God would be called "a house of prayer for all peoples" could not be taken to refer to Jerusalem as a geographical location, but to the catholic church. It was vain for the Jews to hope that "we Israelites will be raised up again, and our city will be rebuilt, but you who proclaim Christ will be put to shame." The Jewish expectation that the Messiah was still to come and that his coming would mean the restoration of Israel as a nation was a false application of such prophecies, which were spoken about the church as the new Israel. It would be "making liars of the prophets" to apply their words to the physical Israel and to its expected Messiah.

The words of Scripture that did apply to the physical Israel were those that had predicted its captivity and destruction. Repeatedly Israel had been conquered by foreign enemies, but the complicity of the Jews in the death of Christ had brought new punishments upon them, just as he had prophesied. Six centuries after crucifying him they were still "desolate and neglected and scattered." The words of 1 Corinthians 2:8, "They crucified the Lord of glory," were taken to mean the Jews. If Christ had been a deceiver, the Jews would have been blessed for crucifying him and would now be ruling in their own land. Instead, they had been disgraced and had in this way, against their will, demonstrated his truthfulness. In fulfillment of the prophecy of Christ, God had "raised up against them Titus and Vespasian and the Greeks, and he cast down their pride," John of Damascus declared in the course of his disputation with the Muslims. For proof

Max.*Ascet*.39 (*PG* 90:948)

Niceph.*Imag*.36 (*PG* 100:624)

Dial.Papisc.9 (McGiffert 60)
Jon.3:3 (LXX)
Max.*Qu.Thal*.64 (*PG* 90:717–20)
Is.56:7

Niceph.*Imag*.46 (*PG* 100:692–93)

ap.Gregent.*Herb*.2 (*PG* 86:676)

Ps.Anast.S.*Jud.dial*.1 (*PG* 89:1213)

Troph.Dam.3.9.3 (*PO* 15:257)

Gregent.*Herb*.2 (*PG* 86:680)

Ps.Anast.S.*Jud.dial*.2 (*PG* 89:1237)
Troph.Dam.2.6.8 (*PO* 15:230)

Thdr.AbuQ.*Mim*.10.14 (Graf 250)

Doct. Jac.3.7 (Bonwetsch 58)
Ps.Anast.S.*Jud.dial*.1 (*PG* 89:1220–21)

Joh.D.*Disp.Sar*. (*PG* 96:1341)

Doct.Jac.1.22 (Bonwetsch 19); Max.*Carit*.2.31 (*PG* 90:993)

Dial. Papisc.16 (McGiffert 79); *Troph.Dam*.2.6.7 (*PO* 15:230)

See vol.1:20
Doct.Jac.1.22 (Bonwetsch 21)
Ps.Andron.Comn.*Jud*.54 (*PG* 133:894)

Is.1:15
Gregent.*Herb*.2 (*PG* 86:725)
Ps.Anast.S.*Jud.dial*.3 (*PG* 89:1249)
Phot.*Amph*.24.9 (*PG* 101:188)
See p. 83 above

See vol.1:241–42
Troph.Dam.4.1.1 (*PO* 15:259)
Niceph.*Antirr*.1.47 (*PG* 100:321); Joh.D.*Imag*.2.19 (*PG* 94:1305)
Bab.*Un*.7 (*CSCO* 80:227[79: 281]); Tim.I.*Ep*.2.7 (*CSCO* 75:44[74:70])
Sev.Ant.*Ep.Thds*. (*CSCO* 103:15[17:24–25])

Ps.Anast.S.*Jud.dial*.1 (*PG* 89:1209); Gregent.*Herb*.1 (*PG* 86:648–49)
ap.*Dial.Papisc*.2 (McGiffert 52)

Gregent.*Herb*.1 (*PG* 86:644)

Doct.Jac.1.27 (Bonwetsch 26)

Gregent. *Herb*.1 (*PG* 86:628); *Dial.Papisc*.2 (McGiffert 52)
Max.*Qu.Thal*.28 (*PG* 90:360)
Ps.Anast.S.*Jud.al*. (*PG* 89:1273–76); Gregent. *Herb*.1 (*PG* 86:625)

Niceph.*Imag*.35 (*PG* 100: 617–20); Gregent.*Herb*.2 (*PG* 86:697)

Hil.Kiev.*Sl*.27 (Müller 71)

that the prophecies against the Jews had been fulfilled, Christians continued to turn to Josephus, whom they described to the Jews as "one of your wise men" or as "Josephus the Hebrew, your historian." At least one anti-Judaic dialogue—not in the original Greek, but in an Old Church Slavic translation—went beyond earlier Christian interpolations and made even more explicitly Christian additions to the text of Josephus. In crucifying Christ, the Jews had fulfilled not only his own prophecies about them, but those of the Old Testament prophets, as, for example, the words of Isaiah: "Your hands are full of blood." They were "Christ-haters" and "Christ-killers"; in fact, the same theory of "communication of properties" between the divine nature and the human nature in Christ which had justified the title "Theotokos" for Mary and the title "ancestor of God" for David also was used to justify the title "God-killers" for the Jews. In casting such epithets and charges against the Jews, the Nestorian opponents of the title "Theotokos" and its Monophysite defenders joined with their Chalcedonian opponents.

The Christian reading of Old Testament prophecies rejected as untenable the Jewish exegesis that applied them to various Old Testament figures. King David had died, and his kingship had not been eternal; therefore the promises of an eternal reign could not have meant David. The Jewish claim that such passages as Psalm 2:7 referred to Solomon was invalidated by the idolatry and lust of which he had been guilty. An apparent correspondence between Old Testament prophecy and the career of Josiah was "totally deceiving." It was an evasion of the clear trinitarian sense of the Old Testament to maintain, as the Jews did, that the term "Son of God" did not refer to Christ but to Israel or to one of its kings. Abraham had taught the doctrine of the Trinity, and the true child of Abraham was one who shared this faith. In short, the election of Israel pertained not to Israel, "but to us from among the Gentiles . . . , namely, to the catholic and apostolic church." Whatever validity there had been to this election had been temporary and belonged to the past. The covenant with Israel "did not extend to other peoples and remained in Judea alone, but the salvation of the Christian is liberal and bountiful, stretching to all the countries of the earth." The historic mission of the people of Israel had been to prepare for the coming of Christ and of Christianity, and now that mission had been discharged. In recognition of this historic mission, the spokesman for Christianity could say to the spokesman for Judaism that "before the descent of the Lord from heaven into the world, I, too, if I had existed, would have been a Jew. For in those times salvation was available only in the law of Israel." At other times Christians said that "the creation is not saved through the law of Moses, but through another and a new law." This presumably did not mean that there had been no salvation under the old law, but that it had been restricted to the people of Israel, while salvation for the whole creation had come only through the new law of Christ.

The question of whether the law of Moses was still binding occupied an important place in the disputes. Sometimes the Christian neglect of the law was the first objection raised by the Jewish party. It seemed to the Jews that the Christians admired what was Christian but despised the laws of Moses. To the Jewish question why they did not observe the Sabbath, the Christians replied that the Sabbath pertained to the first creation, that of Adam, but that in Christ there was a new creation. Christians were not circumcised even though Christ was, because Christ had fulfilled the law as man but had legislated a new covenant for his followers. Dietary laws had been instituted to instruct the people of the Old Testament, but it was foolish for Jews now to refuse pork as unclean and then to eat chicken, the filthiest animal of all. As men before the law of Moses had not yet been obliged to keep the ceremonial law, so now that Christ had come they were no longer obliged to do so. It was necessary to distinguish in the law of Moses between those commands that were to be kept "both in actual fact and in spirit," which were the moral law, and those that were to be kept "in spirit only," which were the ceremonial law. Proof for this concept of the law came from the Old Testament prophets themselves, from Malachi and above all from the promise in Jeremiah 31:31–34 of a new covenant and a new law written in the heart to supersede the law of Moses. This was probably the most consistently quoted authority for the idea that with the coming of Christ the law of Moses had been abrogated. More precisely perhaps, the law had not been so much abrogated in Christ as fulfilled. It amounted to a denial of the fulfillment if, as the Jews sometimes suggested, one sought to have it both

Gregent.Herb.2 (PG 86:673)

Doct.Jac.1.11 (Bonwetsch 9)

ap.Ps.Andron.Comn.Jud.pr. (PG 133:799)

Ps.Andron.Comn.Jud.58 (PG 133:904–6)

Troph.Dam.3.8.1 (PO 15:254)

Thdr.AbuQ.Opusc.39 (PG 95:1597)
Ps.Anast.S.Jud.parv. (PG 89:1272–73)

Doct.Jac.1.28 (Bonwetsch 27)

Max.Carit.2.86 (PG 90:1012)

Doct.Jac.1.19 (Bonwetsch 16); Ps.Andron.Comn.Jud. 50 (PG 133:883)
Doct.Jac.1.10; 1.16 (Bonwetsch 7–8:14); Ps. Andron.Comm.Jud.49 (PG 122:881–82); Troph.Dam. 3.4.3 (PO 15:242–43); Ps. Anast.S.Jud.al. (PG 89:1280); Joh.Cant.Apol.4.14 (PG 154:573); Leo III.Ep. (Jeffery 315–16)
Doct.Jac.1.10 (Bonwetsch 8)

ways, "believing in Christ and confessing him as true God and the Son of God, homoousios with the Father, and yet at the same time observing and keeping the law of Moses, so as in everything to obey both and thus to obtain a double portion of future blessing."

Ps.Andron.Comn.*Jud*.47 (*PG* 133:880)

Underlying this assignment of the Mosaic law to a temporary place in the economy of God's dealings with men was a theology of progressive revelation. God forbade the Jews to eat pork because the Egyptians had worshiped animals and the Jews were in danger of relapsing into such idolatry. The laws about the Sabbath and about un-leavened bread were meant for the "godless Jews," who lived in spiritual darkness, but not for those who now lived in the true light of Christ. The prohibition of images had been "legislated for the Jews . . . because of their inclination toward idolatry, but not for Christians, who serve God alone and have . . . a perfect knowledge of God." Christians were more mature than Jews and no longer needed such prohibitions. God had kept certain things from the Jews lest they attack the prophets and the Scriptures. This view of progressive revelation applied preeminently to the principal doctrinal issues between Jews and Christians, the doctrines of the Trinity and of the incarnation. When the Jew asked why, if Moses taught the Trinity, he had not made it clearer, the Christian replied that God as a good teacher had begun with monotheism because it was elementary and then had gone on to the more perfect revelation of the Trinity. If Moses had dis-closed the doctrine of the Trinity to the Jews, "think of the precipice of polytheism into which your ancestors would have fallen!" They would have supposed that "the Son must also have a Mother in heaven, therefore also a Brother." But now the revelation of God had gone beyond the elementary stage. Jewish monotheism and pagan polytheism had been transcended in "the synthesis of the Logos," on the basis of which Christians, "making the Godhead into a Trinity, proclaim it to be enormous in riches and in authority." This "confession of one God who is trinitarian" was a "Christian synthesis" over against both Judaism and paganism, and a reaffirmation of the paradoxical doctrine by which orthodoxy had sought, while acknowledging the incarnate one as true God, to vindicate its uncompromising monotheism.

Ps.Anast.S.*Jud.parv.* (*PG* 89:1273); *Troph.Dam*.3.6.6 (*PO* 15:248)

Leo Ochr.*Enc*.6 (Will 59–60)

Joh.D.*Imag*.1.8; 3.18 (*PG* 94:1238; 1328) Joh.D.*Imag*.2.20 (*PG* 94:1308)

Troph.Dam.3.8.3 (*PO* 15:255)

Ps.Andron.Comn.*Jud*.3–4 (*PG* 133:804–5)

Troph.Dam.1.3.2 (*PO* 15:197–98)

Gregent.*Herb*.1 (*PG* 86:628)

See vol.1:66–67

Evil and the God of Love

Hussey-Hart(1967) 190

Orthodox Christian monotheism had inherited from the early church not only a continuing debate with Judaism, but also "a constantly recurring and urgent" conflict with the threat of dualism. In the entire period covered by this volume, there was probably no century in which some form of dualism or other did not appear to constitute a clear and present danger to Eastern Christendom. Near the beginning of the period, John of Damascus, who was otherwise a vigorous critic of Judaism, nevertheless acknowledged that "it is better to be converted to Judaism and to die a Jew than to have any fellowship with the

Joh.D.*Man*.67 (*PG* 94:1561)

Manicheans." Five centuries later, Germanus II, patriarch of Constantinople, declared that "although there are many enemies of the cross, such as Jews, Hagarenes [that is, Muslims as descendants of Hagar], and others, neverthe-

Germ.II.*Bog*. (*PG* 140:628)

less these Bogomils are more loathsome and more irreligious than all the others."

It was not clear then—and still is not clear now—how the "Manicheans" of John of Damascus were related to the "Bogomils" of Germanus, or how both were related to other dualist movements. Sometimes the orthodox acknowledged differences among them, but it remains true that "the average orthodox Christian, when faced with

Runciman(1961) 17

any sign of dualism, would cry out 'Manichaean.'" For example, a collection of fourteen anathemas in a synodical protocol, attributed to the late eleventh century, directed itself against a false doctrine variously labeled as Massalian, Phundite, Bogomil, Euchite, Enthusiast, Encratite,

Euth.Zig.*Anath*. (*PG* 131:40)

Psell.*Daem*.4 (*PG* 122:829)

and Marcionite; it was probably the Bogomils who were the object of the anathemas. But when Michael Psellus referred to the Bogomils as "Gnostics" or when Theophylact, patriarch of Constantinople at the middle of the tenth century, called their doctrine "Manicheism, com-

Thphyl.CP.*Ep.Petr.Bulg*.172r (Petrovskij 363)

pounded with Paulicianism," this was an indication that the differences among the several species of dualistic doctrine were less important to the spokesmen for Eastern Christianity than were the common elements shared by all of them. The three principal species were Manicheism, Paulicianism, and Bogomilism. The first of these had been an opponent of Christianity in earlier centuries and had

See vol.1:85

See vol.1:300–301

managed to hold the support of no less a convert than Augustine, at least for several years; but it continued well

Graf(1910)228

Phot.*Man.*1.22 (*PG* 102:73)

Petr.Sic.*Hist.*22 (*PG* 104:1273)

An.Comn.*Alex.*15.8 (Reifferscheid 2:294) Euth.Zig.*Bog.*pr. (Ficker 89); Euth. Zig.*Panop.*27.pr. (*PG* 130:1289)

See vol.1:83–85

Cosm.*Sl.*1 (Popruženko 1–2)

Petr.Sic.*Serm.*1.1 (*PG* 104:1305)

Petr.Sic.*Hist.*1 (*PG* 104:1239)

Euth. Zig.*Anath.*4 (*PG* 131:44)

Joh.D.*Man.*77 (*PG* 94:1576)

into our period, so that for Theodore Abû Qurra at the end of the eighth century "the polemic with the Manicheans was very urgent and relevant." It was, however, the second kind of dualism, Paulicianism, that raised many of the old Manichean questions for the orthodox. The two movements were one in the "soul-destroying fruit" they bore, but the Paulicians were nevertheless a new effort of the devil to shoot his arrows against the church after having emptied his quiver through earlier heresies. When the Bogomils arose, their doctrine was said to be derived from "the godlessness of the Manicheans, which we call the Paulician heresy." It was connected to other movements by its orthodox critics, who noted some of its distinctive emphases. But as the varieties of Gnostic experience were pertinent to our study only as they determined the shape of the orthodox reaction to Gnosticism, so it is the response to dualism that is of interest to us here; and that response, while not altogether indifferent to the varieties, remained substantially the same in its doctrinal content.

Above all, it concentrated on the doctrine of God. The Old Church Slavic treatise against the Bogomils by the presbyter Cosmas declared, in its very first paragraph, the absolute necessity of the dogma of the Trinity as confessed by "the holy fathers at the Council of Nicea." Before the rise of the Bogomils, Peter of Sicily began his first sermon against the Paulicians with a trinitarian confession, and he opened his *History of the Heresy of the Manicheans Also Known as Paulicians* with a declaration of faith in "the Holy Trinity, our only true God." Such was likewise the affirmation of the synodical anathemas summarized under the name of Euthymius Zigabenus, where an anathema was pronounced "upon those who say that, in addition to the holy and life-giving Trinity . . . , there is another trinity." Earlier still, before the Bogomils and the Paulicians, John of Damascus took the Manichean system as an occasion to identify Christian teaching as a faith in "one God, good and just, the Creator of all, the Ruler of all, the Almighty." It seems clear that, whatever the actual intentions of the various dualistic doctrines may have been, the defenders of Christian doctrine saw in them primarily a threat to orthodox trinitarian monotheism.

The deviation of the several groups from orthodox

trinitarianism varied considerably not only between the groups, but within each of them. Against the Manicheans it was necessary to defend the Nicene dogma of the Trinity on the grounds that the three hypostases in the Trinity did not mean a multiplicity of essential principles [ἀρχαί]; for there was in the Trinity a single essential principle, the Father, from whom alone (as the East also contended against Western theology) the Son and the Spirit proceeded. It was reported that the Paulicians, "allegorizing the Holy Trinity in a manner that is illegal and very ignorant, claim to confess [the doctrine of] God" with the church, but in fact denied it. From the polemics of Cosmas against the Bogomils it would seem that they did not maintain any distinctive trinitarian theory and that their chief error in the doctrine of God was their dualism. Although he attacked them for trinitarian heresy, he did not identify any distinctive aberration. On the other hand, the Bogomils were accused by other orthodox theologians of "teaching that the Holy Trinity is unequal." In relation to earlier heresies, some Bogomils were said to have maintained a a "Monarchian" theory, compounding it with their speculations about the origin of Satan and about the betrayal of Christ by Judas. Manicheans, Paulicians, and Bogomils were all, however, out of step with the church because they did not teach the unity of God in the form maintained by orthodoxy.

Against all these dualists, the basic proof text for the unity of God was the same passage of the Old Testament over which the Christians had been disputing with the Jews, the Shema. When the Savior had been asked which was first among the commandments of the law, he replied by quoting the Shema: "Hear, O Israel, the Lord our God is one Lord." In the conflict with the Gnostics, and now again in the conflict with the dualists, the authority of the Old Testament became an issue specifically in connection with the doctrine of God. As part of their argument for a dualistic view of the divine, the Paulicians rejected the Jewish Bible. The church fathers of orthodoxy, who had based so much of their teaching on the Old Testament, also had to be repudiated. One of the theological elements common to the Paulicians and the Bogomils was this rejection of the Old Testament. In opposition to Manicheans, Paulicians, and Bogomils, the orthodox argued that

Joh.D.*Man.*4 (*PG* 94:1509)

Petr.Sic.*Hist.*4 (*PG* 104:1245)

Cosm.*Sl.*26 (Popruženko 62–63)

Euth.Zig.*Panop.*27.23 (*PG* 130:1320)

See vol.1:176–80

Euth.Zig.*Bog.*1 (Ficker 95); Euth.Zig.*Panop.*27.5 (*PG* 130:1293)

Mark 12:28–29

Deut.6:4 Phot.*Man.*2.12 (*PG* 102:113)

ap.Petr.Sic.*Hist.*10 (*PG* 104:1256)

ap.Petr.Sic.*Hist.*19 (*PG* 104:1272)

Euth.Zig.*Bog.*17 (Ficker 98); Euth.Zig.*Panop.*27.1 (*PG* 130:1292)

Phot.*Man*.2.11 (*PG* 102:108)

Phot.*Man*.3.10 (*PG* 102:141)

Phot.*Man*.3.5 (*PG* 102:132)

Phot.*Man*.3.14 (*PG* 102:160)

Joh.D.*Imag*.3.9 (*PG* 94:1332)

Phot.*Man*.3.6 (*PG* 102:133)

See p. 197 above

Joh.D.*Dialex*. (*PG* 96:1324)

Petr.Sic.*Hist*.10 (*PG* 104:1253)

Psell.*Daem*.2 (*PG* 122:824)

ap.Thdr.AbuQ.*Mim*.9.9 (Graf 229)
ap.Petr.Sic.*Serm*.1.4 (*PG* 104:1309)

the God of the Old Testament was identical with the Father of the Lord Jesus Christ. It was "the same dogma" that had been set forth "in the Old [Testament] and in grace [the New Testament]." For if the Old Testament was from the devil, how was it that Christ was born from the people of the law? The God who had not rejected Paul, but had called and elected him, was also the God who had not cast off his ancient people Israel, but would bring it to its consummation through faith in Christ. Therefore the Old Testament should continue to maintain its authority as part of Christian Scripture, but "the shameful, foul, and unclean scripture of the accursed Manicheans" should not. Despite the efforts of the dualists to depict the God of the Old Testament as a God of wrathful justice and the God of the New Testament as a God of kindness, the church confessed that "it is the same God of goodness and love who is the avenger of the righteous man both in the Old [Testament] and in grace."

While maintaining against Judaism that the Shema did not preclude the doctrine of the Trinity, but rather, when correctly understood, included it, orthodox Christian monotheism simultaneously opposed any effort to modify the singleness of the divine nature through the introduction of a double principle [ἀρχή]. The Trinity did not imply any compromise in the fundamental axiom that the divine principle was one, and in opposition to the Filioque this axiom was reinforced. To the dualists the orthodox declared: "For our part, we do not follow your godless ways, nor do we say that there are two principles which are to be separated according to location. But, declaring that there is one Creator of all things and a single principle of all things, we affirm the dogma . . . of the Father and the Son." "The confession of two principles, an evil god and a good one" was understood by the orthodox to be "the first article" of the Paulician creed, taken over from the Manicheans. From the Manicheans and Paulicians the notion of a multiple principle had in turn been taken over by later dualist groups, particularly the Bogomils. Biblical justification for it was found in such passages as Matthew 7:18, which said that there were two different sources for the two different kinds of deeds, or 2 Corinthians 4:3–4, which spoke of "the god of this world." Replying to such exegesis, the orthodox produced biblical evidence that the very rejection of the authority of God by the world was evidence for one principle rather than two; for Christ "came to his own home, and his own people received him not."

Although in later theologians the proof from Scripture took a more prominent role, in the polemics of John of Damascus such proof was heavily reinforced by logic and metaphysics. When the Manicheans contended that the two principles "have absolutely nothing in common," he replied that if they both existed, they had to have at least existence in common. By their very use of the term "principle," the Manicheans contradicted their own dualism, for a principle had to be single. As in mathematics the unit was the principle of every number, so it was in metaphysics. If there was an individual principle for each existing thing, then these many principles had in turn to have a single principle behind them. Otherwise there would not be only the two principles of God and matter, as the dualists taught, but a plurality of them throughout the universe. Not only was this an absurdity on the face of it, but it negated the meaning of the word "principle." Good and evil were not to be explained on the basis of a dual principle, but rather "the good is both the principle and the goal of all things, even of those things that are evil."

"Those things that are evil" had to include even the devil. Although he was "the enemy of God," he was also the "vindicator" and the "servant" of God. The "rod and staff" of which the psalmist spoke represented the cross of Christ, by which the devil, like a snarling dog, was driven off; this proved that he was not a god, not a second principle. From the language of the apostle it was obvious that although idols and devils were called "gods" in the Bible, they were not really gods. The decisive line drawn by Christian ontology was not that between natural and supernatural, nor ultimately that between good and evil, but that between the Creator and his creatures, be they good or evil. For "there is a greater distance between the seraphim and God than there is between the Evil One and the seraphim." "Prince of this world" though he was properly called by Christ himself, Satan remained a creature of the one true God and Creator. Did this mean, the Manicheans asked, that the being of the devil was good? The orthodox replied in the affirmative, adding

Joh.D.*Dialex.* (PG 96:1324); Phot.*Man.*2.8 (PG 102:97)

John 1:11

ap.Joh.D.*Man.*2 (PG 94:1508)

Joh.D.*Man.*11; 16 (PG 94:1516; 1521)

Joh.D.*Man.*3 (PG 94:1509)

Joh.D.*Man.*51 (PG 94:1549)

Joh.D.*Man.*19 (PG 94:1524)

Joh.D.*Man.*9 (PG 94:1513)

Joh.D.*Man.*64 (PG 94:1560)

Max.*Qu.Thal.*26 (PG 90:341)

Ps.23:4

Cosm.*Sl.*13 (Popruženko 24)

1 Cor.8:4–5
Petr.Sic.*Serm.*1.6 (PG 104:1312)

See vol.1:140–41

Joh.D.*Man.*46 (PG 94:1548)
John 14:30

Petr.Sic.*Serm.*1.7 (PG 104:1313)

Joh.D.*Man*.35 (*PG* 94:1540–41)

Matt.4:8–9
Phot.*Man*.3.18 (*PG* 102:172–73)

Job 1:12

Max.*Qu.Thal*.26 (*PG* 90:348)
Petr.Sic.*Serm*.1.5 (*PG* 104:1312)

ap.Joh.D.*Man*.32 (*PG* 94:1540)

Tert.*Praescrip*.7.5 (*CCSL* 1:192)

ap.Joh.D.*Dialex*. (*PG* 96:1325)

Joh.D.*Man*.13–14 (*PG* 94:1517)

Max.*Qu.Thal*.pr. (*PG* 90:253; 257)

Max.*Schol.D.n*.7.2 (*PG* 4:349)

Joh.D.*Man*.14 (*PG* 94:1517)

Max.*Schol.D.n*.4.22 (*PG* 4:239)

Joh.D.*Man*.22–23 (*PG* 94:1528)
Joh.D.*Man*.50 (*PG* 94:1549)

ap.Joh.D.*Man*.34; 68 (*PG* 94:1540; 1568)

Thdr.AbuQ.*Mim*.9.19 (Graf 237–38)

that while being was good simply because it was being, a being that obeyed the will of God was better. It was the devil's heresy, as set forth in the temptation of Christ, to claim that the world belonged to him, not to God. Christ's answer to that temptation confirmed the doctrine of the Book of Job that the devil was able to act against man only by the permission of God rather than by his own authority. The devil had no such authority of his own, but was "a runaway slave and an apostate creature" of God.

If this was the orthodox doctrine of the devil over against dualism, it was reasonable to ask, "What, then, is the wickedness of the devil?" At the root of the conflict between dualism and orthodox monotheism was the question of the relation between evil and the God of love. Tertullian had observed that heretics and philosophers were all concerned with the question, "Whence comes evil?" If, as orthodoxy maintained, there was one God of love who was the Creator, "whence come diseases and death and other evils like those?" A basic element of the orthodox response to such questions was a reassertion of the patristic and classical definition of evil as the privation of good rather than a positive force in its own right. It was an aberration from one's appointed goal, a lack of knowledge about the good cause of all things. In response to the dualists it was necessary to assert that darkness was not a reality but only the absence of light, just as poverty was the absence of riches and blindness the absence of vision. Carried to its logical conclusion, this definition obliged the orthodox to acknowledge that even the demons were good inasmuch as they were created by God, but that the loss of their appointed purpose had made them evil. It also enabled the orthodox to argue that since "being" stood in opposition to "nonbeing," one of the dualists' principles had reality and the other did not. Hence evil must not be eternal, but must be derived from something prior to itself—the God of love, both merciful and just.

Yet this did not answer the question, "Why is it that God, foreknowing that the devil would become evil, made him nevertheless?" Much of the problem of evil was an attempt to resolve the connection between foreknowledge and predestination. The obvious test case was Judas Iscariot, of whom Christ had said: "The Son of man goes as it is written of him, but woe to that man

Matt.26:24

by whom the Son of man is betrayed! It would have been better for that man if he had not been born." The divine election by which the redemption of mankind was carried out achieved its eternal purpose in the events of Christ's death, but Christ nevertheless said that it would have been better for Judas never to have been born. John of Damascus explained that Christ did not say, "It would have been better if that man had not been born," but "better for that man"; for it was good for him to be, but evil for him to be the betrayer. On the basis of this and other passages, it was possible to distinguish between divine foreknowledge and divine will and, by such a distinction, to make clear that God was not the author of evil even though he did foresee it. The other prong of the orthodox attack was the argument that if the dualists were right in making evil a second principle alongside God, "those who sin cannot be held accountable." On the contrary, the very presence of sin and evil and the capacity of a creature to transgress the divine commandments was grim proof for the freedom of the will conferred in creation. By turning the dualists' argument against itself, one could show that the very evil which they sought to reify—and indeed to deify—served ultimately to demonstrate the oneness of God the Creator and the goodness of his creation.

Joh.D.*Man*.70 (*PG* 94:1568)

Joh.D.*Man*.37; 79 (*PG* 94:1544; 1577)

Joh.D.*Man*.29 (*PG* 94:1533); Thdr.AbuQ.*Mim*.9.8 (Graf 228)

Phot.*Man*.2.2 (*PG* 102:88)

See vol. 1:36–37

See vol.1:85

The oneness of God the Creator and his transcendence over the creation had been summarized by the early church in the doctrine of creation ex nihilo. In part, creation ex nihilo was the orthodox answer to the Gnostic theories of emanation, according to which various cosmic "aeons" had proceeded from within the divine being itself. Now that the successors of the Gnostics were once more teaching creation by emanation, it was appropriate to urge that for God "to bring something forth out of his own essence is not an act of creation, but to bring it forth out of nothing is an act of creation." This was the only way to teach that God was the Creator without doing violence to his holy and unchangeable nature. As creation ex nihilo negated the theory of creation through emanation from the divine nature, so in the other direction it also negated the idea that God created as men do, out of previously existing matter. If God was truly "greater than all things that are said or thought," it was more fitting for him to create ex nihilo than to make new things out of old things. The orthodox doctrine of creation, as

Joh.D.*Man*.42 (*PG* 94:1545)

Joh.D.*Man*.6 (*PG* 94:1512)

Joh.D.*Man*.20 (*PG* 94:1524)

confessed in the Nicene Creed, likewise made it possible
for the church to confess that God was the Creator of all
things invisible, none of which had an independent being, and of all things visible, none of which was beneath
the dignity of a God who created ex nihilo.

Phot.*Man*.3.12 (*PG*
102:152)

What had been created ex nihilo by a good God was,
by that very creation, good and not to be despised, for it
had its being from God. God was good, and he was
eternal; his creatures, while they could not be eternal because they had been made ex nihilo and were changeable,
were nevertheless good in their temporality. The inherent
goodness of the creation was shown by the example of
Christ, who said of the animals on which he rode into
Jerusalem: "The Lord has need of them." In these words
he expressed his readiness to identify himself as the
Creator and the Lord of the ass and its foal, confuting
those who regarded such humble beasts as unworthy of
him. The Creator of the world of things and animals was
the same as the Redeemer of mankind, and a hatred of the
material creation amounted to a contempt for him and for
his gifts. According to converts from the Manicheans (or
Paulicians) to orthodox Christianity, it was customary
among these heretics to take a piece of bread in one's
hands and to say, "It was not I who made you," since
it was material and not spiritual. By this action the dualist "hurls curses at the one God, the Highest, and curses
the one who created him." It was blasphemy to say that
"the creation [of this God] is the creation of the devil"
and that "it was not God who made heaven and earth and
the entire visible world."

Joh.D.*Man*.69 (*PG*
94:1568)

Joh.D.*Man*.31 (*PG*
94:1537)

Matt.21:3

Phot.*Man*.3.12 (*PG*
102:149)

Petr.Sic.*Hist*.17 (*PG*
104:1268)

Cosm.*Sl*.17 (Popruženko 32)

Cosm.*Sl*.4 (Popruženko 6)

Perhaps the most striking expression of such hatred
for the created world among the dualists was their asceticism, which evoked the reluctant admiration of their
orthodox adversaries. "They dress like monks," one such
adversary observed. Another reported: "Outwardly the
heretics give the appearance of sheep. They are sweet and
humble, meek . . . , not speaking an idle word nor
laughing out loud nor indulging in crude jests." So impressive was the gravity of their outward demeanor that
it was difficult to distinguish them from "the genuine
Christians." To the orthodox, of course, they were not
genuine Christians at all, but hypocrites. Although they
fasted three days a week, "at someone else's table they
eat and drink like elephants." Their pretense of sexual
continence was negated by a secret self-indulgence, which,

Euth.Zig.*Bog*.29 (Ficker 101);
Euth.Zig.*Panop*.27.24 (*PG*
130:1320)

Cosm.*Sl*.2 (Popruženko 3)

Euth.Zig.*Bog*.32 (Ficker 101);
Euth.Zig.*Panop*.27.24 (*PG*
130:1320)

Phot.*Man.*1.10 (*PG*
102:32)

as Photius noted with regard to the Manicheans, meant
that their doctrine and their life were congruent. Such
accusations had been part of orthodox polemics against
most heresies, particularly against Gnosticism and dualism, in which a hatred of creation seems to have led
sometimes to extreme asceticism and sometimes to extreme libertinism. The orthodox polemic against the
extreme asceticism is more interesting doctrinally than
that against the extreme libertinism, for it made necessary a clarification of the theological differences between
the orthodox denial of the world and the heretical hatred
of the world.

In response to the disparagement of the ascetic life by
some iconoclasts, the orthodox called it "the way of life
of the gospel [εὐαγγελικὴ πολιτεία]" and "imitative of the

Niceph.*Antirr.*2.6 (*PG*
100:345)

angels [ἀγγελομίμητος]." On the basis of the words of
Christ that "in the resurrection they neither marry nor

Matt.22:30

are given in marriage, but are like angels in heaven," the
fathers had argued that Paradise had been like heaven,
so that human sexuality as a means of procreation had
been added to human nature after the original creation.
God had "implanted into mankind, instead of the angelic
majesty of nature, that animal and irrational means by

Gr.Nyss.*Hom.opific.*17 (*PG*
44:189)

which [human beings] now succeed one another." Such
a notion of double creation, the first without sex before
the fall and the second with sex either after the fall or in
foreknowledge of the fall, was taken up from the fathers
by the founders of Byzantine theology, especially Maximus Confessor. He taught that "nature after the trans-
gression drew upon itself carnal conception and birth with

Max.*Ambig.*42 (*PG*
91:1340–41)

corruption." Sexual desire and procreation through sex
were therefore a consequence of the fall and a concession
to man's weakened state after the fall. Although sex was
necessary for the continuation of the human race, it was
in a fundamental sense a necessary evil. By demonstrating
that it was possible to live without sex, the professional
ascetics of the church not only were anticipating the angelic life to be shared by all in the resurrection, but were
also reestablishing the original form of life as it had been
intended before the fall. From such a view it would have
been only one more step—albeit a grave step—to the
doctrine that the body and its sexuality were, while a
necessary evil, more evil than necessary. It was this step
that the Manichean, Paulician, and Bogomil dualists were
prepared to take but that the orthodox refused to take.

When confronted by the dualist form of asceticism, the champions of orthodoxy came to the defense of the body. The material world was not evil, it was simple potentiality—created by God ex nihilo (therefore having no being of its own), but not evil in and of itself. To be "material" meant that it was derivative and dependent, but not that it was despicable. On the basis of the resurrection of Christ, the orthodox argued that the body was not of itself the creation of the Evil One; for if it were, neither the incarnate Christ nor the resurrected Christ nor the resurrected saints would have had a true body. It was, as the Nestorians insisted no less than the Chalcedonians, "a godless slander" to maintain that "matter is evil and consequently our body is also." For the body, which the Manicheans called evil, nevertheless did good works, while the soul, which they called good, was the source of evil works. If, as they contended, the body was the power that compelled the soul to sin, the very presence of good works was evidence that this power was not as overwhelming as they taught and that the body was not intrinsically evil. The body and matter, being neutral, were at the disposal of the power that commanded them. If this power was good, they became good through it; for it was by the power of the good, that is, by the power of God, that matter had originally been called out of nonbeing into being. Therefore when Christ quoted the Old Testament about the creation of man as male and female, he was not only asserting the authority of the books of Moses, but was "bearing witness that the distinction of sex between male and female is the result of an act of creation by God." In this way the orthodox discovered the countervailing force of the doctrine of creation in opposition to a teaching that not only was the explicit dogma of the dualists, but could easily have been the implicit doctrine of some orthodox ascetics.

Orthodoxy was aided in this discovery by the implications of another issue over which it had been contending with its adversaries, the doctrine of icons and of sacraments. During the iconoclastic controversy the orthodox had argued that the physical nature of man made it necessary for the message of the gospel to be communicated through images and for man to worship the invisible God through his visible representations, and they called the opposing spiritualist view "a Manichean notion." Yet the Bogomils asked: "Why is it that you worship [the cross]?

Max.*Schol.D.n.*4.18–19 (*PG* 4:272–76)

Phot.*Man.*3.15 (*PG* 102:161); *Hag.Tom.* (*PG* 150:1233)

Bab.*Evagr.*3.53 (Frankenberg 223[222])

Thdr.AbuQ.*Mim.*9.13 (Graf 233)

Thdr.AbuQ.*Mim.*9.8 (Graf 228)

Joh.D.*Man.*57 (*PG* 94:1552)

Matt.19:5–6

Phot.*Man.*3.1 (*PG* 102:125); Gr.Pal.*Tr.*1.1.22 (Meyendorff 61)

Joh.D.*Imag.*1.16 (*PG* 94:1245)

ap.Cosm.*Sl.*4 (Popruženko 6)
ap.Euth.Zig.*Anath.*11 (PG 131:45)
ap.Germ.II.*Bog.* (PG 140:632)

Euth.Zig.*Bog.*21 (Ficker 99);
Euth.Zig.*Panop.*27.11 (PG 130:1308)

See pp. 109–10 above

For it was on it that the Jews crucified the Son of God, and the cross is the enemy of God." Their terms for the cross were "gibbet [φούλκα]" and "instrument for the murder of Christ." They repudiated the worship of icons and regarded as "orthodox and faithful only the enemies of the icons," especially Emperor Constantine V. Unlike the iconoclasts, however, they did not couple this rejection of images with an emphasis on the Eucharist as the true image of Christ. The orthodox accused the Paulicians of teaching that the eucharistic words, "Take, eat," had been spoken by Christ in a purely symbolic sense; and they accused the Bogomils of teaching that "the communion of the revered body and blood . . . is a communion of ordinary bread and wine." This "disrespect for the mystical and awesome sacrifice" compelled the orthodox to become more explicit than usual about their doctrine of the real presence in the Eucharist: "Visibly it is bread that is set before us, but invisibly it is the Holy Spirit visiting us and consecrating the elements that are set out. They are not symbols [ἀντίτυπα], but in reality the holy body and the revered blood of our Lord and God, who makes them to be this. By [the body and blood] we sinners are sanctified, receiving it for the forgiveness of sins." A dualism that consigned the physical, material world to Satan for the sake of preserving the "spiritual" eventually denied both the material as a creature of God and the spiritual as the nature of God.

Petr.Sic.*Serm.*3.1 (PG 104:1348)

Euth.Zig.*Anath.*12 (PG 131:45)
Euth.Zig.*Bog.*12 (Ficker 96);
Euth.Zig.*Panop.*27.17 (PG 130:1313)

Petr.Sic.*Serm.*3.2 (PG 104:1349)

Once again it was the doctrine of the Virgin Mary that served to safeguard this combination of the material and the spiritual in the incarnation, as it had against Nestorians and iconoclasts. To the orthodox it was evident that all of the dualists had inherited from their Gnostic ancestors a horror at the physical nature of Christ. For this nature, Mary was the guarantee. Immediately after exposing the dualism of the Paulicians, Peter of Sicily turned to their view of Mary, according to which she deserved neither to be called "good," much less holy, nor to be identified as the mother of Christ. Affirming in opposition that she was "second only to God in glory, first among all creatures, invisible and visible," he drew a close logical connection between their heresy in the doctrine of Mary and their heresy in the doctrine of Christ. Similarly, the Bogomils "do not honor the most glorious and most immaculate Theotokos," but heaped all sorts of abuse on

Thphyl.CP.*Ep.Petr.Bulg.*172v (Petrovskij 365)

Euth.Zig.*Panop.*27.8 (PG 130:1304–5)

Petr.Sic.*Hist.*10 (PG 104:1256)

Petr.Sic.*Serm.*2.1 (PG 104:1332)

Petr.Sic.*Serm.*2.6 (PG 104:1337)

Cosm.*Sl*.10 (Popruženko 17)

her. It was even reported that they claimed the title "Theotokos" for every one of their own members, in whom the Holy Spirit was said to dwell, and that they refused to concede any special prerogatives to the real

Euth.Zig.*Bog*.25 (Ficker 100);
Euth.Zig.*Panop*.27.22 (*PG*
130:1317)

Theotokos over the others. If, as the various dualists seem to have believed, the spirituality and sovereignty of the true and highest God could be maintained only by radically separating him from matter, from the human body, and from every other evil, the orthodox doctrines of Christ and of Mary had to be a stumbling block to them.

For orthodoxy, on the other hand, the reality of the incarnation in a material human body was indispensable to salvation and deification. The oneness of the Trinity was not to be surrendered to a duality of spirit and matter or of good and evil, for the incarnate Logos had performed

Phot.*Man*.2.9 (*PG*
102:100)

such miracles as the feeding of the thousands or the healing of the blind by using matter. Creation and incarnation were inseparable in the faith of the church, and what held them together was the doctrine of the Trinity. Every

Phot.*Man*.3.16 (*PG*
102:164)
Phot.*Man*.1.9 (*PG*
102:29)

fatherhood in heaven and on earth was derived from the one Father, as Ephesians 3:14–15 taught. The trinitarian dogma was the mark of true catholic orthodoxy, regardless of the practice of the dualists in referring to themselves as "the catholic church" or as "Christians" and to the or-

Petr.Sic.*Hist*.10 (*PG*
104:1253)

thodox as "Romans." Despite the prominence of the origin of evil as a problem for dualist theology, therefore, the final issue between it and the theology of orthodox Christendom was the Nicene dogma; and it was not a polemical exaggeration, but a valid recognition of the issue, when the presbyter Cosmas declared against the

Cosm.*Sl*.26 (Popruženko
62–63)

Bogomils: "Whoever does not believe in the holy and undivided Trinity, let him be anathema."

The One God—And His Prophet

The seventh century produced a new chapter in the history of relations between Judaism and Christianity; but it was also in that century—as later Byzantine Christians

Joh.Cant.*Or*.1.pr. (*PG*
154:589); *V.Moh*. (*PG*
158:1077)

were wont to say, "in the days when Heraclius was the emperor of the Romans"—that there arose, within the territories of Eastern Christendom, the most powerful organized alternative to Christianity until the rise of the Comintern in the twentieth century, again in the East. Although the Christian contemporaries of Mohammed paid him no heed, the rise of Islam meant that the trini-

tarian monotheism defended by orthodoxy against Jews
and dualists now faced a new challenge from the religion
of the prophet. It was a challenge for which Christian
theology was not well prepared. "In understanding Islam,
the West [as well as the East] could get no help from
antiquity, and no comfort from the present. For an age
avowedly dependent on the past for its materials, this
was a serious matter." Euthymius Zigabenus, in his *Dogmatic Panoply,* devoted the final chapter to "Saracens" or
"Ishmaelites," after having spent the preceding one on
the Bogomils. Anti-Muslim polemics figured prominently
in Byzantine theology during most of the period covered
by this volume, from John of Damascus and Theodore
Abû Qurra to the emperor-theologians of the late Byzantine Empire, John VI Cantacuzenus and his grandson,
Manuel II Palaeologus. Like the anti-Jewish polemics, this
literature sometimes took the form of "dialogues," some
of which also climaxed in the surrender of the opponents
to the orthodox faith. Other literary forms that have been
preserved include: a formula of recantation for converts from Islam to Christianity, which has survived in
at least two different versions; a *Confession of Faith
against the Saracens,* which, because of its quotation from
the Apostles' Creed and the Athanasian Creed, would
appear to be of Western origin, although it is written in
Greek; and what purports to be an exchange of correspondence provoked by the "dogmatic epistle [which
Omar the caliph] sent to Leo [III] the emperor, thinking
that he might persuade him to accept Islam [μαγαρίσαι]."

Whether genuine or pseudonymous, such writings do
give a clear picture of the themes that seemed to the
defenders of Christian orthodoxy to be the most important in their conflict with Islam, although they sometimes misunderstood Muslim doctrine, as well as Muslim
objections to Christian doctrine. After this conflict had
become a standard part of Byzantine theology, it became
necessary to maintain that "our blessed prelates who were
living at the same epoch as your legislator Mohammed"
had written about him in detail, so that it was "unneces-
sary for us to importune you on the subject of your religion." Christians claimed to have mastered the contents
of the Koran, and even to possess an autograph copy of
it in the Church of the Forerunner [ὁ Πρόδρομος, John
the Baptist] in Damascus. In the ninth century a Byzantine

Southern (1962) 4–5

Euth.Zig.*Panop*.28 (*PG*
130:1332–60)
Euth.Zig.*Panop*.27 (*PG*
130:1289–1332)

Man.II.Pal.*Dial*.pr.
(Trapp 6)

Joh.D.*Disp.Sar.* (*PG*
96:1348)

ap.Nicet.Chon.*Thes*.20 (*PG*
140:123–38); *Anath.Sar.*
(Montet 145–63)

Conf.Sar. (*PG* 154:1152)
Leo III.*Ep.* (Jeffery
269–332)

Theoph.*Chron*.A.M.1620
(Boor 1:399)

Leo III.*Ep.* (Jeffery 282)

Barth.Ed.*Agar.* (*PG*
104:1444)

Nicet.Byz.*Arab*.2.26 (*PG* 105:704)
Cydon.*Moh*. (*PG* 154: 1035–52)
Joh.Cant.*Or*.1.4 (*PG* 154:601)

Barth.Ed.*Agar*. (*PG* 104:1392)
Nicet.Byz.*Arab*.19.82 (*PG* 105:776)
Joh.Cant.*Or*.4.1 (*PG* 154:684)

Nicet.Byz.*Arab*.2.28 (*PG* 105:705)

Conf.Sar. (*PG* 154:1157)

ap.Man.II.Pal.*Dial*.1 (Trapp 9)

Khoury (1966) 2:93

Leo III.*Ep*. (Jeffery 295)

Thdr.AbuQ.*Opusc*.22; 35 (*PG* 97:1552–53; 1589); *Conf.Sar*. (*PG* 154:1161)

Nicet.Byz.*Ref.Ep*.2.6 (*PG* 105:829)
Barth.Ed.*Agar*. (*PG* 104: 1444–45)

Meyendorff (1964) 125
Nicet.Byz.*Arab*.2.31 (*PG* 105:709)

scholar, Nicetas, undertook a refutation of the Koran chapter by chapter, and several centuries later the Greek translation of a Latin attack on the Koran provided John Cantacuzenus with additional information about it. Christian critics of Islam could therefore boast of knowing "all your sacred books," which they attacked as "nothing but mythology and witchcraft." Unlike the Old Testament and the New Testament, the Koran was filled with contradictions. Its style was "neither prophetic nor historical nor legislative nor theological," and yet Muslims claimed that it had come down from heaven. Even when it was acknowledged that the Koran contained "many true and clear statements about God and about our Lord Jesus Christ, things that we also confess," this was dismissed as insufficient.

The teachings of the Koran and the practices of Islam gave Christian theologians the occasion to discuss a great variety of religious differences with their opponents. One Muslim presentation of the differences "in a systematic fashion" opened with the question: "What do you think about the nature of the angels, and about the structure of heaven and earth and of the entire cosmos?" "The sensuality of Mohammed . . . as one of the characteristics of his moral description and of his conduct" came in for frequent attention. Christians had to defend themselves against the accusation of sectarianism, and against attacks on the doctrine of the sacraments. Fundamentally, however, the divergence between the two systems was the one voiced in the Shahādah, the Muslim profession of faith: "There is no God but Allah, and Mohammed is his prophet." Christians were acquainted with this profession of faith, sometimes rendering "prophet" with "apostle." While other questions did appear in the debates, the two points of sharpest contention were these: the one God and Mohammed as his prophet.

Contention with Islam produced in Byzantine thought two different views, "the extreme and 'closed' one, which adopted an absolutely negative attitude toward Muhammadanism and considered it a form of paganism, and another, the more moderate one, which tried to avoid burning all bridges and to preserve a measure of common reference, in particular, the recognition of a common allegiance to monotheism." The first of these was by far the more typical. Islam was "a barbaric form of worship," and the prophet himself was "the thrice-accursed and altogether godless Mohammed." He had taken some things from the Old Testament and some things from the New and had invented "a syncretistic religion [σύνθετον θρησκείαν]." It was a summary of all the heresies that had arisen within the church. The Muslim view of God was attributed by the orthodox to Arian influence, while the doctrine of Christ was said to be Nestorian, apparently because it separated the man Jesus from the Logos. Manicheism was the source for Muslim ideas about demons, and Origen was the source for the belief that the demons would be saved. Even "the heretical Donatsists" were blamed for Muslim errors. On the basis of this ancestry, John of Damascus listed Islam in his catalog of Christian heresies. He also called it "forerunner of Antichrist," as had Maximus before him and as later theologians did also, on the basis of the prophecy about the "son of perdition," who would "take his seat in the temple of God." Yet by declaring that "the god of Mohammed is other than the true God," such theologians were raising in acute form the issue of monotheism as in theory a common ground, but in practice the cardinal difference, between Islam and Christianity.

When the Muslims took the Christian adoration of Christ as proof that the Christians taught more than one God, the Christians retorted that "we worship the one true God, Maker of heaven and earth." They quoted the Shema in their response to Muslim criticism, as proof that "the Trinity is united in causality and in essence and in spiration." This was in reply to the attack of the Koran on "those who ascribe associates to God." The defenders of Christian orthodoxy refused to have themselves styled "associationists and participationists [κοινωνταὶ καὶ ἑταιριοταί]" because they attributed to the one God the sort of association and participation that was part of the traditional dogma of the Trinity. The type of monotheism for which Christian thought was contending was different in kind from a definition of God as "altogether single, . . . without any partner." Monotheism formed a basis for a common affirmation between Islam and Christianity, but Christianity had since its earliest beginnings found itself obliged to hold its monotheism in some sort of tension with its no less central conviction that it was

V.Moh. (PG 158:1077)

Barth.Ed.Moh. (PG 104:1457; 1449)
Joh.Cant.Or.1.pr. (PG 154:589)

Thdr.AbuQ.Opusc.25 (PG 97:1557–61); V.Moh. (PG 158:1077)
Joh.Cant.Apol.1.17 (PG 154:417); Joh.Cant.Or.2.24 (PG 154:633)
Nicet.Byz.Arab.2.32 (PG 105:712)

Joh.Cant.Or.2.26; 4.2 (PG 154:649; 685)
Joh.Cant.Or.3.7 (PG 154:673)

Joh.D.Haer.101 (PG 94:764–73)

Max.Ep.14 (PG 91:540)

2 Thess.2:4

Nicet.Byz.Arab.9.63 (PG 105:749); Man.II.Pal.Dial.5 (Trapp 53–54)
Nicet.Byz.Arab.4.46 (PG 105:732)

Joh.Cant.Apol.2.5 (PG 154:453)

Deut. 6:4

Nicet.Byz.Arab.9.61 (PG 105:748); Man.II.Pal.Dial.14 (Trapp 181–82)

Nicet.Byz.Arab.1.12 (PG 105:685)

Thdr.AbuQ.Opusc.20 (PG 97:1545)

See vol.1:173–74

appropriate to speak of Jesus Christ as God. Even more than any of the other contemporary offensives—those from Judaism, Hellenism, and dualism—the Muslim critique imposed on Christian theology the obligation to specify why it was that the dogma of the Trinity did not imply any sort of tritheism.

The importance of this obligation in the Christian case against Islam may be gauged from the prominence assigned to the defense of the trinitarian dogma in the various anti-Muslim tracts, where "the Islamic denial of the Trinity seemed to be the basic point of difference between the religions." "How is it," the Muslim interlocutor was made to ask at the very beginning of one of these tracts, "that you confess a polytheism and introduce 'begetting' into the Godhead, and also that you speak of Father, Son, and Holy Spirit?" Other treatises likewise introduced their replies to Muslim criticism with an affirmation of the dogma of the Trinity, even when this had not come first in the list of Muslim grievances. Nicetas of Byzantium took up the Trinity at the beginning of his first response, and then made it the theme of his second response as well. John VI Cantacuzenus opened the first of his *Apologies* with the doctrine of the Trinity, recurred to it in the third of his *Orations,* and used it in the peroration to his entire anti-Muslim corpus. Almost half of the *Dialogues with a Persian* by Manuel II Palaeologus was devoted to a defense of the doctrine of the Trinity and its corollaries. A neophyte who crossed over from Islam to Christianity was asked to declare: "I anathematize . . . all these things that I have stated, as well as Mohammed himself. . . . And I believe in the Father and the Son and the Holy Spirit." The undated *Confession of Faith against the Saracens* began with an affirmation of the Trinity as "the one most high God, the Creator." Theodore Abû Qurra devoted one of his Arabic discourses to a refutation of the charge that the Trinity represented a compromise of the monotheistic faith, and in his Greek writings sought to prove that Father, Son, and Holy Spirit were one and the same God by asking his Muslim opponent: "If the Koran came down from heaven and is Scripture, do you deny that another book containing [the Koran] is also [one and the same] Scripture?"

Daniel (1960) 175

ap.Euth.Zig.*Sar.*1 (*PG* 131:20–21)

Barth.Ed.*Agar.* (*PG* 104:1384–85)

Nicet.Byz.*Ref.Ep.*1.2; 2.1 (*PG* 105:809; 824)
Joh.Cant.*Apol.*1.1 (*PG* 154:381)
Joh.Cant.*Or.*3.1 (*PG* 154:652)
Joh.Cant.*Or.*4.3 (*PG* 154:692)

Man.II.Pal.*Dial.*10–19 (Trapp 120–241)

ap.Nicet.Chon.*Thes.*20 (*PG* 140:133)

Conf.*Sar.* (*PG* 154:1152)

Thdr.AbuQ.*Mim.*3.7 (Graf 138)

Thdr.AbuQ.*Opusc.*8 (*PG* 97:1528)

The demonstration that trinitarianism was not tritheism involved the clarification of various points of Christian doctrine. "We are accused by you," the Christians said to the Muslims, "of recognizing three gods." But they disavowed the accusation, pronouncing "anathema upon anyone who admits two or three divinities emanating from different origins. For our part, we know only one God." Although they asserted the three hypostases of Father, Son, and Holy Spirit, this did not mean "that we are introducing three gods into the Godhead," for the three hypostases had one nature and were one ousia. It was a slander for the Muslims to charge that such a doctrine was ascribing "associates" to the one God. On the other hand, Christian orthodoxy would not permit the attempt to rescue monotheism by attributing Father, Son, and Holy Spirit to some prior principle of origin; as the Greek East was urging against the Latin West throughout this same period, the Father was the single principle of origin within the Godhead for both the Son and the Holy Spirit. The teaching of the Koran that Christ was to be called "Logos" and "Spirit" permitted Christian apologists to demand: "Do you mean that before he created the Logos and the Spirit, God did not have either Spirit or Logos?" In face of such a question, the Muslim would "turn away from you, having nothing to answer," and the doctrine of the Trinity would be exonerated. The three hypostases were not three gods because "one God" was what they had in common, while Fatherhood, Sonship, and Spirithood were distinctive of the three. The constant Muslim question, "How could God beget a Son without a woman?" was based on a physical misunderstanding of what "begetting" meant when attributed to the divine.

This very question was at the basis of an additional misunderstanding of the dogma of the Trinity. The Christian worship of Mary the Theotokos—and by extension, the cult of saints and icons generally—seemed to the Muslims to be a further violation of the monotheistic faith. "They say," the Christians reported, that the church "worships three persons, the Father and the Mother and the Son." The definition of Mary as Theotokos was taken by Muslim polemics as proof that such was the Christian belief. To this charge the Christians replied: "Listen, and hear that we Christians worship one God . . . and his Son

Leo III.*Ep.* (Jeffery 300–301)

Nicet.Byz.*Arab.*1.19 (*PG* 105:693)

Nicet.Byz.*Ref.Ep.*2.2 (*PG* 105:825)

Nicet.Byz.*Ref.Ep.*1.7 (*PG* 105:816)

See p. 197 above

Joh.D.*Disp.Sar.* (*PG* 96:1341)

Nicet.Byz.*Ref.Ep.*2.4–5 (*PG* 105:828)

Joh.Cant.*Apol.*1.1 (*PG* 154:381); Thdr.AbuQ.*Opusc.* 20 (*PG* 97:1545)

Joh.Cant.*Apol.*pr. (*PG* 154:376)

Barth.Ed.*Agar.* (*PG* 104:1384)

Luke 1:38

Joh.Cant.*Apol*.3.9 (*PG*
154:520)

Euth.Zig.*Sar*.6 (*PG*
131:25)

Joh.Cant.*Apol*.3.12 (*PG*
154:529–32)

Leo III.*Ep*. (Jeffery 322)
Leo III. *Ep*. (Jeffery 320)

See pp. 105–6 above

Nicet.Byz.*Arab*.1.29 (*PG*
105:708); Man.II.Pal.*Dial*.11
(Trapp 134)

Nicet.Byz.*Arab*.18.82 (*PG*
105:776)

and Logos, the Christ." As for Mary, it was orthodox Christian teaching that she was "a creature of God and the handmaid of God," but of a very special sort; for "we also believe and confess that there has never arisen from man and woman, and will never arise until the consummation of the age, any human being who is like her." Theotokos she definitely was, but just as definitely she was not one of the persons of the Trinity. Worship of her was not idolatry, and neither was the worship of the saints and of their images. "Why is it," the Muslims were said to be asking, "that you worship carved pieces of wood, and that you worship icons in a manner appropriate only to God?" Against Muslims, Christians tended to base the defense of icons on their didactic value, rather than on the christological arguments employed against the iconoclasts. If the anti-Muslim letter attributed to the iconoclast emperor, Leo III, is genuine—or is at least based on a genuine original now lost—it shows the loyalty even of the iconoclasts to the veneration of the cross, but their hesitancy about paying a similar homage to pictures. At the same time, Leo spoke out in defense of the cult of relics, "which God declared to be his dwelling." Whether or not the eventual campaign of this emperor against the images was inspired by such contacts with Islam and with Judaism, as his opponents professed to have discovered, the images were an issue in the controversy between Christians and Muslims (as also between Christians and Jews) over the commandment to adore one God and no other.

The counteroffensive of Christian orthodoxy in the controversy sometimes took the form of retorting that Islam was not as monotheistic in fact as it professed to be in theory. For one thing, its doctrine of God was understood by Byzantine polemics to contain the idea that God was "all-spherical [ὁλόσφαιρος]." Based upon a mistranslation of the Arabic, this interpretation of Koranic teaching led to the accusation that the monotheism of Islam was materialistic, so that even when the mistranslation was revised, the Muslim doctrine seemed to be that "God is one, God is made of solid beaten metal [ὁλόσφυρος]." Moreover, the actual religious practice of Islam did not adhere to the rigid monotheism that Muslim theologians professed to be defending against the dogma of the Trinity. John of Damascus drew a lineal connection

Joh.D.*Haer*.101 (*PG*
94:764)

Joh.D.*Haer*.101 (*PG*
94:769)

Nicet.Byz.*Arab*.19.83 (*PG*
105:777)

Nicet.Byz.*Arab*.1.8 (*PG*
105:680)

Becker (1912) 184

Joh.D.*Man*.1 (*PG* 94:1508)

Joh.D.*Disp.Sar*. (*PG*
96:1336–37)

Barth.Ed.*Moh*. (*PG*
104:1452)

Thdr.AbuQ.*Opusc*.35
(*PG* 97:1588)

Nicet.Byz.*Arab*.21.85 (*PG*
105:780)

between the Kaaba shrine at Mecca and the worship of
Aphrodite at the same place before the coming of
Mohammed. "Until the present time," he claimed, it
was possible to see on it "the shadow of the carving"
that had originally been there. The jinns and other inter-
mediaries of Muslim belief were further proof that in
Islam "the name 'one God' is nothing but a screen" for
"an idolatrous adoration of the creature and a paganism" that belied its protestations. The Christian doctrine
of the homoousia of Son and Spirit could be shown to be
consistent with monotheism, but the Muslim practice of
worship could not.

A special form of the conflict over the doctrine of God
was the clash between Muslim teaching about the all-
determining will of Allah and Christian teaching about
free will in both God and man, which was "one of the
principal points in the program of the Christian-Moham-
medan discussion." In some ways this clash paralleled
in its argumentation the debates between orthodoxy and
dualism, for in both the spokesmen for the Christian doctrine of God were pressed to maintain that the one God
was the Creator of all things visible and invisible, but
was not the author of evil. The polemical treatises attributed to John of Damascus against the two sets of
opponents illustrated the parallel, scoring the same points
and employing the same vocabulary in both directions.
His *Dialogue against the Manicheans* introduced the problem of evil in its very first paragraph, and his *Dispute
between a Saracen and a Christian*—at least in its more
complete Greek version—did the same. The Muslim sense
of destiny and the Byzantine sense of mission collided not
only politically, but also theologically, for it was in reaction to Muslim conquests that Greek Christians were
obliged to raise with existential poignancy the very questions of fate and necessity over which they were also disputing theoretically with the philosophers and theologians
of Islam.

It was the widespread belief of Christian theologians
that Islam represented an out-and-out determinism. They
saw in it the teaching that "God does whatever he wishes,
and he is the cause of everything, both good and evil."
Christians made him the cause only of good, Muslims the
cause of evil as well. This meant, of course, that God
must also be "the cause of sin" according to the teachings
of "the godless Mohammed." From its beginnings, Chris-

Joh.D.*Disp.Sar.* (*PG* 96:1336–37)

Barth.Ed.*Agar.* (*PG* 104:1393)

Joh.D.*Disp.Sar.* (*PG* 96:1341)

Nicet.Byz.*Arab.*2.30 (*PG* 105:709)

Joh.Cant.*Apol.*4.8 (*PG* 154:557)

Leo III.*Ep.* (Jeffery 288) *Doct.Jac.*5.17 (Bonwetsch 88); Joh.Cant.*Apol.*1.4 (*PG* 154:393) *V.Moh.* (*PG* 158:1080); Man.II.Pal.*Dial.*7 (Trapp 93)

Man.II.Pal.*Dial.*2 (Trapp 16–17)

Nicet.Byz.*Arab.*5.52 (*PG* 105:737)

tian anti-Muslim polemic denounced this as a notion that made God unjust. But God was the just judge of both good and evil, rendering to each its proper due, and could not be either an unjust judge or the author of evil. Insistent though it was upon a single principle of creation in opposition to dualism, orthodoxy nevertheless held to the paradox that "none of us can stand up or move without God, and yet God does not will that we steal or commit adultery." The question acquired special import when it was applied to the idea of salvation. The implication of the Muslim position was that, since there were some who were not saved, God either did not want to save them or was not able to save them. Both possibilities were blasphemous in Christian eyes. The Christian alternative to such determinism was to assert the universal salvific will of God, but also to assert free will and responsibility in man.

Christian orthodoxy had been prepared for part of this assignment by its confrontation with dualism, but many of the fundamental questions between Christianity and Islam were reenactments of the long-standing dispute between Christianity and Judaism. In fact, the very relation of the Christian-Muslim dispute to the Christian-Jewish dispute was a matter of argument between Muslims and Christians. "I suppose," Emperor Leo III was supposed to have said to the Muslims, "that you are not ignorant of the enmity which exists between us Christians and the Jews." Sometimes Muslims were linked with Jews on the basis of their common opposition to Christianity. The continuity of Muslim customs, such as circumcision, with those of Judaism was an object of Christian attacks. On the other hand, the dispute with Islam gave Christians an opportunity to join forces with Judaism. Although the Jews were "enemies of the faith," said the Christians to the Muslims, they had preserved the primitive documents of revelation and were therefore in complete agreement with the church on such matters as the doctrine of creation. Such joining of forces could reach the point that Christians would defend Judaism against Islam, as in the reply to a Muslim criticism directed against both: "Even though [Mohammed] seeks to make Christians bear this [charge of polytheism] because they confess the all-creating and life-giving Holy Trinity, why does he do the same to the Jews, who claim to hold the faith of Abraham?" As descendants of Abraham through his second

Gen.16:15

Thdr.AbuQ.*Opusc*.9 (*PG*
97:1529); Barth.Ed.*Mob.*
(*PG* 104:1448)

Gen.21:10
Joh.Cant.*Apol*.1.3; 4.2 (*PG*
154:388; 540)

Thdr.AbuQ.*Conc*.(*PG*
94:1596)

Nicet.Byz.*Arab*.10.65 (*PG*
105:753)

Dan.7:7

Leo III.*Ep*. (Jeffery 294)

Barth.Ed.*Agar*. (*PG*
104:1417)

Man.II.Pal.*Dial*.2 (Trapp 18)

Joh.Cant.*Apol*.4.3 (*PG*
154:540)

ap.Thdr.AbuQ.*Opusc*.19
(*PG* 97:1544)
Joh.Cant.*Apol*.4.1 (*PG* 154:
533); Joh. Cant.*Or*.1.10
(*PG* 154:605)

Leo III.*Ep*. (Jeffery 297)

wife, Hagar, and her son, Ishmael, the Muslims came to be called "Hagarenes ['Αγαρηνοί]" or "Ishmaelites ['Ισμαηλῖται]." Although Christian polemicists disputed the Muslim right to such a designation, it did provide them with an opportunity to identify Christianity (not Judaism) with Isaac and in this way to apply against the Muslims the biblical command to "cast out this slave woman [Hagar] with her son [Ishmael]."

Introducing the senior partner, Judaism, into the Muslim-Christian dispute created various complications, not the least of which was some disconcerting similarity between the Muslim case against Christianity and the Christian case against Judaism. When Moses came to a world filled with idolatry, the Muslims asked, which part of the world was right? The Christian would answer: That which followed Moses into Judaism. And when Christ came to Judaism, which part was right? That which accepted Christianity, the Christians replied. Then who was right, now that Islam had come? The Christians continued to reply that those who remained with Christianity were right. There had been a "progressive revelation [προκοπή]" from Moses to Christ, but not a similar progression from Christ to Mohammed. The three ages prophesied by Daniel meant that the coming of Christ had ushered in the final dispensation of human history. Christian opponents of Islam felt themselves to be in a position to maintain that the followers of Mohammed could not really evaluate him; but Christians could, because Christianity was older than Islam. On such a basis they sought to respond to the Muslim acknowledgment of Christ as "the Spirit . . . and the soul and the Logos of the living God," but also as one "who loved Mohammed most of all" and had wanted to save him.

As part of this view of the relation between Moses, Christ, and Mohammed as the three lawgivers, the Muslims accused the church of having deleted from the Gospels the explicit prophecies about Mohammed, such as the statement of Christ: "I shall send you a prophet called Mohammed." Discussion of this accusation became a commonplace in the anti-Muslim literature. Pointing to the wide distribution of the Gospels in many languages, Christians could ask how it was that none of these contained the statement of Christ about Mohammed. In addition, "the truth of the Gospel and the fidelity of Christians are manifested by conserving intact in equal measure both those traits in [Christ] that are the most eminent and those that are the most humiliating." For if, as the Muslims charged, Christians had been tampering with the text of the Gospels, would they not have removed the embarrassment of the passages that spoke of the humiliation of Christ? The Christian interpretation of the entry of Christ into Jerusalem on Palm Sunday as a fulfillment of Old Testament prophecy seemed to justify the Muslim exegesis of another prophecy: "And he saw two riders, a rider on an ass and a rider on a camel." The first was Christ entering Jerusalem, the second Mohammed on the Hegira. According to Christian exegesis, however, the two riders were both prophetic representations of Christ. The quarrel about the proper text of the New Testament and about the proper exegesis of the Old Testament belonged to the dispute over whether biblical prophecy applied not only to Christ, but also to Mohammed. Christians saw the Koran as proof that Mohammed had not even read the Pentateuch. He and his followers claimed to accept the Gospels, but denied them in fact. This was the blasphemy against the Holy Spirit, "which consists in replacing the Holy Spirit by a person completely ignorant of the Holy Scriptures."

Authentic biblical prophecy was that which spoke of Christ and of the church. Specifically, the promise of the coming prophet was not to be sought in such an interpolation as "I shall send you a prophet called Mohammed," but in the authentic words of Moses to the children of Israel: "The Lord your God will raise up for you a prophet like me from among you, from your brethren—him you shall heed." The use of these words against Judaism had prepared Christian exegesis for its conflict with Islam. Moses had prophesied the coming of Christ, and it was an act of loyalty to Moses when one followed Christ; but there had been no similar prophecy about Mohammed, and indeed could not be, for all true prophets had arisen from within Judaism. True, since the death of Moses there had been many prophets, but the prophecy about one like Moses could apply only to that one prophet "who is the most powerful of them, and who announces things difficult to believe." The voice of prophecy unanimously acclaimed Christ as the fulfillment of its predictions and as "the prophet" in a unique sense. Mohammed could cite

Leo III. *Ep.* (Jeffery 311)

Matt.21:4–5
Zech.9:9
Is.21:7(LXX)

Leo III. *Ep.* (Jeffery 327)

Nicet.Byz.*Arab*.11.66 (*PG* 105:756)
Joh.Cant.*Apol*.1.19 (*PG* 154:433)

Matt.12:31

Leo III.*Ep.* (Jeffery 294)

Deut.18:15; Acts 3.22
Ath.*Ar*.1.54 (*PG* 26:125)

Joh.Cant.*Apol*.4.4 (*PG* 154:541)

Leo III.*Ep.* (Jeffery 303)

Joh.Cant.*Apol*.1.5 (*PG* 154: 393–96); Joh.Cant. *Or*.1.4 (*PG* 154:601)

no such testimony in support of his usurpation of the title "prophet." Debate over the legitimacy of that title for him thus joined debate over monotheism, to become the second of the major conflicts between Christian orthodoxy and those whose profession of faith was: "There is no God but Allah, and Mohammed is his prophet."

The commonly accepted definition of a prophet was that "he who prophesies is a true prophet inasmuch as he names Jesus as Lord." This did not preclude his prophesying also about the history of Israel and other such matters, but all of this ultimately pertained to Christ if it was genuine prophecy. There were two marks of a prophet: that he could foretell the future, and that he could perform miracles. A true emissary from God was one who "is announced from of old or one who shows himself trustworthy by miracles." In addition to prophecy and miracles, a prophet distinguished himself by the adornment of his holy life and by his superior knowledge of divine truth. Mohammed lacked all these credentials of the genuine prophet. "Since you call him a prophet," went the Christian challenge to the Muslim, "show me what he has ever prophesied, and in what word he did it, and what he commands, or what sign or marvel he has ever performed." Although Mohammed "called himself a prophet and the apostle of God," he was no such thing, but "the apostle and prophet of the father of lies." If the Muslim affirmed that he knew God through Mohammed and that therefore Mohammed was the prophet, the Christian had to tell him the truth about the so-called prophet. The truth was that he had been a camel-driver and had engaged in other disreputable activities. When his life came to an end, he had died and was buried; and so while Muslims prayed, they stood on the earth, in which their prophet lay buried, and addressed heaven, in which Christ lived and reigned. The Christians meanwhile were "the heirs of the kingdom of heaven, the ambassadors of the orthodox faith, and the followers of the real prophets"; therefore they rejected the claims of Mohammed to be a prophet, and anathematized him as a pretender to such a title.

If the title "prophet" was too magnificent for Mohammed, it was not magnificent enough for Christ. Christ himself had indicated this when he said that "the law

Joh.D.*1 Cor.*12.3 (*PG* 95:664)

Joh.Cant.*Or.*1.3 (*PG* 154:593)

Barth.Ed.*Agar.* (*PG* 104:1392)

Thdr.AbuQ.*Opusc.*19 (*PG* 97:1544)

Nicet.Byz.*Arab.*13.69 (*PG* 105:760)

Barth.Ed.*Agar.* (*PG* 104:1389)
Joh.Cant.*Or.*1.1 (*PG* 154:592)
Nicet.Byz.*Arab.*7.57 (*PG* 105:744)
John 8:44

Barth.Ed.*Agar.* (*PG* 104:1388)

Nicet.Byz.*Arab.*2.32 (*PG* 105:713)

Barth.Ed.*Agar.* (*PG* 104:1412); Euth.Zig.*Sar.*16 (*PG* 131:37)

Barth.Ed.*Agar.* (*PG* 104:1444); Nicet.Chon.*Thes.*20 (*PG* 140:124)

Rom.Mel.*Hymn.*21.13 (*SC* 114:36)

and the prophets were until John [the Baptist]; since then the good news of the kingdom of God is preached." Christ had come as the fulfillment of the prophecy of Moses and the other prophets, and for this reason as the end of prophecy. John the Baptist was the last of the prophets; after him there would be no more prophesiers, now that the prophesied himself had come. Because this had been the place of John in the history of Jewish prophecy, Mohammed was afraid that people would say: "We have no promise of another prophet after Christ. Whence is it, then, that you style yourself an apostle of God and a prophet?" John the Baptist became a favorite topic of Muslim-Christian disputes. If the Muslims agreed with the Christians that he had been a great prophet, the question was: "But what did he prophesy? Evidently nothing else except about Christ." This qualified him as a prophet, but it also disqualified Mohammed; and it put Christ into a position that transcended the category of prophet, as the one to whom all the prophets from Abraham and Moses to John the Baptist had borne witness.

Therefore the convert from Islam to Christianity was called upon to declare: "I anathematize the doctrine of Mohammed which says that Christ is not the Son of God, but an apostle and a prophet." The early Christians had not been satisfied to identify him as apostle or prophet, but had identified him as the Son of God. If he had "been merely a prophet, he would have had to say: 'that they may know thee, the only true God, and Moses with the other prophets, and then Jesus.'" Or, expanding upon the New Testament's comparison of Christ with the angels, one could point out that neither to any of the angels nor to any of the prophets had God said: "Today I have begotten thee." The emphasis of Theodore of Mopsuestia and of the Nestorians on Christ as teacher had helped to discredit the title "prophet" as a term for the Savior. If one used the title at all, Cyril of Alexandria had maintained, one had to recognize that he was "not one prophet among others," and that he had not possessed simply "the grace of prophecy," but the nature of God as his Logos. And therefore, writing apparently without reference to the encounter with Islam, Maximus was able to denounce as Nestorian heresy the idea that Christ was merely a prophet, endowed with the grace of prophecy. The church was not equipped to deal

Luke 16:16

Thdr.AbuQ.*Conc.* (*PG* 94:1597)

Joh.Cant.*Apol.*1.3 (*PG* 154:389-92)

Nicet.Byz.*Arab.*5.50 (*PG* 105:736)
Joh.D.*Disp.Sar.* (*PG* 96: 1348); Thdr.AbuQ.*Opusc.*38 (*PG* 97:1593-96); Man.II. Pal.*Dial.*12 (Trapp 152-53)

Joh.Cant.*Apol.*1.15 (*PG* 154:417)

Joh.Cant.*Apol.*1.17 (*PG* 154:424)

ap.Nicet. Chon. *Thes.*20 (*PG* 140:129); *Anath.Sar.* (Montet 153)

Thdr.AbuQ.*Mim.*2.2 (Graf 129-30)

John 17:3
Leo III.*Ep.* (Jeffery 312)

Heb.1:5

Ps.2:7
Barth.Ed.*Agar.* (*PG* 104:1401)

Cyr.*Chr.un.*(*SC* 97:422-24)

Max.*Opusc.*2 (*PG* 91:40)

Nicet.Byz.*Arab*.2.31 (*PG* 105:712); Barth.Ed.*Moh.* (*PG* 104:1453)

Matt.17:3
Joh.Cant.*Apol*.2.5 (*PG* 154:461)

Joh.Cant.*Or*.4.3 (*PG* 154:689)

Barth.Ed.*Agar.* (*PG* 104:1396)

Nicet.Byz.*Arab*.4.49 (*PG* 105:736)

Joh.Cant.*Or*.3.3 (*PG* 154:653)

Joh.D.*Disp.Sar.* (*PG* 96:1344)

Thdr.AbuQ.*Mim*.3.22 (Graf 156)

Barth.Ed.*Agar.* (*PG* 104:1409)

Barth.Ed.*Moh.* (*PG* 104:1452); Joh.Cant.*Apol*.1.19 (*PG* 154:437); Joh.Cant.*Or.* 1.4 (*PG* 154:657)

Nicet.Byz.*Arab*.28.101 (*PG* 105:800)

with the Muslim use of this title for Christ, despite its impeccably biblical authorization, for it appeared to make him "one prophet among others." Moses and Elijah had appeared with Christ on the mount of transfiguration as prophets to "prove definitely that he is the Sovereign and Lord of all the prophets and of all the creation." As the Muslim understanding of monotheism compelled Christian thought to affirm the dogma of the Trinity, so the Muslim version of prophetism evoked a defense of the dogma of the person of Christ.

The Koran had provided some basis for such a defense when it identified Christ not only as a prophet, but also as the Logos. "If Christ is the Logos of God," Christians could ask, "how is it that you call him a prophet?" One who was, according to the Koran, "the apostle of God and his Logos" had to be more than an apostle. In the Christian Platonism of Byzantine theology, the title "Logos" meant that he had produced "the causes of all things, that is, the paradigms, which are also called ideas," from which in turn the rational and visible worlds had come. This was not the work of a mere prophet. Even when the Platonic doctrine of ideas did not provide the basis for the Christian understanding of Christ as the incarnation of the creating Logos, the witness against Islam took its start from the Logos. For John of Damascus, the proper form of that witness was the declaration: "I confess one single Logos of God, uncreated in his hypostasis." Theodore Abû Qurra, writing in Arabic, formulated it this way: "Allah and his Logos and his Spirit are one God." Bartholemew of Edessa replied to the Koran's use of the Logos: "For my part, I know the Logos of God as 'light from light.'" Because the Muslims rejected the Trinity in their misguided hostility to tritheism, even their use of the Logos doctrine was bound to reflect their error.

So it was also with their interpretation of the birth of Jesus Christ from the Virgin Mary. Christians were repeatedly surprised to discover that, along with various false views about him, Mohammed had taught that Christ was born of a virgin. To explain such unexpected orthodoxy in "the forerunner of the Antichrist," they formulated a principle of interpretation, namely, that "he confesses the virgin birth as an act of effrontery and contrary to his own wishes." The extent of Mohammed's ignorance on the subject of the Virgin Mary could be gauged also

Leo III. *Ep.* (Jeffery 309);
Nicet.Byz.*Arab*.2.29; 3.43
(*PG* 105:708; 728); Joh.
Cant.*Or*.3.8 (*PG* 154:676)
Nicet.Byz.*Arab*.25.93 (*PG*
105:789)

Daniel (1960) 175

Joh.Cant.*Apol*.1.16; 18 (*PG*
154:417; 425)

Barth.Ed.*Agar.* (*PG*
104:1397)

Joh.Cant.*Apol*.2.21 (*PG*
154:477); Thdr.AbuQ.*Opusc.*
32 (*PG* 97:1583–84)

Joh.Cant.*Apol*.2.26 (*PG*
154:488)

Leo III.*Ep.* (Jeffery 284)

Meyendorff (1964) 131–32

from his mistaken supposition that the Christian Trinity consisted of Father, Mother, and Son. Further evidence came from the Koran's identification of Mary, the mother of Christ, with Miriam, the sister of Moses—a confusion on which Christian critics frequently commented, exclaiming: "Oh, the great age of the Virgin!" The fact remained that "there is nothing else in all the Qur'ān to parallel the warmth with which Christ and His mother are spoken of. Christ is presented as a unique being, but His mother's personality appears more vividly. The Qur'ān inspires a devotion to Mary of which Muslims might have made more." When Christians, in response to Islam, emphasized the role of the Virgin in Old Testament prophecy, they were, at least in part, attaching their mariology to that of the Koran. They had to admit that "in the entire Koran there do not occur any praises of Mohammed or of his mother Aminah, such as are found about our Lord Jesus Christ and about the Holy Virgin Mary, the Theotokos." They also acknowledged that, unlike some Christian heresies, Islam did not deny the reality of Christ's human nature, even though it did teach that someone else had been crucified in his stead. Even in such areas of agreement between Muslim doctrine and the christological orthodoxy of the church, then, the adherents of Islam were "deceived about everything that pertains to Christ." They did not see that only as perfect man and perfect God could he be the object of faith.

In relation to the development of doctrine in Eastern Christendom as we have been describing it in this volume, the confrontation with Islam had as its "most important" consequence the result that "for ages Byzantine Christianity was kept on the defensive." This meant that the preoccupation with the liturgical cult, which had been the theme of the iconoclastic controversies, became so dominant for Byzantine Christians that they came to "feel that such an existence was a normal one." Doctrinally, this served to reinforce "the old Byzantine instinct for conservatism, which is both the main force and the principal weakness of Eastern Christianity." Such conservatism was regarded as "the last refuge which could ensure its survival in the face of Islam." In some ways, therefore, the definition of itself that Eastern Christianity formulated in response to the Muslim threat was the most comprehensive and the most faithful, since its shape was de-

Geo.Schol.*Sal.* (Petit
3:434–52)

termined not by internal struggles within Christendom, Eastern or Western, but by the necessity to state in brief compass the heart of the gospel. There was probably no such apologia over against Islam that succeeded more fully than the treatise *Concerning the Only Way for the Salvation of Men,* written by the Aristotelian philosopher and theological scholar, George Scholarius.

Geo.Schol.*Sal.*1 (Petit 3:435)

Geo.Schol.*Sal.*3 (Petit 3:437)

Geo.Schol.*Sal.*5 (Petit 3:438)

Geo.Schol.*Sal.*9 (Petit 3:442)

Geo.Schol.*Sal.*14 (Petit 3:445)

Geo.Schol.*Sal.*21 (Petit 3:452)

In his apologia Scholarius presented an irenic and yet uncompromising exposition of the Christian doctrine of salvation, "without which it is impossible for man to reach his goal." At the heart of this doctrine was trinitarian monotheism. Men lost the way of salvation when they departed from faith in the one true God and turned to the worship of many gods. But God determined to undo the loss, first by giving the natural law, then (when this did not suffice) by sending Moses the lawgiver. As the climax of his revelation and salvation, God sent his Son, whose coming was not the negation but the fulfillment of the law of Moses. Devotion to the Son of God was in fact the only authentic monotheism; for God the Father commanded that the Son be worshiped, and the Son made known the revelation "that there is one God, who is supremely simple, transcending everything composite." Salvation came from "the one and only God in a Trinity of persons," as Scholarius said at the conclusion of his confession. So objective and perceptive a statement of the distinctiveness of the gospel came with special import from Scholarius; for, as Gennadius II, he was the first patriarch of Constantinople after its conquest by the Turks in 1453, and he wrote his confession in response to the request of Sultan Mohammed II for a summary of Christian beliefs.

The God of the Philosophers

Troph.*Dam.*2.2.2 (PO
15:218–19)

See p. 221 above
Psell.*Om.doct.*96
(Westerink 55)

Conflict with these several non-Christian systems made it necessary for orthodox Christian doctrine also to specify its relation to Greek thought. Its apologists against Judaism claimed that Christianity had taken over Judaism from the Jews, had abolished the astrological doctrines of the Persians, and done away with both Platonic and Homeric errors. The definition of evil as not a positive reality in its own right, but only the absence of good, was a mainstay of the antidualist case, but the clarification of the definition was a task for the Christian philosopher. Especially in the debate with Islam, the Greek philosophical tradition and the relation of Christianity to it had an important role to play. In part this was because "the wise and intelligent men of that nation [the Arabs] have learned their wisdom from the Greeks," through a transplantation of books and ideas that has been called "the most astonishing event in the history of thought." Muslim participants in dialogue with Christians were known to demand proof for Christian teaching "not only from your Scripture, but also from universally acknowledged ideas." Christian participants, in turn, claimed that what they were confessing against Islam was "in conformity with the holy gospel and with reason." They professed to share with their Muslim opponents certain common philosophical premises, such as the identity of the essence of God with his attributes, and argued from these for Christian doctrine. Judaism, dualism, and Mohammedanism all required Christianity to clarify its attitude to Hellenism.

Such clarification would have been necessary even if there had been no external opponents, because of the very character of Byzantine culture. In Byzantium, "one became a theologian," not through the study of a formal theological curriculum, but "on the way through the general classical education of the Byzantines, beginning with the study of grammar and going on to rhetoric and philosophy." Many of the leaders of Byzantine theology with whom we have been dealing exemplified this Christian Hellenism in their thought and language; so, for instance, the patriarch Photius. The outstanding representative of Christian Hellenism during the "literary renaissance [that] flourished at Constantinople under the auspices of the Emperor [Constantine Monomachus in the twelfth century]" was Michael Psellus. He had memorized the entire *Iliad* as a child and was able to quote it even for quite incidental information, as, of course, others did also. In his philosophical pursuits, he had passed through arithmetic, geometry, astronomy, and music, all primarily in the form that had been developed by ancient Greece. His own literary and stylistic tastes made him object vigorously to the form taken by certain kinds of edifying and hagiographical literature, which, he thought, made the conflicts of the saints ludicrous and would not persuade or convert anyone. Nevertheless, his Christian Hellenism did not blind him to the "heresy" inherent in "ancient Hellenism"

Joh.Cant.*Or*.2.5 (*PG* 154:617)

Southern (1962) 9

ap.Thdr.AbuQ.*Opusc*.22 (*PG* 97:1552–53)

Conf.Sar. (*PG* 154:1169)

Nicet.Byz.*Arab*.1.8–9 (*PG* 105:680–81)

H. G. Beck (1966) 77

Vogt (1936) 114

Psell.*Om.doct*.180 (Westerink 90)
Nicet.Byz.*Arab*.17.74 (*PG* 105:765)
Psell.*Chron*.6.38–39 (Renauld 1:136)

Psell.*Enc.Sim.Met.* (Kurtz 1:100–101)

Psell.*Acc.Cerul*.8
(Kurtz 1:239–40)

Joh.Cant.*Apol*.1.19 (*PG*
154:433)

Troph.Dam.3.3.3 (*PO*
15:241)

Psell.*Pr.Phil.Sol.* (*PG*
127:707–8)

Psell.*Acc.Cerul*.4
(Kurtz 1:234)

Psell.*Acc.Cerul*.20
(Kurtz 1:258–59)

Psell.*Cant*.2.6; 4.13 (*PG*
122:580; 625)

See vol.1:241–42

Psell.*Cant*.6.8–9 (*PG*
122:660)

Luke 1:26–28

Psell.*Salut*.5; 2 (*PO*
16:522; 518)

Ex.15:20–21

Psell.*Salut*.4 (*PO*
16:521)
Psell.*Salut*.3 (*PO*
16:520)

Psell.*Cant*.1.12 (*PG*
122:560)

Psell.*Acc.Cerul*.16
(Kurtz 1:252)

or heathenism, which could not be reconciled with the Christian gospel. The Byzantines recognized that the Greeks, having neither the Bible nor the prophets, simply did not belong to the same category as the Jews—or even as the Muslims. Although some of the Greeks, and especially the philosophers among them, had known something of God, their knowledge and their hope were quite imperfect in comparison with those of the Jews.

The restriction on any Christian Hellenism, therefore, was the norm of Christian orthodoxy, which took precedence over it. All of these Christian Hellenists preferred "speaking the truth [of the gospel], even with a stammer" to "speaking falsehood, even with the eloquence and power of Plato." It was not permissible to pick and choose within the orthodox tradition, believing some parts and rejecting others. Rather, one was to use the clear and explicit statements of the fathers as a hermeneutical tool for resolving the difficulties of their more obscure statements. Psellus was aware that "the famous Origen . . . was the pioneer of all our theology and laid its foundations, but on the other hand, all heresies find their origin in him." Hence he strove to avoid those elements in the heritage of Greek philosophy that had led Origen astray, and he cultivated the orthodox doctrines by which men's souls were made alive. A test case of a theologian's orthodoxy had long been the doctrine of the Virgin Mary. Not only did Psellus interpret the Song of Solomon as a prophecy of the Theotokos; but in his exposition of the salutation of the angel Gabriel to Mary at the annunciation he proclaimed her the new Eve making good the fall of the first Eve, as well as the new Miriam leading the people of God in their praises. The Logos had been born of her with her virginity unimpaired; earth was mixed with heaven, humanity with divinity, and thus salvation was achieved. Without this salvation, won by Christ and received through baptism in his name, no amount of moral uprightness or virtue would profit a man at all. Admirer of Greek philosophy though he was, Psellus rejected as heresies such Platonic notions as "recollection [ἀνάμνησις]" and "transmigration of souls [μετεμψύχωσις]," which had been condemned by the church.

Aberrations like these did not nullify the legitimate function of philosophy in Christian thought. The theolo-

Max.*Pyrr.* (*PG* 91:296; 345);
Joh.D.*Dialect*.pr. (Kotter
1:52); Thdr.AbuQ.*Opusc*.2
(*PG* 97:1469)

gians of the East had long taken the position that precision in the statement of Christian doctrine required the use of philosophical terms and concepts. It was, if anything, even more important to the Christian philosophers of the East to defend the position that "the use of syllogisms is neither contrary to the dogma of the church nor alien to philosophy, but is in fact the only instrument of truth and the

Psell.*Ep*.175 (Sathas 5:447)

only means of finding what we are looking for." The knowledge gained through philosophy and the knowledge granted through revelation both came "from the single unitary

Psell.*Char.Gr.Theol*.4
(Levy 47)

source [ἀπὸ τῆς ἑνιαίας πῆγης]," which was God. Contrary to the well-known dictum of Blaise Pascal about "the God of Abraham, the God of Isaac, the God of Jacob, not of philosophers and scholars," these philosophers and scholars simply identified "the great Father" with the Prime

Psell.*Acc.Cerul*.47 (Kurtz
1:294)

Mover and First Cause. In doing so they believed themselves to be standing in the succession of the doctors and fathers of the church, who had drawn their knowledge not only from the data of revelation but from the teachings of

Psell.*Char.Gr.Theol*.27
(Levy 56)
Psell.*Char.Gr.Theol*.24
(Levy 54)
Psell.*Enc.Sim.Met*.
(Kurtz 1:95)

the pagan philosophers. The fathers had refused to permit their rhetorical gifts to obscure the philosophical task, but had devoted "the depths of their soul to philosophy."

When Psellus spoke about "philosophy," he was usually referring to Plato and to the way of thinking that drew its inspiration from him. "My Plato!" Psellus wrote, "I do not know how to bear the weight of such a word. Have I not long honored the divine cross above everything else?"

Psell.*Ep*.175 (Sathas
5:444)

Defending his right to sift the correct opinions of Plato from the incorrect ones, he declared: "I may belong entirely to Christ, but I refuse to deny the wiser of our writers or the knowledge of reality, both intelligible and sensible. Interceding with God by prayer according to my capacity,

Psell.*Ep*.175 (Sathas
5:450)

I will eagerly accept whatever may be granted to me." His teacher, the rhetor and poet John Mauropus, prayed in the same spirit that if any heathens were to be exempted from the threat of damnation, it should be Plato and Plutarch, who "in thought and in deed showed how very

Joh.Maur.*Carm*.43.1–5
(Lagarde 24)

near they were to thy laws." Psellus was willing to see in Plato's *Phaedrus* a parallel to the dogma of the Trinity, and

Psell.*Id*. (Kurtz 1:433–34)

he maintained, here as elsewhere, that this was not reading "our doctrine" into the text, but "following Plato himself

Psell.*Exeg.Phdr*. (Kurtz
1:438)

and the theologians among the Greeks." In the same treatise, however, he did not hesitate to call attention to the

Psell.*Exeg.Phdr.* (Kurtz 1:440)
Psell.*Om.doct.*65 (Westerink 43);
Psell.*Acc.Cerul.*16 (Kurtz 1:252)

Psell.*Om.doct.*120 (Westerink 64–65)

Psell.*Om.doct.*199 (Westerink 97)

Psell.*Chron.*6.38 (Renauld 1:136)

Zervos (1920) 255

Psell.*Cant.*2.8 (*PG* 122:581)

Psell.*Char.Gr.Theol.*24 (Levy 54)

Psell.*Char.Gr.Theol.*2 (Levy 46)
Psell.*Char.Joh.Chrys.*1 (Levy 92)

Joannou (1956) 1:6

See vol.1:51

Psell.*Acc.Cerul.*16 (Kurtz 252)

Psell.*Char.Gr.Theol.*15 (Levy 51)

"absurdities" in Plato, and he affirmed his loyalty to dogmatic orthodoxy, even against "thousands of Platos and Aristotles."

As this latter phrase suggests, Psellos's Platonism did not deter him from the study of other philosophies. He set forth a comparison of Plato and Aristotle on the question of whether there was anything beyond heaven, considering the views of the latter in more detail than those of the former. He was at least somewhat acquainted with the teachings of Pythagoras about the mathematical nature of reality. Apart from Plato, most of his favorite philosophers were Neoplatonists—Plotinus, Jamblichus, and above all Proclus. He described how, after wandering over various philosophical seas, he had at last arrived at "the most wondrous Proclus, as at a very great harbor," where he had learned "all kinds of knowledge and the precise truth about concepts." With some qualifications, it still seems fair to characterize the philosophical system of Psellos as eclecticism, but as an eclecticism whose "fundamental dispositions are Neoplatonic." In Psellos's own usage, the term "philosopher" was not reserved for pagan thinkers, but was applied more broadly—for example, to the words of the Virgin as found in the Song of Solomon. It was especially appropriate as a term for the philosophical theologians of Greek Christianity, most of all for "the Theologian," Gregory of Nazianzus. Psellos praised Gregory as superior to Plato, Socrates, Thucydides, Isocrates, and other stars of the Greek firmament, while he hailed John Chrysostom as "our own Demosthenes and Plato." Many of Psellos's philosophical ideas came to him indirectly, through Christian philosophical theology, so that his "direct dependence on ancient philosophy is small."

As in the original encounter between Christian doctrine and classical philosophy, so in this continuation of the discussion, the two themes of "God and the soul" were paramount. Psellos spoke of "Aristotle's doctrine of God and Plato's doctrine of the origin of the soul" as philosophical doctrines that had been rejected by the church, and he observed that "the philosophers have imagined that there are these two realities, the mind and God." He conceded that there was a certain agreement between those "who follow the apostolic word" and Plato in the *Timaeus* as interpreted by Proclus, in that both posited the existence of a spiritual order as a middle be-

Psell.*Om.doct*.54
(Westerink 39)

Psell.*Om.doct*.15
(Westerink 23)

Psell.*Om.doct*.71
(Westerink 45–46)

Psell.*Salut*.2 (*PO* 16:518);
Joh.Maur.*Carm*.2.23
(Lagarde 2)

Psell.*Om.doct*.1
(Westerink 17)

Psell.*Acc.Cerul*.4
(Kurtz 1:234)

Dion.Ar.*D.n*.1.4 (*PG*
3:589)

Psell.*Char.Gr.Theol*.33
(Levy 57)

Psell.*Om.doct*.1
(Westerink 17)
Psell.*Cant*.1.16–17 (*PG*
122:568)

Psell.*Om.doct*.5
(Westerink 18–19)

See vol.1:66–67

ing between God and man; Plato spoke of "the soul of the all," while the apostle spoke of "principalities and powers." Yet it was essential to see that for orthodox Christianity God could not be equated with the mind or the soul any more than he could be equated with the cosmos; not identity, but likeness [ὁμοίωσις] was the appropriate Christian term. The likeness of the soul to God meant something especially important to Eastern Christianity because of the doctrine of salvation as deification. One had to distinguish among various senses of such likeness to God; in the ultimate sense, it meant "the ability to make man divine, to lead him out of the material realm, to deliver him from passions, and to endow him with the ability to deify another—this is the most perfect likeness." Psellus and his associates repeated the standard Eastern formula: the divine Logos had become man so that man might become divine.

Fundamentally, the Christian picture of God was set apart from all other views by its trinitarian monotheism. "The first thing" to be learned was "to worship Father, Son, and Spirit, one God." Psellus opened his compilation of philosophical and theological teachings, *Omnifarious Doctrine,* with a confession of faith in the Trinity, three hypostases and one divine ousia. True piety consisted of the confession of the Holy Trinity and of faith in the evangelical message. One was faithful to God when, in harmony with the decrees of the ecumenical councils, one taught the trinitarian dogma as it had been handed down by the fathers on the basis of the New Testament. The term "monad [μονάς]" had been used by Plato, Aristotle, and Proclus; but in the context of Christian monotheism, as systematized by Dionysius the Areopagite, the divine monad was seen to transcend life and mind, and even being. In his statements about the Trinity, Psellus adhered to the strict line of orthodox Greek theology: he rejected the Filioque, taught that in the incarnation the nature of the Logos had been concealed in the flesh, and defended the doctrine of the homoousios on the basis of "the term 'humanity,' which is common" to several men and yet single in itself. Christian monotheism distinguished itself from Jewish and Muslim monotheism by its trinitarian character, and from Hellenism by its loyalty to the biblical doctrine of God as one.

Hellenism too, had sometimes taught the oneness of

Psell.*Acc.Cerul*.20
(Kurtz 1:259)

Psell.*Om.doct*.102
(Westerink 57–58);
Psell.*Acc.Cerul*.11
(Kurtz 1:245)

Max.*Schol.D.n*.4.7 (PG
4:260)

Psell.*Om.doct*.16
(Westerink 24)

Psell.*Om.doct*.152
(Westerink 79)

Psell.*Salut*.1 (PO
16:517)
Max.*Schol.D.n*.7.1 (PG
4:340)

Psell.*Om.doct*.164
(Westerink 83)

Psell.*Id*. (Kurtz
1:433)

God, but in doing so it had found it difficult to avoid, on the one hand, the doctrine of the eternity of matter or, on the other hand, some form of pantheism. "What do matter and ideas have in common according to our dogmas?" Psellus asked. "But when Aristotle explains that matter has no beginning, then we indeed dissociate the church from this doctrine." According to the Christian doctrine of creation, neither matter nor time could be coeternal with God, who alone possessed true eternity. He also possessed true oneness. The cosmos seen as the all [τὸ πᾶν] could be called one, but only because it had come from the one God. Because of its diversity it must be called many rather than one. On the basis of this Dionysian doctrine, Psellus maintained that in its strict sense the word "one" could be applied only to God. In the sense that there was not a multiplicity of physical cosmoses, the cosmos was one, a universe. "But how can the cosmos be one when it is composite and manifold?" The oneness of God was transcendent, beyond all number and beyond simplicity itself, so that ultimately the cosmos could be called "one" only on account of its participation as creature in the oneness of the Creator. Similarly, God was the beginning [ἀρχή] of all beings, not in the sense that he was the first in a series, but in the sense that he transcended all being and that all beings were dependent on him. It was orthodox doctrine that God was "beyond and above all things that are known and all things that exist." The distinction as well as the link between the Creator and his creation had to be maintained: immanence without pantheistic identification, transcendence without deistic isolation.

The orthodox doctrine of God as Creator meant that he was the ultimate cause of all reality. Discussing the causes of natural phenomena such as earthquakes, Psellus quoted Psalm 104:32: "Who [God] looks on the earth and it trembles"; nevertheless, earthquakes also had a "proximate cause," which was the emission of air from the earth. Considered in its dependence on God as ultimate cause, the world should not be called "self-existent [αὐτοζῷον]," as Plato (actually Proclus) called it. Considered as a coordinated system of natural and proximate causes, it was a proper subject for scientific investigation. Such investigation was, however, illegitimate if, for example, it followed the lead of certain physicians in attributing de-

Psell.*Daem*.14 (*PG* 122:852–53)

Hussey (1937) 88

Psell.*Exeg.Phdr.* (Kurtz 1:439)

Psell.*Om.doct*.19 (Westerink 25)

Psell.*Om.doct*.17; 106 (Westerink 24–25; 59)

Anastasi (1969) 124

Psell.*Om.doct*.201 (Westerink 98–99)

Gr.Naz.*Or*.45.7 (*PG* 36:632)

monic activity not to supernatural forces, but to the "humors." It was, Psellus maintained, "foolish to reject the manifestation of a supernatural power simply because no scientific explanation could be given" for its causation. Psellus took it to be the doctrine of Plato in the *Phaedrus* that all existing things "both remain in their own causes and go forth from them," and that they had "the cause of their turning and rising through Zeus." The connection between causes and effects, the orderliness of nature, the regularity of the movement of the heavenly bodies, as well as "the providence that extends to all things" formed the basis for the natural knowledge of God among men. Belief in divine providence had to be distinguished from any sort of causal determinism, as well as from notions of chance. It was also essential not to permit the idea of providence and of the sovereign will of God to produce "a fatalistic inactivity" instead of "the obligation of man to act," which was the proper response, even in the light of natural knowledge about the ways of God in human history.

As in the doctrine of God, so in the doctrine of the soul, the relation between philosophy and dogma was a complex one. In a candid explanation of the doctrine of the soul, Psellus told his imperial patron that he had collected some of his ideas about the soul "from our own sacred chalices," but that most of them had come "from the briny waters, I mean from those of the Greeks." He had, he explained, done his best to adapt these latter "to our true doctrines," but not with complete success. In any case, he wanted his reader to take his summary of Greek teachings as "an enumeration," in the hope that the doctrines "of our Scriptures, like roses," would stand out in contrast to the poison of pagan teaching. Those aspects of the doctrine of the soul that were no more than a repetition of the Greek doctrine—for example, the division of the soul into its vegetative, animal, and rational parts—are not our concern here, except insofar as they affected Christian doctrine. One point at which they did so was the notion of the preexistence of the soul. The mentor of Psellus and of Eastern thought generally, Gregory of Nazianzus, "the Theologian," had, primarily for the sake of his christological doctrine, taught that the soul and the flesh came into being simultaneously. On the basis of Gregory, Psellus identified this simultaneity

Psell.*Om.doct.*198
(Westerink 97)

Psell.*Acc.Cerul.*11
(Kurtz 1:245)

Psell.*Om.doct.*49
(Westerink 37)

as one aspect of the doctrine of the soul that reflected Christian concerns. "The soul and the body," he wrote, "are different from each other in essence . . . , but according to Christian teaching they are contemporaneous [ὁμοϋπότατα]." It was Christian heretics who had agreed with the Greeks in teaching that "the soul is unbegotten and time is coeternal with God." But the Christian doctrine of creation meant that the soul was not without a beginning or cause, for only God had no cause outside himself.

By combining an impeccable orthodoxy in matters of official dogma with a precise delineation of areas in which Greek philosophy had a valid competence, Michael Psellus was able to maintain, as had Photius two centuries earlier, a position that kept its peace with both the Christian and the classical traditions. When this position clashed with others that regarded it as disloyal to orthodoxy, what was at stake was "not this or that point of dogma," but rather

Stephanou (1949) 35

"a contrast between two ideologies." At the end of the eleventh century, this contrast became a matter of public debate when Psellus's pupil, John Italus, was tried for heresy. He was accused, among other things, of reviving the false teaching of ancient philosophy about the soul and about the eternity of matter and of ideas. For our purposes here, he is interesting as evidence of the "dogmatic conflicts caused by the renaissance of philosophical doctrines, which permit us to follow the uninterrupted march of the work that begins with Psellus across the

Tatakis (1949) 212

last five centuries of Byzantium." Repeatedly during those five centuries, the defenders of the Christian Hellenism represented by Psellus were obliged to reassert its validity within the limits of orthodox dogma. Sometimes the opposition to it came from the exponents of monastic spirituality, whose place in the doctrinal development will occupy us in the next chapter. At other times it came from Western theologians, especially when their systems had begun to aquire an Aristotelian cast, who then objected to the philosophical theology of Byzantium because so much of it was Platonic or Neoplatonic.

Once again, the definitive statement of the orthodox position came in the fifteenth century. Bessarion, a theologian and irenicist whose ecumenical theology will be considered in our last chapter, articulated what was perhaps the most complete statement of the Byzantine case for a

Christian use of Plato. His *Against the Calumniator of Plato* not only defended Plato against various charges of immorality in practice and in teaching, but especially attempted to prove that there were many points of harmony between Platonic and Christian teaching. In opposition to the effort by the detractors of Plato to blame his thought for the heresies of Origen and Arius, Bessarion invoked the authority of Western and of Eastern theologians. Augustine, like Cicero before him, had lauded Plato above all other philosophers. Among the theologians of Greek Christianity, "his theology was so pleasing to our fathers and teachers that they were not ashamed in their writings about God to make use not only of his ideas, but even of the very words of Plato." Dionysius the Areopagite and Gregory of Nazianzus were especially dependent on Plato for their terminology. Plato, while not authentically trinitarian in his doctrine of God, had taught that the Logos was the Creator of the world; some of his disciples had come even closer to Christian orthodoxy, notably Plotinus, who had written about "three hypostases." It was clear that Plato had held to a monotheistic doctrine of God. This was not to try to make him out to have been a Christian, but to urge that his doctrines were more in harmony with the catholic faith than were those of Aristotle.

The fundamental conviction of this Christian Hellenism was that one God was the source of all truth, whatever the medium of its communication, be it philosophy or theology—or even the "many true and clear teachings about God and about our Lord Jesus Christ, which we also confess," but which had been preserved in the Jewish, Manichean, and Muslim traditions. Yet it was only in the Christian dogma of the Trinity that these true and clear teachings all came together, so that—paradoxical though it seemed to the outsider—this dogma was the final vindication of the monotheism professed by its most implacable enemies.

Bess.*Plat*.4.2.1 (Mohler 442–44)

Bess.*Plat*.2.5.8 (Mohler 100–102)

Aug.*Civ*.8.4 (*CCSL* 47:219)
Bess.*Plat*.1.3.2 (Mohler 26)

Bess.*Plat*.2.4.1 (Mohler 88)

Bess.*Plat*.2.5.3 (Mohler 94)
Bess.*Plat*.2.5.5 (Mohler 98)

Bess.*Plat*.2.5.6 (Mohler 98)

Bess.*Plat*.2.4.1 (Mohler 86)

Bess.*Plat*.2.1 (Mohler 80)

Conf.Sar. (*PG* 154:1157)

6

The Last Flowering of Byzantine Orthodoxy

See p. 242 above

See pp. 250–51 above

Thdr.Agall.*Argyr.* (*PG* 158: 1016); Marc.Eph.*Conf.*1 (*PO* 17:436); Marc.Eph.*Or.Purg.* 2.11 (*PO* 15:118)

In many ways the period from the twelfth to the fifteenth century may be identified as the time when Byzantine orthodoxy reached its flowering. Repeatedly throughout our narrative we have been obliged to carry the account of doctrinal development beyond the period being covered in a particular chapter, because a later century—often the fifteenth—was the one in which the summation of that development was set down. So it was in the preceding chapter with the Christian case against Islam, as well as with the orthodox defense of Christian Hellenism. Some parts of what should, by strict chronology, be the story of this final chapter have, therefore, already been told. Other parts of Byzantine cultural and intellectual history in this later period do not pertain directly to our study of the development of doctrine, for they bring nothing new. As everyone agreed, it was not the task of the orthodox theologian to bring something new, but to repeat something old.

Yet it was in this very period that the title "new theologian," which had traditionally been synonymous with "heretic" and was still used that way, came also to be used in a laudatory sense—not meaning, of course, someone who taught a new theology, but a new spokesman for the old theology. Before it had run its course, the mystical way of being a theologian had actually managed to produce not only several new theologians, but a new theology in the strictly technical sense of that word: a new doctrine of God. We shall turn first to this new theology. Among this period's summations of previous developments, at least one involved changes significant enough to warrant treatment on its own. Relations between East and West reached both their nadir (in the Latin sack of Constantinople) and their zenith (in the short-lived reunion at Florence) during these centuries. The doctrinal statement of the differences between East and West likewise flowered on both sides as it had not earlier. Although the issues and the arguments were largely the same, the advances in erudition and refinement achieved during these centuries brought the polemics of Western and of Eastern theologians to a new stage. The phenomenon of separation and isolation belongs to our study of the flowering of orthodoxy in Byzantium, for from their classical and from their biblical sources the Byzantines had learned that the flowering of a plant or of a man or of an entire culture meant "being now in full season, but next withering away and being destroyed by dissolution." For a long time, New Rome believed that this could never happen to it because its empire had the promise that it would last until the end of human history, but eventually it joined the other three Eastern patriarchates under Muslim domination.

Even this catastrophe, however, contributed to a "flowering of Byzantine orthodoxy" after the fall of Constantinople. One additional form of "flowering" was the composition of a systematized dogmatic formulation in which the distinctive doctrines of Eastern Christendom were summarized in a comprehensive confession of faith. Typically, such confessions of faith have been the product of Protestant theology and polemics, and the Eastern confessions of the seventeenth century did owe part of their origin to the Protestant Reformation. They were also, however, a legitimate outcome of Byzantine doctrinal history itself. With the fall of the Byzantine Empire, many institutions, ideas, and practices that had been identified with the orthodoxy of the East for more than a millennium also came to an end. Yet for the history of orthodox doctrine, the continuity between the period before 1453 and the period after 1453 is far more impressive than is the discontinuity. One decisive reason for this continuity is the transplantation of orthodoxy from Byzantine to Slavic soil. In that transplantation, it found yet another flowering. Although most of the history of Christan doctrine in Russia belongs properly to volume 5 of this work, here in this chapter it forms a conclusion to the account of how

Hom.*Il*.13.484

Isa.40:6–8; Ps.103:15

Euth.Zig.*Ps*.102.14 (*PG* 128:1016)

Ps.Anast.S.*Jud.dial*.1 (*PG* 89:1212)

the spirit of orthodox Eastern Christianity developed under the aegis of the Byzantine Empire and managed to survive the demise of Byzantium.

The Mystic as New Theologian

See pp. 243–50 above

From our consideration of Christian Hellenism as it was embodied in Michael Psellus, it is evident that in Byzantine theology the role of philosophy was as significant as it has always been in Christian thought. Less prominent in conventional historical accounts, but if anything even more influential, was the role of monastic piety—or, to use the technical term, "spirituality"—in the shaping of specific doctrines. It has already been visible in such events as the victory of the icons. But during the last several centuries of Byzantine culture the spirituality of the monks contributed even more directly to the development of doctrine by deriving from mystical experience the sort of doctrinal implications that had previously remained inchoate. Formally and technically, orthodox monasticism always claimed to be at least as subservient as any other part of church life to the authority of the fathers and of the dogmatic tradition; this never changed. What changed was that, beginning in the eleventh century and climaxing in the fourteenth, there developed within Byzantine monachism a method of theologizing called "Hesychasm," which found in its practices of devotion and prayer a new resource for Christian doctrine. It had long been recognized by the Greek theologians that "practice is the basis of theory," and that the discipline of Christian devotion, like the discipline of Christian worship, provided a foundation for that vision of God which was the highest contemplation [θεωρία]. Even the critics of the Hesychastic spirituality practiced by the monks on Mount Athos would have had to agree with the principle enunciated by the synod that defended such spirituality: "The matrix of prayer is silence [ἡσυχία], and prayer is the manifestation of the glory of God."

Gr.Naz.Or.4.113 (PG 35:649); Or.Luc.1.5 (GCS 35:9–10)

Syn.Pal. (1341) 13 (Karmirēs 358)

See vol.1:137–40; 198–99

Although an interpretation of Christian doctrine based on the practice of prayer had been a part of Eastern theology all along, it became a major force in the determination of what was orthodox teaching through the thought of Simeon, surnamed "the New Theologian." Among the theologians of the eleventh century, Psellus represented the Christian Hellenism that had helped to shape Eastern speculation since the time of Origen; but in many ways the theological significance of Origen's spirituality was even more pervasive, and this theological spirituality was embodied in the thought of Simeon. Many aspects of the history of Eastern spirituality, such as the evolution of the actual techniques, postures, and gestures of prayer and meditation, cannot concern us here, prominent though they were in the theological polemics, especially during its later stages. What does concern us is the doctrinal implication of such devotional practice: not how the Christian mystic prayed, but what his way of praying meant for Christian teaching about God and about God's saving revelation of himself to the eyes of faith. The full explication of this meaning was the achievement of the fourteenth century, but its foundations were laid by "the New Theologian," who drew in turn upon the Origenist and the Dionysian traditions, as well as upon the writings and ideas that were attributed to the fourth-century mystic, Macarius of Egypt.

In its setting as well as in its style, Byzantine mystical theology was largely the product of monastic communities, which were practically the only places where serious, full-time attention to the evangelical imperatives was possible. The science of contemplative theology was based on a distinction between those who were "novices [ἀρχαῖοι]" and those who were "adepts [τέλειοι]." The sorry fact was that "although Christ is named everywhere, in cities and in villages," there were actually very few genuine Christians. The number of those who "believe the resurrection of Christ" was large, but only a small minority of these were able to "view it purely" or to worship it properly. Those who failed to manifest in their lives the virtues of humility and chastity "are either beasts or demons, even though they may be Christian and orthodox." By contrast, "how blessed is that monk who in prayer stands before God, sees him, and is in turn seen by him." The true monk was one whose dedication to Christ enabled him, by divine grace, to acquire a mystical awareness of the divine presence. The monks were those who had taken on themselves "the image of the angels." Much of Simeon's writing was in the form of monastic exhortations, filled with commonsense advice about the practice of piety and the avoidance of temptation. The monastic brotherhood was a place where the will of God could be

Gr.Pal.*Tr*.1.2.10; 2.11 (Meyendorff 95; 227)

Max.*Ambig*.48 (*PG* 91:1361)

Sim.N.Th.*Eth*.1.12 (*SC* 122:296)

Sim.N.Th.*Catech*.22 (*SC* 104:382)

Sim.N.Th.*Catech*.13 (*SC* 104:196)

Sim.N.Th.*Or*.10 (*PG* 120:363)

Sim.N.Th.*Eth*.10 (*SC* 129:320)

Sim.N.Th.*Or*.17 (*PG* 120:392)
Nil.Sor.*Ustav*.5 (Borovkova-Majkova 44)

Sim.N.Th.*Catech*.18 (SC
104:278)

Sim.N.Th.*Catech*.20 (SC
104:334)

Sim.N.Th.*Eth*.2 (SC
122:326)

2 Pet.1:4
Sim.N.Th.*Or*.11 (PG
120:368)

Sim.N.Th.*Eth*.1.6 (SC
122:226)

Fedotov (1966) 1:28

Sim.N.Th.*Eth*.9 (SC
129:230)
Sim.N.Th.*Eth*.1.10; 3 (SC
122:256; 422)

Sim.N.Th.*Eth*.10 (SC
129:272)

Sim.N.Th.*Or*.14 (PG
120:381)

Sim.N.Th.*Catech*.18 (SC
104:310)

Epiph.M.*V*.*Serg*. (Leonid
44–45)

Sim.N.Th.*Catech*.16 (SC
104:244)
Sim.N.Th.*Catech*.22 (SC
104:372)

Sim.N.Th.*Eth*.1.3 (SC
122:196); Sim.N.Th.*Catech*.22
(SC 104:376)
Sim.N.Th.*Eth*.1.pr. (SC
122:172)

discerned through mutual consultation and admonition, and the monastic director or "spiritual father" was to be regarded, addressed, and respected as a surrogate for Christ himself. Yet the monks had to be reminded on the basis of the teachings of the apostles "that all those who have believed in Christ, be they monks or laymen, have been foreknown and foreseen [by divine predestination] and conformed to the image of the Son of God." Every Christian, not only the monk, had to become a "partaker of the divine nature." Expanding the metaphor of the church as the body of Christ, Simeon assigned various functions to the several "limbs" or "members." Of these, the "thighs" were "those who bear within themselves the generative power of the divine ideas of mystical theology and who give birth to the Spirit of salvation on earth."

The reality of the church as the body of Christ was the presupposition for mystical theology. Because "Byzantium never knew a real tension between ascetic and sacramental spirituality," monastic piety depended upon the sacraments, the liturgy, and the dogmas of the orthodox church. Christian brotherhood was derived in the first instance not from monastic profession, but from "spiritual generation through divine baptism." The contemplative life was nourished by participation in the Eucharist. Even though the sacraments did not work automatically, but only "in the Spirit," they were the normal channels through which grace was communicated; other means were not impossible, but they were exceptional. The monks were obliged to honor the priests and to share in the liturgy as administered by them. Sergius of Radonež partook of the Eucharist as his first act after having been tonsured a monk, and it was said of him that he was assiduous in his attendance upon community worship. It is noteworthy how often a mystical experience came upon someone in the course of the liturgy, as during the chanting of the Trisagion or during the recitation of the Kyrie or of some other prayer of repentance. The mystical ecstasy of the individual and the liturgical ritual of the church were anything but antithetical. Like the sacraments and the liturgy, the dogmas of the church also were the ground of devotion. Mary as Theotokos was a constituent element of authentic piety. True believers were identified as "we who worship the Trinity." Although Simeon's treatment of such dogmatic questions as the

Sim.N.Th.*Or*.3 (*PG* 120:331–32); Sim. N.Th.*Theol*.2 (*SC* 122:136) Sim.N.Th.*Eth*.1.12 (*SC* 122:272)

Sim.N.Th.*Or*.3 (*PG* 120:333)

Filioque did not have a polemical tone and sometimes seemed rather confused, he demanded that the norm of teaching be "the orthodox dogmas of the apostolic and catholic church." It was essential to "believe Christ" personally, not only to "believe in Christ" dogmatically; but the first could not happen without the second.

How "believing in Christ" according to the dogmas of the church could be conducive to "believing Christ" personally is best illustrated by the use of the terms and ideas of Chalcedonian christology as descriptions of the union of the believer with Christ. Christ, according to Simeon, "has a union with the Father similar to the one that we have with [Christ]." The Easter event was mystically reenacted in the believer, so that it was possible to say that "the resurrection of Christ is the same as [ὑπάρχει] our resurrection." Christ was still to be thought of as the victor over the enemies of man and as the divine teacher who instructed the faithful through the Holy Spirit, but it was the traditional concept of Christ as example that received a new emphasis in Simeon's spirituality. Christ was the example whose obedience and humility were the pattern for believers, and especially for the monks. He was this, and more; for "the saints . . . are members of Christ . . . one body of Christ." Or, as Simeon said in one of his hymns, not only had the believers become members of Christ, but Christ had become their member as well: "Christ is my hand and Christ is my foot, . . . and I am the hand of Christ and the foot of Christ." So intimate was this assimilation to Christ that every generation of the church had the same relation to Christ that the apostles had. Nor was the assimilation merely something to be expected in heaven; it was "not only after death, but also now in this present life." The promise of the Beatitudes meant that whoever was "pure in heart" would see God already here and now.

Sim.N.Th.*Eth*.1.6 (*SC* 122:232)

Sim.N.Th.*Catech*.13 (*SC* 104:192–94) Sim.N.Th.*Catech*.5 (*SC* 96:412)

Sim.N.Th.*Catech*.20 (*SC* 104:346)

Sim.N.Th.*Catech*.17 (*SC* 104:262) Sim.N.Th.*Eth*.1.6 (*SC* 122:224)

Sim.N.Th.*Hymn*.15.141–44 (*SC* 156:288)

Sim.N.Th.*Catech*.10 (*SC* 104:140)

Matt.5:8 Sim.N.Th.*Eth*.5 (*SC* 129:88)

The imitation of Christ and identification with Christ became a summons to a life of holiness and love. Fellowship with Christ conferred on the believer three benefits: life, incorruptibility, and humility; it was the third of these that claimed Simeon's special attention. Those who took their faith lightly had to hear the call to obedience: "O man, do you believe that Christ is God? If you do believe this, then keep his commandments with reverence." Although confessing Christ and obeying Christ seemed to

Sim.N.Th.*Or*.8 (*PG* 120:360)

Sim.N.Th.*Catech*.19 (*SC* 104:326)

Sim.N.Th.*Or*.3 (*PG*
120:335)

Sim.N.Th.*Catech*.10 (*SC*
104:142)

Sim.N.Th.*Or*.10 (*PG*
120:365)

Sim.N.Th.*Catech*.1 (*SC*
96:236); Max.*Ascet*.36
(*PG* 90:941)

Sim.N.Th.*Or*.8 (*PG*
120:359)

Sim.N.Th.*Catech*.1 (*SC*
96:234)

Sim.N.Th.*Or*.26 (*PG*
120:451)

See pp. 31–34 above

Lossky (1957) 34

Sim.N.Th.*Theol*.1 (*SC*
122:96)

Sim.N.Th.*Eth*.8 (*SC*
129:210)
Archangel'skij
(1882) 170–73

Nil.Sor.*Ustav*.2
(Borovkova-Majkova 28)

be two things, they were in fact one. The two marks of authentic sanctity were an orthodox faith and a life in conformity with the will of God, for "it is the commandments that make the distinction between the believer and the unbeliever." As lay people had to be reminded that being orthodox and participating in the ritual of the church would not suffice to win salvation for them, so the monks needed to hear that asceticism without love was vain. God in Christ had descended to earth and had humbled himself even unto death for this sole purpose, "to create in those who believe in him a heart that is contrite and humble." In an apostrophe to "holy love," Simeon hailed it as "the teacher of the prophets, the companion of the apostles, the power of the martyrs, the inspiration of the fathers and doctors, the perfection of the saints." Obedience to the demands of this love was at the same time the path to truth, since confession and obedience were one. "Do not," Simeon admonished his brethren, "try to describe ineffable matters by words alone, for this is an impossibility. . . . But let us contemplate such matters by activity, labor, and fatigue. . . . In this way we shall be taught the meaning of such things as the sacred mysteries." Love in action was the most appropriate vehicle for the articulation of a truth that defied positive verbal formulation.

Because such was the nature of truth about God, it called for an apophatic theology, a theology of negation, which was a "religious attitude toward the incomprehensibility of God [that] enables us to transcend all concepts, every sphere of philosophical enquiry. It is a tendency towards an ever-greater plenitude, in which knowledge is transformed into ignorance, the theology of concepts into contemplation, dogmas into experience of ineffable mystery." Simeon opened his *Theological Discourses* on the dogma of the Trinity with the declaration that it was an act of audacity and presumption to speak about God "as though that which is incomprehensible were comprehensible"; and when he was vouchsafed a private revelation, the content of the vision was the message that God was absolute and transcendent. Citing the authority of Simeon, as he often did, Nilus Sorskij spoke of "a light that the world does not see," something "beyond speech and beyond words [neizrečenna i neizglagolanna]." Such a theology of negation stood in the most venerable Eastern

See vol.1:347–48
Thdr.Stud.*Antirr*.1.2
(*PG* 99:329)
Bab.*Evagr*.2.11 (Frankenberg
137[136]); Thos.Ed.*Nat*.7
(Carr 33[42]); Tim.I.*Ep*.2
(*CSCO* 75:22[74:35])

Sim.N.Th.*Or*.9 (*PG*
120:361–62)
Sim.N.Th.*Or*.3 (*PG*
120:331)

Sim.N.Th.*Or*.12 (*PG*
120:373)

Sim.N.Th.*Eth*.4; 5 (*SC*
129:26; 82)

Nil.Sor.*Pred*.
(Borovkova-Majkova 2–3)

Sim.N.Th.*Eth*.1.12 (*SC*
122:272)

Sim.N.Th.*Or*.3 (*PG*
120:333)

Sim.N.Th.*Hymn*.13.87–89
(*SC* 156:264)

Sim.N.Th.*Myst*.33–34 (*SC*
156:152)

tradition, as represented not only by the Dionysian corpus and by Maximus Confessor, but by orthodox theologians in every age; the heretics, too, had supported the thesis that God was utterly incomprehensible. In the hands of the masters of the spiritual life such as Simeon the New Theologian, apophatic theology produced a refusal to pry into the mysteries of the divine being and a concentration on that which could be known. When Simeon classified the various ways of knowing about God, this was a methodological device for emphasizing that the God who could not be known in himself was to be known instead "from his effects." The positive counterpart to the negation that lay at the basis of apophaticism was the identification of personal religious experience as an epistemological principle in theology.

In no sense could this be taken to imply any sort of conflict between experience and the traditional authorities of Eastern dogmatics. On the contrary, the same truth was perceived from Scripture as understood by the church and from experience, since there could not be a contradiction in principle between these sources. Nilus Sorskij opened his exhortation to his monastic disciples with a confession of faith in the Trinity and in the Theotokos. Orthodox dogma was the unquestioned assumption underlying Simeon's theology of experience: Christ had to be what Chalcedonian christology had declared him to be, for only such a Christ could serve as the exemplar of man's union with God. The converse of this was also true: orthodox christology was not intended only to be believed and confessed, but to be believed in and experienced. Simeon's poetry was an expression of thanks to God for permitting him to experience the vision of the divine and for inspiring him to write of it as he did. Yet it was the clear lesson of the experience that man did not always have this vision, even though it was necessary to believe, on the basis of the dogma, that Christ was always present and that his glory and grace continued uninterrupted. The fault for the loss of the vision lay not with Christ, but with man. From the charting of this subjective state in its comings and goings there came an experimental theology, where, in accordance with the patristic axiom, practice was the basis of theory and knowledge of doctrine came through mystical union.

The end result of mystical union was deification

See pp. 10–12 above

Ps.82:6; John 10:34

2 Pet.1:4

Sim.N.Th.*Catech*.15 (*SC* 104:228); Sim.N.Th.*Or*.2 (*PG* 120:330)

Sim.N.Th.*Theol*.2 (*SC* 122:152)

Sim.N.Th.*Eth*.5 (*SC* 129:100–102)

Sim.N.Th.*Eth*.1.10 (*SC* 122:260)

Sim.N.Th.*Catech*.5 (*SC* 96:388–402); Sim.N.Th.*Eth*. 1.2 (*SC* 122:184–94) Sim.N.Th.*Catech*.5 (*SC* 96:406)

Sim.N.Th.*Or*.11 (*PG* 120:367) Sim.N.Th.*Eth*.1.1 (*SC* 122:180); Sim.N.Th.*Catech*.5 (*SC* 96:388–90)

Sim.N.Th.*Or*.14 (*PG* 120:382–83)

Sim.N.Th.*Catech*.4 (*SC* 96:370)

Matt.5:8 Sim.N.Th.*Eth*.5 (*SC* 129:86) Sim.N.Th.*Or*.14 (*PG* 120:384)

Sim.N.Th.*Eth*.1.3 (*SC* 122:202)

[θέωσις], as Eastern theologians had been teaching since the early centuries. From those theologians Simeon learned to quote the biblical statements, "You are gods" and "You become partakers of the divine nature," applying them to the definition of salvation as deification. Echoing these passages, he spoke of "receiving the reward of the vision of God, becoming partakers of the divine nature and becoming gods." For Simeon, as for his tradition, the deification of man was the consequence and the counterpart of the incarnation of God in Christ. In one of his visions God said to him: "Yes, I am God, the one who became man for your sake. And behold, I have created you, as you see, and I shall make you God." Elsewhere Simeon elaborated on a "wondrous and new exchange [συνάλλαγμα]": Christ had received his flesh from his mother and had conferred divinity on her in return; on the other hand, he did not receive flesh from the saints, but conferred upon them his own deified flesh instead. The divergences between the Eastern and Augustinian definitions of Christianity were expressed in connection with this doctrine of deification. For although Simeon spoke at length about the fall of Adam and its disastrous consequences, he was explicit in asserting that the consequences of the fall for subsequent generations were tied to the repetition of Adam's sin; guilt was not transmitted through conception and birth to his descendants. The fall of Adam had as its result that man was "sick, weak, and infirm," but a man's sin was still his own. Only because Adam, despite the fall, had been created as "king" of creation, could salvation mean deification; and only on this basis, for that matter, was it possible to speak of the fall without seeming to deny divine grace and human responsibility.

The spiritual theology of Simeon was summarized in his doctrine of the vision of God as light. Although men were blind as a result of sin and could not see the divine light, the cleansing gift of salvation made it possible for "the pure in heart" to see God, as the Sermon on the Mount promised, and to see him truly. The way to acquire the vision of God was through acts of thanksgiving and love. What was seen by "the saints, both the ancient ones and those who now have spiritual sight," was no mere "form, image, or representation [σχῆμα ἢ εἶδος ἢ ἐκτύπωμα], but the formless light." "A great radiance in the heavens . . .

Epiph.M.*V*.*Serg.* (Leonid 105)

Sim.N.Th.*Theol.*3 (*SC* 122:164)
Max.*Qu.Thal.*8 (*PG* 90:285)

Sim.N.Th.*Eth.*5 (*SC* 129:98)

Matt.17:2
Sim.N.Th.*Catech.*20 (*SC* 104:336)

Sim.N.Th.*Catech.*16 (*SC* 104:246)

exceeding the light of day" came upon Sergius of Radonež during his nocturnal vigil. From such passages as 1 John 1:5, "God is light," it was evident that this light was God himself, the entire Trinity; Maximus Confessor had taught that the true light was the same as God. There was no other way for anyone to come to know God except by the vision of this true light. The supreme manifestation of the light on earth was the transfiguration of Christ, when "his face shone like the sun, and his garments became white as light." What shone here was "the light of the deity" rather than a sign or symbol. Even this emphasis on the identity of the light with God and on the reality of the vision had to be qualified by the reminder that God was transcendent; for the heavenly light, being divine, did not have "an appropriate name of its own." Simeon did not formulate a systematic treatment of the relation between transcendence and the identity of God with the light, but the principal components for such a systematization were present in his thought.

The task of articulating a new theology of the spiritual life, including the doctrine of God as light, was under-taken by Gregory Palamas more than three centuries after Simeon. Yet it was Simeon who acquired the title of "the

Sim.N.Th.*Or.*3 (*PG* 120:334);
Sim.N.Th.*Catech.*5 (*SC* 96:440)

New Theologian." Following Byzantine custom, he him-self employed the title "the Theologian" to refer either to John the apostle (hence the title "John the Divine") or to Gregory of Nazianzus (often identified simply as

Sim.N.Th.*Catech.*5 (*SC* 96:432)

"the Theologian"). The appellation "the New Theolo-gian," as applied to Simeon, "was first used to distinguish him and compare him" in relation to the other two; for "one of the reasons why St. Symeon was called 'ὁ Νέος Θεολόγος' was probably the fact that like St. Gregory of Nazianzus he had also written Theological Orations on

Krivocheine (1954) 323

the Holy Trinity." Gregory Palamas, in one of his very few explicit references to Simeon, called him "the New

Gr.Pal.*Tr.*1.2.12
(Meyendorff 99)

Theologian" and spoke of the miracles made visible in his life. Even though there appears in fact to have been little literary or intellectual connection between Simeon and Palamas, it does seem accurate to identify the latter as the one who took the personal mystical experiences of

Meyendorff (1959) 221

Simeon and gave them a "theological rigor" they had not had before. Palamas followed the custom of calling Greg-

Gr.Pal.*Tr.*1.1.6
(Meyendorff 21)
Gr.Pal.*Tr.*3.1.12
(Meyendorff 581)

ory of Nazianzus "the Second Theologian" or "the one who has acquired 'theology' as a proper name." He also

Gr.Pal.Tr.3.2.4
(Meyendorff 649)
Gr.Pal.Tr.2.1.36
(Meyendorff 299)

Grégoire (1948) 114

Gr.Pal.Tr.2.1.39
(Meyendorff 305)
Gr.Pal.Tr.1.3.42
(Meyendorff 201)

Gr.Pal.Ak.5.6.4
(Contos 317)

Gr.Pal.Tr.1.3.28; 3.1.12;
3.1.23 (Meyendorff 171;
581; 601)

Gr.Pal.Tr.1.1.23; 2.1.39;
2.3.3 (Meyendorff 65–67;
305; 391)

Dion.Ar.E.h.2.pr. (PG
3:392)

Gr.Pal.Theoph. (PG 150:957);
Gr.Pal.Tr.3.3.3 (Meyendorff
699)

Gr.Pal.Tr.1.3.34
(Meyendorff 185)

Gr.Pal.Hom.16 (PG
151:201–4)

referred polemically to his opponent as "this new theologian" because he had departed from the tradition of "the fathers and the whole church of God." The supporters of Palamas were equally opposed to any suggestion of theological novelty. Despite this resistance to the idea of innovation, the theology of Palamas "is a doctrine of surprising boldness, of unexpected novelty," almost as though "Byzantium had sworn to give the lie to her future reputation for dogmatic immobility." The novelty of Palamite theology consisted in the fundamental reinterpretation of emphases going back to Origen and Dionysius the Areopagite, despite a continuing reverence for Dionysius; this issued in a "new theology," even in the narrow sense of the word "theology," for it brought about a further development in the Eastern doctrine of God.

The role of Palamas as a systematizer of Simeon's teachings as these have been outlined above becomes visible when one reviews those teachings as they were rehearsed in the writings of Palamas. Like Simeon, he addressed himself to the monastic practice of the spiritual life and yet insisted that not only monks but all Christians had access to the deifying power of grace. In the theology of Palamas, no less than in that of Simeon, the orthodox tradition, especially as articulated through its liturgy, occupied a normative place and was quoted in support of theological claims. The summons to a life of holiness and love as the most nearly adequate expression of divine truth came, for example, in the frequent quotation of the words of Pseudo-Dionysius: "Assimilation to our God and union with him . . . , as the words of God teach, is consummated only by means of acts of love and reverence in accordance with the most holy commandments." Particularly striking is the similarity between Palamas and Simeon in their assertion of the role of religious experience. What the saints revealed was the content of their own experiences, "for only he who has learned from experience can know the actions of the Spirit." And so, as another of the spiritual ancestors of Palamas had said, "the things of the Spirit are untouched by those who have no experience." Taking up into his thought many of the themes of Byzantine spirituality from these and other sources, Palamas gave expression to the message of salvation as the central element in the Christian gospel. He interpreted salvation as immortality, as the gift of hu-

Gr.Pal.*Hom*.16 (*PG*
151:201–4)
See vol.1:141–55

mility, as the disclosure of authentic humanity, as purification, as the conjunction of divine and human, and above
all, as deification—patristic ideas all, but synthesized into
what must be called a "new theology."

Palamas worked out his synthesis in conscious opposition to alternative positions. The special object of his
polemics was the philosophical theology of Barlaam of
Calabria, in which divine revelation and classical philosophy were said to have the same aim [σκοπός] and therefore to have arrived at one and the same truth, "vouchsafed
to the apostles immediately" but accessible mediately also

ap.Gr.Pal.*Tr*.2.1.5
(Meyendorff 235)

to those who applied themselves to philosophical thought.
This could lead to the thesis that "Plato is nothing other

ap.Gr.Pal.*Tr*.1.1.13
(Meyendorff 33)

than Moses with an Attic accent." The pagan thinkers,
so Barlaam maintained, had been "enlightened by God

Barl.*Ep*.1 (Schirò 262)

and raised above the level of most men." One had only to
compare the sayings of the Greek philosophers with those
of "the great Dionysius in the conclusion of his *Mystical
Theology*" to see that "Plato himself has well understood
divine transcendence" and that other Greeks had "understood that the God who is beyond essence and beyond
name transcends mind, knowledge, and every other

Barl.*Ep*.3 (Schirò
298–99)

achievement." In opposition to such neutralization of the
difference between "the doctrines of the Gospels" and

Gr.Pal.*Tr*.1.1.4
(Meyendorff 15)

"the teachings of the Greeks," Palamas insisted that there
was a "knowledge common to all those who have believed

Gr.Pal.*Tr*.2.3.66
(Meyendorff 525)

in Christ beyond all thought." What all believers shared
was not simply a knowledge of God [γνῶσις], but a union

Gr.Pal.*Tr*.1.3.20
(Meyendorff 153)

with God [ἕνωσις]. The most succinct statement of the
contrast could be found in the difference between the
Socratic axiom, "Know thyself," and the Mosaic exhorta-

Gr.Pal.*Tr*.1.1.10; 1.2.9
(Meyendorff 31–33; 91–93)
Deut.15:9(LXX)

tion, "Take heed unto thyself." The first demanded self-
knowledge, the second self-discipline through the grace
of God. Another way of stating the contrast was the
emphasis of Palamas on what came to be called many

Vilmar (1857)

centuries later "the theology of facts," transcending "all
psychological aspiration or mysticism outside the grace of

Meyendorff (1959) 214

the incarnation." One expression of this theology of facts
was, for example, his propensity for such terms as "in

Gr.Pal.*Ak*.5.6.4
(Contos 317)

very truth [ὡσαληθῶς]" or his stress upon the factual and
nonsymbolic character of such phenomena as the light
of Mount Tabor.

It would be a mistake to suppose, however, that Gregory's theology of facts implied a simplistic reductionism

Gr.Pal.*Theoph.* (PG
150:932)

Gr.Pal.*Cap.*121 (PG
150:1205)

Gr.Pal.*Theoph.* (PG
150:917)

Barl.*Ep.*1 (Schirò
232; 241)

Syn.Pal.(1351)9
(Karmirēs 379)

Gr.Pal.*Tr.*1.3.17
(Meyendorff 147)

Meyendorff (1959) 281

Gr.Pal.*Tr.*1.3.15
(Meyendorff 141)

Gr.Pal.*Tr.*2.3.31
(Meyendorff 449)

that eliminated the ambiguities from doctrinal formulations. On the contrary, he found the secret of orthodoxy in
the fathers to be their capacity "to observe both" aspects
of a truth that was dialectical. For it was a basic methodological principle that "to say now one thing and now
another, both being true, is natural to any man who would
theologize aright." Heresy, then, consisted not so much
in the outright denial of an orthodox dogma as in the
adherence to one pole of a dialectical dogma at the expense of the other pole belonging to that same dogma;
"you will see that almost every wicked heresy originated
from such ambiguities of theology." The correctness of
a heretic's actual teaching was no assurance of his orthodoxy, for it might have been achieved at the cost of
another aspect of the truth from which it was inseparable.
When Barlaam suggested that the differences between
himself and Palamas were "merely over the way of speaking," this was repudiated. "We are," said a Palamite
synod, "contending over dogmas and facts," not over
words. The dogmas and facts were the content of the
orthodox tradition. Gregory Palamas identified the three
basic themes of Eastern Christian spirituality—theology
as apophaticism, revelation as light, and salvation as deification—and redefined them in a way that sought to
correct the formulation of them by Dionysius the Areopagite and his school. Before he had finished this redefinition, Palamas found it necessary to restate even that one
dogma on which orthodoxy had always been thought to
stand or fall, the dogma of the Trinity.

"At the source of the Byzantine theological controversies of the fourteenth century lies the problem of
'apophatic' theology." It became a problem because there
were in the Christian thought of the East at least two
quite different definitions of the unknowability of God:
that which understood God to be unknowable because
of human finiteness, and that which maintained that
theology must be "apophatic" because of divine transcendence. The second of these definitions characterized
the thought of Palamas. He and his opponents were in
agreement, as he said, "with respect to the question of
knowledge," for they all taught that direct knowledge
of God's being was impossible. It was impossible not
only for sinful human beings, but also for the sinless
angels. For Palamas, the basic explanation of this ignorance was the nature of a God who, in the formula of

John of Damascus, "does not belong to the order of existing things, being above existence . . . . so that if all forms
of knowledge relate to existing things, then that which
is above knowing is also above essence." Silence was the
fitting expression of the relation of man to God because
such was the transcendence of God. The silence, then, was
"not a repudiation of theologizing, but rather another
path to knowledge." The knowledge attained by following
this path was genuine knowledge, not merely the absence
of knowledge; it was, therefore, truly positive, not merely
negative. Apophatic theology did not negate or oppose
positive knowledge, for what is said apophatically about
God was true.

The mistake of conventional apophatic theology, according to Palamas, was that it was not apophatic enough.
It needed to recognize that God transcended not only
affirmation, but also negation. Palamas attacked those
whose preoccupation with the apophatic led them to deny
any activity or any vision beyond it. If God transcended
all knowledge, he transcended negative knowledge as well
as positive knowledge. It was customary for theologians
"sometimes to make affirmations, when these carry the
force of a supreme negation," but it was necessary for
theologians to carry the process to its proper conclusion by going beyond negative theology. God was not
only "unknowable"; he was "beyond the unknowable
[ὑπεράγνωστος]." "Negative theology" was only a word,
and it was not to be used in such a way that it undercut
the very practice it was meant to support. "Contemplation
is something other than theology"—also other than apophatic theology. The goal of contemplation was the vision
of God, not indeed according to his ousia, but the true
contemplation of God nevertheless. This, too, was more
than apophatic theology. The same was true of the union
with God to which contemplation and vision led. It
conferred upon the believer a reality to which the apophatic vocabulary was not adequate. Nor could this vocabulary do justice to what went on in the prayer life
of the believer, where he was dealing with a God
whose utter unknowability was a positive fact and a
religious dynamic. In this way Palamas sought to rescue
divine transcendence and its corollary, apophatic theology,
from the Neoplatonic context in which it had often stood,
and to base it instead on the Christian doctrine of
revelation.

Joh.D.*F.o.*4 (Kotter 2:13)

Kiprian (1950) 278

Gr.Pal.*Cap.*123 (*PG*
150:1205)

Gr.Pal.*Tr.*3.3.14
(Meyendorff 723)

Gr.Pal.*Tr.*2.3.53
(Meyendorff 493)

Gr.Pal.*Tr.*3.2.17
(Meyendorff 673)

Gr.Pal.*Ak.*1.6.1
(Contos 11–12)

Gr.Pal.*Tr.*2.3.26
(Meyendorff 439)

Dion.Ar.*Myst.*1.1 (*PG*
3:997)

Gr.Pal.*Tr.*2.3.49
(Meyendorff 487)

Gr.Pal.*Tr.*1.3.4
(Meyendorff 113–15)

Gr.Pal.*Tr.*2.3.35
(Meyendorff 457)

Gr.Pal.*Tr.*2.3.35
(Meyendorff 457–59)

In the process, the doctrine of revelation itself under-
went amplification. It has been suggested that "what is
singular in Palamite theology is the elevation of the
Transfiguration to a degree of importance virtually equal-

ing that of the other acts of the divine economy." Already
in the earlier history of Byzantine mysticism, the story of
Christ on the mount of transfiguration had been an important source of theological ideas. Corresponding as it
did to the emphasis of mystical spirituality on vision as
the instrument and the goal of faith, the centrality of
"light" in that story made it an appropriate vehicle for
inquiry into the means of divine revelation. What was
the light that the disciples saw there? On the one hand, it
was not the ousia of God, which, according to the Bible,
no one had ever seen. On the other hand, it could not have
been an illusion [φάσμα]; for in the order of matins for
August 6, the Feast of the Transfiguration, the church
prayed: "In thy light, which has appeared today on Tabor,
we have seen the Father as light and the Spirit as light."
If the light were not to belong to either of the natures of
Christ, it would have to be a third reality, which would
mean that Christ had three natures. And so, since it was
not part of the human nature that Christ shared with other
men, it must have belonged to his divine nature and must
therefore have been uncreated. The appearance on the
mount of transfiguration, which was a kind of "prelude"
to the second coming of Christ, was also a revelation of
"what we once were and what we are to be" when deified
by him.

When the knowledge of God was called "light" in
biblical and patristic language, this was because it received its inspiration from that light which was truly
God. The ascent of the believer to the vision of God was
not fantasy but truth. Not even the revelations of the
divine light in the Old Testament were to be called "symbolic." Much less could one refer to the light on the mount
of transfiguration as a symbol. Gregory of Nazianzus had
called this light "deity," something he could not have done
"if it had not been truly deity, but merely a created symbol." In fact, the orthodox usage of the word "symbol"
did not refer to a mere symbol. According to Maximus
Confessor, for example, the body of Christ on the cross
was a "symbol" of our bodies, not vice versa. The greater
was a symbol of the lesser, not the lesser of the greater.

Contos (1963) 1:64

Matt.17:1–9

Gr.Pal.Tr.2.3.9 (Meyendorff 405); Gr.Pal.Ak.4.15.3 (Contos 283)

John 1:18
Gr.Pal.Tr.3.1.15 (Meyendorff 587)

Gr.Pal.Tr.3.1.12 (Meyendorff 581)

Gr.Pal.Tr.3.1.17 (Meyendorff 591)

Gr.Pal.Ak.4.5.4 (Contos 254)

Gr.Pal.Tr.1.3.38 (Meyendorff 193)

Gr.Pal.Hom.16 (PG 151:220)

Gr.Pal.Tr.1.3.3 (Meyendorff 111) Gr.Pal.Ak.7.11.3 (Contos 548)

Gr.Pal.Tr.1.3.6 (Meyendorff 119)

Gr.Naz.Hom.40.6 (PG 36:365)

Gr.Pal.Tr.3.1.12 (Meyendorff 581)

Max.Ambig.54 (PG 91:1376) Gr.Pal.Tr.3.1.13 (Meyendorff 583)

Gr.Pal.*Ak*.7.15.4 (Contos 568); Gr.Pal.*Tr*.2.3.20 (Meyendorff 429)

Acts 7:55–56
Gr.Pal.*Tr*.1.3.30 (Meyendorff 175)

Matt.5:8
Gr.Pal.*Theoph*. (PG 150:952)
Gr.Pal.*Tr*.2.3.49 (Meyendorff 487)

Max.*Ambig*.41 (PG 91:1308)

Gr.Pal.*Theoph*. (PG 150:944)

ap.Gr.Pal.*Ak*.5.25 (Contos 393)

ap.Gr.Pal.*Ak*.1.7.23 (Contos 31)

Gr.Pal.*Tr*.3.3.8 (Meyendorff 709–11)

Gr.Pal.*Theoph*. (PG 150:953)
Gr.Pal.*Ak*.3.6.4 (Contos 161)

Gr.Pal.*Tr*.3.1.34 (Meyendorff 625)

Gr.Pal.*Theoph*.(PG 150:933)

Not even this sense of the word "symbol" suited the light of revelation on the mountain, for this was nothing less than God himself. What Stephen, the first martyr, saw when he "gazed into heaven" was neither a symbol nor a fantasy, but, as the text said, "the glory of God." It was not a theory of symbols, but a theology of facts, when Christ promised in the Beatitudes: "Blessed are the pure in heart, for they shall see God." This vision of God transcended all language, even the language of apophatic theology. In one way or another, it was necessary to hold that the light of revelation seen in the vision of God was divine reality.

The emphasis on the reality of the divine in revelation applied also to the divine in deification. Maximus had expressed this unequivocally in the formula: "All that God is, except for an identity in ousia, one becomes when one is deified by grace." Quoting these words approvingly, Palamas was as unwilling to call deification "symbolic" as he was to refer to the light of revelation this way. Yet the reality being discussed in the two questions was not the same; for in the clarification of what it meant to be deified, the qualification added by Maximus, "except for an identity in ousia," proved to be crucial. One of the opponents of Palamas said: "The whole of God deifies me, and when I am deified I am united to the whole of God"; and again: "Uncreated deification is nothing other than the divine nature." A way had to be found, Palamas maintained, to preserve the reality of salvation as deification without implying the absurd and blasphemous idea that those who were deified became "God by nature." The reality was preserved by the teaching that "the Father through the Son in the Spirit deifies those who are deified." Remaining human according to nature, they became divine according to grace. The absurdity and the blasphemy were avoided by the teaching that "the deifying gift of the Spirit is not the superessential ousia of God, but the deifying activity [ἐνέργεια] of the superessential ousia of God." Or, to put the two emphases together, the basic passage on deification, 2 Peter 1:4, spoke of participation in the divine nature—reality, but not identity.

To avoid saying that deification made a human being God by nature, it was necessary to insist that grace was supernatural, that is, beyond nature. For if deifying grace were "according to nature," it would indeed produce an

Hag.Tom. (PG
150:1229)

Gr.Pal.Tr.3.1.26
(Meyendorff 607)

Gr.Pal.Cap.93 (PG
150:1188)

Gr.Pal.Ak.3.4.2
(Contos 152)

Gr.Pal.Ak.5.27.2
(Contos 406)
Gr.Pal.Tr.1.1.22
(Meyendorff 61)

Gr.Pal.Ak.1.7.6
(Contos 17)

Gr.Pal.Theoph. (PG
150:952)

Gr.Pal.Tr.3.2.25
(Meyendorff 689)

Gr.Pal.Theoph. (PG
150:937)

identity of nature and of ousia between the deifying God and the deified man. This was what Palamas took his opponent to be teaching by his doctrine that "the grace of deification is natural." But the illumination and the deifying activity of God which made its recipients participants in the divine nature could not be the very nature of God. The nature of God was not absent from this activity, for it was omnipresent; but the nature of God could not be shared, and hence deification could not be "natural," but had to be "by a certain divine grace." So powerful a reality was this grace that when it was conferred on "those who have a beginning" it could elevate them "above all ages and times and places," giving them—by grace, though not by nature—participation in the very eternity of God, without beginning or end. Here again, it was fundamental to the theology of Palamas that the nature of God be the decisive issue: as God was unknowable, not primarily because of human finiteness but because of divine transcendence, so also here the participation of man in the divine nature through salvation as deification needed to be interpreted in such a way as to safeguard the unchangeability of God, without in any way jeopardizing the reality of the gift of deification. In his divine ousia God remained beyond participation and beyond vision, even for the saints; yet that which they saw and in which they participated was not a symbol of God, but God himself.

The identification of this paradox led Palamas beyond the three themes of apophatic theology, revealing light, and deifying salvation to the sanctum sanctorum of the doctrine of God. The God of Christian devotion was simultaneously absolute and related, incomprehensible in his nature and yet comprehended by the saints, who participated in his nature: he was absolute by nature, related by grace. This was the supreme instance of the principle that orthodoxy consisted in the observance of both aspects of a dialectical truth. "One and the same God is both imparticipable and participable [ἀμέθεκτος ἄρα καὶ μεθεκτός], the former because he is above all essence and the latter because he has the power and activity to create essences." Therefore whenever one heard the fathers speaking of God as imparticipable, this was to be taken in the first sense; and whenever one heard them say that God was participable, this referred to the second. Loyalty to the fathers meant holding to both. The idea of Barlaam and others that the object of contemplation was a symbol or a creature was an effort to preserve the absolute and imparticipable nature of God, but it did so at the cost of the reality. For since the ousia of God "is altogether incomprehensible and incommunicable to all beings, . . . would we have any other means of knowing God truly" if deifying grace and light were not God himself?

Gr.Pal.*Ak*.3.18.5 (Contos 215–16)

The systematic justification for this view of the relation between the participable and the imparticipable in God was a combination of the doctrine of divine actions [ἐνέργειαι], as worked out in the christological controversies, with the doctrine of divine essence [οὐσία], as worked out in the trinitarian controversies. The various distinctions formulated during the controversies with Monenergism were helpful to Palamas and his disciples. Out of the Monenergist controversies had come the teaching that the divine action was eternal and uncreated and yet was distinct from the divine ousia. It was no more than a corollary of this teaching to maintain that the ousia of God was incommunicable, but that the actions of God were communicable. The sending of the Holy Spirit, as the East had argued against the West, had to be distinguished from his eternal procession; for it did not involve the incommunicable ousia of the Trinity, but the "grace, power, and action common to Father, Son, and Holy Spirit," which were nevertheless uncreated and eternal. When the phrase, "grace of God," referred to an action of God, it meant God himself, eternal and uncreated; when it referred to human virtues or "graces," it meant something created and temporal. The actions of God, such as grace, were divine, having neither beginning nor end. Yet they had to be different from the divine ousia; for as Basil had also taught, they were "varied [ποικίλαι]" while the ousia was "simple [ἁπλῆ]." This appeared to call for an extension of the trinitarian dogma, one that would move from the distinction between ousia and hypostasis to the distinction between both of these and action, and yet would acknowledge the ousia, the hypostases, and the actions as God. When the angel said to Mary, "The Holy Spirit will come upon you," he referred to a coming only according to action, not according to hypostasis; for the Spirit did not become man, as the Logos did. Nevertheless it was a genuine coming of God the Holy Spirit. The only other possibilities were either to say that the power, grace, and action of God, as well as his wisdom and

See p. 73 above

See vol.1:219–22

Syn.Pal.(1351)11 (Karmirēs 381)

Gr.Pal.*Tr*.3.3.7 (Meyendorff 707–9)

Gr.Pal.*Theoph*. (*PG* 150:944)

See pp. 193–94 above

Gr.Pal.*Conf*. (Karmirēs 408); Gr.Pal.*Ak*.5.24.4 (Contos 388–89)

Gr.Pal.*Ak*.3.8.4 (Contos 169); Gr.Pal.*Tr*.3.1.8 (Meyendorff 573) Gr.Pal.*Tr*.3.2.8 (Meyendorff 659) Syn.Pal.(1341)32 (Karmirēs 360)

Bas.*Ep*.234.1 (*PG* 32:869)

Syn.Pal.(1351)48 (Karmirēs 402–3)

Luke 1:35

Gr.Pal.*Theoph*. (*PG* 150:952); Theoph. Nic. *Theot*.12.27 (Jugie 160)

truth—all of which were conferred on men—were identical with his ousia or to maintain that they were mere creatures.

The new distinction in the Godhead, "not only according to hypostases but also according to actions," has been called "a resurrection of polytheism" and was so regarded by its contemporary opponents. Yet its supporters maintained that it was the only way to preserve monotheism. From the statement of Pseudo-Dionysius that the God who conferred the grace of deification was "above this deity," that is, "above the deifying gift of God," it might also have seemed possible to conclude that he taught two deities, but this would be contrary to his own explicit statement. Similarly, Palamas dissociated himself from any such implication in his own thought. "I have never thought," he declared, "nor do I think now, that there are two or more deities." It was, he retorted to his critics, his own doctrine of the uncreated grace and action of God, rather than their doctrine, that "preserves the oneness of the Godhead." In sum, he saw in this doctrine, as in the dogma of the Trinity itself, a teaching about God that would confess his oneness while at the same time doing justice to the facts of Christian liturgy and spirituality. Greek theology had long argued that if God was as the Eastern liturgy said he was, the theology of Athanasius was a necessary conclusion. Now it was going on to say that if God was also as Eastern spirituality said he was, the theology of Palamas was a conclusion no less necessary. It was the task of theology to confess the God to whom the church prayed, the God whose eternal light was his authentic revelation and whose eternal grace conferred on the faithful the saving gift of deification.

The Final Break with Western Doctrine

An ever-present reality in the life of Eastern Christendom during the last two centuries of Byzantine history was the prospect of a reunion with the West. Even the growth of mystical theology was involved with the problem of reunion, for Barlaam was identified by the disciples of Gregory Palamas with Western teaching. Not only had he been born in Calabria, although of an Orthodox family; but he also eventually joined the Latin communion, writing an apologia for the West as a refutation to his earlier attack upon papal doctrine. There is also some reason to

Syn.Pal.(1368) (PG 151:699)

Gr.Pal.Ak.5.26.11 (Contos 404)

Vailhé (1913) 768 ap.Gr.Pal.Tr.3.1.24 (Meyendorff 603)

Dion.Ar.Ep.2 (PG 3:1068–69)

Hag.Tom. (PG 150:1228)

Syn.Pal.(1351)9 (Karmirēs 379)

Gr.Pal.Ak.3.16.4 (Contos 204)

See vol.1:206–7

Barl.Un.Rom. (PG 151:1255–80) Barl.Lat. (PG 151:1255–80)

attribute Barlaam's anti-Palamite position at least in part to Augustinian influences on his theology. In fact, the refutation of Western doctrine was frequently the standard means for a Byzantine theologian to win his spurs; and, on the other hand, leading scholastic theologians from Anselm of Canterbury to Thomas Aquinas turned their hands to the composition of treatises with such titles as *Against the Errors of the Greeks.* The place of such treatises in the Christian thought of the West will be part of the subject of volume 3 of this work, and we cannot deal here with Western theology in its own right. Our attention here will be given to the East's defense and elaboration of its historic response to Latin Christianity and to the abortive efforts to create doctrinal formulas that would, after the polemics of centuries, achieve the reunion of the church.

The reunion, like the polemics, was based on many other considerations than the doctrinal ones, so that "the question of the *filioque,* so bitterly debated, . . . masked the vital, underlying problem." Some of the participants in the disputes acknowledged themselves that the schism had not arisen "over ecclesiastical issues," and that what separated the Greeks from the Latins was "not so much a difference in dogma as the hatred of the Greeks for the Latins, provoked by the wrongs that they have suffered." Although both of these statements came from Eastern theologians who eventually defected to the West, partisans of both sides did carry on the doctrinal controversies within the framework of cataclysmic nontheological factors. At the Council of Lyons in 1274, the fourteenth ecumenical council by Western count, Byzantine representatives accepted reconciliation with the Latins. An even more auspicious attempt at reunion came in Florence in 1439, where the Eastern delegates and the Western spokesmen both made basic concessions. These two councils were bracketed by the Latin sack of Constantinople during the Fourth Crusade in 1204 and by the Turkish capture of Constantinople in 1453. The political forces represented by the two conquests of New Rome made the achievements of the two councils a hollow victory, and reunification was declared null and void both times. Nevertheless, the failure of attempts at reunion had roots not alone in politics, whether imperial or clerical, but also in underlying and seemingly irreconcilable differences of doctrine;

Ans.*Proc.* (Schmitt 2:177–219)

Thos.Aq.*Graec.* (Ed. Leon.40:71–105)

Geanakoplos (1966) 105–6

Joh.Bek.*Un.*1.2 (PG 141:17)

Barl.*Or.Un.* (PG 151:1332)

some of these were the continuation of the divergences that had originally helped to divide the two churches, while others were additions to the topics for debate between the two.

As always in the controversy between East and West, the matter of authority in the church seemed to be the most important and to lie at the bottom of other matters. If it could have been resolved, other questions would have become negotiable; until it was resolved, other questions remained hopeless. For example, "the conviction of the Greeks, that the Saints could not err in the faith and therefore must agree" has been cited as "both the explanation and the justification of their accepting union" at Florence. Reunion was based on authority, in this case on the authority of the Latin fathers, who had taught the Western doctrine of Filioque. Not all the Greeks accepted their authority. Despite renditions of Augustine and Aquinas into Greek, there was "a great lack of Greek translations of the Latin ecclesiastical writers." Nor did every private statement by every church father have the same normative standing, for there was a difference between what they had written as individuals and what the church had set down as official dogma. This applied also to Greek fathers such as Gregory of Nyssa, and even more to Latin fathers or to more recent Latin theologians such as "your teacher, Thomas [Aquinas]." Sometimes, as in the case of a controverted passage from Gregory of Nyssa, there had perhaps been interpolations of the text. Therefore it was always necessary to determine whether words of the fathers that one found especially helpful—no less than those that seemed troubling—were authentic or not. It was noteworthy in late Byzantine theology that some important manuscripts, including that of the acts of the Second Council of Constantinople in 553, seem not to have been available to Eastern theologians.

The conflict between East and West was not over the authority of the church fathers, individually or collectively, but over the relation between the authority of the bishop of Rome and all other authority in the church. Strictly speaking, the conflict was not even over the issue of primacy, since all Eastern theologians conceded this to Rome. The question was, however, how it was that Rome had obtained the primacy. The supporters of Roman

Gill (1959) 231

Marc.Eph.*Or.Purg.*
1.6 (*PO* 15:48)
Marc.Eph.*Conf.*2 (*PO* 17:438)
Hofmann (1945) 158

Marc.Eph.*Or.Purg.*2.15 (*PO* 15:122–23)

Marc.Eph.*Or.Purg.* 2.23.3 (*PO* 15:143)

Marc.Eph.*Or.Purg.*1.11 (*PO* 15:53)

Joh.Bek.*Un.*2.1 (*PG* 141:157–81)

Marc.Eph.*Or.Purg.*1.7 (*PO* 15:49)

Nil.Cab.*Caus.Diss.* (*PG* 149:685)

claims, even those who held high position in the East, maintained that the primacy of the bishop of Rome did not derive from secular sources or pertain chiefly to "secular matters [πρὸς τὰ κοσμικά]." On the other hand, the defenders of the East against Roman claims argued that the pope was simultaneously bishop of Rome and first among all bishops; the former of these prerogatives he had from Peter, but the latter had come only "from the blessed fathers and from the pious emperors" in the past. The basis of primacy was the position of Rome as the capital of the empire, "the city that had sovereignty over all other cities." From this premise some Eastern theologians were willing to draw the conclusion that the primacy of the bishop of Rome had lasted only as long as the imperial authority of the city of Rome, so that "when she stopped being the imperial city because she was enslaved by invaders, barbarian tribes, and Goths, under whose rule she still is, then, having lost her imperial standing, she also lost her prerogatives and her primacy."

Even when they did not go quite this far, Eastern theologians did criticize what they charged to be the usurpation by the Roman bishop of authority that properly belonged elsewhere. He was placing himself on the same level as the Scriptures, although "only the canonical Scriptures have the quality of infallibility." By identifying himself with Peter, he seemed to be saying that, like Peter, he could claim the Holy Spirit as the source of what he said; but there was no such promise given to the pope. For that matter, even Peter, despite his primacy, had allowed himself to be corrected by Paul. Not even Peter possessed infallibilty, for he had fallen into error; much less could it be claimed by those who stood in the succession of Peter. The pope was to be obeyed "so long as . . . he preserves order and remains in the truth"; but "if he forsakes the truth," he was to be rejected. The alternative would be to let the authority of the pope claim the same inspiration as Scripture and to assert that "if the tribunal of the pope has competence in these matters, the statements of the blessed fathers will ultimately be useless and superfluous." Obviously, no one was willing to set aside Scripture and tradition; therefore the papal claims were exaggerated.

That was the real issue between East and West: "the refusal to submit matters in controversy to a general ecumenical council, the refusal to arrive at a solution in

Joh.Bek.*Un.*1.6 (*PG* 141:21)

Nil.Cab.*Prim.* (*PG* 149:701)

Nil.Cab.*Prim.* (*PG* 149:704)

Nil.Dox.*Not.* (*PG* 132:1100)

Marc.Eph.*Or.Purg.*2.15 (*PO* 15:124)

Nil.Cab.*Prim.* (*PG* 149:705)

See vol.1:13
Nil.Cab.*Caus.Diss.* (*PG* 149:692)

Nil.Cab.*Prim.* (*PG* 149:705)

Nil.Cab.*Prim.* (*PG* 149:728–29)

Nil.Cab.*Caus.Diss.* (*PG* 149:688)

accordance with the ancient practice of the fathers in such matters, and the wish to set up the Romans as teachers in the disputed question, with the others obliged, in the role of pupils, to obey them." The assertion of an authority alongside that of Scripture and tradition led to a claim of prerogatives over all other structures in the church. According to the Latins, the pope had the same relation to the other patriarchs that the patriarch of Constantinople had to the bishops and clergy under him. Yet in the tradition of the church, the usual title for the pope was simply "bishop of Rome." The captivity of three patriarchs under Muslim rule did not invalidate their authority; therefore the bishop of Rome, as only one patriarch among five, was outvoted by his four other colleagues in his monarchical pretensions. It was the custom of the ancients, moreover, to submit grave issues to "the ecumenical tribunal of the church," that is, to a church council, not to any one person, not even to the prime bishop; "for they were well aware of human weakness." Nor did the prime bishop, or even all the bishops in concert, have the authority to convoke such a council; this authority lay within the purview "of emperors, not of bishops."

To achieve reunion with Rome, however, some representatives of the East were willing to compromise this position in rather striking ways. Such willingness was visible especially at the Council of Florence, where "the successor of Blessed Peter, prince of the apostles, and the true Vicar of Christ" was declared to be "head of the entire church, father and teacher of all Christians, to whom in the person of Blessed Peter the full authority of feeding, ruling, and governing the universal church has been committed by our Lord Jesus Christ." All of this was said to be "in accordance with what is contained in the acts of the ecumenical councils and in the sacred canons." This latter formulation was ambiguous. It could refer to the "twenty-eighth canon" of the Council of Chalcedon, which Eastern prelates regarded as the charter of Constantinople as "New Rome"; or it could refer to the accumulated canonical tradition of Latin Christianity, which by this time included the Pseudo-Isidorian decretals and other affirmations of papal sovereignty, to which we shall be turning again in volume 3. At least some Eastern enthusiasts for reunion were quite unambig-

Nil.Cab.*Caus.Diss.* (PG 149:685)

Nil.Cab.*Prim.* (PG 149:701)

Nil.Cab.*Prim.* (PG 149:720)

Nil.Cab.*Caus.Diss.* (PG 149:696–97)

Nil.Cab.*Caus.Diss.* (PG 149:689)

Nil.Cab.*Prim.* (PG 149:724)

CFlor.(1439)*Def.* (Mansi 31A:1031–32); Eug.IV.*Ep.*176 (Hofmann 1–II:72–73)

uous in their readiness to assert that "the sacred and holy church of Rome possesses the supreme and perfect primacy and rule over the universal catholic church."

Joh.Bek.*Ep.Joh.XXI*
(*PG* 141:945)

Even those most willing to compromise on Roman primacy, however, reserved one proviso, which was most decisive for Eastern churchmanship and theology, namely, that, despite the recognition of Roman primacy, "we must nevertheless abide without change in the rites that have from the beginning obtained in our churches." It is essential for an understanding of the doctrinal compromises demanded by the reunion—and for an understanding of Eastern Christendom in its doctrinal expression generally —to recognize that the doctrinal differences arising between East and West in this new confrontation were differences that had their basis in the Eastern liturgies, whose integrity the West was, at least in principle, pledged to respect. The differences included the chronic dispute over the Filioque and two new disputes, both of which had a pronouncedly liturgical accent, the doctrine of the Eucharist and the doctrine of purgatory. Western theology, which by this period had reached its age of scholasticism and had therefore closed the "theological gap" that had shaped earlier stages of the debate, dealt with such issues in philosophically sophisticated categories. Eastern theology, for all its own philosophical sophistication, approached such theological questions—indeed, all theological questions as far as was possible—in the setting of the liturgy. Yet even issues that came out of the liturgy had to be considered in other contexts as well, as the conflict over the Filioque continued to illustrate.

Joh.Bek.*Ep.Joh.XXI*
(*PG* 141:948–49)

The Filioque had arisen as a liturgical question, and the propriety of the formula as an addition to the text of the Nicene Creed was still the occasion for dispute. Even if the Filioque had been acceptable theologically, it would still have been illegitimate liturgically and legally. A spokesman for the East contended, speaking about the conflict with Nestorianism, that although the title "Theotokos" for the Virgin Mary was "the issue over which the entire struggle was waged," the fathers had not presumed to add it to the text of the creed, but had kept the received form, "and was incarnate by the Holy Spirit from the Virgin Mary." This objection was not really met by the argument that there was no substantive difference of belief between those who had confessed the original

Marc.Eph.*Dial.* (*PO* 17:417)

Joh.Bek.*Ep.Joh.XXI*
(*PG* 141:945)

Marc.Eph.*Dial.* (*PO*
17:416)

See vol. 1:219-20

Ath.*Tom*.8 (*PG* 26:805)

Joh.Bek.*Un*.1.11 (*PG*
141:41); Joh.Bek.*Apol*.4
(*PG* 141:1013)

Joh.Bek.*Un*.1.13; 2.10.3
(*PG* 141:49; 236)

Joh.Argyr.*Proc*.2 (*PG*
158:996)

Joh.Argyr.*Proc*.4 (*PG*
158:996)

Joh.Bek.*Un*.1.8 (*PG*
141:24-25)

Thdr.Agall.*Argyr.* (*PG*
158:1017-18)
Joh.Argyr.*Proc*.10 (*PG*
158:1005)
Joh.Bek.*Ep.Joh.XXI* (*PG*
141:946)
Joh.Bek.*Un*.2.6 (*PG*
141:212-13)

form of the creed at the Council of Nicea, those who confessed the amplified form of the creed as identified with the First Council of Constantinople, and those who confessed the creed as amplified still further through the addition of the words, "and from the Son." The precedent of the addition to the creed by the Council of Constantinople did not authorize an individual see of the church by itself to insert such an addition. Another kind of precedent cited in support of the Filioque was also provided by the Council of Nicea and the decades that had followed it. In the decree at Nicea, as well as in patristic usage elsewhere, the terms "ousia" and "hypostasis" had been used as synonyms. Recognizing that this ambiguity underlay some of the objections to Nicene trinitarianism, Athanasius had declared his unwillingness to let a dispute over words rend the unity of the church. Eastern supporters of the Filioque could refer to the authority of this passage from Athanasius to suggest that here, too, there was the possibility of strife over form rather than over substance. The writings of the fathers, so the defenders of the Filioque urged, did not bear out the Eastern claim that there was a sharp distinction between the eternal "procession [ἐκπόρευσις]" of the Spirit from the Father alone and the "sending [ἐκπέμψις]" of the Spirit economically, which was also from the Son.

Apart from the matter of its liturgical authorization, the principal objection of Eastern theology to the Filioque had been based on its implication of two "sources" and thus two "principles of origin" in the Godhead. Defenders of the Filioque denied that it implied any such thing. Even when they did speak of "principles of origin [ἀρχαί]" in the plural, they insisted that "the Father is the Godhead as source and is the only cause and the only source of the superessential Godhead." It was a fundamental violation of trinitarian orthodoxy to teach that there were two principles in the Trinity, but that was not what the Latins taught. "The holy church of the Romans has never taught two principles in the two [hypostases] as distinct powers," but rather a single production of the Holy Spirit. It was not correct to speak of "two sources" or of "two modes of existence of the Spirit," even though it was correct to say that the Spirit proceeded "from the Father and the Son." The decree on the Trinity adopted at Lyons in 1274 pronounced its anathema upon

CLug.(1274)*Const.*1
(Mansi 24:81)

Thdr.Agall.*Argyr.* (*PG*
158:1017–18)

CFlor.(1439)*Def.* (Mansi
31A:1029–30); Eug.IV.*Ep.*
176 (Hofmann 1–II:71)

Joh.Argyr.*Proc.*8 (*PG*
158:1004)

Joh.Bek.*Un.*1.20 (*PG*
141:60–61)

Thdr.Agall.*Argyr.* (*PG*
158:1040)

Geanakoplos (1966) 102

those who denied the Filioque, but also upon "those who have presumed with audacious temerity to assert that the Holy Spirit proceeds from the Father and the Son as from two principles rather than from one." In spite of these disclaimers, Eastern critics of the Filioque maintained that "there are as many principles of origin as there are hypostases" from whom the Spirit proceeded, so that the Filioque could not avoid a duality of principles. Some other statement of the Western doctrine was necessary to meet the Eastern criticism. The answer was found in the compromise formula, "who proceeds from the Father through the Son [ἐκ Πατρὸς δι᾽ Υἱοῦ]."

At Florence in 1439, therefore, the earlier strictures on any theory of "two principles" were repeated, but the decree went on to declare "that what the holy doctors and fathers say, namely, that the Holy Spirit proceeds from the Father through the Son," led to the position that there was only one principle of origin, but that the Son as well as the Father was this one principle. This made the Son "joint cause [ξυναίτιον]" and, as he was "God from God, light from light" in the creed, so also "principle of origin from principle of origin." Supporters of the West contended that if the Eastern tradition contained—and therefore authorized—the phrase, "through the Son," it was obvious that "there is no difference between saying 'from the Son' and saying 'from the Father through the Son,'" for the two phrases were "identical in force." That was the very objection that Eastern theologians voiced to the compromise, arguing that "through the Son" was a Latin device for foisting the heretical Filioque on the Greeks. Like the reunion at Lyons, this compromise at Florence proved to be too little and too late politically; and even though "the debate over the *filioque,* an endless labyrinth of arguments and counter-arguments, continued for more than eight fruitless months," it also failed to solve the issue theologically, with both sides eventually returning to their historic positions on the doctrine of the Holy Spirit.

The doctrine of the Holy Spirit was also involved, although quite differently, in another conflict between East and West, that over the epiclesis. The epiclesis was a standard part of the Eastern liturgies, for example of *The Clementine Liturgy,* in which the priest, after reciting the words of institution of the Eucharist, prayed:

Lit.Clem. (Brightman 21)

Lit.Bas.; Lit.Chrys. (Brightman 329–30)

Isid.Sev.Eccl.off.1.15.3 (PL 83:753)

Bess.Consec. (PG 161:493) Cyr.H.Catech.23.7 (Reischl-Rupp 2:384)

Petr.Lomb.Sent.4.8.3 (PL 192:856)

Marc.Eph.Consec.5 (PO 17:430)

Chrys.Prod.Jud.1.6 (PG 49:380)

Marc.Eph.Consec.7 (PO 17:434) Chrys.Sac.3.4.179 (Nairn 53)

CFlor.(1439)Decr.Arm. (Mansi 31–A:1057); Eug.IV. Ep.224 (Hofmann 1–II: 129–30)

Bess.Consec. (PG 161:524)

"And send thy Holy Spirit upon this sacrifice . . . so as to make this bread to be the body of thy Christ, and this cup to be the blood of thy Christ." Nearly identical formulas appeared in the eucharistic prayers of *The Liturgy of Basil* and *The Liturgy of Saint John Chrysostom.* Although there had at times been similar prayers in some of the Western liturgies, it had become the standard teaching of Latin theology—partly as a result of the eucharistic controversies during the ninth and eleventh centuries, whose course we shall be tracing in volume 3—that it was the repetition of the words of institution that effected the sacramental miracle of changing bread and wine into the body and blood of Christ. Greek theology, on the other hand, not only "the more recent" but also the earlier, ascribed this power to the invocation of the Holy Spirit. For this it was attacked by the West, which maintained that such an invocation was merely a doxology and that the power to bring about the sacramental miracle came from the original institution by Christ and was applied at each celebration of the Eucharist through the use of the words, "This is my body" and "This is my blood."

According to Eastern polemical teaching, the purpose of these words was "to recall what was done then" by Christ and to "insert the sanctifying power into the things that are being consecrated." But the coming of the Holy Spirit was the action whose grace "accommodates what was said then to what is now present and . . . changes [the elements] set forth into the body and blood of the Lord." Chrysostom had taught that "the word of the Lord, spoken once and for all [by Christ], makes a completed sacrifice." Therefore it did not bring about the real presence, which was accomplished by the invocation of the Spirit. Elsewhere Chrysostom had said that the power of the priest was the power of the Holy Spirit. This meant that all the sacraments, including the Eucharist, were effected by the Holy Spirit. At Florence it was decreed that "by the power of the words [of Christ] the substance of the bread is converted into the body of Christ, and the substance of the wine into his blood." Except for those Greeks who remained in the Western church even after the union of Florence had been dissolved, most Eastern theologians continued the liturgical practice of the epiclesis and the doctrinal stand derived from the epiclesis.

See vol.1:355–56

See vol.1:151

Marc.Eph.*Or.Purg.*2.23.10
(*PO* 15:150)

Marc.Eph.*Or.Purg.*1.11 (*PO* 15:53)

Joh.Bek.*Ep.Joh.XXI*
(*PG* 141:947–48)

Marc.Eph.*Or.Purg.*2.12 (*PO* 15:118)

Lit.Chrys. (Brightman 331)

Marc.Eph.*Or.Purg.*1.3 (*PO* 15:43–44)

Luke 16:22
Marc.Ep.*Or.Purg.*1.14.7
(*PO* 15:58)

2 Macc.12:45

Marc.Eph.*Or.Purg.*1.4; 2.12
(*PO* 15:44–45; 120)

1 Cor.3:15

Marc.Eph.*Or.Purg.*1.5;
2.20–21 (*PO* 15:45; 133–38)

CFlor.(1439)*Def.* (Mansi
31–A:1031); Eug.IV.*Ep.*176
(Hofmann 1–II:72)

The other new question between East and West at Florence was purgatory. There had been anticipations of this doctrine by Augustine and by other Western fathers, and in Gregory the Great it had been set down as the definite teaching of the church; but by that time the mutual isolation between West and East had become pronounced, and the East did not follow the same course. In part, the condemnation of Origen's doctrine of universal salvation served as a cautionary tale for the East, which found the Western doctrine of purgatory disquietingly reminiscent of Origenism. Even though so eminent a saint and doctor of the church as Gregory of Nyssa seemed to have echoed Origen's doctrine, the subsequent identification of "restoration [ἀποκατάστασις]" as heresy made Gregory's doctrine unacceptable now. In their statement of theological demands at Florence, the Latins insisted that the East accept the doctrine of purgatory as apostolic teaching, binding upon the entire catholic church. For the Eastern partisans of reunion, it was sufficient that the church of Rome confessed purgatory, but this was not enough for other Greek theologians. Prayers on behalf of the dead were apostolic tradition, but this did not imply a doctrine of purgatory. *The Liturgy of Saint John Chrysostom* always included prayer for those "who have fallen asleep in faith." This said nothing about their being in an intermediate state from which they would eventually, through cleansing, be translated to heaven. Scripture, too, was silent about this intermediate state. In the parable of Dives and Lazarus, Christ had said that when Lazarus died, he "was carried by the angels to Abraham's bosom" directly and immediately. The words of 2 Maccabees about "atonement for the dead, that they might be delivered from their sin" did not refer to the venial sins for which, according to Western doctrine, purgatory was intended, but to idolatry. For the same reason, the words of the apostle about being "saved, but only as through fire" did not prove purgatory, even though they came closer to doing so than any other biblical passage. The decree at Florence affirmed the Western doctrine that the souls of those who died penitent, but who had not been able to render satisfaction for their sins in this life, "are cleansed by the punishments of purgatory after death." But the failure of the union of Florence meant that the East returned to its view that the state of the soul after death was not clearly defined in Scripture or tradition and that therefore there was not an official orthodox doctrine on the question, but only various private theologoumena, which could not be proved from the norms of the church's teaching. In addition, the East maintained that whatever the "intermediate state" might or might not be, the church on earth did not have the right to claim jurisdiction over it.

Marc.Eph.*Or.Purg*.2.2 (*PO* 15:109)

At no time before or since have the doctrinal differences between the East and the West been discussed as thoroughly as they were in the debates surrounding the Council of Lyons in 1274 and especially in those surrounding the Council of Florence in 1439. The discussion came to naught, and the union failed. But the form given to the doctrinal issues during these two centuries has continued to determine relations between the two churches ever since. The place of the Council of Florence in the theology of reform during the fifteenth century will be assessed in volume 4; but coming as it did less than fifteen years before the fall of Constantinople, the union of Florence, together with its repudiation, must be seen as part of the last flowering of Byzantine orthodoxy. It also helped to prepare the way for the Eastern definitions of orthodox doctrine in the sixteenth and seventeenth centuries.

The Definition of Eastern Particularity

The union negotiations of the late Byzantine period at Lyons and at Florence showed how undefined the Eastern position was on many questions. Repeatedly, it was only in response to a Western attack or to a Western formulation that the East first achieved some conceptual clarity on a doctrine. For example, the Greek word for the miraculous change in the Eucharist was "μετουσίωσις"—a literal rendition into Greek of the scholastic term "transubstantiatio," which would presumably never have become a Greek concept unless it had been imported from the West. That very example suggests, however, that the debates at Lyons and Florence were insufficient in themselves to evoke a definitive statement of Eastern doctrine; for the term "μετουσίωσις," whatever its previous history in Greek theology may have been, did not become an official part of Eastern dogma until the appearance of a third participant in the East-West debate, namely, Protestant theology. The significance of the Reformation for the

Conf.Petr.Mog.1.56; 1.117 (Karmirēs 699; 718); *Conf. Dosith*.17 (Karmirēs 843); Syn.CP.(1691) (Karmirēs 860)

development of doctrine will be the principal theme of volume 4, but it belongs to the present account because of the impact of the Reformation on Greek Christianity.

A common opposition to what they regarded as papal pretensions led the Protestant Reformers to make use of Eastern Christianity for propaganda and polemics. At the Leipzig Debate in 1519, Martin Luther, pressed to defend his view that the authority of the pope was not normative for Christian doctrine and life, cited the example of "the Greek Christians during the past thousand years . . . who had not been under the authority of the Roman pontiff." The following year he declared that "Muscovites, White Russians, Greeks, Bohemians, and many other great lands in the world . . . believe as we do, baptize as we do, preach as we do, live as we do." In Luther's own work this avowal of an affinity with the East did not extend beyond a series of negotiations with the Hussites of Bohemia, who were not part of Eastern Christendom, but had been separated from Rome only a century earlier. What had been only a polemical intuition in Luther became a more substantial ecumenical overture in his colleague, Philip Melanchthon, and in Melanchthon's pupils. The most significant expression of this ecumenical overture was the translation into Greek of the Augsburg Confession, the doctrinal charter of the Lutheran Reformation.

The translation was dispatched to the patriarch of Constantinople with the hope expressed by Melanchthon, as the author of the confession and presumably its translator into Greek, that it would be found to be in conformity with "the Holy Scriptures, both prophetic and apostolic, and the dogmatic canons of the holy councils and the doctrine of your fathers." To this end, the translation did not content itself with a rendition into Greek of the Latin text of the Augsburg Confession, but adapted the doctrines of the confession to its Greek audience. For example, the Latin text followed the teachings of the Reformers in affirming the centrality of the doctrine of justification by grace through faith, without the works of sanctification. But in the effort to interpret this teaching to Eastern Christians, the Latin verb "to be justified [justificari]" became in Greek "to be sanctified [ἁγιάζεσθαι]." Throughout its rendition of the Augsburg Confession into Greek, this translation operated "not with the words of a conceptual dogmatic language as this had been crystallized in

Luth.*Ep.*187 (*WA Br* 1:422)

Luth.*Rom.Leip.* (*WA* 6:287)

Mel.*Ep.*6825 (*CR* 9:923)

C.A.4 (*Bek.*56)

*Act.&script.Wirt.*30

Benz (1949) 104

Chyt.Or.8

Chyt.Or.15

Karmirēs (1937) 36–37

Jer.CP.Ep.Tüb.1.1
(Karmirēs 445)

Jer.CP.Ep.Tüb.1.4
(Karmirēs 449)

Jer.CP.Ep.Tüb.1.10
(Karmirēs 465)
Jer.CP.Ep.Tüb.2.1; 3.1
(Karmirēs 515–30; 556–66)

Jer.CP.Ep.Tüb.1.10
(Karmirēs 481–82)

Jer.CP.Ep.Tüb.1.18; 2.2; 3.2
(Karmirēs 483–85; 530–33;
566–68)

Zernov (1961) 139

a scholastic tradition of many centuries, but with the vocabulary of the Greek liturgy." For their part, the Lutherans interested in Eastern Christendom were impressed that "under the Turkish tyranny not only the doctrine and rituals of the Christian religion," but also the structures of episcopal polity and order were being preserved, even though "the majority of the common people and priests identify the sum of piety with the worship of the Virgin Mary and of the images."

During the sixteenth century very little came of these negotiations, for the Orthodox patriarch "failed to respond to Melanchthon's epistle and did not grasp the hand of fellowship extended to him by the Protestants." A generation later, in a detailed examination of the Augsburg Confession, Patriarch Jeremiah of Constantinople, while voicing his approval of the trinitarian orthodoxy of the Lutherans, declared, in opposition to their doctrine of justification by faith alone, that "the catholic church demands a living faith, one that gives witness of itself through good works." On other points, such as the role of the epiclesis in the consecration of the Eucharist, the patriarch found the Augsburg Confession to be in error because it repeated the usual Latin theory. The same was true of the Lutheran retention of the Filioque. The opposition of the Reformation to the monarchy of Rome in the church and the affinities between the Byzantine and the Lutheran views on the authority of secular government were not sufficient grounds for fellowship; for on some questions, especially on the free will of man, Lutheran theology diverged even further from Eastern teaching than it did from the late medieval teaching in the West. Nevertheless, the theological contacts and the other intellectual traffic between Protestantism and the East continued, as did the influence of Roman Catholicism on Eastern thought. As a result, it was sometimes the case that Eastern "opposition to Rome was based on Protestant principles, and that to the Reformers on Jesuit teaching."

The most dramatic evidence of this anomalous situation was the theology of a seventeenth-century patriarch of Constantinople, Cyril Lucaris. In 1629 he published a confession of faith whose intent it was to achieve a synthesis of Eastern Orthodox dogma and mildly Calvinist theology, in which the genius of each tradition would be articulated without doing violence to the other. The central content of Eastern Orthodox dogma consisted of the doctrine of the Trinity and the doctrine of the person of Christ, as these had been defined by the ancient councils and restated in subsequent centuries. On many other doctrinal matters, the church had not spoken with equal definiteness; for example, the East opposed the Western teaching of purgatory as an effort to elevate private speculation to a normative status in the church. When Cyril Lucaris composed his *Eastern Confession of the Christian Faith,* he strove to adhere to official orthodoxy on the two basic dogmas and to use the official silence of the church on other questions as a warrant to graft Protestantism onto his Eastern Orthodoxy. The outcome of the controversy over his confession showed that the East in fact believed and taught much more than it confessed, but it was forced to make its teaching confessionally explicit in response to the challenge.

Cyr.Luc.*Ep*.92 (Legrand 4:276–77)

In defense of his orthodoxy, which had been impugned, Cyril affirmed the "doctrines of God and of the incarnation of the Logos" as these had traditionally been taught in the East. His confession bore out this affirmation. It

Cyr.Luc.*Ep*.97 (Legrand 4:295)
Cyr.Luc.*Conf*.pr. (Michălcescu 267)

opened with a conventional invocation of the Trinity, and in its first chapter asserted that "we name the all-holy Trinity in one ousia, transcending all creation, eternally blessed, glorified, and worshiped." On the Filioque, the confession followed the compromise formula of the preceding century, teaching that "the Holy Spirit comes forth from the Father through the Son and is homoousios with the Father and the Son." A later chapter identified

Cyr.Luc.*Conf*.1 (Michălcescu 268)

"the God of three hypostases, Father, Son, and Holy Spirit," as "Maker of the visible and of the invisible

Cyr.Luc.*Conf*.4 (Michălcescu 269)

creatures," including the angels. In addition to these echoes of the Eastern doctrinal development, the confession articulated its christological statements in characteristically Eastern ways. Although Mary was not called Theotokos, her perpetual virginity was part of Cyril's

Cyr.Luc.*Conf*.7 (Michălcescu 269)

teaching. The incarnation, moreover, was said to have taken place when Christ "assumed human flesh in his

Cyr.Luc.*Conf*.7 (Michălcescu 269)

own hypostasis"; without going into all the details of the conciliar formulations, the confession thus attached itself to the way of thinking about Christ that saw his one divine hypostasis as the constitutive force in his person also after his having become man. Cyril was able, there-

Cyr.Luc.*Ep*.97 (Legrand 4:296)

fore, to repeat the conventional Eastern strictures against "the church of Rome, the lover of innovations" in dogma; for even the one exceptionable element in his trinitarian formulas, the procession of the Holy Spirit from the Father through the Son, could claim both patristic precedent and at least a sort of conciliar approbation.

Much more surprising in a confession of faith composed by a patriarch of Constantinople were the many concessions to Protestant doctrine. Describing his own discovery of Protestantism, Cyril spoke of "books by evangelical teachers which our East had not only never seen but had not even heard of." On the basis of these books he had undertaken a comparison of Protestant tenets with those of the Greek and Latin churches.

Cyr.Luc.*Ep*.112 (Legrand 4:333)

Through this comparison "it pleased God, the merciful one, to illumine us, so that we discovered in what error we had been standing and began to reflect maturely about what had to be done." On the basis of such statements, it was charged by his opponents that "he is a thief and a Lutheran [κλέπτης ἐστί καὶ λουτεράνος], he teaches in a manner that exceeds the limits [of orthodox dogma], and

ap.Cyr.Luc.*Ep*.92 (Legrand 4:279)

he deceives the people." Although he denied these accusations, his position on some typically Eastern doctrines was certainly an "innovation" by Eastern standards. At one time he had composed a rather conventional defense

Cyr.Luc.*Ep*.112 (Legrand 4:336)

of icons against their critics, but in what called itself an *Eastern Confession of the Christian Faith* he quoted the favorite text of the iconoclasts, the prohibition of graven

See pp. 106–7 above

images in the Decalogue, and proceeded to explain that

Ex.20:4

while "we do not reject painting, which is the art of making symbols, and we leave the possession of icons of Christ and the saints to individual preference," he

Cyr.Luc.*Conf*.q.4 (Michălcescu 276)

rejected any "adoration or worship of them."

In support of this rejection of the worship of icons, Cyril cited the authority of "the Holy Spirit in Holy

Cyr.Luc.*Conf*.q.4 (Michălcescu 276)

Scripture." Throughout the confession, the Scripture was given not only supreme authority but sole authority. "Its authority [Latin, auctoritas; Greek, μαρτυρία] is far superior to the authority of the church," for the church, being

Cyr.Luc.*Conf*.2 (Michălcescu 268)

human, could err. It was, he said later, "true and certain that the church can stray from the path and choose error instead of truth." Only "the doctrine and illumination of

Cyr.Luc.*Conf*.12 (Michălcescu 271)

the Holy Spirit," which was given in Scripture, could counteract this error. On the other cardinal principle of the Reformation, the doctrine of justification, the confession of Lucaris was as forthrightly Protestant as it was on the authority of the Bible. "We believe," it declared, "that man is justified by faith, not by works." "But when we say 'by faith,'" it continued, "we understand the correlative of faith, namely, the righteousness of Christ, which faith, performing the function of a hand, grasps and applies to us for salvation." The function of good works was to be "testimonies of our faith and a confirmation of our calling," but they were "in no way adequate to save man." As "sacraments of the gospel [τὰ εὐαγγελικὰ μυστήρια]" Cyril counted only baptism and the Eucharist; he interpreted the presence of the body and blood of Christ in the latter as something that "faith receives spiritually," and thus he came closer to the Calvinist doctrine than to the Latin or Greek or even Lutheran doctrine of the real presence. All of this was presented as "the very faith which our Lord Jesus Christ has handed down, which the apostles have proclaimed, and which orthodoxy has taught."

The other official representatives of orthodoxy in the East refused to acknowledge Cyril Lucaris's so-called *Eastern Confession of the Christian Faith* as any such thing. "Anathema to Cyril, the wicked new iconoclast!" declared a synod held at Constantinople in 1638, and five years later a synod held at Jassy in Moldavia condemned the confession for "adhering to the Calvinist heresy and diverging as far as possible from the Christian and Eastern form of worship." Particularly alien to Eastern doctrine was its espousal of "Holy Scripture devoid of the exegeses of the holy fathers of the church" and the divinely inspired traditions and conciliar decrees. Although the church fathers were human, they became the instruments of the Holy Spirit, so that when the church was instructed by them it, too, was inspired by the Holy Spirit and could not err. Anyone who held to such doctrines as those in the *Confession* was to be accounted a heathen and a publican; and its author (whom many refused to identify as Cyril, patriarch of Constantinople), by representing "his private faith as an Eastern confession of the Christian faith of the Greeks, when it is in fact a Calvinistic faith," was out of communion with Eastern Christendom. "For our church has never yielded to such dogmas and never will, . . . by the grace of the Spirit who rules it."

Yet in the absence of any official definition of Eastern

Cyr.Luc.*Conf*.13
(Michălcescu 271)
Cyr.Luc.*Conf*.15
(Michălcescu 272)

Cyr.Luc.*Conf*.17
(Michălcescu 273)

Cyr.Luc.*Conf*.con.
(Michălcescu 274)

Syn.CP.(1638)
(Karmirēs 654)

Syn.Jass.(1643)
(Allacci 1082)

Syn.Jass.(1643)
(Allacci 1082–83)

Matt.18:17

Syn.Jass.(1643)
(Allacci 1084–85)

doctrine, who was to determine whether "such dogmas" were permissible or not? Maximus Confessor had observed that even so central a tenet of Eastern Christendom as the doctrine that salvation conferred deification had not been included in the creed or formulated by the councils. In the encounters between East and West it had repeatedly become clear that the adherence of the East to the norm of the ancient councils could become a form of archaism, paralyzing the thought and language of the church when new problems arose on which the fathers and councils had never spoken. Further complicating the treatment of such problems was Eastern polity, according to which a truly ecumenical council ordinarily required the involvement of all five patriarchal sees. Unencumbered by any such inhibitions, the Latin West was able, after the schism with the East, to go on calling its purely Western assemblies "ecumenical councils," but Eastern ecclesiology did not permit such a claim for gatherings that were not universal. By the time of Cyril Lucaris, however, Roman Catholicism had defined its teachings several times, not only in the medieval assemblies such as the Fourth Lateran Council of 1215 (to be discussed in volume 3), but also in the Council of Trent of 1545–63 (to be discussed in volume 4); and the several Protestant communions had likewise formulated their doctrines at great length in such documents as the Lutheran *Book of Concord* of 1580 and the Calvinist *Canons of the Synod of Dort* of 1619. The ongoing conflicts with the various Western churches and the occasional compromises with one or another of them forced Eastern theologians and churchmen to reaffirm the traditional dogmas, but then to go beyond them to a more comprehensive statement—or, more accurately, to several such statements, all drawn up during the seventeenth century and at least partly in reaction to the confession of Lucaris. Some of these carried official sanction, as did the actions of the Synod of Jerusalem in 1672 and those of the Synod of Constantinople in the same year. Others, while bearing the name of an individual, spoke for the church and acquired normative status; this was true especially of the confessions bearing the names of Peter Mogila and of Dositheus. In a special category was the confession written by Metrophanes Critopoulos; it was a private document and one that in some ways represented a concession to Protestantism, but it has re-

Max.*Ambig*.42 (*PG* 91:1336)

peatedly been acknowledged by the spokesmen of Eastern doctrine as an authentic voice of their special understanding of the faith.

Common to all these statements of Eastern doctrine during the seventeenth century was a combination of two theological methods that had not always been easily combined in Eastern thought: the repetition of ancient truths in ancient words and the response to contemporary challenges in words appropriate to them. The combination was articulated in the response of Peter Mogila to the question, "How many parts are there of the catholic and orthodox faith?" There were, his confession declared, "twelve parts, according to the symbol adopted by the first council, that in Nicea, and by the second council, that in Constantinople." In these councils "everything that pertains to our faith" had been set down with such clarity and such finality that nothing further ever needed to be said. Yet while some aspects of this revelation were clear and well-known, others were more "mystical." Therefore it was necessary to explain the less clear in the light of the more clear doctrines. As a result of this combination, the Eastern confessions of the seventeenth century recapitulated the several major doctrines whose rise and development we have recounted here, and they attached their additional formulations to this recapitulation. Thus we are able to review the sequence of developments set forth in our preceding chapters and at the same time to identify the ways in which Eastern Christendom, replying to theological forces within and without, spoke out explicitly about some questions that had not been discrete parts of its dogmatic corpus in the past.

The Eastern symbols reaffirmed the authority of the fathers, but they also clarified the Eastern view of dogmatic authority by defining the doctrine of Scripture and the doctrine of the church with new precision. It did not require a controversy to evoke from Eastern churchmen the definition of the orthodox faith as "that which has been handed down by Christ himself and by the apostles and by the holy ecumenical councils"; this could have been said in these very words by Maximus Confessor or by John of Damascus. The demand that a Christian conform his believing and his teaching to the confession of this orthodox faith was likewise a recurring theme with hallowed precedent. The term "Our Father"

*Conf.Petr.Mog.*1.5
(Karmirēs 675)

*Conf.Dosith.*11
(Karmirēs 835)

Conf.Petr.Mog.2.10
(Karmirēs 729)

Conf.Petr.Mog.2.43; 45
(Karmirēs 736; 737)

Conf.Petr.Mog.1.113
(Karmirēs 722)

Conf.Petr.Mog.1.6–7
(Karmirēs 675)

Conf.Dosith.9
(Karmirēs 831)

Conf.Dosith.12
(Karmirēs 835)

Syn.H.(1672)
(Karmirēs 784)

Luke 1:28

Conf.Petr.Mog.1.41
(Karmirēs 693)

Mark 1:15
Conf.Petr.Mog.1.96
(Karmirēs 714–15)

Conf.Dosith.2
(Karmirēs 827)
Cyr.Luc.Conf.2
(Michălcescu 268)

Conf.Dosith.q.3
(Karmirēs 849–50)

Conf.Petr.Mog.1.96
(Karmirēs 714–15)
Dion.CP.Tom.syn.
(Karmirēs 772)

Conf.Dosith.2
(Karmirēs 827)

in the Lord's Prayer meant that only a son of the orthodox church could pray properly; the Beatitudes in the Sermon on the Mount applied only to those who were orthodox in their doctrine; repentance for sin was useless apart from adherence to the historic faith of the orthodox and catholic church. Affirmations of such fundamental dogmas as the Trinity were normally accompanied by citations from the decrees of the ecumenical councils as the authoritative legislation on the subject. Or when it was necessary to define the word "faith," the definition was attested by a reference to the Councils of Nicea and Constantinople.

In response to the changing theological situation, however, this traditional view of tradition had to be simultaneously emphasized and expanded. There was nothing new in the declaration that the Holy Spirit instructed the church through the fathers, whose authority was joined to that of the Scriptures and of the ecumenical councils. It had long been customary to put "Paul and the ecumenical councils" in tandem. But the controversies of the sixteenth and seventeenth centuries made it important to emphasize, for example, that the church's liturgical and devotional additions to the biblical text of the Ave Maria came from the Holy Spirit; in the same way it was appropriate to expand the inaugural sermon of Jesus to read: "Believe the gospel, but also in all the other Scriptures and conciliar decrees." For the authority of Scripture was that which it possessed in the tradition of the orthodox church. When the authority of Scripture was elevated over that of the church, as it had been by Cyril Lucaris, the essential identity of the two had to be asserted. When, on the other hand, the Council of Trent, as well as certain Reformed statements of faith, enumerated the books that were to be accepted as belonging to Scripture, Eastern Christendom was obliged, for the first time since ancient days, to decree an official canon of the Bible.

No less urgent was the need to define the nature and the authority of the church. The dogmas of the church were entitled to such attributes as "divine" and "divinely inspired." Not only the Scriptures, but also the church had to be called "infallible." In many of its statements about the authority and infallibility of the church, Eastern theology seemed to be echoing Latin ecclesiology. The authoritative witness [μαρτυρία] of the catholic church was in no way inferior to that of Scripture. Some dogmas of the church were contained explicitly in the Bible, but

*Conf.Petr.Mog.*1.4
(Karmirēs 674)

*Conf.Dosith.*10
(Karmirēs 833)

See vol.1:156

Metr.Crit.*Conf.*7
(Michălcescu 216–17)

*Conf.Dosith.*7
(Karmirēs 830)

*Conf.Petr.Mog.*1.42
(Karmirēs 694)

*Conf.Petr.Mog.*1.46
(Karmirēs 695)

others had been handed down orally from the apostles to subsequent generations of the church; both kinds of dogma were equally binding. Although this theory of a twofold source of revealed truth bore many affinities to that of most Roman Catholic theologians after Trent (Trent's own decree on the subject being quite equivocal), the Eastern doctrine of the church did retain its own distinctive emphases. Eastern doctrine, while insisting that the Holy Spirit would not permit the church to capitulate to heresy, continued to describe the church in a manner that did not completely equate its spiritual reality with its institutional structure. Even though the confession of Metrophanes Critopoulos bore traces of Protestant influence, its analysis of the four notes of the church in the Nicene Creed—one, holy, catholic, and apostolic—emphasized, over against the juridical doctrine of the West, that the church, as the bride of Christ and as his body, could not be identified with a legal corporation. Thus neither the biblical spiritualism of the Protestant view nor the juridical institutionalism of the Roman Catholic view could do justice to the Eastern understanding of the authority of the fathers in its dynamic relation to Scripture and the councils.

The Eastern understanding of christology was, in a technical sense, no different from the Western, since both were based on the Council of Chalcedon. It was the orthodox teaching of both that the incarnation took place when "the Son of God . . . assumed human nature in his own hypostasis." Such heretical christological theories as the preexistence of the human nature of Christ were to be rejected. The Nestorian effort to protect the divine nature from involvement in suffering by positing a duality of hypostases was countered with the doctrine that Christ did not suffer "according to the deity," but that "one and the same single hypostasis of Christ," from which neither the deity nor the humanity was ever separated after the incarnation, was that which suffered. These dogmatic affirmations, which represented the answer of Chalcedonian orthodoxy to the denial of the two natures and to the separation of the two natures, carried special force in the East because it had been chiefly there that the defenders of Ephesus and Chalcedon had continued the debate with the Nestorian and the Monophysite christologies.

More recent debates affected the christological articles

of the Eastern confessions in at least two ways, in both of which the difference between the Greek and the Latin communions was a question more of emphasis than of opposition. Because of the controversies of the Reformation over the doctrine of justification by faith, it was the work of Christ rather than the person of Christ that became an issue. Despite the Greek interpretation of salvation as deification, the confessions of the seventeenth century contented themselves with more common ideas such as divine sonship or the vision of God when they came to define what the work of Christ had conferred on men. They also demanded, in opposition to the Reformation, that the justification of the sinner did not take place "simply through faith," but that saving faith had to be "activated through love." Part of the Reformation doctrine of justification was also the insistence that since Christ was the sole mediator between God and man, not even the Virgin Mary could be assigned a mediatorial function. The doctrine of Mary had always been a part of othodox christology, especially in the East. The Eastern confessions reasserted her claim to the title "Theotokos." She was declared to be free of any sin. Moreover, the mediatorial office of Christ did not in any way negate her role, as "the utterly immaculate Mother of the very Logos of God," to act as "intercessor." Such statements as these, which constituted a "more precise dogmatic expression than [Eastern] Orthodoxy had ever found" on the doctrine of Mary, were nevertheless far less detailed than the contemporary Western disputes over the immaculate conception of Mary (to be discussed in volume 4) or the Roman Catholic definition of that doctrine in 1854 (to be discussed in volume 5). They also continued the Eastern tendency of locating the doctrine of Mary more in liturgy and devotion than in dogma and theology.

This they did especially by reasserting the historic defense of orthodox worship in such a way as to clarify not only the place of the saints and of their icons, but also the doctrine of the sacraments, in Eastern Christianity. Such reassertions of the standard arguments for icons were based on the writings of the defenders of images and on the decrees of "the holy and ecumenical seventh council," with the reminder that "we accept only seven ecumenical councils." It is noteworthy that the christological argument for the icons, which had been so prominent in the later stages of the iconoclastic controversy, did

*Conf.Petr.Mog.*2.10; 56
(Karmirēs 729; 742)

Conf.Dosith. 13; 9
(Karmirēs 835; 831)

1 Tim.2:5

*Conf.Petr.Mog.*1.38
(Karmirēs 692)
*Conf.Dosith.*6
(Karmirēs 830)

*Conf.Dosith.*8
(Karmirēs 831)

Georgi (1940) 48

*Conf.Dosith.*q.4
(Karmirēs 850)

Metr.Crit.*Conf.*15
(Michălcescu 236–37)

Conf.Petr.Mog.3.55
(Karmirēs 761)

Conf.Dosith.q.4
(Karmirēs 850)
Dion.CP.Tom.syn.
(Karmirēs 773)

Conf.Petr.Mog.1.51
(Karmirēs 698)

Conf.Petr.Mog.1.88
(Karmirēs 712)

Conf.Dosith.16
(Karmirēs 839)

See vol.1:305–6

Conf.Petr.Mog.1.98
(Karmirēs 715);
Dion.CP.Tom.syn.
(Karmirēs 770);
Conf.Dosith.15
(Karmirēs 837)

Metr.Crit.Conf.5
(Michălcescu 213–14)

Conf.Dosith.15
(Karmirēs 838)
Conf.Petr.Mog.1.106
(Karmirēs 718)

Conf.Dosith.q.4
(Karmirēs 850)
Conf.Dosith.17
(Karmirēs 842)

not receive significant attention here. The use of icons was altogether different from the worship of graven images prohibited in the Decalogue. The worship paid to them was an act of "honor [τιμή]," not one of "adoration [λατρεία]." It had, moreover, come down by tradition to the church "from apostolic times." Other Eastern liturgical usages were accorded normative confessional status, including the distinctive manner in which Eastern believers made the sign of the cross (from the right shoulder to the left). "An orthodox Christian" was one who observed the festivals of the church year in accordance with the calendar set down by the church.

Very little of this was new. What was new was the need to articulate the Eastern doctrine of the sacraments against Western doctrines, especially against Protestant ones. Such articulation drew not only upon the usual Eastern sources, but even upon such Western theologians as Augustine. Not from Augustine, whose own usage of the word "sacrament" was still ambiguous, but from later scholasticism came the identification of seven sacred acts as "sacraments [μυστήρια]" in the technical sense. The Eastern confessions of the seventeenth century took over this identification of seven sacraments. Metrophanes Critopoulos sought to introduce a distinction between the four other sacraments and baptism, the Eucharist, and penance, partly because these three could claim institution by Christ in a more explicit sacramental sense and partly "as a sign of the . . . Trinity"; but this distinction did not gain broad support among Eastern theologians at the time. The relation between sacrament and icon had been an issue in earlier controversies, but it was in need of further clarification through distinction. The sacraments could not be subsumed under a general theory of "signs [σημεία]," for they were "active instruments [ὄργανα δραστικά]." Among the sacraments, the Eucharist had a special position, "rising above all the others." It was also the one whose relation to the icons had to be specified with the greatest precision.

This required, on the one hand, that while the worship paid to the icons was one of honor rather than of adoration, the worship paid to the Eucharist was one of adoration rather than merely of honor, because the presence in the Eucharist was that of the Lord himself. Similarly, when it came to the definition of the presence, it would not suffice to say that the body and blood of Christ were

Conf.Dosith.17
(Karmirēs 841)

Dion.CP.Tom.syn.
(Karmirēs 770);
Conf.Dosith.17
(Karmirēs 841)

Heiler (1937) 206

Metr.Crit.Conf.9
(Michălcescu 225)

Conf.Dosith.17
(Karmirēs 843)

Metr.Crit.Conf.1
(Michălcescu 187–200)
Conf.Petr.Mog.1.71
(Karmirēs 705–6);
Conf.Dosith.1
(Karmirēs 827)

present "in a manner appropriate to symbols or icons [τυπικῶς, εἰκονικῶς]," for the presence was more real than such terms could express. Just how real the presence was, Eastern theology had to learn from the West to describe with precision; this was apparently how it acquired the Greek word for "transubstantiation [μετουσίωσις]," which now became a technical term in Eastern theology. Eastern theologians made a number of efforts to specify the real presence, most of them variations on the several themes of "factually, truly, and exactly." If there was a difference between such Eastern specifications and the corresponding Western definitions, it was once more, as in the doctrine of Mary, a certain "reverential reserve" about the metaphysical details. The "manner [τρόπος]" of the presence was "unknown," according to Metrophanes Critopoulos; and even the rather scholastic decrees of the *Confession of Dositheus* made a point of urging that the manner of the change from bread and wine to the body and blood of Christ was beyond human perception. It is quite clear that the two principal stimuli to these sacramental definitions by Eastern Christendom, after so many centuries, lay outside its own territory, in the scholastic theology of the sacraments as this had evolved in the Middle Ages, and in the Protestant challenge to scholastic theology as this had arisen during the sixteenth and seventeenth centuries.

Not only in the doctrine of the sacraments, but in its entire definition of doctrinal particularity, the Eastern theology of the seventeenth century was offering a rejoinder to Western theology, whether Roman Catholic or Protestant. Therefore its treatment of the doctrinal issues in the schism between East and West (including the issues that had arisen in the late Middle Ages and the period of the Reformation) was an essential part of these confessional formulations. Although the Filioque had not been very important in the dogmatic negotiations between Protestantism and the East, it bulked large in the confessions. It was the first, and by far the lengthiest, article in the confessional summary of Metrophanes Critopoulos, which was devoted to a careful defense of the Eastern doctrine of the Holy Spirit and a polemic against the Western doctrine of Filioque. The other confessions also were sure to rehearse the Eastern rejection of the Filioque—Mogila at some length, Dositheus more briefly

Cyr.Luc.*Conf*.1
(Michălcescu 268)

—at least partly because Cyril Lucaris had compromised the Eastern position in his acceptance of the formula "from the Father through the Son." Against Protestantism and especially against Roman Catholicism, the Eastern confessions defined the catholicity of the church as a universality that could not be confined to any particular church, not even to that of Rome; if any local church had a universal claim, it was Jerusalem as "mother" of the others.

Conf.Petr.Mog.1.84
(Karmirēs 709–10)

These two issues between East and West had arisen during the controversies of the ninth century, but the later issues were not overlooked by the Eastern confessions. In their statements of the doctrine of the Eucharist, despite the concession to scholasticism represented by the doctrine of transubstantiation, they made a considerable point of requiring that the bread in the sacrament be "made of wheat and leavened," in opposition to the Western azymes. They also maintained that the eucharistic miracle took place "by the action of the Holy Spirit" with the recitation of the epiclesis, not with the repetition of the words of institution, as the West taught. Yet another difference between East and West came to expression in the demand that both the consecrated bread and the consecrated wine be distributed to all communicants, including laymen. Also the later controversies between East and West over the doctrine of purgatory found their way into the confessions. Purgatory was taught neither by Scripture nor by the orthodox fathers. Yet, once the question had been asked, the Eastern confessions did feel obliged to posit some sort of "purgation after death," even though they taught that there was only heaven or hell. In some ways the most interesting, though certainly not the most important, affirmations of these confessions were those in which the contemporary theological trends were reflected. For example, Mogila repeated the idea that Christ was prophet, priest, and king all in one. It was a perfectly orthodox idea, having had one of its first expressions in Eusebius; but it had not really become a topic of Christian dogmatics until the *Institutes* of John Calvin, whence it came into the doctrinal works of various denominations.

Conf.Petr.Mog.1.107
(Karmirēs 718); Metr.Crit.
Conf. (Michălcescu 221–24)

Dion.CP.*Tom.syn*.
(Karmirēs 770);
Conf.Petr.Mog.1.107
(Karmirēs 718–19)

Conf.Petr.Mog.1
107 (Karmirēs 719);
Conf.Dosith.17
(Karmirēs 841)

Conf.Petr.Mog.1.66
(Karmirēs 703)

Conf.Dosith.18
(Karmirēs 844–48)

Conf.Petr.Mog.1.34
(Karmirēs 690)

Eus.*H.e*.1.3.8–18
(*GCS* 9:32–36)

Calv.*Inst*.(1559)2.15
(Barth-Niesel 3:471–81)

Metr.Crit.*Conf*.23
(Michălcescu 248–52)

Despite the predicament of Eastern churches under Muslim domination, which sometimes appeared as a theme of the Greek confessions, "the vindication of trini-

Deut.6:4
Conf.Petr.Mog.1.8
(Karmirēs 674–75)
Conf.Dosith.1
(Karmirēs 827)

See vol.1:299–301

Conf.Petr.Mog.3.20
(Karmirēs 748–49);
Conf.Dosith.6
(Karmirēs 830)
Dion.CP.Tom.syn.
(Karmirēs 770–71);
Conf.Dosith.16
(Karmirēs 839)
Conf.Petr.Mog.1.24
(Karmirēs 686)

See vol.1:318–31

Conf.Dosith.14
(Karmirēs 836)

Syn.H.(1672)
(Karmirēs 784)

Conf.Dosith.3
(Karmirēs 829)
Syn.H.(1672)
(Karmirēs 784)

tarian monotheism" did not bulk as large here as it had in earlier encounters between Christian thought and its Jewish and Muslim opponents. As in those encounters, the Shema was cited in support of the doctrine of "one God in a holy Trinity." Father, Son, and Holy Spirit were "three hypostases in one ousia, the all-holy Trinity." Since, except for the Filioque, the dogma of the Trinity was not a matter of controversy with either Roman Catholicism or Protestantism, the Eastern confessions did not go beyond these simple affirmations of trinitarian monotheism. The point at which traditional monotheistic affirmations needed to be reinforced in the seventeenth century was the relation of the one God to evil, the question over which orthodoxy had contended against various dualistic systems; but now it was not a metaphysical dualism, but the Reformation's version of the Augustinian doctrine of original sin that provoked a new defense of the goodness of God the Creator.

Confrontation with the Augustinian West obliged the East to define a doctrine of original sin in more detail than it had for the preceding fifteen centuries. Although it was possible to find passages in various Greek fathers to support such a doctrine, it was in a basic sense a new development when Eastern confessions spoke of "ancestral sin [τὸ προπατορικὸν ἁμάρτημα]" as the sin committed by Adam in Paradise and transmitted to his posterity. Even though this ancestral sin was said to be forgiven through baptism, the fact remained that "no human being is conceived except in sin." As the debates after Augustine had demonstrated, it was very difficult to maintain such a doctrine of original sin without jeopardizing the doctrine of the free will of man and eventually the doctrine of the goodness of God. Unaccustomed as it was to coping with this conflict, Eastern theology insisted nevertheless upon both of these cardinal tenets. The will of man was free, even before grace, to choose between good and evil. "The affirmation of free will is both profound and necessary," the East continued to declare. It was even more unequivocal in its continued witness to God as simultaneously the source of all things and yet the cause only of what was good. The divine nature was "beyond the reach of the very experience of evil" and "in no sense the cause of things that are evil." In the doctrine of predestination, it was necessary not

Conf.Dosith.3
(Karmirēs 828)
Metr.Crit.Conf.2
(Michălcescu 200)

Conf.Dosith.14
(Karmirēs 836)

only to rule out any theory of a double predestination, to damnation as well as to salvation, but to make a point of calling God "the supremely good one" and even "the one who is good and beyond the good." Any theology that did not include these two cardinal tenets about God and man would be equivalent to saying "that nature is evil," and nothing would be more blasphemous. Even though it was compelled by the situation to say more than it had ever said before about original sin, Eastern theology continued to hold to the doctrine of the Creator and of the creation that it had formulated in early centuries and that it had supported against the Manicheans and their successors.

The treatment of original sin in the Eastern confessions of the seventeenth century suggests their ambivalent status. On the one hand, they were an authentic expression of what was being believed, taught, and confessed in the churches of Eastern Christendom, as this had been elicited by internal and especially by external controversy. As such, they were long overdue in a communion that hesitated, for both theological and canonical reasons, to legislate dogma. Yet the form that such legislation took when it finally achieved a normative codification was in a basic way alien to the spirit of Eastern Christendom. Evidence for this came both from the role of

Karmirēs (1968) 667

"Latin scholastic prototypes" in determining its style and language and from its constant reiteration of the liturgy as the appropriate point of reference for doctrinal statements. To grasp the Eastern understanding of the church and of its doctrine, "one has to return from the schoolroom to the worshipping Church and perhaps to change the school-dialect of theology for the pictorial and

Florovsky (1972) 1:58

metaphorical language of Scripture." Despite their scholastic terminology and systematic tidiness, the Eastern confessions retained this sense—and thus defined Eastern particularity even more faithfully.

The Heir Apparent

There is still another sense in which we may speak of a last flowering of Byzantine orthodoxy, namely, its establishment and growth in Russia and in other Slavic cultures. Throughout the second half of this volume we have repeatedly had occasion to cite Slavic writers, even though the actual history of doctrine has been prin-

Florovskij (1937) 8

cipally Byzantine. The reason for this way of handling Slavic sources is that "it is not appropriate to speak of the 'independence' of these writers." To a large extent, therefore, such sources might just as well have been written in Greek.

Thus in the controversies between East and West, the early Slavic texts were either translations from Greek or compositions in Old Church Slavic by Greek authors; they repeated the polemics against the Latin church that had been formulated by the spokesmen for Constantinople. Slavic Christianity also figured as an issue between the two parts of the church, when the conversion of Moravia and that of Bulgaria produced a jurisdictional dispute in which both territories were claimed by both Rome and Constantinople, with one of them eventually coming under the authority of each. The role of the Slavs in "the

See p. 158 above

vindication of trinitarian monotheism" was more direct, and that for at least two reasons. The conversion of the Khazar dynasty to the Jewish faith meant that whereas Byzantine apologists were dealing largely with isolated groups of Jews within Christian territory, early Russian theologians saw in Judaism a more substantial threat,

See p. 202 above

politically and militarily but also doctrinally. The threat of "Manichean" dualism was a grave one for the Christian Slavs, particularly in Bulgaria; and the defense of orthodoxy against the Bogomils by Cosmas is an important

See pp. 216–27 above

source of information about them. Earlier in this present chapter, the spirituality of Sergius of Radonež and of Nilus Sorskij formed part of the account of Hesychast mysticism.

In all these ways, the theologians of the Slavic lands "stand under the overwhelming influence of Byzantine

Florovskij (1937) 8

literature," and there would have been no justification for treating them separately. It is, however, no less true that "Christianization was the awakening of the Russian

Florovskij (1937) 4

spirit." Byzantium, as a Christian empire (or, more precisely, as *the* Christian empire), had also been the subject of theological affirmations and had possessed a vivid sense of its manifest destiny. But something new came into existence when Byzantine Christianity was exported to Russia. A Christian philosophy of history became a constituent element of Russian theology as early as Hilarion of Kiev, whose polemics against Judaism put special emphasis on the interpretation of history. This aspect of

Hilarion's thought "is not simply a part of Greek tradition, since history is not a favored Greek approach to theology, particularly a national interpretation of history. Here Cyrillo-Methodian thought left its mark upon the Russian writer." It was "Cyrillo-Methodian" because the apostles to the Slavs, Cyril and Methodius, had brought not only the gospel of Christ, but also the consciousness of national vocation, to their converts. This was true in some ways also of Western missionaries, but the dominance of the Latin Mass carried with it the obligation to impose on the several nations of Western Europe a single —and foreign—liturgical language. By contrast, Cyril and Methodius "were anxious to give to the Slavs the whole body of Byzantine liturgical texts in their own language." The national consciousness of the Slavs owed much of its origin to their conversion, and on the other hand Slavic "theological thought was first awakened by meditation upon the religious destiny of the nation."

At first, such meditation formed part of a general religious culture that continued to be heavily dependent upon Byzantium. The events of the fifteenth century changed all of that, when "the last will and testament of the Byzantine renaissance" came to the Slavs. The Russians did not accept the union that had been negotiated at the Council of Florence and hence were in schism with Constantinople. Soon after Florence, New Rome fell to the Turks. The implication of these events for the future destiny of Russian Christianity did not become evident right away; but a century or so after the fall of Constantinople, Russian leaders in church and state concluded that it was time for them to assert a greater measure of independence. At a synod held in Moscow, the tsar declared: "I desire, if it be pleasing to God and if the divine Scriptures do not oppose it, that there be erected a most exalted patriarchal throne [prestol patriaršeskij] in the ruling city of Moscow." In 1589 this desire became a reality, with the approval of the four Eastern patriarchs and of other church leaders. The patriarch of Constantinople journeyed to Moscow to install the new patriarch, because, he said, "under the sun there is [now] only one pious tsar . . . ; it is fitting that the ecumenical patriarch should be here, while in old Car-grad [Constantinople] the Christian faith is being driven out by the infidel Turks for our sins." Whether or not these sentiments were

Fedotov (1966) 1:88

Dvornik (1970) 107

Fedotov (1966) 1:92

Florovskij (1937) 27

*Vosk.Chron.*6945
(*PSRL* 8:100–109)

Patr.Mosc.
(*DAI* 2:191[no.76])

Patr.Job.
(*RIB* 2:318[no.103])

actually expressed by Patriarch Jeremiah of Constantinople, they were taken up by the Muscovites. A Russian
monk, Philotheus of Pskov, had asserted that "two Romes
have fallen, and the third is still standing, and a fourth
there shall not be." Whoever may have been its originator,
the idea of Moscow as the third Rome was an apt expression for the theological interpretation of Russia's historic
role. "The third Rome became a thoroughgoing theocracy.
. . . In the East, especially in Moscow, church doctrine
acquired a more exclusive dominance [than in the West].
There was no classical tradition in Moscow. . . . The summit of all knowledge was theology."

It was not until the modern period that Russian theology—including the notion of the third Rome—came
into its own. While volume 3, *The Growth of Medieval
Theology*, and volume 4, *Reformation of Church and
Dogma,* will be taken up exclusively with the development of Christian doctrine in the West, the modern era
was the time when the two parts of the church that had
been divided by the schism of East and West began once
more to face the same doctrinal problems—sectarianism
and heterodoxy, rationalism and unbelief. In volume 5,
Christian Doctrine and Modern Culture, therefore, we
shall turn again to the sixteenth and seventeenth centuries in Russia, examining orthodox and sectarian doctrine in the East as part of "the crisis of orthodoxy East
and West." Later periods of Russian and Greek thought
will likewise be dealt with there. Yet none of that would
be intelligible apart from "the spirit of Eastern Christendom" as this had evolved from the seventh to the
seventeenth century.

Philoth.*Posl.*
(Malinin 2:55)

Masaryk (1930) 1:49–50

Selected Secondary Works

GENERAL

Adeney, Walter Frederic. *The Greek and Eastern Churches.* New York, 1932.

Atiya, Aziz Suryal. *History of Eastern Christianity.* Notre Dame, Ind., 1968. Especially helpful for the understanding of the non-Chalcedonian churches, both Jacobite (pp. 167–235) and Nestorian (237–302).

Attwater, Donald. *The Christian Churches of the East.* 2 vols. Milwaukee, 1947–48. The first volume deals with Eastern churches that are in communion with Rome, the second with those that are not.

Baumstark, Anton. *Geschichte der syrischen Literatur, mit Ausschluß der christlich-palästinischen Texte.* Bonn, 1922.

Beck, Hans-Georg. "Stand und Aufgaben der theologischen Byzantinistik." *Ostkirchliche Studien* 6 (1957): 14–34.

———. *Kirche und theologische Literatur im byzantinischen Reich.* Munich, 1959. The one indispensable reference work in the field.

Benz, Ernst. *Geist und Leben der Ostkirche.* 2d ed. Munich, 1971. An English translation of the first German edition appeared under the title, *The Eastern Orthodox Church, Its Thought and Life* (Garden City, N. Y., 1963).

Böhlig, Gertrud. *Untersuchungen zum rhetorischen Sprachgebrauch der Byzantiner, mit besonderer Berücksichtigung der Schriften des Michael Psellos.* Berlin, 1956.

The Cambridge Medieval History. 1st ed. Vol. 4: *The Eastern Roman Empire (717–1453).* Cambridge, 1936.

———. 2nd ed. Vol. 4: *The Byzantine Empire.* Cambridge, 1966–67.
The two editions of this symposium are altogether different. The first is amplified and corrected, but by no means superseded, by the second.

Dvornik, Francis. *The Idea of Apostolicity in Byzantium and the Legend of the Apostle Andrew.* Cambridge, Mass., 1958.

———. *Early Christian and Byzantine Political Philosophy: Origins and Background.* 2 vols. Washington, 1966.

Ehrhard, Albert. "Theologie." In Krumbacher, Karl. *Geschichte der byzantinischen Litteratur von Justinian bis zum Ende des Oströmischen Reiches,* pp. 37–218. 2d ed. Munich, 1897.

Elert, Werner. *Der Ausgang der altkirchlichen Christologie: Eine Untersuchung über*

Theodor von Pharan und seine Zeit als Einführung in die alte Dogmengeschichte. Edited by Wilhelm Maurer and Elisabeth Bergsträsser. Berlin, 1957. An examination of Monophysite christology in the context of its earlier and later history.

Fedotov, George P. *The Russian Religious Mind.* 2 vols. Cambridge, Mass., 1966. Fedotov's analysis of "Russian Byzantinism" illumines both the Byzantine and the Russian development.

———. ed. *A Treasury of Russian Spirituality.* New York, 1948.

Florovskij, G. V. *Vizantijskie otci V-VIII* [The Byzantine fathers of the fifth to the eighth (centuries)]. Paris, 1933.

Florovsky, Georges. *Collected Works.* Belmont, Mass., 1972–. The first volume bears the subtitle, *Bible, Church, Tradition: An Eastern Orthodox View.*

Gass, Wilhelm. *Symbolik der griechischen Kirche,* 1872.

Geanakoplos, Deno John. *Greek Scholars in Venice: Studies in the Dissemination of Greek Learning from Byzantium to Western Europe.* Cambridge, Mass., 1962.

———. *Byzantine East and Latin West: Two Worlds of Christendom in Middle Ages and Renaissance.* New York, 1966. The chapters on "Church and State in the Byzantine Empire: A Reconsideration of the Problem of Caesaropapism" (pp. 55–83) and on "The Council of Florence (1438–39) and the Problem of Union between the Byzantine and Latin Churches" (pp. 84–111) are the most relevant for the history of doctrine.

Gibbon, Edward. *The History of the Decline and Fall of the Roman Empire.* Edited by J. B. Bury. 7 vols. London, 1896–1900. Gibbon's caricatures have helped to shape the stereotype of the Byzantine Empire ever since.

Graf, Georg. *Geschichte der christlichen arabischen Literatur.* 5 vols. Rome, 1944–53. Although Graf's account of Christian anti-Muslim polemics in Arabic is the most obviously pertinent, his summary and interpretation of other literature is also valuable.

Grégoire, Henri. "The Byzantine Church." In *Byzantium: An Introduction to East Roman Civilization,* edited by Norman H. Baynes and H. St. L. B. Moss, pp. 86–135. Oxford, 1961. A brilliant summary of the author's special insights.

Grumel, Venance. *La chronologie.* Bibliothèque byzantine: Traité d'études byzantines, vol. 1. Paris, 1958.

Hammerschmidt, Ernst, et al. *Symbolik des orthodoxen und orientalischen Christentums.* Stuttgart, 1962.

Harnack, Adolf von. *Lehrbuch der Dogmengeschichte.* 3 vols. 5th ed. Tübingen, 1931–32.

Hauck, Albert, ed. *Realencyklopädie für protestantische Theologie und Kirche.* 22 vols. 3d rev. ed. Leipzig, 1896–1908.

Heiler, Friedrich. *Urkirche und Ostkirche.* Munich, 1937. This was the first volume of a projected (but never completed) work entitled *Die katholische Kirche des Ostens und Westens.*

Holl, Karl. *Gesammelte Aufsätze zur Kirchengeschichte.* 3 vols. Tübingen, 1928. The second volume, *Der Osten,* contains several articles that pertain directly to our work, including Holl's edition of the fragments of Epiphanius against the worship of images (see "Editions and Collections").

Hussey, Joan Mervyn. *Church and Learning in the Byzantine Empire 867–1185.* Oxford, 1937.

Jones, Arnold Hugh Martin. *Were Ancient Heresies Disguised Social Movements?* Philadelphia, 1966. A critique of social determinism.

Jugie, Martin. *Theologia dogmatica Christianorum Orientalium ab ecclesia Catholica dissidentium.* 5 vols. Paris, 1926–35. While overly systematic in its organization and often quite polemical, this is a work of industry and erudition.

Krumbacher, Karl. *Geschichte der byzantinischen Litteratur von Justinian bis zum Ende des Oströmischen Reiches.* 2d ed. Munich, 1897. Krumbacher continues to be needed especially for those works (some of them quite theological) with which Beck does not deal.

Kurz, Josef. et al., eds. *Slovník jazyka staroslověnského* [Lexicon of the Old Slavic language]. Prague, 1958–. Particularly helpful because it relates Old Slavic words not only to their counterparts in modern Slavic languages, but also to Greek terms.

Lampe, Geoffrey William Hugo. *A Patristic Greek Lexicon.* Oxford, 1961–69. Unfortunately, the period covered by Lampe does not extend very far into the period covered by the present volume, but Byzantine traditionalism meant that many patristic words continued to be used for centuries.

Lemerle, Paul Émile. *Le premier humanisme. Notes et remarques sur enseignement et culture à Byzance des origines au Xe siècle.* Paris, 1971. A fruitful new approach to the problems of Byzantine culture, including the relation of Christianity and classicism.

Lopuchin, A. P., and Glubokovskij, N. N., eds. *Pravoslavnaja bogoslovskaja enciklopedija ili bogoslovskij enciklopedičeskij slovar'* [Orthodox theological encyclopedia or theological encyclopedic dictionary]. 9 vols. in 12. Petrograd, 1900–11. Although no match in learning for the works of Hauck and Vacant, this is the most complete theological encyclopedia in Russian.

Lossky, Vladimir. *The Mystical Theology of the Eastern Church.* Translated by members of the Fellowship of St. Alban and St. Sergius. London, 1957.

Meyendorff, John. *Christ in Eastern Christian Thought.* Washington, 1969. Important not only for the second chapter, but for the entire narrative of this volume.

Payne Smith, Robert, et al., eds. *Thesaurus Syriacus.* 2 vols. Oxford, 1879–1901. *Supplement,* edited by J. P. Margoliouth. Oxford, 1927. Special value for the study of biblical and theological terms.

Polnyj pravoslavnyj bogoslovskij enciklopedičeskij slovar' [Complete encyclopedia dictionary of Orthodox theology]. 2 vols. St. Petersburg, 1913. A convenient reference for definitions and identifications.

Preobraženskij, A. G. *Etimologičeskij Slovar' russkago jazika* [Etymological dictionary of the Russian language]. 3 vols. Reprint edition. New York, 1951. More than a dictionary, this work documents Russian social (and religious) history through the history of words.

Rudakov, Aleksandr P. *Očerki vizantijskoj kul'tury po dannym grečeskoj agiografii* [Outlines of Byzantine culture on the basis of Greek hagiography]. Reprinted with an introduction by Dimitri Obolensky. London, 1970.

Sophocles, Evangelinus Apostolides. *Greek Lexicon of the Roman and Byzantine Periods (from B.C. 146 to A.D. 1100).* 3d ed. New York, 1900. Although it tends to be weak in its definition of technical theological terms, Sophocles's lexicon is often the only place to turn for the meaning of a word in Byzantine Greek.

Urbina, Ignacio Ortiz de. *Patrologia syriaca.* Rome, 1958.

Vacant, Jean-Michel-Alfred, et al., eds. *Dictionnaire de Théologie Catholique.* 15 vols. Paris, 1903–50. Such scholars as Émile Amann and Martin Jugie make this Roman Catholic work a basic tool for the study of Eastern theology.

Vailhé, Siméon. "Greek Church." *The Catholic Encyclopedia* 6 (New York, 1913): 752–72.

Vasiliev, Alexander A. *History of the Byzantine Empire 324–1453.* 2 vols. Reprint. Madison, Wis., 1958.

Vernadsky, George, and Karpovich, Michael. *A History of Russia.* 5 vols. New Haven,

1959–69. The first two volumes, particularly the second, tell the story behind the development of early Russian Christianity.

Ware, Timothy. *The Orthodox Church*. London, 1963.

Zernov, Nicolas. *The Church of the Eastern Christians*. London, 1942.

―――. *Eastern Christendom: A Study of the Origin and Development of the Eastern Orthodox Church*. New York, 1961.

Through these and other works, Zernov has done much to interpret Eastern theology and spirituality to the English-speaking world.

1. THE AUTHORITY OF THE FATHERS

Balthasar, Hans Ur von. "Das Scholienwerk des Johannes von Skythopolis." *Scholastik* 15 (1940): 16–38. An effort to disentangle the scholia of Maximus Confessor from later accretions.

―――. *Kosmische Liturgie. Maximos der Bekenner: Höhe und Krise des griechischen Weltbildes*. Freiburg, 1941.

Bardy, Gustave. "La littérature patristique des 'Quaestiones et responsiones' sur l'Écriture Sainte." *Revue biblique* 41 (1932): 210–36; 341–69; 515–37; 42 (1933): 14–30; 211–29; 328–52. Deals with the hermeneutics of Greek theologians as well as of Latin ones.

Boer, S. de. *De anthropologie van Gregorius van Nyssa*. Assen, 1968. Because of its discussion of deification, this is a helpful guide also to Byzantine theology.

Bornhäuser, Karl. *Die Vergottungslehre des Athanasius und des Johannes Damascenus*. Gütersloh, 1903.

Epifanovič, S. L. *Prepodobnyj Maksim Ispovědnik i vizantijskoe bogoslovie* [Saint Maximus Confessor and Byzantine theology]. Kiev, 1915. The basic work on the thought of Maximus.

Gross, Jules. *La divinisation du chrétien d'après les pères grecs: Contribution historique à la doctrine de la grâce*. Paris, 1938.

Hausherr, Irénée. *Philautie: De la tendresse pour soi à la charité, selon saint Maxime le confesseur*. Rome, 1952.

Loosen, J. *Logos und Pneuma im begnadeten Menschen bei Maximus Confessor*. Münster i. W., 1941. The idea of salvation as union with the Trinity.

Pelikan, Jaroslav. "'Council or Father or Scripture': The Concept of Authority in the Theology of Maximus Confessor." In *The Heritage of the Early Church: Essays in Honor of The Very Reverend Georges Vasilievich Florovsky*, edited by David Neiman and Margaret Schatkin, pp. 277–88. Rome, 1973. A fuller examination of some of the issues raised in this chapter.

Schermann, Theodor. *Geschichte der dogmatischen Florilegien vom V. bis zum VIII. Jahrhundert*. Leipzig, 1904. A preliminary study of the untapped resources available in these compilations.

Sherwood, Polycarp. *An Annotated Date-List of the Works of Maximus the Confessor*. Rome, 1952.

―――. *The Earlier "Ambigua" of Saint Maximus the Confessor and His Refutation of Origenism*. Rome, 1955.

―――. "Exposition and Use of Scripture in St. Maximus as Manifested in the 'Quaestiones ad Thalassium.'" *Orientalia Christiana Periodica* 24 (1958): 202–7.

Almost singlehandedly, Polycarp Sherwood introduced the theology and spirituality of Maximus Confessor to American and British readers.

Thunberg, Lars. *Microcosm and Mediator: The Theological Anthropology of Maximus the Confessor.* Lund, 1965.

Viller, Marcel. "Aux sources de la spiritualité de S. Maxime: Les oeuvres d'Évagre le Pontique." *Revue d'ascétique et de mystique* 41 (1930): 156–84; 239–68; 331–36.

Völker, Walther. "Der Einfluss des Pseudo-Dionysius Areopagita auf Maximus." In *Universitas: Festschrift für Albert Stohr,* 1:243–54. Mainz, 1960.

2. UNION AND DIVISION IN CHRIST

Abramowski, Rudolf. *Dionysius von Tellmare, jakobitischer Patriarch von 818–845: Zur Geschichte der Kirche unter dem Islam.* Leipzig, 1940.

Badger, George Percy. *The Nestorians and Their Rituals.* 2 vols. London, 1852.

Bergsträsser, Elisabeth. "Philoxenus von Mabbug. Zur Frage einer monophysitischen Soteriologie." In *Beiträge zur historischen und systematischen Theologie: Gedenkschrift für D. Werner Elert,* edited by F. Hübner, pp. 43–61. Berlin, 1955.

Bonwetsch, G. Nathanael. "Ein antimonophysitischer Dialog." *Nachrichten von der Königlichen Gesellschaft der Wissenschaften zu Göttingen, Philosophisch-historische Klasse, 1909,* pp. 123–59. Berlin, 1909.

Caspar, Erich. "Die Lateransynode von 649." *Zeitschrift für Kirchengeschichte* 51 (1932): 75–137. A determination that the Greek and the Latin versions of the *Acts* of the synod are independent witnesses to its transactions.

Chabot, Jean Baptiste, ed. *Documenta ad origines monophysitarum illustrandas.* 2 vols. Louvain, 1952–55. Essential materials and comments not available elsewhere.

Codrington, Humphrey William. *Studies of the Syrian Liturgies.* London, 1952.

Cramer, Maria, and Bacht, Heinrich. "Der antichalkedonische Aspekt im historisch-biographischen Schrifttum der koptischen Monophysiten (6–7. Jahrhundert)." In *Das Konzil von Chalkedon,* 2:315–38. (See Grillmeier and Bacht, below.)

Diekamp, Franz, ed. *Doctrina patrum de incarnatione Verbi.* Münster, 1907.

Dorner, Isaac August. *Entwicklungsgeschichte der Lehre von der Person Christi vom Ende des vierten Jahrhunderts bis auf die Gegenwart.* Berlin, 1853. Despite its evident dependence on Hegelian categories for the interpretation of the dialectic in the history of christology, a work of great learning and brilliant analysis.

Downey, Glanville. *A History of Antioch in Syria from Seleucus to the Arab Conquest.* Princeton, 1961. Basic for an understanding of the tangled political and cultural development underlying the doctrinal history.

Draguet, René. *Julien d'Halicarnasse et sa controverse avec Sévère d'Antioche sur l'incorruptibilité du corps du Christ.* Louvain, 1924.

Engberding, Hieronymus. "Das chalkedonische Christusbild und die Liturgien der monophysitischen Kirchengemeinschaften." In *Das Konzil von Chalkedon,* 2:697–733. (See Grillmeier and Bacht, below.)

Evans, David Beecher. *Leontius of Byzantium: An Origenist Christology.* Washington, 1970. A reinterpretation.

Frend, W. H. C. *The Rise of the Monophysite Movement: Chapters in the History of the Church in the Fifth and Sixth Centuries.* Cambridge, 1972.

Grillmeier, Aloys, and Bacht, Heinrich, eds. *Das Konzil von Chalkedon: Geschichte und Gegenwart.* 3 vols. Würzburg, 1951–52. For the present volume, it is especially the studies in the second volume that are pertinent, dealing as they do with the post-Chalcedonian and anti-Chalcedonian developments.

Grillmeier, Aloys. *Christ in Christian Tradition: From the Apostolic Age to Chalcedon (451)*. Translated by J. S. Bowden. New York, 1965.

Grumel, Venance. "Un théologien nestorien, Babaï le Grand." *Échos d'Orient* 22 (1923): 153–81; 257–80; 23 (1924): 9–33; 162–77; 257–74; 395–99.

———. "Recherches sur l'histoire du monothélisme." *Échos d'Orient* 27 (1928): 6–16; 257–77; 28 (1929): 19–34; 272–82; 29 (1930): 16–28.

Hage, Wolfgang. *Die syrisch-jakobitische Kirche in frühislamischer Zeit: Nach orientalischen Quellen.* Wiesbaden, 1966.

Helmer, Siegfried. *Der Neuchalkedonismus: Geschichte, Berechtigung und Bedeutung eines dogmengeschichtlichen Begriffes.* Bonn, 1962. A study in the recent historiography of doctrine.

Hjelt, Arthur. *Études sur l'Hexaméron de Jacques d'Edesse notamment sur ses notions géographiques contenues dan le 3ième Traité.* Helsinki, 1892.

Kawerau, Peter. *Die Jakobitische Kirche im Zeitalter der syrischen Renaissance: Idee und Wirklichkeit.* Berlin, 1955.

Kayser, C. *Die Canones Jacob's von Edessa übersetzt und erläutert, zum Theil auch zuerst im Grundtext veröffentlicht.* Leipzig, 1886.

Kleyn, Hendrik Gerrit. *Jacobus Baradeüs: De Stichter der syrische monophysietische kerk* [Jacob Baradaeus, the founder of the Syrian Monophysite church]. Leiden, 1882.

Koffler, Hubert. *Die Lehre des Barhebräus von der Auferstehung der Leiber.* Rome, 1933.

Labourt, Jerome. *De Timotheo I. Nestorianorum patriarcha (728–823): Accedunt XCIX eiusdem Timothei definitiones canonicae e textu syriaco inedito nunc primum latine redditae.* Paris, 1904.

Lebon, Joseph. "La christologie de Timothée Elure d'après les sources syriaques inédites." *Revue d'histoire ecclésiastique* 9 (1908): 677–702.

———. *Le monophysisme sévérien: Étude historique, littéraire et théologique sur la résistance monophysite au concile de Chalcédoine jusq'à la constitution de l'église jacobite.* Louvain, 1909.

———. "La christologie du monophysisme syrien." In *Das Konzil von Chalkedon,* 1:425–580. (See Grillmeier and Bacht, above.)

Lebon has taught Western theologians to begin to appreciate the deeper meaning of "one incarnate nature of God the Logos."

Merx, Adalbert. *Historia artis grammaticae apud Syros.* Reprint edition. Nendeln, Liechtenstein, 1966.

Moberg, Axel. *On Some Syriac Fragments of the Book of Timotheus Ailuros against the Synod of Chalcedon.* Lund, 1928.

Moeller, Charles. "Le chalcédonisme et le néo-chalcédonisme en Orient de 451 à la fin du VIe siècle." In *Das Konzil von Chalkedon,* 1:637–720. (See Grillmeier and Bacht, above.)

Oswepian, G. *Die Entstehungsgeschichte des Monotheletismus nach ihren Quellen geprüft und dargestellt.* Leipzig, 1897.

Parente, Pietro. "Uso e significato del termine Θεοκίνητος nella controversia monotelitica" [The use and significance of the term Θεοκίνητος (moved by God) in the Monotheletist controversy]. *Revue des études byzantines* 11 (1953): 241–51.

Peitz, W. M. "Martin I. und Maximus Confessor: Beiträge zur Geschichte des Monotheletenstreites in den Jahren 645–668." *Historisches Jahrbuch* 38 (1917): 213–36; 429–58. An attempt to clarify the chronology.

Raes, Alphonse. "L'étude de la liturgie syrienne, son état actuel." *Miscellanea liturgica in honorem L. Cumberti Mohlberg,* 1:333–46. Rome, 1948.

Roey, Albert van. "La lettre apologétique d'Elie à Léon, syncelle de l'évêque chalcédonien de Harran." *Le Museon* 57 (1944): 1–52.

———. "Les débuts de l'église jacobite." In *Das Konzil von Chalkedon,* 2:339–60. (See Grillmeier and Bacht, above.)

Rozemond, Keetje. *La christologie de Saint Jean Damascène.* Ettal, 1959. Philosophical, dogmatic, and polemical aspects.

Rücker, Adolf, ed. *Die syrische Jakobosanaphora nach der Rezension des Ja'qôb(h) von Edessa.* Münster, 1923.

———. "Aus dem mystischen Schrifttum nestorianischer Mönche des 6.–8. Jahrhunderts." In *Orientalische Stimmen zum Erlösungsgedanken,* edited by Franz Gustav Taeschner, pp. 38–54. Leipzig, 1936.

Sachau, Eduard. *Zur Ausbreitung des Christentums in Asien.* Berlin, 1919.

Samuel, Vilakuel Cherian. "The Council of Chalcedon and the Christology of Severus of Antioch." Ph.D. dissertation, Yale University, 1957.

Straubinger, E. *Die Christologie des hl. Maximus Confessor.* Bonn, 1906.

Unger, Dominic J. "The Incarnation—A Supreme Exaltation for Christ according to St. John Damascene." *Franciscan Studies* 8 (1948): 237–49.

Urbina, Ignacio Ortiz de. "Das Glaubenssymbol von Chalkedon—sein Text, sein Werden, seine dogmatische Bedeutung." In *Das Konzil von Chalkedon,* 1:389–418. (See Grillmeier and Bacht, above.)

Vine, Aubrey Russell. *The Nestorian Churches: A Concise History of Nestorian Christianity in Asia from the Persian Schism to the Modern Assyrians.* London, 1937. A popular account.

Vööbus, Arthur. *History of Asceticism in the Syrian Orient: A Contribution to the History of Culture in the Near East.* 2 vols. Louvain, 1958–60.

———. *History of the School of Nisibis.* Louvain, 1965.

Vööbus's research has been fundamental in opening up the treasures of Syriac literature.

Vries, Wilhelm de. *Sakramententheologie bei den Nestorianern.* Rome, 1947.

———. "Die syrisch-nestorianische Haltung zu Chalkedon." In *Das Konzil von Chalkedon,* 1:603–35. (See Grillmeier and Bacht, above.)

———. *Der Kirchenbegriff der von Rom getrennten Syrer.* Rome, 1955.

3. IMAGES OF THE INVISIBLE

Alexander, Paul J. "Hypatius of Ephesus: A Note on Image Worship in the Sixth Century." *Harvard Theological Review* 45 (1952): 177–84.

———. "The Iconoclastic Council of St. Sophia (815) and Its Definition (Horos)." *Dumbarton Oaks Papers* 7 (1953): 35–66.

———. *The Patriarch Nicephorus of Constantinople: Ecclesiastical Policy and Image Worship in the Byzantine Empire.* Oxford, 1958.

Antoniadis, Sophie. *Place de la liturgie dans la tradition des lettres grecques.* Leiden, 1939. A cultural study, with significant doctrinal implications.

Bastgen, Hubert. "Das Capitulare Karls d. Gr. über die Bilder oder die sogenannten Libri Carolini." *Neues Archiv der Gesellschaft für ältere deutsche Geschichtskunde* 35 (1911): 631–66; 36 (1912): 13–51; 455–533. A monograph in preparation for Bastgen's edition of the *Caroline Books* in the *Monumenta Germaniae Historica.*

Baynes, Norman H. "The Icons before Iconoclasm." *Harvard Theological Review* 44 (1951): 93–106. Argues that "iconoclasm was primarily religious in its inspiration."

Bornert, René. *Les commentaires byzantins de la divine liturgie du VIIIe au XVe siècle.* Paris, 1966.

Campenhausen, Hans von. "The Theological Problem of Images in the Early Church." In *Tradition and Life in the Church: Essays and Lectures in Church History*, pp. 171–200. Translated by A. V. Littledale. Philadelphia, 1968.

Caspar, Erich. "Papst Gregor II. und der Bilderstreit." *Zeitschrift für Kirchengeschichte* 52 (1933): 28–89. Includes a new edition (though not a "critical edition," which Caspar says is impossible) of Gregory's letters.

Chevalier, Célestin. *La Mariologie de saint Jean Damascène.* Rome, 1936.

————."Mariologie de Romanos." *Recherches de science religieuse* 28 (1938): 48–69.

Dalton, Ormonde Maddock. *Byzantine Art and Archaeology.* Oxford, 1911.

Dobschütz, Ernst von. *Christusbilder: Untersuchungen zur christlichen Legende.* Leipzig, 1899. An early study of the place of "images" in the first centuries of Christian history.

Dvornik, Francis. "The Patriarch Photius and Iconoclasm." *Dumbarton Oaks Papers* 7 (1953): 67–97.

Elliger, Walter. *Die Stellung der alten Christen zu den Bildern in den ersten vier Jahrhunderten nach den Angaben der zeitgenössischen kirchlichen Schriftsteller.* 2 vols. Leipzig, 1930–34.

Florovsky, George. "Origen, Eusebius, and the Iconoclastic Controversy." *Church History* 19 (1950): 77–96. Iconoclasm as a theological outgrowth of certain tendencies within Origenism.

Funk, Franz Xaver. "Ein angebliches Wort Basilius des Gr. über die Bilderverehrung." *Theologische Quartalschrift* 70 (1888): 297–98.

Geischer, Hans-Jürgen, ed. *Der byzantinische Bilderstreit.* Gütersloh, 1968. A collection of some of the most important sources, compiled from other editions.

Goldschmidt, Rudolf Carel. *Paulinus' Churches at Nola: Texts, Translations and Commentary.* Amsterdam, 1940.

Grabar, André. *Martyrium: Recherches sur le culte des reliques et l'art chrétien antique.* 2 vols. Paris, 1943–46. Especially valuable for the discussion in the second volume of the relation between the cult of relics and the cult of icons.

————. *L'iconoclasme byzantine.* Paris, 1957.

Hoeck, J. M. "Stand und Aufgaben der Damaskenos-Forschung." *Orientalia Christiana Periodica* 17 (1951): 5–60.

Kitzinger, Ernst. "The Cult of Images in the Age before Iconoclasm." *Dumbarton Oaks Papers* 7 (1954): 85–150.

————. "On Some Icons of the Seventh Century." In *Studies in Honor of A. M. Friend, Jr.*, pp. 132–50. Princeton, 1955.

————. "Byzantine Art in the Period between Justinian and Iconoclasm." In *Berichte zum XI. Internationalen Byzantinisten-Kongress*, pp. 1–50. Munich, 1958. An almost unique correlation of the history of art and the history of theology.

Koch, Hugo. *Die altchristliche Bilderfrage nach den literarischen Quellen.* Göttingen, 1917.

Koch, Lucas. "Zur Theologie der Christus-Ikone." *Benediktinische Monatschrift zur Pflege religiösen und geistlichen Lebens* 19 (1937): 375–87; 20 (1938): 32–47; 281–88; 437–52.

————. "Christusbild—Kaiserbild. Zugleich ein Beitrag zur Lösung der Frage nach dem Anteil der byzantinischen Kaiser am griechischen Bilderstreit." Ibid. 21 (1939): 85–105.

Kotter, Bonifatius. *Die Überlieferung der "Pege gnoseos" des hl. Johannes von Damaskos.* Ettal, 1959. Part of the work in preparation for the new edition (See "Editions and Collections," above.)

Ladner, Gerhart B. "Der Bilderstreit und die Kunst-Lehren der byzantinischen und abendländischen Theologie." *Zeitschrift für Kirchengeschichte* 50 (1931): 1–23.

――――. "Origin and Significance of the Byzantine Iconoclastic Controversy." *Medieval Studies* 2 (1940): 127–49.

――――. "The Concept of the Image in the Greek Fathers and the Byzantine Iconoclastic Controversy." *Dumbarton Oaks Papers* 7 (1953): 1–34.

Lazarev, Viktor Nikitič. *Mozaiki Sofii Kievskoj* [The mosaics of (St.) Sophia in Kiev]. Moscow, 1960. The earliest great monument of the transplantation of Greek religious art to Russia.

Martin, Edward James. *A History of the Iconoclastic Controversy.* New York, 1930.

Mathew, Gervase. *Byzantine Aesthetics.* London, 1963.

Menges, Hieronymus. *Die Bilderlehre des hl. Johannes von Damaskus.* Kallmünz, 1937.

Nersessian, Siraprie der. "Un apologie des images du septième siècle." *Byzantion* 17 (1944/45): 58–87. Translation and discussion of an Armenian source.

Ostrogorskij, Georgij. "Soedinenie voprosa o sv. ikonach s christologičeskoj dogmatikoj v sočinenijach pravoslavnych apologetov rannjago perioda ikonoborčestva" [The combination of the problem of the holy icons with christological dogmatics in the works of the orthodox apologists of the early period of iconoclasm]. *Seminarium Kondakovianum: Recueil d'études* 1 (1927): 35–48.

Ostrogorsky, Georg. *Studien zur Geschichte des byzantinischen Bilderstreites.* Breslau, 1929. Includes an attempt at reassembling the fragments of the iconoclastic writings of Emperor Constantine V.

Ouspensky, Leonid, and Lossky, Wladimir. *Der Sinn der Ikonen.* Bern, 1952. A profound essay.

Richter, Gerhard. *Die Dialektik des Johannes von Damaskos: Eine Untersuchung des Textes nach seinen Quellen und seiner Bedeutung.* Ettal, 1964.

Runciman, Steven. "Some Remarks on the Image of Edessa." *Cambridge Historical Journal* 3 (1929–31): 238–52.

Shepherd, Dorothy G. "An Icon of the Virgin: A Sixth-Century Tapestry Panel from Egypt." *The Bulletin of the Cleveland Museum of Art* 56 (1969): 90–120. Probably the oldest icon in America.

Skrobucha, Heinz [Heinz Paul Gerhard]. *The World of Icons.* Translated from the third German edition. New York, 1971.

Schwarzlose, Karl G. *Der Bilderstreit: Ein Kampf der griechischen Kirche um ihre Eigenart und ihre Freiheit.* Gotha, 1890. Still a useful summary.

Studer, Basilius. *Die theologische Arbeitsweise des Johannes von Damaskos.* Ettal, 1956.

Trubeckoj, Evgenij Nikolaevič. *Umozrenie v kraskach: Tri očerka o russkoj ikone* [Theory of colors: Three studies of the Russian icon]. Paris, 1965. An effort to identify intellectual trends in ancient Russian icon-painting.

Uspenskij, K. N. "Očerki po istorii ikonoborčeskogo dviženija v vizantijskoj imperii v VII-IX. vv.: Feofan i ego chronografija" [Studies in the history of the iconoclastic movement in the Byzantine Empire during the eighth and ninth centuries: Theophanes and his *Chronography*]. *Vizantijskij Vremennik,* n.s. 3 (1950): 393–438; 4 (1951): 211–62. A recent examination of the issues from a Marxist viewpoint.

Uspenskij, Leonid. "Sed'moj vselenskij sobor i dogmat ob ikonopočitanij" [The seventh ecumenical council and the dogma concerning the worship of icons]. *Žurnal Moskovskoj Patriarchii* (December, 1958): 40–48.

Visser, Anne Jippe. *Nikephoros und der Bilderstreit: Eine Untersuchung über die Stellung des Konstantinopeler Patriarchen Nikephoros innerhalb der ikonoklastischen Wirren.* The Hague, 1952.

Weitzmann, Kurt. *Frühe Ikonen.* Vienna, 1965. Art history with a keen sense of intellectual and doctrinal issues.

Wellen, G. A. *Theotokos: Eine ikonographische Abhandlung über das Gottesmutterbild in frühchristlicher Zeit.* Utrecht, 1960.

Wellesz, Egon. *The Akathistos Hymn.* Copenhagen, 1957. A defense of the thesis—which we have accepted—that the author of the hymn was Romanus the Melodist.

———. *A History of Byzantine Music and Hymnography.* 2d ed. Oxford, 1961. The standard work, by the leading authority in the field.

4. The Challenge of the Latin Church

Bilz, Jakob. *Die Trinitätslehre des hl. Johannes von Damaskus, mit besonderer Berücksichtigung des Verhältnisses der griechischen zur lateinischen Auffassungsweise des Geheimnisses.* Paderborn, 1909. Did John of Damascus teach some version of the Filioque doctrine?

Bréhier, Louis. *Le schisme oriental du XI siècle.* Paris, 1899.

———. "The Greek Church: Its Relations with the West up to 1054." In *Cambridge Medieval History,* 1st ed., 4:246–73. (See "General" section, above.)

———. "Attempts at Reunion of the Greek and Latin Churches." Ibid., pp. 594–626.

Butler, Cuthbert. *The Vatican Council 1869–1870.* Edited by B. C. Butler. Westminster, Md., 1962.

Chapman, John. *The Condemnation of Pope Honorius.* London, 1907.

Chevalier, Irénée. *S. Augustin et la pensée grecque: Les relations trinitaires.* Fribourg, 1940. Origins of the Filioque.

Dobroklonskij, Aleksandr Pavlovič. *Prepodobnyj Feodor, ispovědnik i igumen studijskij* [Saint Theodore, confessor and abbot of Studios]. 2 vols. Odessa, 1913–14. The best study of this subject in any language.

Dölger, Franz. "Rom in der Gedankenwelt der Byzantiner." In *Byzanz und die europäische Staatenwelt,* pp. 70–115. Speyer, 1953.

Dvornik, Francis. *Les Slavs, Byzance et Rome au IXe siècle.* Paris, 1926.

———. *Les légendes de Constantin et de Méthode, vues de Byzance.* Prague, 1933. Contains the *Vitae* of both.

———. *The Photian Schism: History and Legend.* Cambridge, 1948.

———. *Byzantium and the Roman Primacy.* New York, 1966.

———. *Byzantine Missions among the Slavs: SS. Constantine-Cyril and Methodius.* New Brunswick, N. J., 1970.

More than any other Western scholar, Dvornik has worked to set straight the narrative of East-West relations during the ninth century.

Erickson, John H. "Leavened and Unleavened: Some Theological Implications of the Schism of 1054." *St. Vladimir's Theological Quarterly* 14–3 (1970): 3–24.

Evans, Ernest, ed. *Q. Septimii Florentis Tertulliani Adversus Praxean Liber.* London, 1948.

Freeman, Ann. "Further Studies in the *Libri Carolini*. III. The Marginal Notes in Vaticanus Latinus 7207." *Speculum* 46 (1971): 597–612.

Galtier, Paul. "La première lettre du pape Honorius." *Gregorianum* 29 (1948): 42–61.

Gill, Joseph. "St. Theodore the Studite against the Papacy?" In *Polychordia: Festschrift Franz Dölger zum 75. Geburtstag,* 1:115–23. Amsterdam, 1966.

Gross, Julius. "Hat Johannes von Damaskus die Erbsünde gelehrt?" *Zeitschrift für Religions- und Geistesgeschichte* 5 (1953): 118–35.

Grumel, Venance. "Photius et l'addition de *Filioque* au symbole du Nicée-Constantinople." *Revue des études byzantines* 5 (1947): 218–34.

Guillou, André. *Régionalisme et indépendance dans l'empire byzantine au VIIe siécle: L' exemple de l'exarchat et de la Pentapole d'Italie.* Rome, 1969.

————. *Studies on Byzantine Italy.* London, 1970.

Haacke, Walter. *Die Glaubensformel des Papstes Hormisdas im Acacianischen Schisma.* Rome, 1939.

Haendler, Gert. *Epochen karolingischer Theologie: Eine Untersuchung über die karolingischen Gutachten zum byzantinischen Bilderstreit.* Berlin, 1958. The *Caroline Books* and the Western misunderstanding of both sides in the dispute over images.

Hergenröther, Joseph Adam Gustav. *Photius, Patriarch von Constantinopel. Sein Leben, seine Schriften und das griechische Schisma.* 3 vols. Regensburg, 1867–69. The standard work until Dvornik.

Hofmann, Georg, ed. *Photius et ecclesia Romana.* 2 vols. in 1. Rome, 1932. The pertinent documents with explanatory notes.

————. "Johannes Damaskenos, Rom und Byzanz (1054–1500)." *Orientalia Christiana Periodica* 16 (1950): 177–90.

Jugie, Martin. *De processione Spiritus Sancti: Ex fontibus revelationis et secundum Orientales dissidentes.* Rome, 1936.

————. *Le schisme byzantine, aperçu historique et doctrinal.* Paris, 1941.

Laourdas, Basil S. "Εἰσαγωγή" to Φωτίου ὁμιλίαι ["Introduction" to *The Homilies of Photius*]. Thessalonica, 1959.

Laurent, Vitalien. "Le symbole Quicumque et l'église byzantine. Notes et documents." *Échos d'Orient* 39 (1936): 385–404.

Leib, Bernard. *Rome, Kiev et Byzance à la fin du XIe siècle.* Paris, 1924.

Ludwig, Josef. *Die Primatsworte Mt. 16, 18. 19 in der altkirchlichen Exegese.* Münster, 1952.

Mango, Cyril, ed. *The Homilies of Photius, Patriarch of Constantinople.* Cambridge, Mass., 1958. Although we have cited the *Homilies* according to the Greek text as edited by Laourdas, Mango's translations and comments have been helpful.

Martin, Thomas Owen. "The Twenty-Eighth Canon of Chalcedon: A Background Note." In *Das Konzil von Chalkedon,* 2:433–59. (See Grillmeier and Bacht, in works for chapter 2 above.)

Meyendorff, John. "St. Peter in Byzantine Theology." In *The Primacy of Peter,* pp. 7–29. London, 1963. How the East acknowledged Peter as prince of the apostles without accepting Roman claims.

Michel, Anton. *Humbert und Kerularios: Quellen und Studien zum Schisma des XI. Jahrhunderts.* 2 vols. Paderborn, 1924–30.

————. "Von Photios zu Kerullarios." *Römische Quartalschrift* 41 (1933): 125–62.

————. *Amalfi und Jerusalem im griechischen Kirchenstreit (1054–1090).* Rome, 1939. The dispute over the use of "azymes" in the Eucharist.

Noesgen, Karl Friedrich. *Geschichte der Lehre vom Heiligen Geiste.* Gütersloh, 1899.

Norden, Walter. *Das Papsttum und Byzanz: Die Trennung der beiden Mächte und das Problem ihrer Wiedervereinigung bis zum Untergange des byzantinischen Reiches (1453).* Berlin, 1903. A massive history.

Pelikan, Jaroslav. *Development of Doctrine: Some Historical Prolegomena.* New Haven, 1969. Includes chapters on the Filioque, on Mary, and on original sin as differences between East and West.

————. "The Doctrine of Filioque in St. Thomas and Its Patristic Antecedents." In *St. Thomas Aquinas 1274–1974: Commemorative Studies,* edited by Armand A. Maurer, 1:315–36. Toronto, 1974.

Plannet, Wilhelm. *Die Honoriusfrage auf dem Vatikanischen Konzil.* Marburg, 1912.

Prestige, George Leonard. *God in Patristic Thought.* 2d ed. London, 1956.

Rackl, Michael. "Die griechischen Augustinusübersetzungen." In *Miscellanea Fr. Ehrle,* 1:1–38. Rome, 1924.

Runciman, Steven. *A History of the Crusades.* 3 vols. Cambridge, 1951–54. Describes the Fourth Crusade of 1204 (3:107–31) and concludes: "There was never a greater crime against humanity than the Fourth Crusade."

————. *The Eastern Schism: A Study of the Papacy and the Eastern Churches during the XIth and XIIth Centuries.* Oxford, 1955.

Salaville, Sévérien. "La primauté de saint Pierre et du pape d'après saint Théodore Studite (759–826)." *Échos d'Orient* 17 (1914): 23–42.

Schindler, Alfred. *Wort und Analogie in Augustins Trinitätslehre.* Tübingen, 1965.

Schmaus, Michael. *Die psychologische Trinitätslehre des heiligen Augustinus.* Münster, 1927.

Schulz, Hans-Joachim. "Die 'Höllenfahrt' als 'Anastasis': Eine Untersuchung über Eigenart und dogmengeschichtliche Voraussetzungen byzantinischer Osterfrömmigkeit." *Zeitschrift für katholische Theologie* 81 (1959): 1–66. Why the doctrine of the atonement takes a different cast in the East.

Sherrard, Philip. *The Greek East and the Latin West: A Study in the Christian Tradition.* London, 1959. An original and provocative, if not altogether convincing, hypothesis.

Simonetti, Manlio. "La processione dello spirito santo nei Padri latini." *Maia* 7 (1955): 308–24. Deals especially with Ambrose and Marius Victorinus.

Southern, Richard William. *Western Society and the Church in the Middle Ages.* London, 1970. Volume 2 of "The Pelican History of the Church," which has no volume on Eastern Christendom.

Stanislav, Ján, ed. *Ríša veľkomoravská: Sborník vedeckých prác* [The Greater Moravian Empire: a symposium of scholarly studies]. Prague, 1935.

Swete, Henry Barclay. *On the History of the Doctrine of the Procession of the Holy Spirit, from the Apostolic Age to the Death of Charlemagne.* Cambridge, 1876. Judicious and balanced, although now outdated.

Valoriani, S. "Massimo Planude traduttore di s. Agostino." *Studi Bizantini* 7 (1953): 234.

Zlatarski, Vasil Nikolov. "Veľká Morava a Bulharsko v IX. storočí" [Greater Moravia and Bulgaria in the ninth century]. In *Ríša Veľkomoravská,* pp. 275–88. (See Stanislav, above.)

5. THE VINDICATION OF TRINITARIAN MONOTHEISM

Abd El-Jalil. *Marie et l'Islam.* Paris, 1950.

Anastasi, Rosario. *Studi sulla "Chronographia" di Michele Psello.* Catania, 1969.

Anawati, George C. "Islam and the Immaculate Conception." In *The Dogma of the Immaculate Conception: History and Significance,* edited by Edward Dennis O'Connor, pp. 447–61. Notre Dame, Ind., 1958.

Andrae, Tor. *Der Ursprung des Islams und das Christentum.* Uppsala, 1926.

Angelov, Dimitŭr Simeonov, et al., eds. *Bogomilstvoto v B"lgarija, Vizantija i zapadna Evropa v izbori.* [Bogomilism in Bulgaria, Byzantium, and Western Europe: Selections]. Sofia, 1967. A comprehensive collection of sources from various languages, translated into Bulgarian.

Beck, Hans-Georg. "Bildung und Theologie im frühmittelalterlichen Byzanz." In *Polychronion: Festschrift Franz Dölger zum 75. Geburstag,* edited by Peter Worth, pp. 69–81. Heidelberg, 1966. A critique of Dvornik's view of how one "studied theology" in Byzantium.

Beck, Hildebrand. *Vorsehung und Vorherbestimmung in der theologischen Literatur der Byzantiner.* Rome, 1937. Especially helpful for the encounter with Islam.

Becker, C. H. "Christliche Polemik und islamische Dogmenbildung." *Zeitschrift für Assyriologie* 26 (1912): 175–95.

Chidiac, Robert, ed. Al-Ghazzālī. *La réfutation excellente de la divinité de Jésus Christ d'après les Évangiles.* Paris, 1939. An able statement of the Muslim case.

Conybeare, Frederick, ed. *The Key of Truth: Manual of the Paulician Church of Armenia.* Oxford, 1898.

Cumont, Franz. "Une formule grècque de renonciation au judaisme." *Wiener Studien* 24 (1902): 462–72.

d'Alverny, Marie Thérèse. "Deux traditions latines du Coran au Moyen Age." *Archives d'histoire doctrinale et littéraire du Moyen Age* 16 (1948): 69–131.

Daniel, Norman. *Islam and the West: The Making of an Image.* Edinburgh, 1960.

Döllinger, Ignaz von. *Beiträge zur Sektengeschichte des Mittelalters.* 2 vols. Munich, 1890. Although replaced in many ways by the works of Grundmann and others, this is still a comprehensive account of value.

Dräseke, Johannes. "Zu Michael Psellos." *Zeitschrift für wissenschaftliche Theologie* 32 (1889): 303–30.

―――. "Johannes Mauropus." *Byzantinische Zeitschrift* 2 (1893): 461–93.

Eichner, Wolfgang. "Die Nachrichten über den Islam bei den Byzantinern." *Der Islam* 23 (1936): 133–62; 197–244. A study of rumor, propaganda, and theology.

Ficker, Gerhard. *Die Phundagiagiten: Ein Beitrag zur Ketzergeschichte des byzantinischen Mittelalters.* Leipzig, 1908. Contains (pp. 89–111) a critical edition of the treatise of Euthymius Zigabenus against the Bogomils.

Fritsch, Erdmann. *Islam und Christentum im Mittelalter: Beitrag zur Geschichte der muslimischen Polemik gegen das Christentum in arabischer Sprache.* Breslau, 1930. The other side of the story.

Gass, Wilhelm. *Gennadius und Pletho, Aristotelismus und Platonismus in der griechischen Kirche (nebst einer Abhandlung über die Bestreitung des Islam im Mittelalter).* 2 vols. Breslau, 1844.

Graf, Georg, ed. *Die arabischen Schriften des Theodor Abû Qurra.* Paderborn, 1910.

Grundmann, Herbert. *Religiöse Bewegungen im Mittelalter.* Reprint edition. Darmstadt, 1961. Includes not only the original appendix on "Die Ketzerei im 11. Jahrhundert," with its discussion of relations between Western "Cathari" and Eastern "Bogomil-Manicheans," but also a later essay by the author, where this relation is treated in more detail.

Grégoire, Henri. "Mahomet et le monophysisme." *Mélanges Charles Diehl.* 1:107–19. Paris, 1930.

―――. "Les sources de l'histoire des Pauliciens." *Bulletin de la classe des lettres de l'Académie royale* 22 (1936): 95–114.

Hick, John Harwood. *Evil and the God of Love.* New York, 1966. A reconsideration of the classic alternatives—and the source of our subhead "Evil and the God of Love" (with permission).

Hussey, J. M., and Hart, T. A. "Byzantine Theological Speculation and Spirituality." In *Cambridge Medieval History,* 2d ed., 4:185–205. (See "General" section, above.)

Ivánka, Endra. *Hellenisches und christliches im frühbyzantinischen Geistesleben.* Vienna, 1948. The relation of patristic and Byzantine "Hellenism."

Ivanov, Ior. *Bogomilski knigi i legendi* [Bogomil books and legends]. Sofia, 1925. As distinguished from the collection of Angelov et al., this contains only materials of the Bogomils themselves.

Joannou, Perikles. *Christliche Metaphysik in Byzanz.* Vol. 1: *Die Illuminationslehre des Michael Psellos und Joannes Italos.* Ettal, 1956.

Khoury, Adel-Theodore, *Les théologiens byzantins et l'Islam.* 2 vols. Lyons, 1966. The second volume contains French translations of some of the sources.

Klinge, Gerhard. "Die Bedeutung der syrischen Theologen als Vermittler der griechischen Philosophie an den Islam." *Zeitschrift für Kirchengeschichte* 58 (1939): 346–86.

Kritzeck, James. *Peter the Venerable and Islam.* Princeton, 1964.

Lerch, David. *Isaaks Opferung christlich gedeutet: Eine auslegungsgeschichtliche Untersuchung.* Tübingen, 1950.

Lipšic, E. "Pavlikianskoe dviženie v Vizantii v VIII i pervoj polovine IX vv." [The Paulician movement in Byzantium in the eighth and the first half of the ninth century]. *Vizantijskij Vremennik,* n.s. 5 (1952): 49–92. Despite its preoccupation with making the Paulicians a movement of social protest, a useful summary, based largely on Photius and Peter of Sicily.

Meyendorff, John. "Byzantine Views of Islam." *Dumbarton Oaks Papers* 18 (1964): 115–32. Judicious, informed, and balanced.

Michel, A. *L'Église et les églises.* Chevetogne, 1954. Contains (pp. 351–440) Michel's previously published essay on Psellus.

Moeller, Carl Rudolf. *De Photii Petrique Siculi libris contra Manichaeos scriptis.* Bonn, 1910. Photius was, at least in part, dependent on Peter of Sicily.

Obolensky, Dmitri. *The Bogomils: A Study in Balkan Neo-Manichaeism.* Cambridge, 1948. Differs with Runciman (see below) at significant points.

Pines, Salomon. " 'Israel, My Firstborn' and the Sonship of Jesus: A Theme of Moslem Anti-Christian Polemics." In *Studies in Mysticism and Religion Presented to Gershom G. Scholem,* pp. 177–90. Jerusalem, 1967.

Puech, Henri-Charles, and Vaillant, André, eds. *Le traité contre les Bogomiles de Cosmas le prêtre.* Paris, 1945. Although we have used the text of the edition by Popruženko, the translations and notes in this edition have been very useful.

Rambaud, Alfred Nicolas. *Études sur l'histoire byzantine.* Paris, 1912. Includes an essay on Psellus as philosopher and statesman.

Renauld, Émile. *Étude de la langue et du style de Michel Psellos.* Paris, 1920.

Runciman, Steven. *The Medieval Manichee: A Study of the Christian Dualist Heresy.* New York, 1961.

Salaville, Sévérien. "Philosophie et théologie ou épisodes scolastiques à Byzance de 1059 à 1117." *Échos d'Orient* 29 (1930): 132–56.

Smith, Wilfred Cantwell. "Some Similarities and Differences between Christianity and Islam." In *The World of Islam: Studies in Honor of Philip K. Hitti,* edited by James Kritzeck and R. Bayly Winder, pp. 47–59. London, 1960.

Southern, Richard William. *Western Views of Islam in the Middle Ages.* Cambridge, Mass., 1962. Although this book deals explicitly only with the Latin church, many of its astute observations pertain at least as much to the Greek and Syriac churches.

Stein, Ludwig. "Die Kontinuität der griechischen Philosophie in der Gedankenwelt der Byzantiner." *Archiv für Geschichte der Philosophie* 9 (1896): 225–46.

Stephanou, Pelopidas Étienne. *Jean Italos: Philosophe et humaniste.* Rome, 1949.

Tatakis, Basile Nicolas. *La philosophie Byzantine.* Paris, 1949.

Vogt, Albert. "The Macedonian Dynasty from 976 to 1057 A.D." In *Cambridge Medieval History,* 1st ed., 4:83–118. (See "General" section, above.)

Vryonis, Speros. "Late Byzantine Views of Islam." *Greek, Roman and Byzantine Studies* 12 (1971): 263–86.

————. *The Decline of Medieval Hellenism in Asia Minor and the Process of Islamization from the Eleventh through the Fifteenth Century.* Berkeley and Los Angeles, 1971.

Walzer, Richard. *Greek into Arabic: Essays on Islamic Philosophy.* Oxford, 1963.

Wolfson, Harry A. "The Muslim Attributes and the Christian Trinity." *Harvard Theological Review* 49 (1956): 1–18.

Ždanov, I. N. *Sočinenija* [Works]. 3 vols. St. Petersburg, 1904. Includes a study of Hilarion of Kiev.

Zervos, Chr. *Un philosophe néoplatonicien du XIe siècle: Michel Psellos, sa vie, son oeuvre, ses luttes philosophiques, son influence.* Paris, 1920.

Zlatarski, Vasil Nikolov. *Istorija na b"lgarskata d"ržava prez srednite vekove* [History of the Bulgarian state during the Middle Ages]. Reprint. 1 vol. in 2. Sofia, 1970–71.

Zöckler, Otto. *Geschichte der Apologie des Christentums.* Gütersloh, 1907. Includes a discussion (pp. 236–53) of anti-Muslim apologetics.

6. The Last Flowering of Byzantine Orthodoxy

Ammann, Albert Maria. *Die Gottesschau im palamitischen Hesychasmus: Ein Handbuch der spätbyzantinischen Mystik.* 2d ed. Würzburg, 1948. A translation and a study of the *Centuries* by Callistus II and a monk named Ignatius.

Andreyev, Nikolay. *Studies in Muscovy: Western Influence and Byzantine Inheritance.* Reprinted in Russian and English. London, 1970.

Archangel'skij, Aleksandr Semonivič. *Nil Sorskij i Vassian Patrikčev: Ich literaturnye trudy i idei v drevnej Rusi* [Nilus Sorskij and Vassian Patrikčev: their literary works and ideas in ancient Russia]. St. Petersburg, 1882. The basic monograph on Nilus Sorskij.

Benz, Ernst. *Wittenberg und Byzanz: Zur Begegnung und Auseinandersetzung der Reformation und der östlich-orthodoxen Kirche.* Marburg, 1949.

Biedermann, Hermegild Maria. *Das Menschenbild bei Symeon dem Jüngeren dem Theologen, 942–1022.* Würzburg, 1949.

Bulgakov, Sergej. "Evcharisticeskij dogmat" [The dogma of the Eucharist]. *Put'* 20 (February 1930): 3–46; 21 (April 1930): 3–33. Despite the author's special ideas about the personal Wisdom of God, an acute presentation of the Eastern position.

Candal, E. "El 'Teófanes' de Gregorio Pálamas." *Orientalia Christiana Periodica* 12 (1946): 238–61. A point-by-point analysis and summary.

Contos, Leonidas C. *The Concept of Theosis in Saint Gregory Palamas. With Critical Text of the "Contra Akindynum."* 2 vols. Los Angeles, 1963.

Dujčev, Ivan. *Slavia Orthodoxa: Collected Studies in the History of the Slavic Middle Ages.* Reprint in Russian and Czech. London, 1970.

Florovskij, G. V. *Puti russkago bogoslovija* [The ways of Russian theology]. Paris, 1937. Probably the masterwork of the author's rich and varied scholarship.

Florovsky, George. "An Early Ecumenical Correspondence (Patriarch Jeremiah II and the Lutheran Divines)." In *World Lutheranism of Today: A Tribute to Anders Nygren,* pp. 98–111. Lund, 1950.

———. "Saint Gregory Palamas and the Tradition of the Fathers." *Sobornost'* 4 (1961): 165–76.

Geanakoplos, Deno John. *Emperor Michael Palaeologus and the West, 1258–82.* Cambridge, Mass., 1959. The Second Council of Lyons and its failure.

Georgi, Curt R. A. *Die Confessio Dosithei (Jerusalem 1672): Geschichte, Inhalt und Bedeutung.* Munich, 1940.

Gill, Joseph. *The Council of Florence.* Cambridge, 1959. The summation of years of research.

Hausherr, Irénée. "La méthode d'oraison hésychaste." *Orientalia Christiana* 9 (1927): 101–210. The foundation (with Karl Holl's work) of modern Western study of Byzantine mysticism.

Hofmann, Georg. *Il beato Bellarmino e gli orientali.* Rome, 1927. Contains source material on Bellarmine's relations with the Greeks and the Slavs.

———. "Patriarch Johann Bekkos und die lateinische Kultur." *Orientalia Christiana Periodica* 11 (1945): 141–64.

Holl, Karl. *Enthusiasmus und Bussgewalt beim griechischen Mönchtum: Eine Studie zu Symeon dem Neuen Theologen.* Leipzig, 1898.

Jugie, Martin. "Le mot transsubstantiation chez les Grecs avant 1629, at après 1629." *Échos d'Orient* 10 (1907): 5–12; 65–77.

———. "La Confession orthodoxe de Pierre Moghila à propos d'une publication récente." Ibid. 28 (1930): 414–30.

Kapterev, N. F. *Charakter otnošenij Rossii k pravoslavnomu vostoku v XVI i XVII stoletijach* [The nature of the relations between Russia and the Orthodox East during the sixteenth and seventeenth centuries]. 2d ed. Sergiev Posad, 1914. A long chapter (pp. 26–102) on "the third Rome."

Karmirēs, Iōannēs N. Ὀρθοδοξία καὶ Προτεσταντισμός [Orthodoxy and Protestantism]. Athens, 1937.

———. ed. Τὰ δογματικὰ καὶ συμβολικὰ μνημεία τῆς ὀρθοδόξου καθολικῆς ἐκκλησίας [The dogmatic and symbolic monuments of the Orthodox Catholic Church]. 2 vols. 2d ed. Athens and Graz, 1960–68.

Kijprian, Archimandrite. "Epikleza. (Molitva prizivan'a Sv. Ducha) u aleksandrijskim liturgijama" [Epiclesis. The prayer of invocation of the Holy Spirit in the Alexandrian liturgies]. *Bogoslovie* 7 (1932): 290–335.

Kiprian, Archimandrite. *Antropologija Sv. Grigorija Palamy* [The anthropology of Saint Gregory Palamas]. Paris, 1950. A careful theological monograph.

Krivocheine, Basile. "The Writings of St. Symeon the New Theologian." *Orientalia Christiana Periodica* 20 (1954): 298–328. The first comprehensive attempt to explain the literary and chronological relations between the several collections.

———. "La thème de l'ivresse spirituelle dans la mystique de Saint Syméon le Nouveau Théologien." In *Studia Patristica,* 3:368–76. Berlin, 1962.

Loenertz, R. "Pour la biographie du cardinal Bessarion." *Orientalia Christiana Periodica* 10 (1944): 116–49. A lengthy critique of the work of Ludwig Mohler.

Lossky, V. "Le problème de la 'Vision face a face' et la tradition patristique de Byzance." In *Studia Patristica,* 2:512–37. Berlin, 1957. The origins of the Western opposition to Palamism.

Maloney, George A. *The Spirituality of Nil Sorsky.* Westmalle, Belgium, 1964. The only full-length study in English, done with care and sympathy.

Masaryk, Tomáš Garrigue. *Rusko a Evropa: Studie o duchovních proudech v Rusku* [Russia and Europe: studies in intellectual trends in Russia]. 2 vols. 2d ed. Prague, 1930–33. The author had great difficulty comprehending Eastern piety, but his insights into the history of ideas are sometimes brilliant. (An English translation was made by Eden and Cedar Paul from an earlier German edition; it has now been revised and reissued: *The Spirit of Russia: Studies in History, Literature and Philosophy.* 2d ed. London, 1955–67.)

Meyendorff, Jean. "Note sur l'influence dionysienne en Orient." In *Studia Patristica,* 2:547–52. Berlin, 1957.

————. *Introduction a l'étude de Grégoire Palamas.* Paris, 1959. Contains, as the English translation does not, an annotated list of the works of Palamas, published and unpublished, as well as an exhaustive bibliography.

————. *A Study of Gregory Palamas.* Translated by George Lawrence. London, 1964.

Le millénaire du Mont Athos 963–1963: Études et mélanges. 2 vols. Wetteren, Belgium, 1963. Several essays on Palamas.

Mohler, Ludwig. *Kardinal Bessarion als Theologe, Humanist und Staatsmann.* 3 vols. Paderborn, 1923–42. (See also "Editions and Collections," above.)

Robertson, J. N. W. B. *The Acts and Decrees of the Synod of Jerusalem.* London, 1899.

Romanides, John S. "Notes on the Palamite Controversy and Related Topics." *Greek Orthodox Theological Review* 6 (1960/61): 186–205; 9 (1963/64): 225–70. A critique of Meyendorff's study, and an effort to show that Barlaam stood in the Augustinian tradition.

Schlier, Richard. *Der Patriarch Kyrill Lukaris von Konstantinopel: Sein Leben und sein Glaubensbekenntnis.* Marburg, 1927.

Spáčil, T. "Doctrina theologiae Orientis separati de sanctissima Eucharistia." *Orientalia Christiana* 13 (1928): 187–280; 14 (1929): 1–173. An extensive bibliography on the question of the epiclesis.

Špidlík, Thomas. *Joseph de Volokolamsk: Un chapitre de la spiritualité russe.* Rome, 1956.

Valacopoulos, Apostolos E. *Origins of the Greek Nation: The Byzantine Period, 1204–1461.* Translated by Ian Moles. New Brunswick, N. J., 1970. A useful chapter (pp. 86–103) on "The Church at Bay."

Vernadsky, George, et al., eds. *A Source Book for Russian History from Early Times to 1917.* 3 vols. New Haven, 1972. A vademecum through the labyrinth of Russian historical collections.

Vilmar, August. *Die Theologie der Thatsachen wider die Theologie der Rhetorik: Bekenntnis und Abwehr.* 3d ed. Marburg, 1857.

Völker, Walther. *Scala paradisi: Eine Studie zu Johannes Climacus und zugleich eine Vorstudie zu Symeon dem Neuen Theologen.* Wiesbaden, 1968.

Zachariadēs, Georg Elias. *Tübingen und Konstantinopel: Martin Crusius und seine Verhandlungen mit der griechisch-orthodoxen Kirche.* Göttingen, 1941.

Zernov, Nicolas. *St. Sergius—Builder of Russia.* Translated by Adeline Delafeld. London, 1939.

Index

Biblical

General

THE CHRISTIAN TRADITION, Volume 2

Designed by Joseph Alderfer.
Composed by Typoservice Corporation
in Linotype Garamond with display lines
in Foundry American Garamond.
Printed by Photopress Inc.
on Warren's Olde Style.
Bound by A. C. Engdahl Co. in Joanna Arrestox Vellum
and stamped in amber and gold.
The symbol on the cover shows an arch
with cross and candlesticks.
It is adapted from a mosaic of the eleventh century,
the original of which is in
St. Sophia's Cathedral
in Kiev, U.S.S.R.